THE ILLUSTRATED DIRECTORY OF

Trees &
Shrubs

THE ILLUSTRATED DIRECTORY OF

Trees &
Shrubs

ALLEN J. COOMBES

CHARTWELL
BOOKS, INC.

A Salamander Book

Published by
CHARTWELL BOOKS, INC.
A Division of BOOK SALES, INC.
114 Northfield Avenue
Edison, New Jersey 08837

©Salamander Books 2002

A member of **Chrysalis** Books plc

ISBN 0-7858-1622-4

Designed, edited, and produced by Hilton/Sadler
Indexer Kathie Gill

Author's Acknowledgments

I would like to thank all at Salamander, particularly Charlotte Davies for asking me to work on this project. Special thanks go to Jonathan Hilton and Margaret Sadler, with whom it was a pleasure to work, for their thorough and professional work on the layouts and for keeping me on target. Finally I am indebted to both Justyn Willsmore and David Brown for their fine photography.

Picture Credits

All pictures by Justyn Willsmore except:
Salamander Picture Library: half title; artworks on pp. 10–13; p. 26b; p. 27b; p. 31tl; p. 36b; p. 38b; p. 42t; p. 46tl; p. 52b; p. 57; p. 58b; p. 61; p. 65t; p. 66br; p. 68b; p. 75; p. 77br; p. 78tr; p. 79ml; p. 82; p. 83bl; p. 87tr; p. 88ml, mr; p. 91m; p. 96; p. 103bl; p. 117tl; p. 118; p. 133ml; p. 137;p. 138tl; p. 142br; p. 143; p. 144; p. 145t; p. 149tr; p. 153; p. 158tl, ml; p. 159tl; p. 169t; p. 173b; p. 174; p. 183; p. 187t; p. 188b; p. 198b; p. 208; p. 214b; p. 225m; p. 232t; p. 241; p. 243b; p. 245t; pp. 270–3; p. 274br; p. 275br; p. 276; p. 277tr, mr; pp. 278–80; pp. 282–94; p. 295tr; p. 297tl, b; p. 298
Allen Coombes: p. 109
Gardens used in the book: pp. 16, 17t Hampton Court Palace flower show
p. 17b Mr and Mrs J Willsmore, Southampton pp. 9, 14 Mr and Mrs Ward
All others from:The Sir Harold Hillier Gardens and Arboretum, RHS Wisley, Westonbirt Aboretum, Kew Gardens

Contents

Introduction

The trees, shrubs, climbers, and conifers described in this book are all woody plants, so they do not die back into the soil in winter. They may, however, be deciduous, meaning they lose their leaves in winter, or evergreen. They are normally long-lived and permanent garden features.

The wide range of ornamental features displayed by woody plants makes them ideal for providing a design structure for your garden, a backbone of planting around which you can add annuals, herbaceous perennials, and the like. From upright to spreading, pendulous, or creeping, woody plants can be found for virtually any situation or size of garden, perhaps as striking specimens in a lawn or woodland setting or as attractive screens and hedges, ground cover, or as plants for a mixed border. If combined thoughtfully, they can produce flowers throughout the year, while additional features, such as ornamental foliage or bark, can give additional autumn color and winter interest.

Decoding plant names

Plants are referred to in the following chapters by their scientific names. Although many people often refer to

Right: *Traditional climbers, in this case Clematis 'Jackmanii' and Boston ivy (Parthenocissus tricuspidata), around a doorway create a welcoming, cottage-garden effect. The raised bed, with its mixture of small shrubs and herbaceous perennials sloping to a stone pathway, brings the planting visually close to the house without actually encroaching on it.*

plants by common names, this is frequently a source of confusion. Many plants do not have common names for a start and, in addition, many common names apply to more than one plant. To add to the problem, different countries or even different regions within countries, will often have their own common name for a particular plant. In fact, the scientific name is the only internationally recognized method of plant naming.

Plants are listed alphabetically by genus, after which the family name is given. A description of that genus including any cultivation requirements follows, after which individual species in the genus are listed. As an example, the genus *Abelia* contains about 30 species. It is placed in the family Caprifoliaceae, which includes related genera (the plural of genus) such as *Lonicera* and *Viburnum*.

Within the genus *Abelia* several species are listed, such as *A. chinensis*. This is a species that is grown in gardens but occurs naturally in China. Some species are hybrids between two others, denoted by an x between the name of the genus and the species epithet. An example of this is *Abelia* x *grandiflora*—a hybrid that occurs only in gardens. Both naturally occurring species and garden hybrids can have named selections or cultivars. These have been selected for a particular feature. In the case of *A.* x *grandiflora*, several cultivars have been selected. The cultivar epithet is placed in inverted commas—for example, *Abelia* x *grandiflora* 'Confetti'.

Sometimes a cultivar is not placed under any species, particularly if it has a complicated or unknown parentage. *Abelia* 'Edward Goucher' is an example of this. The purpose of naming a cultivar is that plants grown under that name are relatively uniform. When a selection is not uniform but is based on a variable feature, it may be referred to as a Group. For example, *Abeliophyllum distichum* Roseum Group includes all plants with pink flowers and no specific selection. Some plants are most commonly listed under selling or trademark names. This is particularly common in roses. In this case, the selling name is given first without inverted commas, followed by the accepted cultivar epithet, such as *Rosa* Blue Moon ('Tannacht').

Choosing a plant

As woody plants are intended to be long-lived in the garden, it is particularly important to choose healthy specimens. Reputable garden centers will normally sell plants only when they are ready for planting out. With plants that have been grown in containers, this is throughout the year. Don't necessarily choose the largest plant; instead, look for one that is growing strongly and has no obvious signs of damage or disease. Pot-bound plants, those with a mass of roots circling the pot or emerging from the base through the drainage holes, should be avoided.

Trees may also be sold bare root—with no or little soil and usually wrapped in hessian. Check that the roots are healthy and not congested and have not dried out. Root-balled trees are sold with a ball of soil wrapped in hessian. Check that the root ball is firm and has not dried out. Both bare root and root-balled trees are generally available only between autumn and early spring.

Planting

After choosing a plant it is important to make sure that it does not dry out before it is planted in your garden. Place the plant in a sheltered position and keep the root ball or roots moist until it is safely in the ground. Those in containers should be soaked in water for about 30 minutes before planting.

Avoid planting in frosty conditions or when the weather is very dry. The planting hole should be two to three times the width of the root ball and deep enough for the soil level in the pot to match that of the ground. Refill the hole with soil mixed with organic matter. Most trees should be staked on planting. Water well after planting and frequently in the first year. Applying a mulch at the base of a plant will help to conserve water around the roots by inhibiting evaporation and so prevent desiccation.

Hardiness zones

Throughout the following chapters, plant entries have been given a hardiness rating. Hardiness is a measure of a plant's ability to resist low winter temperatures. Plants that will survive winters in a particular area are often termed "hardy," while those that will not are referred to as "tender." Hardiness, however, is a relative term, and a plant that is tender in one area or region may well be perfectly hardy in a slightly warmer one. The hardiness zones used here are based on those developed by the United States Department of Agriculture, and are shown on the maps below and opposite. If the hardiness rating for a plant is given as Zone 7, for example, it will survive winters in Zones 7 and above, but is likely to be damaged by typical winter conditions in Zones 6 and below. In spite of this, it is often well worth trying plants that should only be hardy in a warmer area—for example, Zone 8 plants in Zone 7. Within a typical garden, even a small one, there is likely to be a

Minimum winter temperature
Zone 1: Below -50° F (Below -45° C)
Zone 2: -50 to -35° F (-45 to -37° C)
Zone 3: -35 to -20° F (-37 to -29° C)
Zone 4: -20 to -10° F (-29 to -23° C)
Zone 5: -10 to -5° F (-23 to -21° C)

Zone 6: -5 to 5° F (-21 to -15° C)
Zone 7: 5 to 10° F (-15 to -12° C)
Zone 8: 10 to 20° F (-12 to -7° C)
Zone 9: 20 to 30° F (-7 to -1° C)
Zone 10: 30 to 40° F (-1 to 4° C)
Zone 11: Above +40° F (Above +5° C)

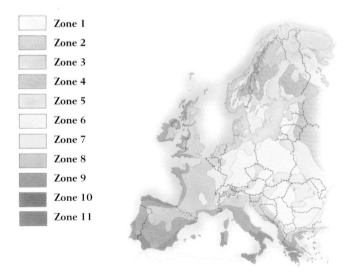

Zone 1
Zone 2
Zone 3
Zone 4
Zone 5
Zone 6
Zone 7
Zone 8
Zone 9
Zone 10
Zone 11

Western Europe

limited range of "microclimates"—sheltered areas that will often
be slightly warmer during winter than a more exposed site lying
just a little distance away. A planting position against a wall or
under tree cover are just two examples where the worst effects
of winter conditions may be lessened, and in such places many
plants regarded as tender can be tried.

Winter temperature, however, is not the only factor that
influences hardiness. Some plants require very hot summers in
order to ripen their growth, and without this heat they will not
survive a cold winter. Other plants are successful only if the
winters are dry rather than mild, and if it is wet, they are likely to
succumb to the unfavorable conditions. In yet other situations,
plants that grow naturally in high northerly or southerly latitudes
may not thrive in warmer regions. Some of these plants may
require a permanently moist soil, which may be difficult to provide
in areas with a long, dry season, or they may come into growth very
early and then fall victim to late spring frosts.

North America

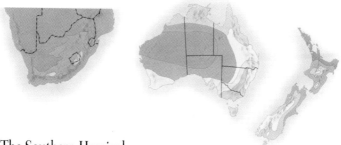

The Southern Hemisphere

Tree and leaf shapes

Trees are extremely varied in many of their most obvious features, such as their leaves and growth habit. The shape of leaves and how they are arranged can be very useful guides to identification. When leaves are said to be opposite, they are arranged in pairs, one opposite the other. Some trees with superficially similar leaves can be distinguished in this way—for example, the opposite-leaved *Liquidambar* from the alternate-leaved maples (*Acer*). Unless otherwise stated, plants described in the working chapters of the book have alternate leaves.

Compound leaves

When a leaf is divided into several leaflets it is said to be "compound." There are different types of compound leaves, however, for example, the ashes (*Fraxinus*) with their pinnately (leaflets growing opposite each other in pairs either side of the leaf

Tree shapes

Low branching

Narrowly conical

Spreading

stalk) compound leaves, and the horse chestnuts (*Aesculus*) with
their palmately (hand-shaped) compound leaves.

Types of growth

While the shape of a tree's leaves will affect its appearance, the
shape of the tree itself is vital in aiding its placement in the
garden, and especially its relationship with other garden plants.
Thus, shape is an important feature to consider when buying a
tree. For example, a very narrow, columnar tree will not be
effective for use as a screen—perhaps to provide privacy from
neighboring gardens or to help divide a garden up into different
areas, or "rooms"—but it may be excellent as a focal point if the
available space is restricted—perhaps at the end of a well-planted
mixed border. While a wide-spreading or weeping tree may create
just the desired effect, remember that it will cast a good deal of
shade and will need plenty of space.

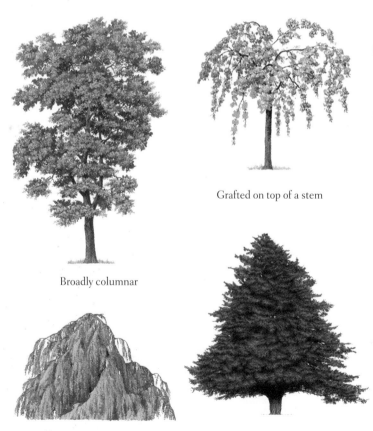

Grafted on top of a stem

Broadly columnar

Weeping

Broadly conical

Leaf shapes

Alternate leaves

Toothed

Juniperus chinensis
with adult and
juvenile foliage on
same plant

Opposite leaves

Pinnate

Cordate (heart-shaped)

Trifoliolate (with three
leaflets)

Toothed and lobed

Male and female flowers

Palmately compound

Chamaecyparis—scale-like leaves of forms with adult (*above left*) and juvenile foliage (*above right*)

Untoothed, unlobed

Ovate

Palmately lobed

Pendulous cones

Upright cones

Male and female catkins on same plant

Fern-leaved and copper beech showing variation in foliage in same species

Pruning

While many plants will grow happily without any intervention on your part, there are several reasons why a plant may need to be pruned. In each case it is important to understand why the pruning is necessary, what it is intended to achieve, and how best to go about the task. The object of pruning may be to remove damaged or diseased wood, for example, or it could be to remove suckers from grafted plants, encourage a bushy habit, stimulate fresh growth, restrict overall size, balance a misshapen specimen, renovate old plants, or to create special effects, such as coppicing, hedging, or topiary.

In each case, you will minimize potential damage to the plant if you use sharp, clean tools. Plants that you prune regularly should also be given regular doses of a balanced fertilizer. Where relevant, pruning recommendations are given under each genus.

Pruning trees

Trees do not normally need a great deal of pruning. Most formative pruning is carried out in the nursery, but small trees may need to be trained by gradually removing the lower shoots. If you purchase what is known as a "feathered" tree, it will be a young plant with branches almost to the base. If a standard tree is required, one with a clear stem, you will have to remove the lower branches over a period of a few years.

Pruning is normally carried out when the tree is dormant. In the first year, remove any shoots growing from the lower third of the stem. Cut back by about a half the shoots arising from the middle one-third of the stem, pruning to an outward-facing bud. In the second and third years, remove the shoots shortened in the previous year, cutting them back to the main stem, and cut back by two-thirds the shoots arising from the middle third of the stem. The following year, remove all side shoots to the desired height. Any pruning of the upper part of the tree is restricted to removing congested, diseased, or damaged wood.

Once the tree is fully established, continue to remove any congested, diseased, or damaged wood, reverting shoots on

Left: *The association of stonework and rock garden plants is made more intimate by the seclusion created by shrubs and trees in the* *background. Shrubs, which have been sensitively pruned, also hide the destination of the path, inviting further exploration.*

variegated plants, and any shoots that arise from the base of the trunk. Unless you are experienced, any major work that is necessary on large trees should be carried out by professional tree surgeons.

Pruning shrubs

Shrubs vary tremendously in their pruning requirements. Many benefit from regular intervention to encourage new growth from the base or to remove older shoots that often do not flower or fruit as effectively as younger growth. It is not unusual for old shrubs to become tall and leggy; if so, they can often be renovated by cutting them back hard to the base. Take care, however, as some shrubs will not recover if pruned too hard.

When pruning shrubs, the time of pruning is often a crucial factor. Shrubs that flower late in the year, for example, should often be pruned in the early spring. This then promotes young growth that will bear flowers later in that same year. For shrubs that flower early in the year, however, such a pruning regime would result in the loss of an entire season's flowers, and for this reason these shrubs should be pruned after flowering has finished. The resulting growth then bears flowers in the following year. Shrubs grown for their attractively colored winter shoots can be hard pruned in spring, just before the new season's growth starts. How often you prune, however, depends largely on a shrub's vigor and the eventual size you want it to reach in the garden.

Bamboos usually require very little attention in the garden, but well-established clumps will benefit by having some of the old or dead culms cut right back to the base in spring. Some bamboos can be invasive, however, and the spread of these may need to be checked by removing unwanted culms.

Pruning climbers

The pruning of climbers depends on how they are to be grown. While those that are encouraged to scramble into a tree can be left unpruned, those that are grown on a wall or over a trellis will probably require pruning at some time to restrict their growth. Climbers that produce several shoots from the base can have the older growths removed if necessary while some, such as *Clematis* and *Wisteria*, have specific pruning requirements designed to promote flowering. If you wish to train a climber to grow in a particular direction, make your pruning cuts to buds facing the way you want them to grow.

Pruning conifers

Conifers mostly need very little in the way of pruning, if they are given the space they need. Allowed to reach their full size in an open situation, those that make large trees can look magnificent when fully clothed with branches sweeping right down to the ground. As trees mature, however, it often becomes necessary to remove some of the lower branches as they become shaded, either by the upper canopy or by surrounding trees. Dwarf conifers occasionally produce reverting shoots, which can grow strongly and quickly dominate the plant. These you should cut back to their point of origin as soon as you notice them.

Conifers that are used for hedging require the most pruning. Their dense habit and vigorous growth, as well as their tolerance of frequent pruning, make conifers such as *Chamaecyparis*, *Thuja* and x *Cupressocyparis* popular subjects for this treatment. These plants should be pruned regularly from an early age—in this way you avoid the necessity of cutting into old wood, which will not generate new growth. This is the best way to ensure that a conifer hedge remains dense and well clothed with foliage.

Designing a garden

Whether you are intending to remodel an existing garden or merely adding to it, or if you are about to start work on an entirely new site, the design stage can be an exciting and a rewarding process. Many gardens simply evolve through the acquisition and loss of plants over a period of many years. While the gradual development of a garden in this fashion has its advantages and rewards—for example, it allows for frequent changes of mind regarding the content of the garden and its use—it is the planning of a completely new garden or a major development of an existing one that presents the greatest challenge.

The initial design

When planting a new garden, there is always a temptation to rush to the garden center, choose from the many attractive plants on sale, and get them into the ground as soon as possible. However, a better effect usually results from first thinking carefully about how the garden will be used. Will it be mainly for recreation, or as a showcase for your plant collection? How much of it will be lawn? Is any hard landscaping needed, such as decking or stonework?

Below: A clever use of color and of hard landscaping makes the link between living area and garden in this water garden. The intimate association created effectively makes the garden part of the house, and the house part of the garden.

Will screening be required, such as that provided by hedges? Make a rough plan to scale showing the position of any important features—lawns, paths, where hedges are needed, and the places where trees will be planted—and then add in the positions of any special plants you intend to grow, borders, raised beds, screes, and so on. Once you have worked out the structure of the garden, then you can think about choosing specific plants.

Garden conditions

To be able to choose plants suitable for your garden, first you need to know the conditions that prevail there. How cold does it get in winter? Is it susceptible to late spring frosts? Which areas are in shade and which in full sun? What is the pH of the soil? Does the soil dry out very quickly? A look at other gardens in the same area will give you a very good idea of how local conditions will affect your choice of plants. If rhododendrons and camellias are common locally, then the soil is likely to be acid and not too dry. If

Left: *Don't be afraid to mix hard landscaping with associated plantings. Here, a rustic wooden walkway is softened with closely planted foliage plants. In this way, any structure can be linked to the rest of the garden and close contact with the plants around it increase overall enjoyment of the entire garden.*

common hydrangeas are lush, then conditions are likely to be moist, without too many late frosts. Hedges of escallonias or fuchsias indicate relatively mild conditions. Above all, talk to local gardeners about what they grow, and why.

Placing trees

Trees can be used to frame a view or to hide it, to enclose a garden, or to provide a window onto the landscape outside. As well, a tree can highlight an area rather than dominate it.

Since trees are the largest and most permanent plants in a garden, careful thought needs to be given to their selection and position. Never be tempted to rely on pruning to restrict a tree's growth—this is simply not a practical solution in the long run. Instead, choose a specimen that has an eventual size and spread that is suitable for its intended position. Exceptions to this include the forms of *Salix alba*, which can regularly be cut back hard to a short stem to encourage the production of young colored shoots.

Where space is tight, trees of a narrow or upright habit are useful, while spreading or weeping trees can create microclimates in which shade-loving plants will thrive.

Specimen plants

Depending on the size of your garden, choose specimen trees and shrubs for focal positions. These plants should have several ornamental qualities so that they remain interesting over more than a single season. They may, for example, combine an upright habit with ornamental foliage, as in *Taxus baccata* 'Standishii', or a weeping habit with silvery leaves, as in *Pyrus salicifolia* 'Pendula'. Trees with ornamental bark, such as the snake bark maples (*Acer*), are particularly useful as specimens as the bark is visible through-out the year. Specimen plants need not be at the center of a garden; they could become the focal point of a side border or draw the eye to a more secluded part of the garden.

Borders

Borders are ideal for combining a wide range of plants. Choose them according to the size and aspect of the area under cultivation and look for examples that can be combined to give contrasts of shape, color, texture, and flowering times. In this way, a border of shrubs and herbaceous perennials can be attractive throughout the year. Large shrubs, combined according to taste, at the back of a border can create an effective and ornamental screen, in colors ranging from shades of muted green to striking contrasts—such as that between purple-leaved *Cotinus* and *Philadelphus coronarius* 'Aureus'. Smaller shrubs can be accommodated toward the front, perhaps using a selection of aromatic plants here. There is always the danger in a border that plants will become too large and grow into adjacent ones. For this reason, those shrubs that tolerate, or even welcome, hard pruning are useful for providing ground cover, such as *Cornus*, *Hypericum*, and *Caryopteris*.

Right: *Climbers are very effective at hiding or softening hard structures in the garden. In this case, Virginia creeper (*Parthenocissus quinquefolia*) scrambles over stonework to provide an effective contrast with its striking autumn color. Sticky pads on the tendrils enable this useful plant to cling to almost any surface.*

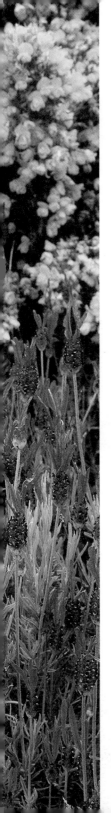

Trees, shrubs, and bamboos

The great variation in the habit, foliage, stems, and flowers of woody plants provides an almost endless choice of ornamental features to be used either singly or in combination. Although many plants are selected for their flowers, it is wise not to rely on this feature alone for ornamental effect in the garden. Many trees and shrubs also have attractive young foliage, such as the red new leaves of many *Pieris* and *Photinia*, while others have colored or variegated foliage. Variegated evergreens can be particularly valuable, especially if they have other desirable assets. For example, the holly *Ilex* x *altaclerensis* 'Lawsoniana' not only has boldly variegated leaves, but also red berries in the autumn and winter seasons.

Don't be tempted to use too many trees and shrubs with colored or variegated foliage: use just a few well-chosen examples to highlight or draw attention to particular areas, contrasting them with green foliage from, for example, a clump of bamboo. Variegated plants will usually not flower as freely as their green-leaved counterparts, and they usually grow more slowly—a factor that may well be an advantage in small gardens.

Trees and shrubs can be used in combination to provide a succession of flower color throughout the year, but other qualities can also be used to extend the seasonal attractions of your planting scheme. Fruiting shrubs, such as *Pyracantha* and *Cotoneaster*, provide autumn displays, while striking autumn color can be provided by such plants as *Euonymus alatus*. The winged shoots of the *Euonymus* also provide an extra winter attraction, and this can be supplemented by winter-flowering plants such as *Hamamelis* (the witch hazels) and *Daphne*.

Abelia
Caprifoliaceae

The 30 species in this genus of
shrubs include evergreen as well as
deciduous specimens with opposite
leaves grown for their attractive
foliage and their usually small, but
profusely borne, tubular- or funnel-
shaped, sometimes fragrant flowers.
In some forms the foliage is
variegated. Additional attractions of
this genus include the young foliage,
which is often colored, and the
sepals, which can be tinted and
enlarged after flowering is over.

They are generally easy-to-grow
shrubs and tend to do best if planted
in a sunny position in a border. Prune
as necessary to control growth,
depending on the space available;
established plants can be cut back
hard in early spring.

In particularly cold areas, it is best
to grow them against a sunny wall,
but even if they are cut down by
severe winter frosts they will often
regrow from the base. They are native
plants of East Asia, from the
Himalayas to Japan, and Mexico.

Abelia 'Edward Goucher'

Abelia x *grandiflora*

Abelia chinensis

A deciduous shrub of spreading habit
with glossy, dark green leaves to 1½ in
(4 cm) long, sometimes bronzy when
young. The small, white or pink-
tinged and fragrant, funnel-shaped
flowers are borne in dense clusters
over a long period during summer
and autumn. As the flowers fade, the
sepals around them turn from green
to pink.

Native range: China
Height: 5 ft (1.5 m)
Spread: 6 ft (2 m)
Hardiness: Zone 7

Abelia 'Edward Goucher'

This semi-evergreen shrub is a
hybrid between *A.* x *grandiflora*
and *A. schumannii*. It has a vigorous,
spreading habit with arching

branches bearing glossy, green leaves
to 2 in (5 cm) long, bronze-colored
when young. The clusters of funnel-
shaped, lilac-pink flowers open over a
long period throughout the summer
and autumn months.

Height: 5 ft (1.5 m)
Spread: 6 ft (2 m)
Hardiness: Zone 6

Abelia floribunda

This striking species is among the
most attractive of the entire genus,
but it is also the most tender. It
makes a large, vigorous, evergreen
shrub with arching branches and
glossy, dark green leaves up to 2 in
(5 cm) long. The tubular, bright
magenta-pink flowers are 2 in (5 cm)
long and hang in small clusters from

Abelia x grandiflora 'Francis Mason'

the shoots during summer and through to autumn. It can be grown to good effect if trained against a wall for protection.

Common name: Mexican abelia
Native range: Mexico
Height: 6 ft (2 m) or more
Spread: 10 ft (3 m) or more
Hardiness: Zone 8

Abelia x *grandiflora*

The most popular plant in the genus, this semi-evergreen shrub is a hybrid between *A. chinensis* and *A. uniflora*. It makes a vigorous bush with attractive, arching branches. The glossy, dark green leaves are about 2 in (5 cm) long and often turn bronze in the cold weather. The small, funnel-shaped, white or pink-tinged, and slightly fragrant flowers are borne in clusters over a long period during summer and autumn. As the flowers fade, the sepals turn to a pink hue, thus extending the long period of color this shrub brings to the garden.

Common name: Glossy abelia
Height: 10 ft (3 m)
Spread: 13 ft (4 m)
Hardiness: Zone 6
Variants: *Abelia* x *grandiflora* has given rise to several forms, often with variegated foliage, that do not tend to be as striking in flower as those with green leaves. 'Confetti' is a smaller shrub, reaching a height of about 3 ft (1 m) and a spread of 5 ft (1.5 m), with slender leaves that are narrowly edged with white or pink. 'Francis Mason' has yellow-green

Abelia triflora

leaves edged with yellow and reaches
a height and spread of 5 ft (1.5 m).
Some plants under this name
include 'Goldsport', which is a little
less vigorous, with completely yellow
leaves. 'Sunrise' is low growing, up to
3 ft (1 m) tall and 5 ft (1.5 m) across,
with dark green leaves edged with
bright yellow.

Abelia schumannii

A vigorous and particularly hardy,
deciduous species with purple young
shoots and arching branches. The
mid-green leaves are about 1 in
(3 cm) long and are bronze when
young. The funnel-shaped flowers
are slightly fragrant and lilac-pink,
with a conspicuous orange blotch in
the throat. They are borne in clusters
during summer and autumn, and the
sepals turn pink with age.

Native range: China
Height: 6 ft (2 m)
Spread: 10 ft (3 m)
Hardiness: Zone 6

Abelia triflora

This less commonly seen species is a
very distinct treelike shrub with a
vigorous, upright habit, developing a
stout trunk with ridged bark. The
branches arch with age and the
large, hairy leaves, to 3 in (8 cm)
long, are occasionally lobed. The
fragrant, white or pink-tinged,
tubular flowers have red sepals and
are borne in clusters during summer.

Native range: W Himalayas
Height: 13 ft (4 m)
Spread: 8 ft (2.5 m)
Hardiness: Zone 6

Abeliophyllum distichum
Oleaceae

The single species in this genus is
native to Korea and is related to
Forsythia. Being a winter-flowering
shrub, it makes a valuable addition
to the garden at a time of year when
color is usually at a premium.

The shrub is easy to cultivate in any reasonable soil, but it prefers a sunny position in a border if it is to flower at its best. In areas that experience relatively cool summers, *Abeliophyllum distichum* will benefit from the additional warmth that comes from being grown against a wall. Old plants that have become straggly do better if they are cut back hard after flowering.

This deciduous, spreading shrub has opposite leaves that grow up to 3 in (8 cm) long. They are matt dark green in color, but often turn a deep red-purple in autumn before falling. The young shoots in winter are also a deep red-purple color, as are the buds, which open in late winter to early spring. The flowers are white, four-lobed, and fragrant—sometimes pink-tinged as they emerge.

Common name: White forsythia
Native range: Korea
Height: 5 ft (1.5 m)
Spread: 6 ft (2 m)
Hardiness: Zone 5
Variants: Roseum Group includes plants that have pink flowers.

Abutilon
Malvaceae

This large and varied genus contains some 150 different species of annual and perennial herbaceous plants. In addition, the genus encompasses deciduous and evergreen trees and shrubs that are widely distributed throughout the tropical and subtropical regions of the world.

The often lobed leaves of *Abutilon* species are variegated in some forms. They are valued for their showy, bell- or saucer-shaped flowers, which are borne in a variety of colors. They are suitable only for milder garden temperatures, however, and while they will survive in any reasonable soil, they prefer a site that is sheltered from any strong winds— either in a border or against a wall in a sunny position.

Prune these plants in early spring before growth starts, either by trimming as required to restrict growth or by cutting back hard to create a low framework of branches. Many tender *Abutilon* species not described here are grown as conservatory plants or for summer bedding.

Abutilon 'Kentish Belle'
This semi-evergreen shrub has slender shoots and dark green, slightly lobed leaves that grow to 1½ in (4 cm) long. The pendulous, bell-shaped flowers, which are also about 1½ in (4 cm) long, are borne from the growing shoots over a long period during summer and autumn. Each flower has red sepals and pale apricot petals, from which protrudes a cluster of purple stamens. It is best trained against a wall as it grows.

Height: 8 ft (2.5 m)
Spread: 8 ft (2.5 m)
Hardiness: Zone 8

Abutilon megapotamicum
A vigorous, semi-evergreen shrub with slender shoots and dark green, unlobed leaves to 5 in (12 cm) long. The pendulous, bell-shaped flowers,

Abutilon vitifolium 'Veronica Tennant'

Abutilon megapotamicum

1½ in (4 cm) long, hang from arching shoots during summer and autumn. The flowers have conspicuous, bright red sepals, from the mouths of which appear yellow petals and clusters of purple stamens. It is best grown trained against a wall.

Common name: Trailing abutilon
Native range: Brazil
Height: 6 ft (2 m)
Spread: 6 ft (2 m)
Hardiness: Zone 8
Variant: 'Variegatum' has leaves that are densely mottled with yellow.

Abutilon x *suntense*
This hybrid is a cross between *A. ochsenii* and *A. vitifolium*. It makes a vigorous, treelike, deciduous shrub with bold, heart-shaped, lobed and toothed, green to gray-green leaves that grow to a length of about 5 in (12 cm). The color of the saucer-shaped flowers, which are up to 2½ in (6 cm) across, varies from white to deep violet. The shrub comes into flower in late spring or early summer, depending on conditions.

Height: 16 ft (5 m)
Spread: 8 ft (2.5 m)
Hardiness: Zone 8
Variants: Selections of this hybrid include 'Gorer's White', which has white flowers; 'Jermyns', a shrub with deep mauve flowers; 'Ralph Gould', which has strikingly large violet-colored flowers; and 'Violetta', with deep violet-blue flowers.

Abutilon vitifolium
This vigorous, treelike, deciduous shrub has stout, felted shoots and large, gray-haired leaves that are markedly lobed and toothed. The leaves grow up to 6 in (15 cm) in length. The saucer-shaped flowers of

Abutilon vitifolium, which grow up to 3 in (8 cm) across, vary in color from white to mauve, and they are profusely borne in the late spring and summer.

Native range: Chile
Height: 16 ft (5 m)
Spread: 8 ft (2.5 m)
Hardiness: Zone 8
Variants: var. *album* has white-colored flowers; 'Tennant's White' is another white-flowering form of *Abutilon*, but it has particularly large flowers; and 'Veronica Tennant' has large and attractive mauve flowers.

Acacia
Leguminosae

A very large genus of more than 1,000 species of mainly evergreen trees and shrubs, with some herbaceous species, widely distributed in tropical and subtropical regions of Australia, Africa, and South and Central America. They are mainly grown for their attractive, often fragrant flowers, which, although individually tiny, are borne in dense clusters. Many also have attractive foliage, which in some is composed of leaves with numerous leaflets, while in the

Acacia baileyana

mature plants of others the leaves are reduced to an expanded leaf stalk (phyllode).

Acacias are suitable for growing outside only in mild or nearly frost-free areas. They prefer a sunny position and make specimen plants in such locations. In areas with cooler winters, they can be grown if afforded the protection of a wall. Ideally sited in a neutral to acidic soil, Acacias can show signs of chlorosis on shallow alkaline soils. Cut back lightly after flowering if necessary, and remove any damaged or dead wood in early spring.

Acacia baileyana
This is a small, evergreen tree, sometimes shrubby, with a spreading habit, and with blue-green leaves up to 2 in (5 cm) long, finely divided into numerous tiny leaflets. Small, rounded heads of bright yellow flowers open in large clusters, up to 4 in (10 cm), long during the late winter and early spring.

Common name: Cootamundra wattle
Native range: New South Wales (Australia)
Height: 20 ft (6 m)
Spread: 20 ft (6 m)
Hardiness: Zone 8
Variant: 'Purpurea' is a very attractive form in which the young leaves are deep purple, later turning to blue-green.

Acacia dealbata
This is a fast-growing, evergreen tree with fernlike, blue-green leaves, reaching up to about 5 in (12 cm) long, finely divided into small leaflets. The large clusters, about 8 in (20 cm) long, of small, rounded heads of fragrant, yellow flowers open during the late winter and early spring.

Common name: Silver wattle
Native range: SE Australia,

Acacia dealbata

Tasmania
Height: 50 ft (15 m) or more
Spread: 33 ft (10 m)
Hardiness: Zone 8

Acacia pravissima

This is an unusual and large-growing, evergreen shrub featuring slender, arching branches. The leaves have been reduced to densely arranged, blue-green, triangular, spine-tipped phyllodes, growing up to about ¾ in (2 cm) in length. Clusters of small, bright yellow, fragrant flowerheads, up to about 4in (10 cm) long, open during the late winter and early spring. This species looks particularly effective when it is grown against a wall.

Common name: Ovens wattle
Native range: SE Australia
Height: 20 ft (6 m)
Spread: 26 ft (8 m)
Hardiness: Zone 8

Acacia retinodes

This species can be grown as a small, evergreen tree or as a large shrub with arching shoots and willow-like foliage. The leaves have been reduced to slender, slightly curved, blue-green phyllodes that grow up to about 8 in (20 cm) in length. The small, rounded heads of yellow flowers are borne in clusters up to about 1½ in (4 cm) long during the summer, and then intermittently throughout the year.

Native range: SE Australia, Tasmania
Height: 26 ft (8 m)
Spread: 23 ft (7 m)
Hardiness: Zone 8

Acca
Myrtaceae

Of the two or three species in this
small genus of South American
evergreen shrubs, only the following
example is commonly found in
garden cultivation.

Grown for its unusual flowers, it
is suitable for any reasonable soil as
long as it is provided with a sunny
position. In cold regions, it should be
grown against a wall for the
protection it provides, while in mild
regions it can be used as a free-
standing specimen shrub or planted
as hedging. In warm climates it is
cultivated for its edible fruit.

Pruning is not usually required;
however, a light trimming back of
over-long shoots in spring will help
to retain a compact habit.

Acca sellowiana

This evergreen shrub has opposite,
gray-green, untoothed leaves that
grow up to about 3 in (7 cm) long.
The leaves have a dense felt of gray
hairs beneath. The showy flowers are
about 1½ in (4 cm) across and are
borne during the summer months.
The striking flowers have four rather
fleshy petals, deep red above and
curling upward at their edges to
show a starkly contrasting white
undersurface. At the center of each
bloom is found a dense brush of
conspicuous, red stamens. In warm
climates edible, egg-shaped, green
fruits, up to about 2 in (5 cm), long
are produced.

Synonym: *Feijoa sellowiana*
Common name: Pineapple guava
Native range: Brazil, Uruguay
Height: 6 ft (2 m)
Spread: 8 ft (2.5 m)
Hardiness: Zone 8
Variant: 'Variegata' is a form in which
the leaves are narrowly edged with
creamy white.

Acca sellowiana

Acer
Aceraceae

The maples are an important and
very varied genus of plants consisting
of more than 120 species of mainly
deciduous trees, with some shrubs,
widely distributed throughout the
Northern Hemisphere.

All maples have opposite-growing
leaves, which, in most species, are
palmately (hand-shaped) lobed,
occasionally unlobed, and sometimes
divided into separate leaflets. The
flowers are small and usually green
in color, but they can be an attractive
feature when they open in spring and
are then followed by the familiar
winged fruits.

While maples are grown principally
for their striking foliage, which can
provide a spectacular autumn display,
some species—such as the snakebark
maples—have attractively striped
bark to recommend them. Such
species include *A. capillipes*,
A. davidii, *A. grosseri* var. *hersii*,
A. pensylvanicum, and *A. rufinerve*.

Maples are generally easy to grow
in any good garden soil. The Japanese
maples (*A. palmatum* and
A. japonicum) are subject to damage
by late frosts and cold winds in
spring, and so are best planted in a
sheltered position. The following
plants are all deciduous.

Acer capillipes

Acer cappadocicum 'Rubrum'

Acer cappadocium 'Aureum'

Acer buergerianum

This is a rather slow-growing tree suitable for the small garden. It has glossy dark green leaves to 3½ in (9 cm) long, blue-green beneath and three-lobed at the tip. Late in autumn or early winter the leaves turn yellow, orange, and red before dropping. Its small yellow-green flowers are rather inconspicuous among the foliage as it emerges in spring. Mature specimens benefit from the appearance of attractive, flaking, red-brown bark.

Common name: Trident maple
Native range: E China, Korea
Height: 33 ft (10 m)
Spread: 30 ft (9 m)
Hardiness: Zone 5

Acer campestre

This is a densely branched, spreading or rounded tree with dark green, slender-stalked leaves, three- to five-lobed, turning butter-yellow in autumn. Small, greenish flowers are inconspicuous as the leaves emerge. This is a tough, small tree for a variety of situations, from streets to small gardens. It also responds well to pruning and makes a very effective dense hedge.

Common name: Hedge maple
Native range: Europe, N Africa, W Asia
Height: 33 ft (10 m) or more
Spread: 33 ft (10 m)
Hardiness: Zone 5
Variant: 'Carnival' is a form in which the leaves are broadly edged in creamy white.

Acer capillipes

This snakebark maple is a small tree. The young shoots are red and the main trunk and branches streaked with white. The dark green leaves, 5 in (12 cm) long, are prominently three-lobed with slender, tapering tips, and turn striking shades of red in autumn. The green flowers appear in drooping clusters in spring as the leaves emerge.

Native range: Japan
Height: 33 ft (10 m)
Spread: 33 ft (10 m)
Hardiness: Zone 5

Acer cappadocicum

This is a vigorous tree of a spreading habit with bold, bright green leaves up to 6 in (15 cm) across, each with five to seven lobes ending in slender, tapering points. Often bronzy or red when young, the leaves turn to an attractive butter-yellow color in autumn. The tree bears small clusters of yellow flowers in spring.

Common names: Caucasian maple, Coliseum maple

Native range: Turkey to China
Height: 65 ft (20 m)
Spread: 50 ft (15 m)
Hardiness: Zone 5
Variants: 'Aureum' is a smaller sized tree that grows up to about 50 ft (15 m) tall. It has bright yellow young foliage that turns green in summer and then back to yellow once more in the autumn. The young foliage of 'Rubrum' is deep blackish-red in color.

Acer circinatum

A relative of the attractive Japanese maples A. palmatum and A. japonicum, A. circinatum makes a small, shrubby tree with a spreading habit. The rounded leaves are up to 5 in (12 cm) across and have seven to nine toothed lobes. Leaves turn to shades of orange, yellow, and red in autumn. Small, purple and white flowers are borne in clusters in spring. A useful tree that thrives well in dry, shady positions.

Common name: Vine maple
Native range: W North America
Height: 16 ft (5 m)
Spread: 16 ft (5 m)
Hardiness: Zone 5

Acer davidii

Perhaps the best known of the snakebark maples, this small tree has arching branches and green bark on the main trunk, attractively streaked with white. The oval, mid- to dark green leaves are up to 6 in (15 cm) long, unlobed or with two small lobes, with taper-pointed tips. Leaves often turn orange and yellow in autumn. Pale green flowers open in drooping clusters in the spring.

Common name: David maple
Native range: China
Height: 50 ft (15 m)
Spread: 40 ft (12 m)
Hardiness: Zone 5
Variants: 'Ernest Wilson' has pale green leaves turning orange-yellow in

Acer davidii 'George Forrest'

autumn. 'George Forrest' has bold, dark green, unlobed leaves, up to 8 in (20 cm) long, that usually fall without coloring. 'Serpentine' has small, dark green leaves, up to 4 in (10 cm) long, and purple-colored shoots.

Acer griseum

This species is among the most striking and most sought-after of all trees for its bark. *Acer griseum* is slow-growing but, once they are mature, trees develop a spreading habit and their attractive, cinnamon-brown bark starts to peel in thin flakes on the main trunk and even the smallest branches. The dark green leaves have three leaflets growing up to 4 in (10 cm) long and these can turn orange and red in autumn, when the tree is often laden with contrasting pale green fruits.

Common name: Paperbark maple
Native range: China
Height: 33 ft (10 m)
Spread: 33 ft (10 m)
Hardiness: Zone 5

Acer grosseri var. *hersii*

A vigorous snake-bark maple with arching branches, which, like the main trunk, are green and attractively marked with white streaks. The broadly oval, glossy, green leaves are taper-pointed at the tip and have two small lobes at the base, turning bright yellow to orange-yellow in autumn.

Native range: China
Height: 50 ft (15 m)
Spread: 40 ft (12 m)
Hardiness: Zone 5

Acer japonicum

A bushy, spreading tree, often branching low and shrubby, with rounded leaves, up to 5 in (13 cm) long, edged with up to 11 sharply toothed lobes. Silky hairy when young, leaves become dark green then turn to shades of orange and red in autumn. Pendulous clusters of small, red and purple flowers open in spring with the emerging leaves.

Common name: Fullmoon maple
Native range: Japan
Height: 33 ft (10 m)
Spread: 33 ft (10 m)
Hardiness: Zone 5
Variants: 'Aconitifolium' has leaves that are deeply cut, nearly to the center, into sharply toothed lobes, turning deep crimson in autumn. 'Vitifolium' has very large leaves that turn brilliant orange, red, and purple in autumn.

Acer maximowiczianum

This is a spreading tree, the leaves of which are divided into three stalked leaflets that have few, if any, teeth. Leaves are up to 4 in (10 cm) long, dark green above, blue-green beneath with a layer of soft hairs. The leaves take on bright autumn colors at the end of the season. Drooping clusters of small, yellow flowers open with the young leaves in spring.

Acer griseum

Acer japonicum 'Aconitifolium'

Synonym: *A. nikoense*
Common name: Nikko maple
Native range: Japan, China
Height: 33 ft (10 m)
Spread: 26 ft (8 m)
Hardiness: Zone 5

Acer negundo

A very fast-growing tree of broadly columnar habit with leaves up to 8 in (20 cm) long, each with from three to seven separate, sometimes lobed, leaflets. Leaves can turn yellow in autumn, but they can also drop

Acer maximowiczianum

without coloring. Male and female flowers are borne on separate plants in pendulous, tassel-like clusters before the leaves appear in the spring. It is normally grown only as one of the forms listed below. Those with variegated leaves often produce green-leaved reversions, which must be removed as soon as possible.

Common name: Box elder
Native range: North America
Height: 65 ft (20 m) or more
Spread: 50 ft (15 m)
Hardiness: Zone 3
Variants: 'Elegans' has leaflets that are broadly edged with yellow and it grows to a height of about 33 ft (10 m). 'Flamingo' is similar, but the margin of its leaves are pink at first and later turn to white. The leaves of 'Variegatum' have a white margin from the outset.

Acer palmatum

This is among the most popular of all the maples and grows into a rounded tree, usually branching low down, with slender shoots. The dark green leaves are deeply cut into five or seven taper-pointed and toothed lobes, and leaves turn various shades of orange, yellow and red in the autumn. The drooping clusters of red-purple flowers open with the young leaves in spring.

Common name: Japanese maple
Native range: Japan, China, Korea

Acer palmatum

Height: 26 ft (8 m)
Spread: 33 ft (10 m)
Hardiness: Zone 5
Variants: Numerous garden
selections have been made, varying in
size, leaf shape, and color.
'Atropurpureum' has red-purple
leaves that turn bright red in autumn.
'Bloodgood' has deeply cut, deep red-
purple leaves, turning red in autumn.
'Butterfly' is a dainty, slow-growing,
upright form reaching a height of 6 ft
(2 m) or more, and its small leaves
have margins of pink and cream.
'Chitoseyama' is shrubby, up to about
6 ft (2 m) tall, with arching branches
and deeply cut, bronze-colored leaves
that turn deep red in autumn.
'Crimson Queen' grows to about 10 ft
(3 m) with pendulous shoots and
finely cut, deep red-purple foliage,
turning red in autumn. 'Dissectum' is
similar to 'Crimson Queen', but with
green foliage turning orange-yellow in
autumn, while 'Garnet' has rich
garnet-red foliage turning red in
autumn. 'Inaba-shidare' has large,
red-purple leaves deeply cut into
slender lobes, turning red in autumn.
'Osakazuki' has dark green, seven-
lobed leaves turning a brilliant deep
red in autumn. 'Red Pygmy' is slow-
growing and bushy, up to about
5 ft (1.5 m) tall, and its deep red-
purple leaves are deeply cut into
narrow lobes. 'Sangokaku' ('Senkaki'),
known as the coral-bark maple, has
pale green leaves, turning orange-
yellow in autumn, and its young
shoots are bright pink in winter.
'Seiryu' resembles 'Dissectum' with
its finely cut leaves, but it is upright,
reaching about 13 ft (4 m) or more.
'Trompenburg' has deep red-purple
leaves, but the margins of the lobes
are rolled under, which makes them
appear narrow.

Acer pensylvanicum

This is the only snakebark maple that
is native outside of East Asia. It is a
vigorous tree and its green bark is
attractively marked with white
stripes. The bold, rather pale green
leaves grow to a length of 6 in
(15 cm) or more, and have three
conspicuous, taper-pointed lobes at
the tip. Leaves turn a striking butter-
yellow in autumn. Its slender,

Acer palmatum 'Bloodgood'

drooping clusters of pale green flowers open as the leaves are emerging in spring.

Common name: Moosewood
Native range: E North America
Height: 26 ft (8 m)
Spread: 23 ft (7 m)
Hardiness: Zone 3
Variant: 'Erythrocladum' has yellow-green foliage and yellow bark. The young shoots are brilliant pink in winter. It is best grown as a shrub rather than trained as a single stem.

Acer platanoides

A vigorous large tree that is normally taller than it is wide—suited only to large gardens. The bold, bright green leaves are up to 6 in (15 cm) long and are divided into five lobes edged

Acer palmatum 'Osakazuki'

Acer pensylvanicum 'Erythrocladum'

Acer platanoides 'Crimson King'

Acer pseudoplatanus 'Brilliantissimum'

Acer platanoides 'Drummondii'

with taper-pointed teeth. Leaves turn yellow, occasionally red, in autumn. Among the best of the maples for flowers, it has conspicuous clusters of yellow blooms opening in spring before the leaves emerge.

Common name: Norway maple
Native range: Europe, SW Asia
Height: 80 ft (25 m) or more
Spread: 50 ft (15 m)
Hardiness: Zone 5
Variants: 'Crimson King' has deep red-purple foliage and red-tinged flowers. 'Crimson Sentry' is compact and upright in habit,

reaching 40 ft (12 m) tall, with
leaves that are red when young,
becoming deep purple-green.
'Drummondii' has leaves with a
broad, creamy yellow margin when
young, turning to creamy white, but
often produces reverting shoots with
all-green leaves. It reaches a height
of about 40 ft (12 m).

Acer pseudoplatanus

A large, vigorous, and very tough tree
of rounded habit. The dark green
leaves are blue-gray beneath, up to
6 in (15 cm) or more long, with five,
toothed lobes. Leaves do not usually
color in autumn. Dense, pendulous
clusters of small, yellow-green
flowers without petals open with the
young leaves. Useful in exposed and
coastal positions.

Common name: Sycamore maple
Native range: Europe, SW Asia
Height: 100 ft (30 m)
Spread: 80 ft (25 m)
Hardiness: Zone 4
Variants: The leaves of
'Atropurpureum' are deep red-purple
beneath. 'Brilliantissimum' is useful
in small gardens, reaching about
20 ft (6 m) in height. Its young leaves
are bright pink in spring, turning
yellow-green. 'Leopoldii' has leaves
mottled with creamy yellow, pink
when young. 'Prinz Handjéry' is
similar to 'Brilliantissimum', but its
leaves are purple beneath. 'Simon-
Louis Frères' has pink young leaves,
later turning green blotched with
creamy white. 'Worley' ('Worleei') has
pale yellow young leaves on red
stalks, later turning green.

Acer rubrum

This is a fast-growing member of the
maple family with a broadly
columnar to rounded habit when
mature. The glossy, dark green leaves
have between three and five lobes
each, and grow up to about 4 in
(10 cm) long. The leaves are colored
blue-white on their undersurfaces

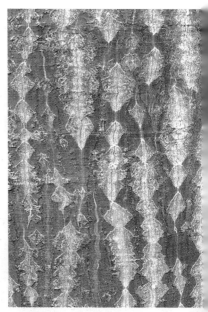

Acer rufinerve

and often turn a brilliant red in
autumn, but sometimes yellow.
Dense clusters of deep red flowers
open on the bare shoots in early
spring. If *Acer rubrum* is grown on
dry, alkaline soils, it may not develop
the type of autumn color for which it
is valued.

Common name: Red maple
Native range: E North America
Height: 80 ft (25 m)
Spread: 50 ft (15 m)
Hardiness: Zone 4
Variants: 'October Glory' has reliably
good, bright red autumn color.
'Scanlon' exhibits a compact form of
columnar habit and grows to about
50 ft (15 m) in height and with a
16-ft (5-m) spread. It, too, has good
red autumn color.

Acer rufinerve

This striking snakebark maple makes
a compact tree suitable for most
small gardens. It has arching
branches and green bark
conspicuously streaked with white.
The dark green leaves grow up to

Acer saccharinum

about 5 in (13 cm) in length and are
sharply toothed and shallowly three-
lobed. In autumn, its foliage turns
from green to orange-yellow and red-
purple. The small, yellow-green
flowers produced in spring are
followed by fruits which often have
distinctly red-flushed wings.

Native range: Japan
Height: 33 ft (10 m)
Spread: 26 ft (8 m)
Hardiness: Zone 5

Acer saccharinum

A. saccharinum is a vigorous tree with
a broadly columnar to spreading
habit. Its large leaves grow up to 6 in
(15 cm) long and they are deeply cut
into usually five lobes. These, in
turn, are lobed and toothed. Rather
a pale green color above, the leaves
have a distinct blue-white tint to
their undersurfaces and they turn
yellow or orange in autumn. Like
A. rubrum, the small flowers open
on the bare shoots in early spring,
but they are less conspicuous as
they are yellow-green.

Common name: Silver maple
Native range: E North America
Height: 80 ft (25 m)
Hardiness: Zone 3

Acer saccharum

Probably best known as the tree from which maple syrup is obtained, this species is also one of the best for its striking autumn color. It is a large specimen with a normally broadly columnar habit, whose five-lobed leaves grow up to 6 in (15 cm) long and the same size across. Mid- to dark green above, the leaves are blue-green beneath, and they turn attractive shades of orange, yellow, and red in autumn. Many selections have been made of this species for their habit and autumn color.

Common name: Sugar maple
Native range: E North America
Height: 80 ft (25 m)
Spread: 50 ft (15 m)
Hardiness: Zone 4

Acer shirasawanum

This is a rather bushy tree with a rounded habit, and it is closely related to *A. japonicum*. In fact, so similar are these maple species that they are sometimes confused with each other in gardens. The bright green, rounded leaves grow up to about 5 in (12 cm) in length and they are edged with, usually, 11 toothed lobes. The leaves turn to attractive colors of orange and red in autumn. Small, upright clusters of pink and cream flowers open with the leaves in spring.

Native range: Japan
Height: 33 ft (10 m)
Spread: 33 ft (10 m)
Hardiness: Zone 5
Variant: The most commonly found form of this tree in garden cultivation is 'Aureum' (*A. japonicum* 'Aureum'). This is a slower-growing tree and attains a maximum height of up to about 20 ft (6 m). As implied by its name, it produces bright yellow foliage.

Acer shirasawanum 'Aureum'

Acer tataricum

Due to its extreme hardiness, *A. tataricum* is an extremely useful tree to grow in areas that experience cold winters. This tough tree is also a fast-growing and small specimen, features that makes it an extra bonus in gardens where space is tight. It has a spreading habit, and its bright green, toothed, but usually unlobed leaves are up to about 4 in (10 cm) long. The leaves break through early in the spring season, turning yellow or red before dropping in the autumn. Fragrant, white flowers are borne in small clusters in the late spring after the leaves have emerged, and these are followed by red-winged fruits.

Common name: Tatarian maple
Native range: SE Europe, SW Asia
Height: 20 ft (6 m) or more
Spread: 16 ft (5 m)
Hardiness: Zone 3
Variants: The most commonly seen form is subsp. *ginnala* (*A. ginnala*), Amur maple, which differs from *A. tataricum* in that it has distinctly three-lobed leaves. This tree is native to China and Japan.

Acradenia frankliniae

Acradenia
Rutaceae

The two species that make up this small genus are evergreen shrubs native to Australia. Only the following species, however, is commonly found in cultivation, and it is grown principally for its aromatic foliage and small white flowers.

This species is best planted in soil that is not too dry, and in cold regions it should be given a position where it is sheltered from the effects of strong winds. Apart from the removal of any damaged, diseased, or unwanted growth, pruning is not usually necessary.

Acradenia frankliniae
This evergreen shrub has an upright habit and is broadly columnar. The dark green, opposite, leathery leaves have three leaflets, up to 2 in (5 cm) long, and are pleasantly aromatic when crushed. Small clusters of starry, white flowers are produced in late spring and sometimes again in autumn.

Common name: Whitey wood
Native range: Tasmania
Height: 10 ft (3 m)
Spread: 5 ft (1.5 m)
Hardiness: Zone 8

Aesculus
Hippocastanaceae

The horse chestnuts and buckeyes comprise a small genus of about 15 species of deciduous trees and shrubs that are native to North America, southeast Europe, and East Asia. They all have opposite leaves divided into several leaflets. They are mainly grown for their flowers, which are borne in conical clusters at the ends of the shoots in spring or summer. They prefer a good, but not too dry soil and are mainly planted as specimen trees.

Aesculus x carnea
This deciduous tree is a hybrid between *A. hippocastanum* and *A. pavia* and is known only in cultivation. It is most often planted as a street tree and in parks, and it has a rounded habit when mature. Its dark green leaves have between five and seven leaflets, growing to a length of up to 10 in (25 cm), and they can turn orange-red in autumn. Large clusters of pink flowers, blotched yellow, open in late spring, followed by rounded, slightly prickly fruits.

Common name: Red horse chestnut
Height: 65 ft (20 m)
Spread: 50 ft (15 m)
Hardiness: Zone 4
Variant: 'Briotii' is a good selection to consider with its particularly glossy, green leaves and deep red-colored flowers.

Aesculus flava
This broadly conical-to-rounded, deciduous tree is a particularly good choice for autumn color. The dark green leaves usually have five leaflets and grow up to 6 in (15 cm) long; leaves turn a bright orange-red in autumn. In late spring to early summer it produces large clusters of pale yellow flowers tinged with pink, followed by smooth, rounded-to-pear-shaped fruits.

Aesculus hippocastanum

Synonym: *A. octandra*
Common names: Sweet buckeye,
yellow buckeye
Native range: E United States of
America
Height: 80 ft (25 m) or more
Spread: 50 ft (15 m)
Hardiness: Zone 4

Aesculus hippocastanum

A fast-growing, deciduous tree with
stout shoots and large sticky buds.
The long-stalked leaves have
between five and seven leaflets,
each growing up to 12 in (30 cm)
long, and leaves can turn yellow in
autumn. The large clusters, up to
12 in (30 cm) long, of white flowers

Aesculus flava

are blotched with red and open in late spring. These are followed by rounded, very spiny fruits.

Common name: Common horse chestnut
Native range: SE Europe
Height: 100 ft (30 m)
Spread: 80 ft (25 m)
Hardiness: Zone 4
Variant: 'Baumannii' is a form that has double flowers, but it produces no fruit.

Aesculus indica

This very elegant species of tree provides a welcome change from the more commonly seen members of the genus, in that it flowers much later in the year. It has a broadly columnar-to-rounded habit and is of a large size. The leaves of A. indica are large, dark green in color, and bear five to seven leaflets up to 10 in (25 cm) long. Leaves are bronze when young and turn orange and yellow in autumn. White and pink flowers with a yellow blotch open in clusters up to 12 in (30 cm) long in midsummer, and these are followed by smooth, pear-shaped fruits.

Common name: Indian horse chestnut
Native range: NW Himalayas
Height: 65 ft (20 m)
Spread: 50 ft (15 m)
Hardiness: Zone 7

Aesculus x neglecta 'Erythroblastos'

This striking-looking tree is a garden selection of a naturally occurring hybrid between A. flava and A. sylvatica. It is a slow-growing, medium-sized tree of essentially columnar habit with leaves that are divided into five leaflets. When the leaves first emerge in the spring, they are a brilliant pink color and they then slowly turn whitish as the season advances. Finally the leaves become green flushed with yellow.

The small flowers are creamy white with a pink flush, but they are relatively inconspicuous when they open in the early summer.

Common name: Sunrise horse chestnut
Height: 33 ft (10 m)
Spread: 16 ft (5 m)
Hardiness: Zone 6

Aesculus parviflora

This deciduous shrub forms dense mounds and spreads by producing suckers. The dark green leaves have between five and seven leaflets, and grow up to 8 in (20 cm) long. Leaves are bronze when young, turning yellow in autumn. The long, slender clusters of flowers that appear in mid-summer reach 12 in (30 cm), and their most striking feature is the long white stamens with red anthers that project from each flower. An excellent plant as a lawn specimen or in a shrub border.

Common name: Bottlebrush buckeye
Native range: SE United States of America
Height: 10 ft (3 m)
Spread: 16 ft (5 m) or more
Hardiness: Zone 4

Ailanthus
Simaroubaceae

This small genus of just five species of deciduous trees, all of which are natives of the region from China to Australia, is mainly represented in cultivation by the following species.

It is an extremely fast-growing tree and is able to flourish almost anywhere. It also suckers extensively and has become naturalized in many parts of the world and is considered a weed. Flowering and fruiting are best in regions experiencing hot summers, but some trees may be all male and produce no fruit.

Ailanthus altissima

Ailanthus altissima

A very vigorous, large, deciduous tree of broadly columnar-to-spreading habit with stout shoots. The leaves are truly impressive, being up to 24 in (60 cm) long, and are divided into numerous leaflets. They are bronze when young, becoming dark green, but show no autumnal change of color. Large clusters of small, yellow-green flowers open in mid- to late summer, and these are followed by small, pale green winged fruits that turn red as they ripen.

Common name: Tree-of-heaven
Native range: China

Height: 80 ft (25 m)
Spread: 50 ft (15 m)
Hardiness: Zone 4

Albizia
Leguminosae

The 150 or so species in this genus of deciduous trees, shrubs, and climbers are widely distributed throughout the warm regions of the world. The elegant leaves are finely cut into numerous small leaflets and the showy part of the flowers are the long stamens. Only the following is commonly grown. It thrives in any

Albizia julibrissin f. rosea

well-drained soil and does best when planted in full sun. Although it is hardy in all but the coldest areas, it requires hot summer temperatures to ripen the growth, and without this summer heat it can suffer from frost damage during the winter months.

Albizia julibrissin f. rosea

An elegant, spreading, deciduous tree with fernlike, dark green leaves growing up to 20 in (50 cm) long cut into many small leaflets. The individual flowers are small, but are borne in clusters made conspicuous by long, pink-colored stamens. Flowers open in early summer in warm climates, but in late summer to early autumn where summers are cool, followed by flattened pods up to 6 in (15 cm) long.

Common name: Silk tree
Native range: Iran to E Asia
Height: 26 ft (8 m)
Spread: 33 ft (10 m)
Hardiness: Zone 6

Alnus
Betulaceae

The alders are a genus of some 35 species of deciduous, catkin-bearing trees and shrubs widely distributed in the Northern Hemisphere and extending into the Andes of South America. Male and female catkins are borne separately on the same tree: the male catkins are long and pendulous, opening, in most of the cultivated species, in early spring before the leaves appear; the female catkins mature into persistent, woody, conelike fruits.

Alders are useful for growing in very poor, even wet soils, and via bacteria in their roots they are able to enrich soils with nitrogen. They are best planted in full sun.

Alnus cordata

This handsome and vigorous, large-growing tree is among the finest of all the cultivated alders. It has a conical form and glossy, dark green leaves growing up to 4 in (10 cm) in length with a heart-shaped base. The yellow male catkins are up to 3 in (7.5 cm) long and open in late winter or early spring before the leaves emerge.

Common name: Italian alder
Native range: Corsica, S Italy
Height: 80 ft (25 m)
Spread: 26 ft (8 m)
Hardiness: Zone 5

Alnus glutinosa

This is a vigorous tree that is extremely tolerant of poor-quality and wet soils. It is mainly planted in gardens as one of the selected forms, but it is also useful in wet soil by riverbanks, where it is frequently seen. The dark green leaves grow up to 4 in (10 cm) long and they are broadest toward the tip. The leaves are edged with small teeth or lobes. The yellow-brown male catkins open in late winter or early spring.

Common name: European alder
Native range: Europe, N Africa, W Asia
Height: 80 ft (25 m)
Spread: 33 ft (10 m)
Hardiness: Zone 4

Alnus cordata

Variant: 'Aurea' is a smaller tree growing up to about 40 ft (12 m) with golden yellow young foliage. 'Imperialis' is smaller again and its leaves are deeply cut into slender lobes. It reaches a height of about 33 ft (10 m).

Alnus incana

A good choice for poor, dry, or wet soils, it is a broadly conical-shaped tree, very tough and hardy. The dark green leaves grow up to 4 in (10 cm) long and are blue-green beneath, pointed at the tip, and edged with small, sharp teeth. The yellow-brown catkins are 4 in (10 cm) long and open in late winter or early spring. They are tinged red at first.

Common name: Gray alder
Native range: Europe, Caucasus
Height: 65 ft (20 m)
Spread: 40 ft (12 m)
Hardiness: Zone 2

Alnus glutinosa 'Imperialis'

Amelanchier lamarckii

Variant: 'Aurea' is a smaller tree, reaching a height of about 33 ft (10 m). Its young leaves are flushed with yellow and the shoots and catkins are colored orange-pink during winter.

Aloysia
Verbenaceae

The 35 or so species in this genus comprise both deciduous and evergreen shrubs that are native from the southwest of the United States of America to Central and South America. Only the following is commonly grown—primarily for its aromatic foliage. It requires a well-drained soil in full sun and is suitable for growing or training against a sunny wall. The long shoots produced in summer are best cut back hard in spring.

Aloysia triphylla
A. triphylla is a deciduous shrub that is capable of reaching a large size. It

is normally restricted to about 5–6 ft (1.5–2 m), however, by being cut back annually. The glossy green leaves grow to 4 in (10 cm) long and are normally borne in whorls of three. Leaves are rough to the touch and are very strongly lemon-scented. Large, open clusters of tiny, pale lilac flowers open in late summer.

Synonym: *Lippia citriodora*
Common name: Lemon verbena
Native range: Chile, Argentina
Height: 10 ft (3 m)
Spread: 10 ft (3 m)
Hardiness: Zone 8

Amelanchier
Rosaceae

Variously known as serviceberries, Juneberries, and snowy mespilus, this genus, consisting of about 25 species of deciduous trees and shrubs, is widely distributed in North America, Europe, and Asia.

Grown for their foliage, which is ornamental in spring and autumn, as well as for their flowers and fruits, they require a lime-free soil and are an excellent choice for providing spring interest in the garden among other trees and shrubs, or when planted in a shrub border.

Amelanchier canadensis

This is a deciduous shrub that forms thickets of upright stems. The silky, hairy young leaves, up to 2 in (5 cm) long, mature to a dark green color and then turn orange-yellow in autumn. Slender, upright clusters of white flowers open as the leaves begin to unfold, and these are followed by edible blue-black fruits. Some plants grown under this name are *A. lamarckii*.

Common name: Shadblow
Height: 16 ft (5 m)
Spread: 8 ft (2.5 m)
Hardiness: Zone 3

Amelanchier x grandiflora

Many forms of this hybrid, between *A. arborea* and *A. laevis*, have originated in gardens. It is a vigorous, deciduous tree with a spreading habit, sometimes shrubby, with dark green leaves up to 3 in (7.5 cm) long, silky and bronze when young, turning orange and red in autumn. White flowers in drooping clusters open in the spring as the leaves unfold, and these are followed by edible blue-black fruits.

Height: 40 ft (12 m)
Spread: 40 ft (12 m)
Hardiness: Zone 4
Variants: Many selections have been made, including 'Ballerina', with profusely borne, large white flowers and red and purple autumn color. 'Rubescens' has pale pink flowers, deeper in bud.

Amelanchier lamarckii

This is a spreading, shrubby, deciduous tree, often with several main stems. The young leaves, which grow up to 3 in (7.5 cm) long, have silky hair, and become bronzy and then dark green before turning orange and red in autumn. Arching clusters of white flowers appear as the leaves open, followed by edible purple-black fruits.

Native range: Europe
Height: 33 ft (10 m)
Spread: 33 ft (10 m)
Hardiness: Zone 4

Andromeda
Ericaceae

This small genus, comprising just two species of evergreen shrubs, is native over a wide area of the Northern Hemisphere, where it is found in northerly latitudes and on mountains farther south. The following species is the most commonly seen in garden cultivation and requires a cool, moist position in a peaty, lime-free soil. It is suitable for a peat garden among plants requiring similar conditions. It does best in full sun, but it needs to be grown in the shade where summers or soil conditions are dry.

Andromeda polifolia

This is a dwarf and extremely hardy, evergreen shrub with slender, glossy, dark green or blue-green, leathery leaves up to 1½ in (4 cm) long, blue-white beneath. Clusters of small, nodding, urn-shaped, pale pink or white flowers open during the late spring and early summer.

Common name: Bog rosemary
Native range: North temperate regions
Height: 18 in (45 cm)
Spread: 24 in (60 cm)
Hardiness: Zone 2
Variants: 'Alba' is compact, up to 6 in (15 cm) tall, with white flowers. 'Compacta' reaches 12 in (30 cm), with blue-green foliage and bright pink-colored flowers.

Aralia elata

Arbutus x *andrachnoides*

Aralia
Araliaceae

Containing about 40 species of herbaceous perennials and climbers as well as trees and shrubs, Aralias are widely distributed in East and South Asia, as well as in North and South America. The following woody species is grown for its bold foliage, autumn color, and flowers.

It does best in a good, not too dry, soil and should be given some shelter from strong winds, which can damage its large leaves. It may be necessary to remove suckers if they become invasive.

Aralia elata
A vigorous, deciduous shrub that spreads by suckers. It has stout, erect, sparsely branched, and spiny shoots, and sometimes forms a spreading tree. The very large leaves can be 3 ft (1 m) or more long and are divided into numerous leaflets. In late summer and early autumn large clusters of small, white flowers open at the ends of the shoots as the huge leaves turn to orange, yellow, and purple. This is followed by small, black fruits. It is sometimes grown as *A. chinensis*.

Common name: Japanese angelica tree
Native range: E Asia
Height: 33 ft (10 m)
Spread: 33 ft (10 m)
Hardiness: Zone 4
Variants: The following variegated forms are slower-growing and smaller, reaching only about 16 ft (5 m) or less. Any shoots with green leaves that arise at the base should be removed. 'Aureovariegata' has the leaflets edged with yellow when young, becoming similar to 'Variegata', which has leaflets edged with creamy white.

Arbutus
Ericaceae

These valuable evergreens provide a range of ornamental features for the garden, from attractive bark to winter flowers and fruits. The genus comprises about 15 species of trees and shrubs, found in Europe and the west of North America, Mexico, and Central America.

The following species will grow on any well-drained soil, including chalky soils. In cold areas they should be protected from the effects of strong winds.

Arbutus x andrachnoides

Arbutus x *andrachnoides*

This naturally occurring hybrid of *A. andrachne* and *A. unedo* is among the finest in the genus. A large, evergreen shrub or spreading tree with glossy, dark green leaves, up to 4 in (10 cm) long, it bears nodding clusters of small, urn-shaped, white flowers in autumn and sporadically during winter, sometimes followed by warty red fruits. The warm reddish-brown bark peels attractively in thin strips.

Native range: Greece
Height: 33 ft (10 m)
Spread: 33 ft (10 m)
Hardiness: Zone 7

Arbutus 'Marina'

This small-to-medium-sized, spreading tree is of uncertain origin, but is proving to be a handsome addition to gardens. It has cinnamon-brown, peeling bark and glossy, dark green-colored leaves to 5 in (12 cm) long, bronze when young. The drooping, urn-shaped flowers are white flushed with deep pink and open in large, upright panicles in summer and autumn, followed by yellow, then red fruits.

Height: 33 ft (10 m)
Spread: 33 ft (10 m)
Hardiness: Zone 8

Arbutus *unedo*

This well-known plant makes a spreading, evergreen tree with rough, red-brown bark and smooth, glossy,

Arctostaphylos uva-ursi

Aronia arbutifolia

dark green leaves to 4 in (10 cm) long. Drooping clusters of small, urn-shaped, white or pink-tinged flowers open at the ends of the shoots in autumn—the warty red fruits, which are about ¾ in (2 cm) across, ripening at the same time from the previous year's flowers.

Common name: Strawberry tree
Native range: Mediterranean region, SW Ireland
Height: 33 ft (10 m)
Spread: 33 ft (10 m)
Hardiness: Zone 7
Variant: Deep pink flowers are found on f. *rubra*.

Arctostaphylos
Ericaceae

This genus, which contains about 50 species of evergreen shrubs and small trees, is mainly confined to California, with the exception of the following, which is probably the most commonly cultivated of all the species. Given a lime-free soil, it is easy to grow, and it prefers a position where it receives full sun. It is an excellent plant for providing dense ground cover and it is a good choice for a large rock garden.

Arctostaphylos uva-ursi

This is a vigorous, creeping, evergreen shrub that, unless checked, forms an extensive carpet, with small, leathery, glossy ,dark green leaves growing up to 1½ in (4 cm) in length. It bears clusters of small, urn-shaped, white or pink-tinged flowers that open in late spring and summer. The flowers are followed by small, glossy red fruits.

Common name: Bearberry
Native range: North temperate regions
Height: 12 in (30 cm)
Spread: 10 ft (3 m) or more
Hardiness: Zone 2
Variants: Several selections have been made, the most popular of which are 'Massachusetts', which has small, glossy, green leaves and pink-tinged flowers, and 'Vancouver Jade', which has attractive red shoots, bright green leaves that turn to

shades of bronze in winter, and pink-colored flowers.

Aronia
Rosaceae

The chokeberries are a genus of two species of deciduous shrubs native to eastern North America. Valued in gardens for their toughness as well as their flowers, autumn color, and fruits, they will grow in almost any soil, but they may become chlorotic in shallow, dry, alkaline soils.

They do best in full sun, but will tolerate shade.

Aronia arbutifolia
A deciduous shrub with upright branches, forming thickets by producing basal suckers. Glossy, dark green leaves, up to 4 in (10 cm) long, are gray-felted beneath and turn brilliant red to purple in autumn. In mid- to late spring, small clusters of white flowers open, followed by bright red fruits.

Common name: Red chokeberry
Native range: E North America
Height: 8 ft (2.5 m)
Spread: 5 ft (1.5 m)
Hardiness: Zone 4

Aronia melanocarpa
This is a vigorous, upright, deciduous shrub with smooth, glossy, dark green leaves up to 4 in (10 cm) long. Its clusters of small, white flowers in spring are followed by glossy, black fruits.

Common name: Black chokeberry
Native range: E North America
Height: 8 ft (2.5 m) ·
Spread: 6 ft (2 m)
Hardiness: Zone 3

Atriplex
Chenopodiaceae

The 100 or so species in this genus are annual and perennial herbs as well as shrubs, and are widely distributed. The following is useful for its ability to withstand full coastal exposure, thriving on sea cliffs and similar situations. In colder inland areas it may need more shelter. It does best in a not-too-rich, well-drained soil in full sun.

Atriplex halimus
An evergreen or semi-evergreen shrub of compact habit with arching branches and diamond-shaped, silvery gray, scaly leaves up to 2½ in (6 cm) long. The tiny, yellow-green flowers in long clusters at the ends of the shoots in late summer are relatively inconspicuous and are not always produced.

Common name: Tree purslane
Native range: S Europe
Height: 6 ft (2 m)
Spread: 6 ft (2 m)
Hardiness: Zone 7

Aucuba
Aucubaceae

This is a genus made up of three or four species of evergreen shrubs, all native from the Himalayas to East Asia. Only the following species is commonly grown, principally for its bold, often variegated leaves and fruits. It will thrive in almost any situation, except very wet soils, and is very shade-tolerant. Male and female flowers are borne on separate plants and both are needed to produce fruits. Overgrown or leggy plants can be cut back hard in early spring before growth starts.

Aucuba japonica
A strong-growing and compact, evergreen shrub with stout, green shoots and glossy green leathery leaves to 8 in (20 cm) long, usually edged with a few teeth. Tiny flowers open in clusters at the ends of the shoots in spring, followed, on females, by glossy red fruits. Usually grown as one of many selected forms, often with variegated foliage.

Common name: Japanese aucuba
Native range: Japan
Height: 10 ft (3 m)
Spread: 10 ft (3 m)
Hardiness: Zone 7
Variants: 'Crotonifolia' is a female form, the leaves of which are heavily speckled with golden yellow. 'Golden King' is male with leaves heavily blotched yellow. 'Rozannie' is a compact female and free-fruiting form up to 5 ft (1.5 m) tall, with dark green leaves. 'Sulphurea Marginata' is female and its leaves have a broad, pale yellow margin. 'Variegata' is female with yellow-spotted leaves.

Azara
Flacourtiaceae

The ten species in this genus of evergreen trees and shrubs are all natives of South America and are grown for their handsome foliage as well as their yellow flowers—the prominent feature of which are their long, yellow stamens.
    They prefer a moist but well-drained soil in a position sheltered from strong winds.

Azara microphylla
This is an evergreen tree with slender shoots and small, glossy, dark green leaves that grow only up to about 1 in (2.5 cm) long. The small clusters of vanilla-scented yellow flowers open on the undersides of the shoots in the late winter or early spring, and these are sometimes followed by small, orange-red berries.

Native range: Argentina, Chile
Height: 33 ft (10 m)

Aucuba japonica 'Variegata'

Spread: 16 ft (5 m)
Hardiness: Zone 8
Variant: 'Variegata' is much slower-growing and usually only about half the size. Its leaves have a yellow margin.

Azara serrata

A vigorous, evergreen shrub with upright branches and glossy, dark green leaves that grow up to 2½ in (6 cm) in length. This is the most striking species of the genus in flower, its clusters of fragrant, golden yellow blooms, which are about ¾ in (2 cm) across, open in late spring and are followed by small, blue-tinged, white berries. In cold areas it benefits from the protection of being trained against a wall.

Native range: Chile
Height: 13 ft (4 m)
Spread: 10 ft (3 m)
Hardiness: Zone 8

Ballota
Labiatae

In this genus there are about 35 species of perennial herbs and subshrubs that are all natives of Europe, mainly in the Mediterranean region, North Africa, and Southwest Asia. The following low-growing species is cultivated principally for its attractive foliage, and the plant does best in soil that is not too rich. It also prefers a position in full sun.

The plant needs to be cut back hard in spring before growth starts in order to maintain a compact habit.

Ballota pseudodictamnus

An evergreen, mound-forming subshrub that has thickly woolly shoots and rounded gray-green leaves up to 1 in (3 cm) long. The small, two-lipped flowers, borne in whorls in the leaf axils in late spring and early summer, are white with a pink

Berberis darwinii

tinge, but they are relatively
inconspicuous in comparison to
the surrounding large, shield-
shaped calyx.

Native range: E Mediterranean
region
Height: 24 in (60 cm)
Spread: 3 ft (1 m)
Hardiness: Zone 8

Berberis
Berberidaceae

The barberries are a large genus
comprising about 450 species of
both deciduous and evergreen, spiny
shrubs that are widely distributed in
the Northern Hemisphere and
throughout South America. The
species are vary variable in terms of
foliage—their leaves range from

those that are untoothed to others
that are edged with spiny teeth, while
the deciduous species often provide
good autumn color, and also include
many selections that have colored
leaves. Purple-leaved forms color
best if they are planted in full sun.

The flowers of the barberries are
usually small and yellow and are
followed by small fruits that range in
color from red to black. They are not
demanding plants in cultivation and
will grow in most types of soil, except
those that are very wet.

Little pruning is required, except
for the removal of stray branches to
maintain shape, and this should be
carried out when flowering is over.

Berberis candidula
A very dense, mound-forming,
evergreen shrub useful for ground

Berberis x frikartii 'Amstelveen'

Berberis x stenophylla 'Corallina Compacta'

cover. The narrow leaves, up to 1 in (3 cm) long, end in a spiny tip and are glossy dark green above and blue-white beneath. Leaves can turn bronze in cold weather. Bright yellow flowers open singly in the leaf axils in spring, followed by egg-shaped, blue-black, bloomy berries.

Native range: China
Height: 24 in (60 cm)
Spread: 5ft (1.5 m)
Hardiness: Zone 6

Berberis darwinii

This is a vigorous, evergreen shrub with arching shoots and sharply toothed, glossy, dark green leaves up to 1½ in (4 cm) long. The dense, drooping clusters of rich orange flowers hang from the shoots in mid-to late spring, followed by spherical, blue-black, bloomy berries.

Native range: Chile, Argentina
Height: 10 ft (3 m)
Spread: 10 ft (3 m)
Hardiness: Zone 7

Berberis x frikartii 'Amstelveen'

A vigorous, evergreen hybrid between B. candidula and B. verruculosa,

making a dense shrub with arching shoots. The glossy, green leaves, up to 1 in (3 cm) long, are white beneath and edged with spiny teeth. Small clusters of yellow flowers open in late spring followed by blue-black berries.

Height: 3 ft (1 m)
Spread: 5 ft (1.5 m)
Hardiness: Zone 6

Berberis julianae

This vigorous, evergreen shrub forms a large, dense mound with glossy, green, leathery leaves, up to 3 in (8 cm) long, edged with numerous spiny teeth. Dense clusters of yellow flowers wreath the shoots in late spring, followed by blue-black, bloomy, egg-shaped fruits. A good species for hedging.

Native range: China
Height: 10 ft (3 m)
Spread: 11–12 ft (3.5 m)
Hardiness: Zone 6

Berberis x lologensis

This is a naturally occurring hybrid between B. darwinii and B. linearifolia. It makes a large, evergreen shrub with arching shoots and with glossy, dark green, spine-

Berberis x *ottawensis* 'Superba'

toothed leaves up to 2 in (5 cm) long.
It bears dense clusters of rich,
orange-colored flowers in late spring,
and often periodically at other times
of the year, followed by spherical
blue-black berries.

Native range: Argentina
Height: 13 ft (4 m)
Spread: 13 ft (4 m)
Hardiness: Zone 6
Variants: 'Apricot Queen' is more
upright with large, bright orange-
colored flowers, 'Mystery Fire' has
profuse orange-yellow flowers,
deeper in bud. 'Stapehill' has profuse,
rich orange-colored flowers.

Berberis x *media*

A hybrid that originated in cultivation
between *B.* 'Chenaultii' and *B.*
thunbergii, making a small semi-
evergreen shrub. The leaves are up to
1 in (3 cm) long and are untoothed or
edged with a few spines. Small
clusters of yellow flowers open in late
spring, and these are followed by dull
red fruits. It is grown only in the two
forms noted below.

Height: 6 ft (2 m)
Spread: 8 ft (2.5 m)
Hardiness: Zone 5
Variants: 'Parkjuweel' has dark green
leaves, some turning bright red in
autumn. 'Red Jewel' has bronze-
purple young foliage, later becoming
dark green.

Berberis x *mentorensis*

This garden-raised hybrid shrub is
a cross between *B. julianae* and
B. thunbergii. It is semi-evergreen
with a rounded habit and is a useful
plant for hedging, with long-
persistent, dark green leaves that are
either untoothed or have just a few
teeth toward the tip. Leaves turn
orange-yellow before they fall in
autumn. Clusters of yellow-colored
flowers tinged with red are followed
by dull red-brown fruits.

Common name: Mentor barberry
Height: 5 ft (1.5 m)
Spread: 6 ft (2 m)
Hardiness: Zone 5

Berberis x ottawensis

This is a vigorous and very hardy hybrid of garden origin between B. vulgaris and B. thunbergii. It is a large, rounded, deciduous shrub with arching shoots and usually untoothed leaves up to 1 in (3 cm) long. The shrub is commonly grown only as forms with purple leaves, which have small clusters of pale yellow flowers tinged with red in spring, followed by egg-shaped red berries.

Height: 8 ft (2.5 m)
Spread: 10 ft (3 m)
Hardiness: Zone 3
Variants: 'Silver Miles' has leaves flushed with silvery gray. The most commonly seen form is 'Superba' ('Purpurea'), which has deep red-purple foliage turning red in autumn.

Berberis x stenophylla

This vigorous, garden hybrid between B. darwinii and B. empetrifolia makes a dense, wide-spreading, evergreen shrub with long, slender, arching shoots bearing slender, spine-tipped, glossy, dark green leaves up to 1 in (2.5 cm). In mid-spring the shoots are wreathed in dense clusters of deep yellow flowers followed by bloomy, blue-black berries.

Height: 10 ft (3 m)
Spread: 16 ft (5 m)
Hardiness: Zone 5
Variants: 'Claret Cascade' has rich orange-colored flowers flushed with red, and purple-tinged young foliage. 'Corallina Compacta' is very compact, up to 24 in (60 cm) tall, with orange flowers from red buds. 'Irwinii' is compact, up to 6 ft (2 m) tall, with orange-yellow flowers. 'Lemon Queen' ('Cream Showers') has creamy white flowers. '

Berberis thunbergii

A very hardy, deciduous shrub of dense, rounded habit. Untoothed leaves to 1 in (3 cm) are bronzy when young, becoming bright green and

Berberis thunbergii 'Aurea'

turning bright orange and red in autumn. Small clusters of pale yellow flowers tinged with red open in mid- to late spring followed by glossy, red, persistent berries. There are numerous and varying selections.

Native range: Japan
Height: 5 ft (1.5 m)
Spread: 8 ft (2.5 m)
Hardiness: Zone 4
Variants: For deep red-purple foliage there is f. atropurpurea. 'Atropurpurea Nana' ('Crimson Pygmy') is compact to 24 in (60 cm), also with red-purple foliage. 'Aurea' has bright yellow young foliage and does best in semishade. 'Bagatelle' is similar to 'Atropurpurea Nana' but more compact. 'Harlequin' has red-purple leaves heavily blotched with white and pink. 'Rose Glow' has red-purple foliage mottled with white and pink.

Berberis verruculosa

A dense, mound-forming, evergreen shrub with rough shoots and small, glossy, dark green, spine-toothed

Berberis wilsoniae

leaves up to 1½ in (4 cm) long, blue-white beneath. Golden yellow flowers in late spring are followed by small, blue-black fruits, which are covered with a white bloom when they are young.

Native range: China
Height: 5 ft (1.5 m)
Spread: 5 ft (1.5 m)
Hardiness: Zone 6

Berberis wilsoniae

A deciduous or semi-evergreen shrub with arching shoots and small blue-green leaves up to 1 in (2.5 cm) long. Leaves are untoothed or have few teeth and turn orange and red in autumn. Clusters of pale yellow flowers in late spring and summer are followed by brilliant coral-red fruits.

Native range: China
Height: 3 ft (1 m)
Spread: 5 ft (1.5 m)
Hardiness: Zone 6

Betula
Betulaceae

The birches are a genus of some 60 species of catkin-bearing deciduous trees and shrubs widely distributed in north temperate regions. The separate male and female catkins open on the same tree in spring before or as the leaves are emerging. The male catkins are pendulous.

Birches are useful in gardens for their fast growth; graceful habit; attractive, sometimes peeling bark; their foliage, which colors in autumn; and their catkins.

These trees are easy to grow in most types of soil and do best in full sun, although they will tolerate light shade. The typical bark color is not usually shown by trees until they are a few years old.

If any pruning is needed, carry it out in summer, as birches bleed sap if their stems are cut in spring.

Betula albosinensis
A conical tree with attractive, orange-red to coppery red bark peeling in horizontal strips to reveal creamy white bark beneath. The glossy, green, sharply toothed leaves, 3 in (7.5 cm) long, end in a tapered point and turn yellow in autumn. In spring it bears pendulous male catkins 2½ in (6 cm) long.

Common name: Chinese paper birch
Native range: China
Height: 80 ft (25 m)
Spread: 33 ft (10 m)
Hardiness: Zone 5
Variant: var. *septentrionalis* has less glossy leaves and buff-pink bark.

Betula alleghaniensis
When young, this is a conical tree, but it spreads as it matures. Young

Betula ermanii

Betula ermanii (catkins)

Betula albosinensis

Betula nigra

shoots are scented with oil of wintergreen when they are scratched and it has yellow-brown peeling bark. This is among the best species for autumn color, when the deep green, finely toothed leaves up to 4 in (10 cm) long turn to a beautiful butter-yellow color. Pendulous male catkins, up to 4 in (10 cm) long, open in the spring.

Synonym: *Betula lutea*
Common name: Yellow birch
Native range: E North America
Height: 65 ft (20 m)
Spread: 50 ft (15 m)
Hardiness: Zone 3

Betula ermanii

This is a broadly conical tree with rough shoots and striking white bark. The bark is conspicuously marked with horizontal, gray-brown bands that are creamy colored when freshly exposed. Glossy, green, finely toothed leaves, up to 3 in (7.5 cm) long, turn yellow in autumn. Male catkins open in the spring.

Native range: NE Asia, Japan
Height: 65 ft (20 m)
Spread: 33 ft (10 m)
Hardiness: Zone 5

Betula nigra

Betula nigra

A vigorous tree, conical when young and spreading with age. The striking bark varies from cream to pink, gray, and brown, and on young trees it peels conspicuously in numerous thin, shaggy layers. Older trees have ridged, gray-brown bark. The sharply toothed, rather blue-green leaves, up to 4 in (10 cm) long, turn yellow in autumn and pendulous male catkins, about 3 in (7.5 cm) in length, open in the spring.

Common name: River birch
Native range: E United States of America
Height: 65 ft (20 m)

Spread: 50 ft (15 m)
Hardiness: Zone 4
Variant: 'Heritage' is a form selected for its vigorous growth and excellent bark.

Betula papyrifera

A vigorous and very tough conical tree. It has white bark that peels in thin strips, pinkish orange when freshly exposed, becoming marked with black on old trees. Taper-pointed and sharply toothed, dark green leaves, up to 4 in (10 cm) long, turn yellow to orange-yellow in autumn. It bears pendulous male catkins 4 in (10 cm) long in spring.

Betula pendula 'Tristis'

Common name: Canoe birch
Native range: North America
Height: 65 ft (20 m)
Spread: 40 ft (12 m)
Hardiness: Zone 2

Betula pendula

A fast-growing, conical tree with distinctive slender, pendulous branches, which give it a very graceful appearance. The white bark does not peel and develops conspicuous blackish cracks toward the base of mature trees. Taper-pointed, glossy, dark green and sharply toothed leaves up to 2½ in (6 cm) long turn yellow in autumn, and pendulous male catkins up to 2½ in (6 cm) long open in spring.

Common name: European birch
Native range: Europe, N Asia
Height: 80 ft (25 m)
Spread: 33 ft (10 m)
Hardiness: Zone 2
Variants: 'Laciniata' (often grown under the name 'Dalecarlica') has finely cut leaves. 'Tristis' has slender, very pendulous shoots, hanging vertically. 'Youngii' (Young's weeping birch) is a mop-headed, small, spreading tree, to about 26 ft (8 m) or less, with pendulous shoots.

Betula utilis

This variable and widely distributed species contains some of the best birches for their bark. It is a broadly conical tree with dark green leaves up to 4 in (10 cm) long that turn a rich yellow in autumn. The bark is variable in color, ranging from coppery brown to pure white, and the striking male catkins can be up to 7 in (18 cm) in length.

Common name: Himalayan birch
Native range: Himalayas, China
Height: 80 ft (25 m)
Spread: 50 ft (15 m)
Hardiness: Zone 5
Variants: var. *jacquemontii* has white bark and good selections of this form include 'Grayswood Ghost', 'Jermyns', and 'Silver Shadow'.

Brachyglottis
Compositae

This genus contains approximately 30 species of evergreen trees and shrubs, as well as herbaceous perennials, and all are natives of New Zealand and Tasmania.

Many of the species now listed here were previously classified under *Senecio*, to which they are closely related.

The most frequently cultivated members of the genus are the evergreen shrubs, which are commonly grown in borders both for their foliage and flower interest. They are easy to grow in any well-drained soil, preferring a position in full sun, and although they are not hardy in the coldest areas, they will withstand full coastal exposure.

Pruning is not usually necessary, but they can be cut back lightly after flowering has finshed.

Brachyglottis monroi
Making a compact, mound-forming, evergreen shrub, *B. monroi* features small, leathery, wavy-edged leaves that grow up to 1½ in (4 cm) long. The leaves are deep green in color above and are covered beneath with a dense layer of white hairs. The bright yellow, daisy-like flowerheads are about ¾ in (2 cm) across and they

Brachyglottis monroi

open in clusters throughout the summer months.

Synonym: *Senecio monroi*
Native range: New Zealand
Height: 30 in (75 cm)
Spread: 5 ft (1.5 m)
Hardiness: Zone 8

Brachyglottis 'Sunshine'
This is an evergreen shrub that develops into a spreading mound. It has leathery, dark green leaves, up to about 3 in (7 cm) long, gray and hairy above when young and covered with white hairs beneath. Large clusters of bright yellow, daisy-like flowerheads open over a long period during the summer season and early autumn. This shrub can be used for hedging.

Synonym: *Senecio* 'Sunshine' (sometimes grown as *Senecio greyi*)
Height: 5 ft (1.5 m)
Spread: 8 ft (2.5 m)
Hardiness: Zone 8

Broussonetia papyrifera (female)

Broussonetia
Moraceae

This is a small genus consisting of just seven species, encompassing deciduous trees and shrubs. All are native from East Asia to Polynesia. Only the following is commonly found in cultivation, however, principally for its handsome foliage as well as its unusual flowers and fruits.

Male and female flowers are borne on separate plants and both are needed in order to produce fruits. It can be grown in any well-drained soil in full sun, but it is more likely to reach treelike proportions in regions where summers are hot.

In cooler areas, growth may not ripen sufficiently and young shoots can then be damaged by winter frosts.

Broussonetia papyrifera

A small and fast-growing, deciduous tree or large shrub, *B. papyrifera* has stout shoots and large, dark green leaves that can reach up to 6 in (15 cm) across. The leaves are roughly hairy above and have soft hairs on their undersurfaces. The leaves are also very variable in shape and are often deeply three-lobed. Male plants bear stout, drooping clusters of white flowers in the spring or early summer, while female plants bear spherical clusters of purple flowers. The female flowers are followed by heads of small red fruits.

Common name: Paper mulberry
Native range: China, Japan
Height: 20 ft (6 m) or more
Spread: 20 ft (6 m)
Hardiness: Zone 6

Buddleja alternifolia

Buddleja crispa

Buddleja
Buddlejaceae

The 100 or so widely distributed species that make up this genus are deciduous and evergreen shrubs and trees. The plants are native to Africa and Asia, as well as the region from the southern United States of America to Mexico, and Central and South America.

Most species in this genus have opposite leaves and small, often fragrant, flowers borne in large conical clusters at the ends of their shoots. The flowers can be highly attractive to butterflies. They will grow in most good soils, but they do best if positioned in full sun. It may be necessary to train less-hardy species against a sunny wall.
B. davidii is best if it is cut back hard to create a low framework of branches in early spring, before the new season's growth starts.

Buddleja alternifolia
A graceful, deciduous shrub with slender, arching shoots and slender, alternate, dark green leaves, growing up to 4 in (10 cm) in length, with gray-white undersurfaces. In early summer, dense clusters of fragrant, lilac-purple flowers open along the shoots that grew in the previous year. Cut branches back after flowering if necessary to maintain shape or to restrict growth.

Native range: China
Height: 10 ft (3 m)
Spread: 10 ft (3 m)
Hardiness: Zone 5
Variant: 'Argentea' has very silvery foliage.

Buddleja crispa
This is a choice garden species, with the double appeal of attractive foliage and extravagant flowers.
B. crispa is a deciduous shrub with graceful, arching shoots. The soft, gray-green leaves, up to 5 in (12 cm) long, have scalloped margins, are hairy white when young, and are borne on white downy shoots. Large clusters of fragrant, lilac flowers open over a long period during summer. This is a good species for training against a wall.

Native range: Himalayas, China

Buddleja davidii 'White Profusion'

Height: 10 ft (3 m)
Spread: 10 ft (3 m)
Hardiness: Zone 7

Buddleja davidii

The most popular species in the genus, *B. davidii* makes a deciduous shrub of vigorous growth with long, arching branches bearing slender, pointed leaves. The large leaves grow up to 10 in (25 cm) in length and are dark green to gray-green above with a layer of white hairs on their undersurfaces. The large, dense, terminal clusters of fragrant flowers can be up to 12 in (30 cm) long and they open over a long period during the summer and autumn. It is grown mainly as selected forms, which vary in color from white, pink, or red to blue and purple.

Common name: Orange eye butterfly bush
Native range: China
Height: 13 ft (4 m)
Spread: 16 ft (5 m)
Hardiness: Zone 5
Variants: The flower color of 'Black Knight' is very deep purple, while 'Dartmoor' has large, branched clusters of flowers red-purple in color. 'Empire Blue' has violet-blue flowers. 'Harlequin' has deep red-purple flowers and its leaves have margins colored an attractive creamy white. 'Nanho Blue' makes a compact plant, up to 6 ft (2 m) tall, with very slender leaves and small clusters of lilac-blue flowers. 'Nanho Purple' is similar to 'Nanho Blue', but with strikingly colored magenta-purple flowers. 'Royal Red' has rich red-purple flowers. For a cooler color

Buddleja davidii 'Dartmoor'

Buddleja davidii 'Empire Blue'

theme, consider 'White Bouquet', which produces large clusters of white flowers, each with a distinctive orange eye. 'White Profusion' is another option that also makes very large clusters of white flowers, but here with a yellow eye.

Buddleja fallowiana

This deciduous shrub is somewhat like a refined and more compact version of *B. davidii*, and it makes a particularly desirable addition to the garden because of its attractive foliage, which maintains interest even when the flowers are spent. The young leaves of *B. fallowiana* emerge covered in white down from white woolly shoots before becoming gray-green in color and growing up to 5 in (12 cm) in length. It may require

Buddleja globosa

shelter in exposed sites. The conical clusters of fragrant, lavender flowers, each with an orange eye, reach about 6 in (15 cm) in length and open in the summer and autumn. Like *B. davidii*, it can be cut back hard in the spring.

Native range: China
Height: 10 ft (3 m)
Spread: 10 ft (3 m)
Hardiness: Zone 7
Variant: var. *alba* has creamy white flowers and silvery gray foliage.

Buddleja globosa

This very distinct species makes a large, semi-evergreen, treelike shrub with dark green, prominently veined

Buddleja lindleyana

large, deep violet-purple flowers are borne in long, arching clusters, reaching up to 8 in (20 cm) long, during the summer and autumn months. Remove spent flowerheads to promote further flowering and extend the season.

Native range: China
Height: 6 ft (2 m)
Spread: 6 ft (2 m)
Hardiness: Zone 7

Buddleja 'Lochinch'

This vigorous, deciduous shrub is a garden-raised hybrid between *B. davidii* and *B. fallowiana*. The arching shoots bear gray-green leaves up to 8 in (20 cm) in length. The leaves are covered in white hairs when they are young. During late summer and autumn, the shrub produces large clusters of fragrant lavender-blue flowers, up to 8 in (20 cm) long, each with an orange eye. Like *B. davidii*, *B.* 'Lochinch' can be cut back hard in the spring to maintain its shape or to restrict height and spread.

Height: 8 ft (2.5 m)
Spread: 10 ft (3 m)
Hardiness: Zone 6

leaves that grow up to 8 in (20 cm) in length. The striking, orange-yellow fragrant flowers are borne in dense, spherical clusters in early summer. This species does best if it is not pruned.

Common name: Globe butterfly bush
Native range: Chile, Argentina
Height: 16 ft (5 m)
Spread: 10 ft (3 m)
Hardiness: Zone 7

Buddleja lindleyana

This unusual deciduous or semi-evergreen shrub species makes a thicket of upright and arching shoots bearing glossy, dark green leaves up to 4 in (10 cm) long. The particularly

Buddleja x weyeriana

These vigorous, deciduous shrubs are garden hybrids between *B. davidii* and *B. globosa* with dark green leaves growing up to 8 in (20 cm) in length. The rounded heads of usually yellow-colored flowers are grouped into large clusters, up to 12 in (30 cm) long, at the ends of the shoots. It is normally grown as one of the selected forms listed below.

Height: 13 ft (4 m)
Spread: 10 ft (3 m)
Hardiness: Zone 7
Variants: 'Golden Glow' has orange-yellow flowers flushed with lilac, while 'Sungold' has deep orange-colored flowers.

Bupleurum
Umbelliferae

The members of this genus, which number about 100 or so species, are mainly annual and perennial herbs and are widely distributed throughout the north temperate regions, as well as South Africa.

The following shrubby species is grown for its attractive foliage and unusual flowers and is suitable for the garden border; where it is of questionable hardiness, it can be grown against a wall for additional protection from the elements. It is best given a well-drained soil in full sun and will thrive in exposed coastal positions. No pruning is usually needed, but it can be cut back in spring, if necessary, to improve its habit or to remove stray, crossing, or unwanted shoots.

Bupleurum fruticosum
This is an evergreen, sparsely branched shrub with a naturally compact habit, with glossy, blue-green leaves that grow up to 3 in (8 cm) in length. Open, rounded heads of small, starry shaped, mustard-yellow flowers open over a long period during summer and early autumn.

Buxus sempervirens 'Suffruticosa'

Common name: Shrubby hare's ear
Native range: Mediterranean region
Height: 5 ft (1.5 m)
Spread: 6 ft (2 m)
Hardiness: Zone 7

Buxus
Buxaceae

The boxes are a genus of some 30 species of evergreen shrubs and trees widely distributed in Europe, Asia, Africa, Mexico, and Central America. All have opposite, rather leathery leaves and very small flowers that are borne in clusters in the leaf axils. The only conspicuous part of the male flowers are the yellow anthers.

In gardens, box plants are grown for their neat habit and attractive foliage and, especially, for their tolerance of hard pruning, which makes them suitable for hedging, topiary, and ground cover. These very adaptable plants thrive in most conditions, as long as the soil is well drained, and although they will tolerate being positioned in either sun or shade, box does particularly well in partial shade.

Prune hedges and edging box in summer as necessary to maintain their size and shape, while old plants—or those that have become neglected—can be renovated by cutting them back to the base before the new growth starts in spring.

Buxus microphylla
The plant grown under this name is probably a Japanese garden selection of a species widely distributed in several forms in East Asia. It is an evergreen shrub of a dense habit forming a low, spreading mound. The small, dark green leaves, growing up to about ¾ in (2 cm) long, are narrow and oblong in shape and can turn bronze in very cold weather.

Height: 3 ft (1 m)
Spread: 3 ft (1 m)
Hardiness: Zone 6

Buxus sempervirens 'Elegantissima'

Variants: A variable species with several geographical variants and numerous garden selections. The very hardy var. *koreana* is good for cold areas, while var. *japonica* can reach 6 ft (2 m).

Buxus sempervirens

This species of box develops into an evergreen shrub or small tree with mature leaves that are glossy and very dark green in color. When they are young, the leaves are usually more blue-green. The leaves, which form a dense mass, grow up to about 1 in (2.5 cm) in length, and are often notched at their tips. The small, but numerous, yellow-green, fragrant flowers add interest and attract insects in spring. B. sempervirens, which is much valued by topiarists, makes an excellent dense hedge and is commonly seen clipped into a wide variety of animal, geometric, or other unusual shapes.

Common name: Common box
Native range: Europe, North Africa, SW Asia
Height: 16 ft (5 m)
Spread: 16 ft (5 m)
Hardiness: Zone 5
Variants: 'Aureovariegata' has a very compact growth habit, reaching up to about 8 ft (2.5 m) in height, and has leaves that are conspicuously blotched and streaked a creamy yellow color. 'Elegantissima' is a very dense form. It is slow-growing, however, eventually reaching a height of up to about 5 ft (1.5 m). It produces tiny leaves that are narrowly edged with white. 'Suffruticosa' is dwarf and upright in habit, reaching up to 3 ft (1 m) in height, but in gardens it is usually cut back to form low edging to paths or borders.

Callicarpa bodinieri var. giraldii 'Profusion'

Callicarpa
Verbenaceae

There are approximately 140 species of shrubs and trees in this genus. Although they are largely tropical in origin, they also include some very hardy species providing striking displays of brilliantly colored fruits. Known as the beautyberries, they have opposite leaves and clusters of small flowers in summer. They can be grown in any well-drained soil, preferably in a sunny position such as a shrub border, where they can add valuable autumn interest.

Pruning is not essential, but in order to restrict growth or renovate old plants, they can be cut back hard before growth starts in spring.

Callicarpa bodinieri

A deciduous shrub of upright growth with dark green, taper-pointed leaves. In summer, clusters of small, pink flowers open in the axils of the leaves, followed by violet fruits.

Native range: China
Height: 10 ft (3 m)
Spread: 8 ft (2.5 m)
Hardiness: Zone 6
Variant: var. *giraldii* 'Profusion' is the best form of this species, with young, bronze-tinged foliage and dense clusters of deep violet fruits.

Callicarpa dichotoma

This elegant, deciduous shrub has slender shoots that become arched with age, and bright green, slender-pointed leaves. Pale pink flowers open in small, dense clusters during summer and these are followed by violet-colored fruits. Given hot summers, this is the hardiest species of the genus.

Native range: China, Korea, Japan
Height: 5 ft (1.5 m)
Spread: 5 ft (1.5 m)
Hardiness: Zone 5

Callistemon
Myrtaceae

The bottlebrushes are a group of very showy evergreen shrubs and trees, related to the myrtles, and are best known for their flower clusters, which are likened to bottlebrushes.

With about 30 species in Australia, they have slender, sometimes aromatic leaves, often attractively tinted as they emerge. The flowers are arranged in dense, cylindrical clusters on the shoots and are made conspicuous by their long, colorful, and showy stamens.

Bottlebrushes are mostly suitable for milder regions, but even where they are borderline hardy, they can still be grown if they are given the protection of a wall. They prefer a lime-free soil in a sunny position and are suitable for coastal positions. Cut back after flowering if necessary.

Callistemon citrinus

This popular species makes a large shrub, treelike in mild areas, with dark green, pointed leaves that are bronze when young and strongly lemon-scented when crushed. The dense, showy clusters of crimson flowers open during spring or summer, and sometimes at other times of the year as well.

Common name: Lemon bottlebrush
Native range: SE Australia
Height: 6 ft (2 m) or more
Spread: 10 ft (3 m)

Callistemon citrinus 'Splendens'

Hardiness: Zone 8
Variant: 'Splendens' has profuse clusters of bright crimson-colored flowers.

Callistemon rigidus

This relatively hardy species makes a rigidly branched shrub with long, narrow, sharply pointed, gray-green leaves. The dense, short clusters of red flowers open during the late spring or early summer.

Common name: Stiff bottlebrush
Native range: E Australia
Height: 6 ft (2 m)
Spread: 8 ft (2.5 m)
Hardiness: Zone 8

Callistemon salignus

A striking but tender species reaching tree size in suitable locations, with narrow, willow-like leaves that are bronze or pink when young. The flowers vary in color from white, green, and pale yellow to pink, red, and mauve, and are borne in dense clusters in spring or summer.

Common name: Willow bottlebrush
Native range: SE Australia
Height: 16 ft (5 m) or more
Spread: 16 ft (5 m)
Hardiness: Zone 9

Calluna vulgaris 'Darkness'

Calluna vulgaris
Ericaceae

The single species in this genus is an evergreen shrub widely distributed across northern Europe and Asia, occurring on mountains in the south. The tiny, scalelike leaves densely clothe the shoots in opposite pairs, and small urn-shaped flowers, varying in color from white to pink and purple, are produced in long spikes during late summer and autumn. It needs a well-drained, acidic, peaty or sandy soil in full sun. Cut back lightly in spring to maintain its compact habit.

Common name: Heather
Native range: Europe, W Asia
Height: 24 in (60 cm)
Spread: 3 ft (1 m)
Hardiness: Zone 4
Variants: 'Beoley Gold' has bright yellow foliage and white flowers. 'County Wicklow' is dwarf, to 10 in (25 cm), with pale pink, double flowers. 'Darkness' is compact, to 12 in (30 cm), with dark green foliage and deep purple-pink flowers. 'Gold Haze' has yellow foliage and white flowers. 'HE Beale' has long spikes of bright pink, double flowers. 'JH Hamilton' is compact, to 10 in (25 cm), with deep pink, double flowers. 'Kinlochruel' has bright green foliage and white, double flowers. 'Robert Chapman' has golden yellow foliage, red in winter, and purple flowers. 'Silver Queen' has silvery gray foliage and pale mauve flowers. 'Sir John Charrington' has yellow foliage, turning orange and red in winter, and lilac-mauve flowers. 'Spring Cream' is vigorous with dark green foliage, tipped cream in spring, and long spikes of white flowers. 'Wickwar Flame' has orange-yellow foliage, turning red in winter, and mauve-pink flowers.

Calluna vulgaris 'Wickwar Flame'

Calycanthus
Calycanthaceae

This small genus consisting of three species of deciduous shrubs is restricted to North America. Species have opposite, aromatic leaves. As well as handsome foliage, they also have unusual, often fragrant, flowers, which are composed of numerous strap-shaped petals.

These shrubs are suitable for planting in a large border or woodland clearing and they prefer a moist, humus-rich soil.

Calycanthus floridus

This bushy, spreading shrub has bold, dark green leaves, aromatic when crushed, that sometimes turn yellow in autumn. The flowers, which can have a spicily aromatic scent, open in late spring and sporadically through summer, and they have many straplike red or red-brown petals.

Calycanthus floridus

Common name: Carolina allspice
Native range: SE United States of America
Height: 8 ft (2.5 m)
Spread: 13 ft (4 m)
Hardiness: Zone 5

Camellia x *williamsii* 'Donation'

Camellia
Theaceae

Containing some 250 named species, this genus of evergreen shrubs and trees originates in East and Southeast Asia. A small number of the total available species provides most garden selections and hybrids. These are all characterized by having dark green, leathery leaves and showy flowers, which vary in color from white to pink and red, with some having yellow centers. While most garden species of camellia flower in the spring, the forms of C. *sasanqua* are unusual in that they bloom in the autumn and winter seasons.

Camellia japonica 'Elegans'

Ideally, camellias should be sited in a border or among other shrubs and trees. In order to thrive, they require a well-drained, moist, lime-free soil bulked out with abundant organic matter. The buds of camellias are susceptible to damage by early-morning frosts late in the spring season and so may need some protection until the danger period has passed.

The flowers of camellias vary considerably in both shape and in the number of their petals, and the central cluster of stamens often forms a conspicuous and distinguishing feature of the bloom. In the species descriptions on the following pages, the flower terms used are defined as meaning:
Single Flowers with up to eight petals arranged in a single row, and with a conspicuous central cluster of stamens.
Semidouble Flowers with the petals arranged in two or more rows, and with the center of the flower usually having a conspicuous cluster of stamens.
Double Flowers with numerous overlapping petals and a concave

Camellia japonica 'Adolphe Audusson'

center of stamens when the bloom is fully open.

Formal double Flowers with numerous overlapping petals and no stamens.

Anemone-form Flowers with the outer petals in one or more rows, with a dense central cluster of stamens mixed with stamen-like petals.

Peony-form A rounded flower composed of mixed petals and stamen-like petals, often with some stamens in the center.

Camellia 'Cornish Snow'

This garden-raised hybrid makes a fast-growing, medium-sized, and rounded evergreen shrub. It has an essentially open, upright, bushy habit, arching shoots, and taper-pointed leaves sometimes described as lancelike. When young, the leaves are bronze in color, turning dark green as they mature. Small, cup-shaped, single, white or pink-tinged flowers open during spring. Pruning is not usually necessary; however, dead, damaged, or unwanted branches can be removed in late spring to maintain shape after flowering has finished.

Height: 8 ft (2.5 m)
Spread: 10 ft (3 m)
Hardiness: Zone 7

Camellia 'Inspiration'

Camellia 'Inspiration'

This is a medium-sized shrub, vigorous, large-growing, frost-hardy, and evergreen. It has an upright habit and dark green, oval-shaped, leathery leaves. The flowers of C. 'Inspiration' are large and semidouble in form. They are a rich deep pink color, and are profusely borne during the spring season. Pruning is not usually necessary, but dead, damaged, or unwanted branches can be removed in late spring, after flowering has finished.

Height: 13 ft (4 m)
Spread: 10 ft (3 m)
Hardiness: Zone 7

Camellia japonica

This is by far the most popular species in garden cultivation, and has given rise to many selections and hybrids, with plants varying enormously in terms of flower size, form, and color. Making a dense, usually rounded shrub with glossy, dark green foliage, C. japonica bears flowers during the spring, and blooms can be single, semidouble, or fully double, ranging in color from white to pink or red, sometimes variegated.

Common name: Common camellia
Native range: China, Korea, Japan
Height: 10 ft (3 m) or more
Spread: 16 ft (5 m) or more
Hardiness: Zone 7
Variants: 'Adolphe Audusson' has large, semidouble, deep red flowers, while 'Akashigata' ('Lady Clare') has large, deep pink, semidouble flowers. 'Alba Simplex' has large, white, single flowers with a conspicuous center of bright yellow stamens. 'Apollo' is a vigorous shrub with small, red, semidouble flowers. 'Betty Sheffield' has large, white, semidouble flowers attractively blotched pink. 'Blood of China' is a vigorous and compact plant with large, deep red, semidouble flowers. 'Debutante' is vigorous and upright in habit with pale pink, peony-form flowers. 'Drama Girl' benefits from having very large, deep salmon-pink, semidouble flowers, while 'Elegans' has a spreading habit and bears large, peach-pink, anemone-form flowers. 'Guilio Nuccio' has vigorous growth and an upright habit, with large, rose-pink, semidouble flowers. 'Hagoromo' ('Magnoliiflora') has pale pink, semidouble flowers. 'Hakurakuten' is vigorous and upright with large, white, semidouble flowers. 'Jupiter' is vigorous with single to semidouble, deep pink flowers with conspicuous stamens. 'Kramer's Supreme' is a compact shrub with an upright habit with very large, peony-form, slightly fragrant, red blooms. 'Lady Vansittart' bears white, semidouble flowers that are striped pink or red, while 'Lavinia Maggi' has large, white, formal double flowers striped in deep pink. 'Mars' has large, red, semidouble flowers. 'Nobilissima' flowers very early in the season and has white, peony-form blooms. 'RL Wheeler' is vigorous and has large, semidouble, rose-pink flowers. 'Silver Anniversary' is vigorous and upright in growth and bears large, semidouble, white flowers. 'Tricolor' has single to semidouble flowers that are streaked with white, pink, and red

Camellia 'Leonard Messel'

This garden-raised hybrid has an open, rounded habit with large, oval-shaped, dark green, leathery leaves. Its striking, semidouble, rich clear pink flowers open during the spring season. Flower shape can be flattish to cup-shaped.

Height: 8 ft (2.5 m)
Spread: 10 ft (3 m)
Hardiness: Zone 8

Camellia sasanqua

A rather elegant species with glossy, dark green leaves, varying in habit from spreading and shrubby to upright and treelike. The normally white flowers can be pink or red in garden selections. They are fragrantly scented and open in autumn and early winter.

Native range: Japan
Height: 10 ft (3 m) or more
Spread: 10 ft (3 m)
Hardiness: Zone 7
Variants: 'Crimson King' has single red flowers, while 'Narumigata' has large white flowers.

Camellia 'Spring Festival'

This is a very distinct garden-raised hybrid, a seedling of *C. cuspidata*, which makes an evergreen shrub of compact, narrowly upright habit and has glossy, dark green leaves. The small, formal double, pink flowers fade in mid- to late spring to pale pink after opening.

Height: 10 ft (3 m)
Spread: 3 ft (1 m)
Hardiness: Zone 8

Camellia x williamsii

These garden-raised hybrids between *C. japonica* and *C. saluenensis* have provided some of the finest camellias found in garden cultivation. They are normally very vigorous and most selections grow into large shrubs with glossy, dark green leaves. The flowers vary in form and color from single to formal double and from white to deep pink. Blooms are produced during spring.

Height: 10 ft (3 m) or more
Spread: 10 ft (3 m) or more
Hardiness: Zone 8
Variants: 'Anticipation' is upright in habit with large, deep pink, peony-form flowers. 'Bow Bells' has single, bright pink, funnel-shaped flowers over a long period. 'Brigadoon' has a compact and upright habit with semidouble, rose-pink flowers. 'China Clay' bears semidouble, white flowers, while 'Debbie' has large, rich pink, peony-form flowers. 'Donation' is among the most popular of all, with large, semidouble, pink flowers and an upright habit. 'EG Waterhouse' has pale pink, formal double flowers and 'Elegant Beauty' has large, deep rose-pink, anemone-form flowers. 'Elsie Jury' bears large, clear pink, peony-form flowers and 'ETR Carlyon' is vigorous with arching shoots and semi-double to double white flowers. 'Francis Hanger' has an upright shape with single, white flowers and wavy edged leaves. 'Golden Spangles' has small, single, pink flowers and leaves that are blotched yellow-green in their centers. 'JC Williams' has single pink flowers and 'Jury's Yellow' has anemone-form white flowers, the centers of which contain many yellow petal-like stamens. 'Saint Ewe' has large, single, rich pink flowers and 'Water Lily' has large, fully double, rich pink flowers.

Caragana
Leguminosae

These deciduous and often spiny shrubs and small trees make up a genus comprising some 80 species that are native in Eastern Europe and Asia. They have leaves that are divided into several leaflets and they bear small, pealike, usually yellow, flowers. The following plant is the only commonly grown species and it is valued for its extreme hardiness and its ability to grow in poor soils. For best results, grow it in any well-drained soil in full sun; it will also tolerate exposed positions. Little pruning is required, but selected forms are usually grafted and so it may sometimes be necessary to remove suckers from the base, below the graft point.

Caragana arborescens
A fast-growing, deciduous and spiny shrub, whose upright branches bear

Camellia x williamsii 'Bow Bells'

bright green leaves, each divided up into 12 small leaflets. Small, pealike, bright yellow flowers open singly or in clusters during spring and these are followed by slender, brown seed pods later in the year.

Common name: Siberian pea tree
Native range: Siberia, N China
Height: 16 ft (5 m)
Spread: 13 ft (4 m)
Hardiness: Zone 2

Variants: 'Lorbergii' is a very graceful shrub with slender shoots, narrow leaflets, and smaller flowers. 'Pendula' is a weeping form, grafted on the top of a stem, usually about 3–5 ft (1–1.5 m) tall. 'Walker' is similar to 'Pendula', but it has foliage that is more like 'Lorbergii'.

Carpinus betulus

Carpenteria
Hydrangeaceae

The single species in this genus is an evergreen shrub with opposite leaves, native to California, and is grown in gardens for its handsome flowers. It should be given well-drained soil and a sunny position, where it will be suitable for a shrub border or, in cooler areas, a sunny wall. Cut back lightly in spring if necessary, removing any dead or crossing wood at the same time.

Carpenteria californica
This is an evergreen shrub with opposite, glossy, dark green leaves.

Carpenteria californica

The showy, white, anemone-like flowers have a conspicuous center of yellow stamens and the attractive blooms open in clusters toward the ends of the shoots in the summer months.

Common name: Evergreen mock orange
Native range: California
Height: 6 ft (2 m)
Spread: 5 ft (1.5 m)
Hardiness: Zone 8

Carpinus
Carpinaceae

The hornbeams comprise a genus of about 35 species of deciduous, catkin-bearing trees, mainly found in China, but also widely distributed throughout Europe, Asia, and North America.

The following species is useful both as a specimen tree and as hedging. It will grow on any well-drained soil, even shallow chalk soils. Hedges can be cut in late summer.

Carpinus betulus
This is a deciduous tree that has a broadly conical-to-rounded habit

with a smooth, gray, fluted trunk and sharply toothed, conspicuously veined leaves turning yellow in autumn. Separate male and female catkins are borne on the same tree in spring: the males yellow and drooping; the females green and forming attractive, green fruit clusters, later turning yellow-brown in color.

Common name: European hornbeam
Native range: Europe, SW Asia
Height: 80 ft (25 m)
Spread: 65 ft (20 m)
Hardiness: Zone 5
Variant: 'Fastigiata' is dense and narrowly upright when young, later rounded, up to 50 ft (15 m) tall.

Carya
Juglandaceae
The hickories are a genus of some 20 species of generally fast-growing, deciduous trees that are related to the walnuts (*Juglans*). Hickories are natives of North America and Southeast Asia. Suitable for larger gardens only or parks, hickories are mainly large trees grown for their stately habit and bold foliage, which colors in autumn, often turning a clear yellow. Several species produce edible nuts, including the pecan (*Carya illinoinensis*). They require a good, fertile, well-drained soil, and should also be planted when they are small in order to prevent any possible damage to the tap root.

Carya ovata
A deciduous tree with gray-brown bark, which, on mature trees, peels in long, vertical strips. The leaves are deep green and are usually made up of five individual leaflets. In autumn, leaves turn golden yellow. Male and female flowers are borne separately on the same tree: the male flowers in pendulous catkins growing in clusters of three; the small female flowers developing into thick-shelled and edible nuts.

Common name: Shagbark
Native range: E North America
Height: 80 ft (25 m)
Spread: 50 ft (15 m)
Hardiness: Zone 4

Caryopteris
Verbenaceae

This small genus consists of only about six species of deciduous shrubs and herbaceous perennials, all of which are native to East Asia. The following is the most commonly seen shrubby representative of the genus in cultivation and it is grown for its blue flowers.
   In order to do well, it needs to be grown in a well-drained, but not overly rich soil, and it requires a position where it receives full sun. The shrub is suitable for the front of a garden border or for growing against a sunny wall. Cut it back hard in spring before growth starts.

Caryopteris x clandonensis
This is a garden-raised hybrid between *C. incana* and *C. mongolica* that makes a deciduous, mound-forming shrub with aromatic, gray-green leaves that are silvery white beneath. Clusters of blue flowers open during the late summer and autumn seasons. Several selections have been raised and these vary in flower color. In particularly cold regions, the shrub may be treated as a herbaceous perennial and be cut down to soil level in autumn.

Height: 35 in (90 cm)
Spread: 3 ft (1 m)
Hardiness: Zone 6
Variants: 'Arthur Simmonds' has purple-blue flowers. 'Ferndown' has deep blue-violet flowers. 'Heavenly Blue' has very dark blue flowers. 'Kew Blue' has dark blue flowers. 'Worcester Gold' has yellow to yellow-green foliage and lavender blue-colored flowers.

Caryopteris x clandonensis 'Heavenly Blue'

Cassiope
Ericaceae

In this genus there are about 12 species of unusual heather-like, evergreen shrubs with a restricted native range taking in the arctic and alpine regions. They have small, densely overlapping leaves and bear small, white, nodding flowers in late spring and early summer. They require a moist, acidic, peaty soil and are at their best in cooler climates, where they are suitable for a rock or peat garden.

Cassiope 'Edinburgh'
This garden-raised hybrid grows into an attractive, dwarf, evergreen shrub ideal for a rock garden. It has sparsely branched, upright shoots bearing slender, dark green leaves, and its small, pendulous, white flowers, which open in the late spring, are notable for having contrasting red-edged sepals.

Height: 8 in (20 cm)
Spread: 8 in (20 cm)
Hardiness: Zone 3

Cassiope lycopodioides
This low-growing and mat-forming, evergreen shrub spreads by sending out slender, creeping or ascending shoots with tiny, dark green leaves. In late spring, C. *lycopodioides* bears small, nodding, white, bell-shaped flowers with attractively contrasting red sepals and stalks.

Native range: Japan, Alaska
Height: 4 in (10 cm)
Spread: 10 in (25 cm)
Hardiness: Zone 3
Variants: 'Beatrice Lilley' is a compact form and bears profuse flowers.

Castanea
Fagaceae

This small genus of 12 species, which encompasses the sweet chestnut, contains deciduous trees and shrubs that are natives of north temperate regions. They all have sharply toothed leaves and bear their fragrant flowers in upright, slender catkins that are followed by fruits enclosed in conspicuous spiny husks.

The following species is the most commonly grown of the genus. It does best if planted in a good, acidic soil and it is also suitable for planting where soils are very sandy.

Castanea sativa
This is a fast-growing, large, deciduous tree with smooth, gray bark when young. The bark becomes brown and spirally furrowed with age. The bold, glossy, dark green leaves are edged with numerous bristle-tipped teeth. Masses of creamy, fragrant catkins appear in summer and these are followed by very spiny fruits containing large, brown, and edible seeds.

Common names: Spanish chestnut, sweet chestnut
Native range: S Europe, SW Asia, North Africa
Height: 100 ft (30 m)
Spread: 65 ft (20 m)
Hardiness: Zone 5
Variant: 'Albomarginata' has its leaf margins colored creamy yellow when foliage is young, becoming creamy white with age.

Catalpa
Bignoniaceae

The 11 species that make up this genus are all deciduous trees and their native range is North America and East Asia. They make wide-spreading trees with bold leaves that are opposite or borne in whorls of three. Large clusters of white,

Catalpa x erubescens 'Purpurea'

foxglove-like flowers, variously spotted with purple, are conspicuously borne in summer at the ends of the shoots of older trees, and these are followed by long, pendulous, beanlike seed pods.

These trees will grow in any good soil, as long as it is well-drained, and they do best where they receive full sun. They make striking specimen trees if given adequate room to spread, but they can also be grown as shrubs. In this case, they need to be cut back annually to just above the base before the new growth starts in spring. If treated as a shrub, they will produce vigorous shoots and very large leaves, but no flowers.

Catalpa bignonioides
This is a vigorous, deciduous, spreading tree that has large, rounded, taper-pointed leaves emerging in late spring. The large, upright, conical clusters of white, bell-shaped flowers are heavily spotted with purple and yellow and open in summer. The flowers are followed by slender, pendulous pods, which persist on the tree. It requires an open site to be seen at its best.

Common name: Southern catalpa
Native range: SE United States of America
Height: 50 ft (15 m)
Spread: 50 ft (15 m)
Hardiness: Zone 5

Catalpa bignonioides 'Aurea'

Variant: 'Aurea' is a smaller-growing tree, attaining a maximum height of about 33 ft (10 m), and has bright yellow foliage.

Catalpa x *erubescens*

This garden-raised hybrid makes a deciduous tree of spreading habit with large, angularly three-lobed, dark green leaves. Conical clusters of white, bell-shaped, fragrant flowers are heavily spotted with yellow and purple. The flowers open in late summer and these are followed by long, slender, pendulous pods.

Height: 50 ft (15 m)
Spread: 50 ft (15 m)
Hardiness: Zone 5
Variant: 'Purpurea' has particularly attractive foliage. The young leaves are deep blackish-purple, maturing to a purple-green color before turning dark green.

Ceanothus
Rhamnaceae

Sometimes known as the California lilacs, this genus contains about 55 species of evergreen and deciduous trees and shrubs. They can have opposite or alternate leaves and are found mainly in California, although some do occur in other parts of North and Central America. Showing a wide variation in both habit and foliage, they are valued for their small, but profusely borne, clustered flowers. The flowers are usually blue, but they can also be pink or white.

The plants in this genus all require a well-drained soil and a sunny position. They can be used as specimen plants, grown against a wall, or the low-growing specimens are suitable for ground cover. The deciduous plants can be cut back hard in spring, while the evergreens should be only lightly pruned.

Ceanothus arboreus

This vigorous species makes a large, spreading, evergreen shrub or small tree with glossy, dark green leaves densely covered with gray hairs beneath. The blue flowers open in large, showy, conical clusters in late spring and early summer.

Common name: Feltleaf ceanothus
Native range: California
Height: 16 ft (5 m)
Spread: 20 ft (6 m)
Hardiness: Zone 8
Variant: 'Trewithen Blue' is a form with particularly rich-blue flowers.

Ceanothus 'Autumnal Blue'

This garden-raised hybrid is one of the hardiest of the evergreen forms and it makes an outstanding plant for the border. The shrub is of an essentially upright habit and has glossy, dark green, distinctly three-veined leaves. A profusion of conical clusters of sky-blue flowers open in late spring and often there is a repeat flowering in the late summer and autumn.

Height: 10 ft (3 m)
Spread: 8 ft (2.5 m)
Hardiness: Zone 8

Ceanothus 'Blue Mound'

This fast-growing and very tough garden hybrid makes a dense, evergreen mound of spreading habit with small, glossy, dark green, wavy-edged, and finely toothed leaves. Clusters of deep blue flowers open in the late spring and often there is a repeat flowering in the late summer and early autumn.

Height: 8 ft (2.5 m)
Spread: 13 ft (4 m)
Hardiness: Zone 8

Ceanothus 'Cascade'

This large, vigorous shrub of spreading habit has arching branches bearing glossy, dark green, finely toothed leaves. The dense, rounded clusters of powder-blue flowers are profusely borne over a long period in late summer and early autumn.

Height: 13 ft (4 m)
Spread: 16 ft (5 m)
Hardiness: Zone 8

Ceanothus 'Concha'

This is a vigorous, garden-raised hybrid making a spreading, evergreen shrub with arching shoots bearing narrow, glossy, dark green leaves. Dense clusters of deep blue flowers open from red buds during spring.

Height: 8 ft (2.5 m)
Spread: 13 ft (4 m)
Hardiness: Zone 8

Ceanothus x delileanus

This group of garden hybrids between C. americanus and C. coeruleus contains some of the finest deciduous Ceanothus. Vigorous and upright, they bear dark green leaves and large clusters of blue flowers during summer and autumn.

Height: 6 ft (2 m)
Spread: 5 ft (1.5 m)
Hardiness: Zone 7
Variants: Several of the most popular garden forms belong here. For example, 'Gloire de Versailles' bears large clusters of powder-blue flowers, 'Henri Desfossé' has deep blue flowers, while 'Topaze' has indigo-blue flowers.

Ceanothus griseus

This vigorous and spreading, evergreen shrub has glossy, green, toothed, and wavy-edged leaves covered with gray hairs on their undersurfaces. The flowers of C. griseus varies in color from lilac to deep blue, and flowers open in large, rounded clusters during the late spring and early summer.

Ceanothus 'Blue Mound'

Common name: Carmel ceanothus
Native range: California
Height: 10 ft (3 m)
Spread: 16 ft (5 m)
Hardiness: Zone 8
Variant: var. *horizontalis* 'Yankee Point' is a low-growing selection with a compact habit, growing to about 24 in (60 cm) tall, and with deep blue flowers.

Ceanothus impressus

This species is popular in gardens, as well as being the parent of several hybrids. It makes a compact, rounded, evergreen bush with small, dark green, deeply veined leaves. Small, dense, rounded clusters of deep blue flowers open in late spring.

Common name: Santa Barbara ceanothus
Native range: California
Height: 6 ft (2 m)
Spread: 8 ft (2.5 m)
Hardiness: Zone 8

Ceanothus x pallidus

These are garden hybrids between *C. x delileanus* and *C. ovatus*. Like the forms of *C. x delileanus*, they make deciduous shrubs of upright growth and bear large flower clusters at the ends of their shoots in the summer and autumn. They can be cut back in spring if necessary before the new season's growth starts. There are several selections varying in flower color.

Ceanothus 'Concha'

Ceanothus x pallidus 'Perle Rose'

Height: 5 ft (1.5 m)
Spread: 3 ft (1 m)
Hardiness: Zone 7
Variants: 'Marie Simon' has pale pink
flowers, while 'Perle Rose' has
carmine-pink flowers.

Ceanothus thyrsiflorus

This is a vigorous and spreading
evergreen shrub, sometimes treelike
in form, with glossy, dark green,
finely toothed, and three-veined
leaves. Among the most striking and
hardy of the evergreens, it produces
large clusters of bright blue flowers
during spring.

Common name: Blue blossom
ceanothus
Native range: California
Height: 16 ft (5 m)
Spread: 20 ft (6 m)
Hardiness: Zone 7
Variant: var. *repens* (creeping blue
blossom) is the most commonly
grown form. It makes a dense bush
of low, spreading habit about 3 ft
(1 m) tall.

Ceratostigma
Plumbaginaceae

This is a small genus consisting of
about eight species of herbaceous
perennials and subshrubs that are
natives of Africa and from the

Ceratostigma willmottianum

Himalayas to East Asia. The few species in cultivation are valued for their unusual blue flowers, which are borne late in the season.

The following is the most popular and easiest species to grow. It is suitable for a garden border or for planting against a wall, and prefers a well-drained soil in a position where it receives full sun. It does best if cut back hard in the spring before growth starts or it may behave as a herbaceous perennial in cold areas.

Ceratostigma willmottianum

This is a small-growing, compact, and deciduous subshrub with slender, upright, sparsely branched red shoots and bristly red-edged leaves. The leaves turn red in autumn. Clusters of attractive blue flowers open over a long period during the late summer and autumn.

Native range: China
Height: 3 ft (1 m)
Spread: 3 ft (1 m)
Hardiness: Zone 7

Cercidiphyllum
Cercidiphyllaceae

The two species of trees in this genus are both deciduous and are native to Japan and China. Having very distinctive foliage, they are grown mainly for their autumn leaf color.

These trees do best in a good, moist, neutral or acidic soil, and they also benefit from the shelter offered by other nearby trees. The foliage emerges very early in the year and can be damaged by late frosts. Established plants can survive this, but young plants can be killed.

Cercidiphyllum japonicum

This is a strongly growing deciduous tree. When young, it is essentially conical in shape, but as it ages it becomes more spreading in habit. Its leaves are opposite or alternate, rounded, and shallowly toothed, bronze when young and becoming green to blue-green. The very small red flowers—males and females are borne on separate trees—open before the leaves emerge. The leaves turn

Cercis siliquastrum

startling hues in autumn, ranging from yellow to orange and red, and colors are more striking if the tree is grown on acid soils. Unusually, the leaves smell of burned sugar after they have fallen.

Common name: Katsura tree
Native range: Japan, China
Height: 65 ft (20 m)
Spread: 65 ft (20 m)
Hardiness: Zone 4
Variants: 'Pendulum' forms a mound of arching shoots up to 20 ft (6 m) tall. 'Rotfuchs' is upright in habit, with deep red-purple foliage.

Cercis
Leguminosae

The redbuds are a small genus of some seven species of very distinct deciduous trees native from the eastern Mediterranean region to Central and East Asia, and in North America, with untoothed, rounded leaves that are distinctly heart-shaped at the base. Popular in gardens for their small but profuse flowers, borne before or as the leaves emerge, they are suitable for all well-drained soils, including chalk, and they do best in a warm, sunny position

CERCIS — CESTRUM 'NEWELLII' 101

Cercis canadensis

This is a deciduous tree that has a rounded-to-spreading habit. It bears heart-shaped, bright green leaves, which are bronze-colored when young, ending in short, tapered points. The pealike flowers vary in color from white to pale or deep pink, and open in clusters on the shoots before the leaves emerge in the spring. The flowers are followed by flattened seed pods, which are green colored when young and turn red and then brown as they mature and ripen.

Common name: Eastern redbud
Native range: North America
Height: 26 ft (8 m)
Spread: 33 ft (10 m)
Hardiness: Zone 4
Variant: 'Forest Pansy' produces leaves that are deep red-purple in color.

Cercis siliquastrum

A spreading, deciduous tree, often branching low down, with broad, rounded leaves deeply heart-shaped at their bases. Pealike flowers, pink to deep pink or sometimes white, open in clusters before or as the leaves emerge in the spring. The flowers are occasionally seen in dense bunches on the main trunks, and these are followed by flattened pods that turn from pink to brown.

Common name: Judas tree
Native range: E Mediterranean region
Height: 33 ft (10 m)
Spread: 33 ft (10 m)
Hardiness: Zone 7

Cestrum
Solanaceae

This is a genus comprising some 175 New World species of both deciduous and evergreen shrubs. They are characterized by their mostly narrow, simple leaves and are natives of the warm regions from Mexico to South America.

The main attraction of these species is their striking tubular, sometimes fragrant flowers, commonly seen in colors of yellow, red, white, or greenish. These plants are suitable for any reasonable soil in a sunny position, but they will grow in an open situation—as a specimen shrub, perhaps—only in mild, nearly frost-free gardens. In colder climates, however, they can be trained on a warm, sun-facing wall. Alternatively, they can be grown in containers and moved to the glasshouse or conservatory during winter.

Cestrum aurantiacum

This is an evergreen shrub, sometimes treelike or with a tendency to develop somewhat climbing shoots when mature. Its leaves are wavy-edged, taper-pointed, and aromatic. Large, conical clusters of bright orange, tubular flowers open during late spring and summer followed by white berries.

Native range: Guatemala
Height: 10 ft (3 m) or more
Spread: 10 ft (3 m)
Hardiness: Zone 9

Cestrum elegans

This is a vigorous, evergreen shrub with stout, arching shoots and taper-pointed, deep green leaves. The drooping clusters of bright red to purple-red, tubular flowers open over a long period during summer and autumn.

Synonym: Cestrum purpureum
Native range: Mexico
Height: 10 ft (3 m)
Spread: 10 ft (3 m)
Hardiness: Zone 9

Cestrum 'Newellii'

A garden selection of uncertain origin making a vigorous, evergreen shrub

Cestrum elegans

with slender, arching shoots. Large clusters of deep crimson, tubular flowers open at the ends of the shoots in the spring.

Height: 6 ft (2 m)
Spread: 10 ft (3 m)
Hardiness: Zone 9

Cestrum parqui

This deciduous shrub is the hardiest of the genus, and it has slender, pointed leaves. The large, conical clusters of bright yellow-green flowers open during the summer and are fragrant at night. In cold regions, this shrub may behave more as a herbaceous perennial.

Native range: Chile
Height: 5 ft (1.5 m)
Spread: 6 ft (2 m)
Hardiness: Zone 8

Chaenomeles x superba 'Crimson and Gold'

Chaenomeles
Rosaceae

The ornamental flowering quinces are a small genus consisting of just three species, all bearing alternate, toothed leaves. These sometimes spiny deciduous shrubs are East Asian natives, and are found in China and Japan.

Valuable in gardens for their dense habit and profuse, early flowers, as well as their apple-like ornamental fruits, they are easy to grow in any soil and can be used as specimen shrubs, in the border, for growing against a wall or for hedging. They can be cut back as required to maintain their shape or size in spring.

To rejuvenate old or neglected plants, cut back hard in spring. The fruits of some types can be used for making preserves.

Chaenomeles speciosa

A vigorous and deciduous spreading shrub with spiny shoots and glossy, dark green leaves, usually bronze in color when young. The variously colored (single or double), white, pink, or red flowers open in showy clusters in the spring, the first ones before the leaves emerge. Flowering is followed by the appearance of aromatic, spherical-shaped fruits.

Native range: China
Height: 8 ft (2.5 m)
Spread: 10 ft (3 m)
Hardiness: Zone 4
Variants: 'Geisha Girl' is a variety that bears double, apricot-peach flowers. 'Moerloosei' ('Apple Blossom') has apple-blossom pink and white flowers. 'Nivalis' has white flowers. 'Simonii' has double, deep red flowers.

Chaenomeles speciosa 'Nivalis'

Chaenomeles x *superba*

This garden-raised hybrid between
C. japonica and *C. speciosa* makes a
dense, bushy, deciduous shrub with
spiny shoots and glossy, green leaves.
Showy clusters of single or double,
white to pink, orange or red flowers
open in spring, and these are
followed by aromatic fruits.

Height: 5 ft (1.5 m)
Spread: 8 ft (2.5 m)
Hardiness: Zone 4
Variants: 'Crimson and Gold' is low
and spreading, growing to 3 ft (1 m)
tall, and its deep red flowers have
conspicuous yellow stamens. 'Knap
Hill Scarlet' is vigorous and compact
in habit, with large, deep orange-red
flowers. 'Pink Lady' has profusely
borne, deep pink flowers.

Chamaecytisus
Leguminosae

The 30 species that make up this
genus include both deciduous and
evergreen shrubs. The shrubs are all
natives of Europe and bear leaves
that are divided into three distinct
leaflets.

The following is the most popular
species of the genus and is still often
listed as being a species of *Cytisus*, to
which it is related. It requires a well-
drained soil in a sunny position in
order to thrive. It is particularly
suited to growing in a rock garden,
as long as the drainage is good.

Chamaecytisus purpureus

This dwarf, deciduous shrub has a
compact habit with arching shoots
bearing small, dark green leaves, each
divided into three leaflets. The small,
pealike, pink flowers open during the
late spring or early summer.

Synonym: *Cytisus purpureus*
Common name: Purple broom
Native range: SE Europe
Height: 24 in (60 cm)
Spread: 35 in (90 cm)
Hardiness: Zone 6
Variant: 'Atropurpureus' has
attractive, deep purple-pink flowers.

Chimonanthus praecox

Chamaerops
Palmae

The single species, *C. humilis*, that
makes up this small genus is an
evergreen shrubby palm, which
grows into a dense mound of foliage.
The plant sometimes develops a
stem and then becomes more treelike
in form.

Chamaerops humilis
The bold, long-stalked, fan-shaped,
deep green to blue-green leaves of
this evergreen palm are deeply cut
into numerous segments and are very
striking in appearance. Clusters of
small, yellow flowers emerge from
near the base of the plant in the late
spring or summer. *C. humilis* is one
of only two palms that are native in
Europe.

Common name: Mediterranean palm
Native range: Mediterranean region
Height: 6 ft (2 m)
Spread: 10 ft (3 m)
Hardiness: Zone 9

Chimonanthus
Calycanthaceae

This is a small genus comprising six
species of both deciduous and
evergreen shrubs, all with opposite
leaves, and all natives of China. Only
the following species, however, is
commonly found in garden
cultivation.

Its unusual and very fragrant
flowers, which are borne in the
winter, make it particularly valuable
in gardens at a time of year when
color and scent are often largely
absent. The shrub can be grown as a
free-standing specimen or, in colder
climates, it will benefit from the
protection afforded by being trained
against a sunny wall.

It is suitable for growing in any
reasonably good soils but will flower
best if given a position in full sun.
Wall-grown plants can be cut back as
necessary just after flowering has
finished to maintain their shape or
restrict their size. At the same time,
remove any damaged, dead, diseased,
or crossing wood.

Chionanthus virginicus

Chimonanthus praecox

This is a large and vigorous deciduous shrub of upright habit. The plant has glossy, dark green leaves that are rough to the touch. The very fragrant, nodding, bell-shaped flowers are yellow and conspicuously marked with purple inside. They open to startling effect on the bare shoots during the winter. Flowers can sometimes be damaged by hard frosts.

Common name: Wintersweet
Native range: China
Height: 16 ft (5 m)
Spread: 10 ft (3 m)
Hardiness: Zone 7
Variants: 'Grandiflorus' has large leaves and flowers; 'Luteus' has large, pure yellow flowers.

Chionanthus
Oleaceae

This is a large genus consisting of approximately 100 species of deciduous and evergreen shrubs and trees. All species have opposite-growing leaves and they are widely distributed throughout the tropical regions.

The following is the most commonly grown garden species and its popularity is due to its showy and fragrant white flowers. It is suitable for any good, well-drained soil, but it flowers best in regions with hot summers—even so, it will still benefit from being positioned in full sun. The similar native Chinese species, *C. retusus*, is also sometimes grown.

Chionanthus virginicus

This is a deciduous shrub, sometimes grown on a single stem as a tree, with a habit ranging from conical to spreading. The plant has bold, dark green, oblong-shaped leaves, growing up to 8 in (20 cm) long, turning yellow in the autumn. The fragrant, slender-petalled flowers are individually small, but they open in impressively large clusters, 8 in (20 cm) in length, during the late spring or summer. Flowers are followed by egg-shaped, blue-black fruits.

Choisya 'Aztec Pearl'

Common name: Fringe tree
Native range: E United States of America
Height: 13 ft (4 m)
Spread: 13 ft (4 m)
Hardiness: Zone 4

Choisya
Rutaceae

The five species in this genus are evergreen, aromatic shrubs native to the southwest of the United States of America and Mexico. They all have opposite leaves that are divided, fanlike, into several leaflets.

These species are grown for their attractive foliage as well as their showy, fragrant, white flowers. They are suitable for any fertile, well-drained soil, where they can be planted either in a shrub border or against a wall. They will tolerate shade but prefer a sunny position, and to produce their best display of flowers, full sun is essential. They can be pruned after flowering, if necessary to maintain their shape or restrict their size.

Choisya ternata

Choisya 'Aztec Pearl'
This garden-raised hybrid makes a compact bush, and its elegant and attractively aromatic leaves are divided into three to five slender leaflets. Its especially prolific clusters of fragrant, pink-tinged, white flowers open at the ends of the shoots in late spring, and usually there is a second flowering in autumn.

Chusquea culeou

Height: 5 ft (1.5 m)
Spread: 6 ft (2 m)
Hardiness: Zone 7

Choisya ternata

This bushy, evergreen shrub, which is grown for its foliage and flowers, has a compact habit and provides year-round garden interest. The glossy, dark green, aromatic leaves are divided into three untoothed leaflets. Clusters of fragrant, white flowers open in late spring and again in autumn. It can be affected by severe frosts.

Common name: Mexican orange
Native range: Mexico
Height: 6 ft (2 m)
Spread: 8 ft (2.5 m)
Hardiness: Zone 7
Variant: 'Sundance' has golden yellow young foliage when it is given a

position in full sun; foliage turns yellow-green if it is planted in the shade, and it is less free-flowering as a result.

Chusquea
Gramineae

This is a large genus consisting of about 100 species of evergreen bamboos native to Mexico and central America and the Andes of South America.

Only the following species is commonly found in garden cultivation, however, where it is grown principally for its densely leafy and graceful habit. Plant in a good, moist but well-drained soil that is rich in humus. It requires a sheltered position that offers it some protection from strong winds.

Chusquea culeou

This is a vigorous, clump-forming bamboo with upright, arching shoots and stout, solid, yellow-green to green culms. The culms are made more attractive by the presence of persistent, white-colored leaf sheaths. The long, slender, and taper-pointed leaves are borne in dense clusters.

Common name: Chilean bamboo
Native range: Chile
Height: 16 ft (5 m)
Spread: 16 ft (5 m)
Hardiness: Zone 7

Cistus
Cistaceae

Chusquea culeou

These evergreen shrubs, commonly known as rock roses, comprise a genus of some 20 species found throughout the Mediterranean region, from Turkey to the Canary Islands and North Africa.

They are easy to grow in any well-drained soil, as long as it is not too rich, and they need full sun to thrive. They are ideally suited to a border, rock garden, or against a sunny wall.

The individual flowers are short-lived, but they are profusely borne. Light pruning after flowering has finished helps to retain their attractive and compact habit.

Cistus x aguilarii

A naturally occurring hybrid that makes a spreading shrub with bright green, wavy-edged, sticky leaves. Large white flowers with centers of golden yellow stamens are freely borne in summer.

Native range: SW Europe, North Africa
Height: 3 ft (1 m)
Spread: 5 ft (1.5 m)
Hardiness: Zone 8
Variant: 'Maculatus' produces flowers that are blotched in the center with deep red.

Cistus albidus

A mound-forming, bushy shrub with gray, hairy shoots and felted, oblong-shaped leaves. The contrasting lilac-pink, saucer-shaped flowers have a conspicuous yellow center and are abundantly produced in summer.

Native range: SW Europe, North Africa
Height: 24 in (60 cm)
Spread: 35 in (90 cm)
Hardiness: Zone 8

Cistus x cyprius

This is a naturally occurring hybrid that makes a rounded, bushy shrub with taper-pointed, gray-green, wavy-edged, and sticky leaves borne on sticky shoots. The large, white flowers open in succession during summer and are conspicuously blotched with red and a center of yellow stamens.

Native range: France, Spain
Height: 5 ft (1.5 m)
Spread: 6 ft (2 m)
Hardiness: Zone 8

Cistus x dansereaui

This naturally occurring hybrid develops into an upright shrub with

Cistus x aguilarii 'Maculatus'

Cistus albidus

Cistus x skanbergii

sticky shoots and dark green, wavy-edged, sticky leaves. Its large, white flowers, which are borne during the summer months, are conspicuously blotched with red in their centers.

Synonym: *Cistus x lusitanicus* of gardens
Native range: SW Europe
Height: 3 ft (1 m)
Spread: 5 ft (1.5 m)
Hardiness: Zone 8
Variant: 'Decumbens' is a low-growing form with a wide, spreading habit, about 24 in (60 cm) tall.

Cistus x *hybridus*

A bushy shrub of dense, rounded habit with small, dark green, wavy-edged leaves. Masses of small, white flowers, yellow in the center, open from red buds during late spring and summer.

Synonym: *Cistus x corbariensis*
Native range: S Europe

Cistus x purpureus

Height: 3 ft (1 m)
Spread: 5 ft (1.5 m)
Hardiness: Zone 8

Cistus ladanifer

This is a strongly growing shrub with an upright habit and lancelike, dark green, sticky leaves, which are aromatic when bruised. Its very large, white flowers have attractively frilled petals, and each flower is blotched with deep red at its center. The flowers open at the ends of the shoots during the summer and the shrub requires a position in full sun in order to thrive.

Common name: Gum rock rose
Native range: SW Europe, North Africa
Height: 6 ft (2 m)
Spread: 5 ft (1.5 m)
Hardiness: Zone 8
Variant: var. albiflorus bears white flowers with no central blotches.

Cistus laurifolius

This is a stoutly branched and vigorous shrub. When young it has an upright habit, but its shape changes to a more rounded form as the plant matures. Its dark green leaves, with white undersurfaces, are leathery, sticky, and wavy-edged. Clusters of large, white flowers, colored yellow in their centers, open throughout the summer. This is a particularly hardy species that looks its best when positioned in full sun.

Native range: SW Europe, North Africa
Height: 5 ft (1.5 m)
Spread: 6 ft (2 m)
Hardiness: Zone 8

Cistus x pulverulentus

A naturally occurring hybrid that makes a compact, low shrub with a spreading habit and with wavy-edged, gray, hairy leaves. The profusely

borne, showy, pink flowers open
during summer.

Native range: SW Europe
Height: 24 in (60 cm)
Spread: 3 ft (1 m)
Hardiness: Zone 8
Variant: 'Sunset' has deep cerise-pink
flowers.

Cistus x *purpureus*

This is a naturally occurring hybrid
making a rounded shrub with sticky
red shoots and slender, pointed, and
slightly wavy-edged, dark green
leaves. The deep pink flowers have
yellow stamens and crinkled petals
marked with deep red at the base.

Native range: SW Europe
Height: 3 ft (1 m)
Spread: 5 ft (1.5 m)
Hardiness: Zone 8
Variant: 'Alan Fradd' has white
flowers that are blotched with red.

Cistus x *skanbergii*

This naturally occurring hybrid makes
a low-growing, compact shrub with
white, hairy shoots and narrow, gray-
green leaves. Clusters of delicate,
soft pink flowers with yellow stamens
at their centers open during summer.

Native range: Greece
Height: 24 in (60 cm)
Spread: 30 in (75 cm)
Hardiness: Zone 8

Cladrastis
Leguminosae

The five species in this genus are
deciduous trees mainly natives of
China, but only the following—the
most commonly grown—is found in
North America. The leaves are
divided into several leaflets and the
pealike flowers are borne in large
clusters. It is suitable for any well-
drained soil and flowers best in
climates with hot summers.

Clerodendrum trichotomum var. fargesii

Cladrastis kentukea

This is a deciduous tree with bold,
bright green leaves that divided into
11 untoothed leaflets turning yellow
in autumn. The white, slightly
fragrant, pealike flowers open in the
summer in large, drooping clusters
from the ends of the shoots, and the
flowers are then followed by
flattened seed pods.

Synonym: *Cladrastis lutea*
Common name: Yellow wood
Native range: SE United States of
America
Height: 50 ft (15 m)
Spread: 40 ft (12 m)
Hardiness: Zone 4

Clerodendrum
Verbenaceae

This is a large genus of plants encompassing approximately 400 species of trees, shrubs, and climbers, both deciduous and evergreen, native mainly to the tropical regions.

While several species are commonly found growing in conservatories and outside in tropical regions, two species are hardy enough to be planted outside in temperate regions. They are cultivated for their showy clusters of flowers rather than their individual blooms, and they are more likely to thrive if provided with a good, well-drained soil and a position in full sun.

Clerodendrum bungei
A vigorous, deciduous shrub that spreads by suckers. It has upright shoots and bold, heart-shaped, dark green leaves, flushed with purple when young. The large, dense, dome-shaped clusters of deep pink, very fragrant flowers open at the ends of the shoots in the late summer and autumn. It can be treated like a herbaceous perennial in cold areas.

Common name: Glorybower
Native range: China

Clerodendrum bungei

Height: 5 ft (1.5 m)
Spread: 6 ft (2 m)
Hardiness: Zone 8

Clerodendrum trichotomum

This is a deciduous tree of upright habit, often shrubby with several stems, and with broad, dark green, softly hairy leaves. The very fragrant, white flowers have contrasting red sepals and they open in broad clusters during the late summer and autumn. The flowers are followed by fruits colored a bright metallic blue.

Common name: Harlequin glorybower
Native range: China, Japan
Height: 20 ft (6 m)
Spread: 16 ft (5 m)
Hardiness: Zone 7
Variants: 'Carnival' has blue-green and gray-green leaves that are irregularly margined with creamy white; var. *fargesii* has smooth leaves that are colored bronze when young, and it usually fruits more freely.

Clethra
Clethraceae

The 60 or so species that make up this genus comprise both deciduous and evergreen shrubs and trees. They have a very wide distribution, occurring from North through Central and South America, East Asia, and Madeira. The following species is the most commonly found one in cultivation and it requires a moist, humus-rich, acidic soil in order to thrive. Despite this, it is not a difficult plant to grow, but it does benefit from being provided with more shade in areas that experience dry summers.

Clethra alnifolia

This is a deciduous shrub that spreads by producing suckers. It is upright when young, but becomes progressively more rounded as it matures. It has glossy, green leaves that often turn yellow in autumn. *C. alnifolia* produces slender, upright spikes of very fragrant, small, creamy white clusters of flowers that open over a long period in late summer and early autumn. Pruning is not normally necessary, but damaged or unwanted branches can be removed in early spring.

Common name: Summersweet
Native range: E United States of America
Height: 8 ft (2.5 m)
Spread: 6 ft (2 m)
Hardiness: Zone 4
Variants: 'Hummingbird' has very dark green leaves, yellow in autumn, and large, profusely borne flower spikes. 'Pink Spires' has pink flowers.

Clianthus
Leguminosae

The two species that make up this genus are Southern-Hemisphere, evergreen shrubs, natives of Australia and New Zealand. Their leaves are

Clethra alnifolia

divided into numerous leaflets and they bear flowers with an unusual appearance—they have been likened in shape to a lobster's claw. The following species is usually grown trained against a sunny wall in more temperate regions and it is suitable for any good, well-drained soil, as long as it receives sun and shelter. Cut back long shoots by about one-third after flowering.

Clianthus puniceus

This is a vigorous, evergreen or semi-evergreen shrub with long scandent, or climbing, shoots bearing dark green leaves made up of as many as 25 leaflets. The showy, drooping clusters of large, bright red flowers open over a long period during the summer months.

Common name: Red parrot beak
Native range: New Zealand (North Island)
Height: 10 ft (3 m)
Spread: 10 ft (3 m)
Hardiness: Zone 8
Variants: 'Albus' has white flowers, while 'Roseus' has deep pink flowers.

Colletia
Rhamnaceae

This is a small genus of plants comprising just five species of very unusual, spiny, and distinct deciduous shrubs that are native to South America. The branches of the shrubs often have a thickened and flattened appearance.

These shrubs are either leafless or are very sparsely leafy, but they have

Clianthus puniceus 'Roseus'

prominent, opposite thorns. Small, fragrant flowers are profusely borne in the late summer or early autumn, in clusters from below the thorns.

They are easy plants to grow and are suitable for any well-drained soil, as long as they are provided with a sunny position. Little pruning is usually required apart from the removal of any dead, crossing or diseased wood.

during late summer and autumn, are tubular, white, and fragrant and open in clusters.

Synonym: *Colletia armata*
Native range: Chile
Height: 8 ft (2.5 m)
Spread: 10 ft (3 m)
Hardiness: Zone 8
Variant: 'Rosea' produces pink-colored flowers.

Colletia hystrix

Deciduous and nearly leafless, this distinctive shrub has rigid shoots and stiff, sharply pointed, dark green spines. Its flowers, which are borne

Colletia hystrix 'Rosea'

Colquhounia
Labiatae

The three species in this small genus are evergreen shrubs with bold, opposite leaves, and are natives of the Himalayas and China. The following is the most commonly seen and is cultivated for its striking flowers. It can be grown in any good, well-drained soil in full sun. In cold areas it can behave almost like a herbaceous perennial, regrowing from the base in spring. Cut back any dead shoots to the base as the new growth appears.

Colquhounia coccinea
This is a vigorous, upright, evergreen or semi-evergreen shrub with stout, square, felted shoots and aromatic, sage-green leaves. It produces upright clusters of showy, bright orange-red flowers, which open at the ends of the shoots in the late summer months.

Native range: Himalayas, China
Height: 8 ft (2.5 m)
Spread: 6 ft (2 m)
Hardiness: Zone 8

Colutea
Leguminosae

This widely distributed genus of some 25 species of deciduous shrubs can be found throughout Europe, as well as North Africa to the Himalayas. Plants have leaves that are divided into several leaflets, and their pealike, usually yellow flowers are followed by conspicuous bladder-like pods.

These shrubs are easy to grow in any well-drained garden soil. They are particularly tolerant of poor, dry soils and are useful in a shrub border due to their long flowering and fruiting season.

Little pruning is usually necessary, but to restrict their size they can be cut back hard if required. They are best pruned in the early spring, before the new season's growth gets started.

Colutea arborescens
This tough, vigorous deciduous shrub has bright green leaves divided into as many as 13 leaflets. Clusters of yellow, pealike flowers, marked with orange in their centers, are followed by pale green, later gray, inflated, bladder-like pods.

Common name: Bladder senna
Native range: S Europe, North Africa
Height: 10 ft (3 m)
Spread: 8 ft (2.5 m)
Hardiness: Zone 5

Convolvulus
Convolvulaceae

This is a g genus of about 250 species of mainly annual and perennial herbs, with some shrubs, widely distributed but mainly in temperate regions. The following is the most popular shrubby species and is grown for its attractive foliage and flowers. It needs a well-drained, not too rich soil in full sun and is suitable for the front of a sheltered border, a rock garden, or a sunny wall. Prune lightly after flowering to retain its compact habit.

Convolvulus cneorum
This is a dense, mound-forming, evergreen shrub with slender, silky haired, silvery gray leaves. The contrasting funnel-shaped flowers are pink in bud, opening white, and are profusely borne in the late spring and early summer.

Native range: Mediterranean region
Height: 24 in (60 cm)
Spread: 3 ft (1 m)
Hardiness: Zone 8

Colutea arborescens

Cordyline
Agavaceae

This genus comprises some 15 species of evergreen, palm-like trees and shrubs that are natives of Southeast Asia, Australasia, and the Pacific Islands. All species are characterized by their densely clustered, swordlike leaves. While many are grown as conservatory specimens in temperate regions, the following species is hardy in mild areas, although it may require some frost protection. It is suitable for any good, well-drained soil and does best if given a sunny position.

Cordyline australis
This upright, evergreen tree has a single trunk until it is mature and then it branches sparsely. The bold, swordlike leaves are borne in large tufts toward the ends of the shoots.

The leaves are upright at first, but later become more arching. Mature trees bear large clusters of small, white flowers during the summer season.

Common name: Giant dracena
Native range: New Zealand
Height: 33 ft (10 m)
Spread: 10 ft (3 m)
Hardiness: Zone 9
Variants: Several variegated forms are also grown, including 'Albertii', with leaves striped green and pink, and 'Purpurea', which has purple leaves.

Cornus
Cornaceae

The dogwoods comprise a genus of some 45 species of usually deciduous shrubs and trees, usually with opposite leaves, that are widely distributed in north temperate

Cornus alba 'Aurea'

regions. The genus also includes examples of herbaceous perennials.

The individual flowers are small, but they are usually borne in dense clusters, which, in some species, are surrounded by conspicuous bracts. They have a variety of ornamental features: some are grown for their highly colored winter shoots; some for their foliage, with many variegated selections; and yet others for their showy flowerheads.

Forms of *C. alba*, *C. sanguinea*, and *C. stolonifera* grown for their winter shoots can be cut back hard in early spring, before the new season's growth starts.

Cornus alba

A vigorous, thicket-forming shrub with upright shoots turning bright red in winter. Dark green leaves show autumn colors of orange to red and purple. Flattened heads of small white flowers appear in late spring to early summer and these are followed by small white fruits.

Common name: Siberian dogwood
Native range: N Asia
Height: 10 ft (3 m)
Spread: 10 ft (3 m)
Hardiness: Zone 3
Variants: 'Aurea' has golden yellow foliage. 'Elegantissima' has leaves with irregular white margins. 'Ivory Halo' is compact with white-edged leaves. 'Sibirica' has brilliant red shoots in winter. 'Sibirica Variegata' has leaves with broad, irregular white margins. 'Spaethii' has yellow-margined leaves.

Cornus controversa

Cornus alternifolia

This is conical-to-spreading, large, deciduous shrub or small tree, often multi-stemmed, with alternate leaves usually clustered at the ends of the shoots and turning red and purple in the autumn. Flattened heads of white flowers appear in the early summer and these are followed by small blue-black fruits.

Common name: Alternate-leaved dogwood
Native range: E North America
Height: 20 ft (6 m)
Spread: 20 ft (6 m)
Hardiness: Zone 3
Variant: 'Argentea' is a beautiful form. Its most attractive feature is its small leaves, which are strikingly margined with creamy white. It is a compact-growing bush to about 10 ft (3 m) in height.

Cornus controversa

This is a spreading, deciduous tree with characteristically layered branches and alternate, glossy, dark green leaves that turn purple in the autumn. Broad, flattened heads of creamy white flowers appear between early and midsummer, and these are later followed by small blue-black fruits.

Native range: E Asia
Height: 50 ft (15 m)
Spread: 50 ft (15 m)
Hardiness: Zone 5
Variant: 'Variegata' is a smaller-growing tree, the leaves of which have a broad, creamy yellow margin when young. The leaf margins turn creamy white as the leaves mature.

Cornus florida 'Cherokee Chief'

Cornus 'Eddie's White Wonder'

This is a garden-raised hybrid that develops into a conical, deciduous tree with dark green, taper-pointed leaves. In autumn, the leaves turn to colors of brilliant orange, red, and purple. The dense, button-like heads of small, greenish-colored flowers that open in late spring are surrounded by four large and conspicuous, white or pink-tinged bracts.

Height: 20 ft (6 m)
Spread: 13 ft (4 m)
Hardiness: Zone 6

Cornus florida

The dark green leaves of this deciduous, spreading tree turn red to red-purple in autumn. Dense clusters of small, greenish-colored flowers in spring are surrounded by four conspicuous bracts, which are usually white but can occasionally be various shades of pink.

Common name: Flowering dogwood
Native range: E North America
Height: 26 ft (8 m)
Spread: 33 ft (10 m)
Hardiness: Zone 5
Variants: There are numerous selections, such as 'Cherokee Chief', with deep pink bracts. 'Rainbow' has leaves with yellow margins, the margins turning to red-purple and edged in scarlet in autumn. Its bracts are white.

Cornus kousa

This is a deciduous tree that is conical when young but takes on a spreading habit as it matures. It has peeling, pale and dark brown bark and dark green, wavy-edged leaves that turn red-purple in autumn. The small, green flowers open in dense heads in the early summer and are

Cornus kousa

surrounded by four large, taper-pointed, creamy white bracts. The flowers are followed by pendulous, strawberry-like red fruits.

Native range: Japan
Height: 26 ft (8 m)
Spread: 20 ft (6 m)
Hardiness: Zone 5
Variants: var. *chinensis* is similar, but its leaf margins are not wavy. It generally performs better in gardens and many of the selected forms belong here. 'China Girl' has large flowerheads that are borne profusely, even on young, small plants. 'Gold Star' has leaves that are attractively blotched in their centers with golden yellow, turning red, edged with purple in the autumn. 'Satomi' has deep pink-colored bracts.

Cornus mas

This vigorous, deciduous, spreading shrub has dark green leaves that sometime turn red-purple in the autumn. The small, yellow flowers open in clusters on the bare shoots in late winter, and these are followed by glossy red, edible, fleshy fruits that mature in late summer.

Common name: Cornelian cherry
Native range: Europe, W Asia
Height: 16 ft (5 m)
Spread: 20 ft (6 m)
Hardiness: Zone 4
Variants: 'Aurea' is a striking form that has golden yellow foliage. 'Aureoelegantissima' is smaller in size, reaching a height of about 8 ft (2.5 m), and its leaves are edged with yellow and tinged pink. 'Golden Glory' is upright in habit with handsome, glossy foliage and dense clusters of bright yellow flowers followed by freely borne fruits. 'Variegata' is a compact shrub, up to about 6 ft (2 m) in height, and its leaves are margined with creamy white.

Cornus mas

Cornus 'Norman Hadden'

This garden-raised hybrid between
C. *capitata* and C. *kousa* makes a
semi-evergreen, spreading tree—
some of its pale-colored green leaves
turn pink in autumn before dropping;
others remain throughout the winter.
The densely-borne heads of small,
creamy white flowers that appear in
early summer are surrounded by
conspicuous bracts. These open
creamy white, then turn white, and
finally change to a deep pink color
in midsummer. In autumn, the
strawberry-like fruits ripen to deep
red and hang down on long stalks.
'Porlock' is similar in appearance and
has been distributed under this
name.

Height: 26 ft (8 m)
Spread: 26 ft (8 m)
Hardiness: Zone 7

Cornus nuttallii

A vigorous, deciduous tree with a
conical habit and dark green leaves
that can turn red in autumn. Dense
heads of small, creamy flowers open
at the ends of the shoots in late
spring, surrounded by creamy white
bracts. This striking species does best
when given good, deep soil and a
woodland situation.

Common name: Pacific dogwood
Native range: W North America
Height: 40 ft (12 m)
Spread: 26 ft (8 m)
Hardiness: Zone 7
Variants: Selected forms with large
flowerheads include 'Colrigo Giant'
and 'Portlemouth'.

Cornus sanguinea

This is a vigorous, fast-growing,
deciduous shrub, fully frost-hardy,
with an essentially upright habit. The
young shoots of C. *sanguinea* are
flushed with red and its dark green
leaves turn to red or purple-red in the
autumn. Small, white flowers open in
flattened heads in early summer and
these are followed by small, blue-
black fruits. This shrub is dense
enough to make successful hedging.
Apart from the removal of unwanted,
dead, or crossing branches, no
pruning is usually necessary. Any
pruning that does take place is best
carried out in spring.

Common name: Bloodtwig dogwood
Native range: Europe
Height: 16 ft (5 m)
Spread: 13 ft (4 m)
Hardiness: Zone 4
Variants: 'Midwinter Fire' and the
similar 'Winter Beauty' ('Winter
Flame') are lower-growing, with
bright orange-red and yellow shoots
in winter.

Cornus stolonifera

This is a vigorous, thicket-forming,
deciduous shrub, fully hardy, that is
valuable in the garden because of its

Cornus mas

Cornus nuttallii 'Portlemouth'

Cornus nuttallii 'Colrigo Giant'

Cornus stolonifera 'Flaviramea'

Cornus stolonifera 'Flaviramea'

bright red winter shoots. It is similar to *C. alba*, except that it spreads by suckers. The taper-pointed, dark green leaves turn red to purple-red in autumn. Flattened heads of small, white flowers appear in late spring and early summer, and these are followed by small, white fruits.

Synonym: *Cornus sericea*
Common name: Red osier dogwood
Native range: North America
Height: 8 ft (2.5 m)
Spread: 10 ft (3 m)
Hardiness: Zone 2
Variants: 'Flaviramea' has yellow-green winter shoots and looks extremely effective when grown in association with *C. alba*. 'Kelseyi' is a dwarf, growing to a maximum height of only about 35 in (90 cm), with slender shoots, red-tipped in winter. 'White Gold' has leaves that are edged with creamy white, and yellow winter shoots.

Corokia
Rhamnaceae

The three species that make up this genus of plants are all evergreen shrubs native to New Zealand. Due to their attractive habit, flowers, fruits, and foliage, they can make versatile additions to the garden.

Species have small, yellow flowers followed by orange, yellow, or red fruits. They are suitable for any fertile, well-drained soil, and they do best when given protection from strong winds. They also appreciate a position in full sun or they can be planted against a wall for the shelter it provides.

Pruning to restrict their size can be carried out after the flowering period has finished.

Corokia cotoneaster
This is an intricately branched, evergreen shrub with slender, wiry shoots and spoon-shaped, bronze-green leaves that are silvery beneath. Small, star-shaped, yellow, fragrant flowers open in late spring, followed by small yellow or red fruits.

Common name: Cotoneaster corokia
Native range: New Zealand
Height: 6 ft (2 m)
Spread: 6 ft (2 m)
Hardiness: Zone 7

Corylopsis spicata

Coronilla valentina subsp. *glauca*

Coronilla
Leguminosae

This is a genus comprising about 20 species of deciduous and evergreen shrubs, as well as annual and perennial herbaceous plants. They are natives mainly of Europe and the Mediterranean region and they are grown principally for their flowers and foliage.

The leaves of the species are usually divided into several leaflets and they bear clusters of yellow, pealike flowers. They should be grown in well-drained soil that is not too rich, and in a position where they will receive full sun. Plant against a sunny wall in regions where they are not fully hardy.

Coronilla valentina

A bushy, evergreen shrub with bright green leaves divided into 13 wedge-shaped leaflets. Long-stalked clusters of small, golden yellow, pealike flowers open over a long period during spring.

Native range: Mediterranean region
Height: 5 ft (1.5 m)
Spread: 5 ft (1.5 m)
Hardiness: Zone 8
Variants: The most commonly seen is subsp. *glauca*. It has blue-green leaves with up to seven leaflets. Selected forms of this are 'Citrina', with pale yellow flowers, and 'Variegata', in which the leaflets are edged with white.

Corylopsis
Hamamelidaceae

This is a genus of about seven species of deciduous shrubs, all closely related to the witch hazels (*Hamamelis*), and popular in gardens for their early-opening flowers.

These plants are natives of East Asia and bear hazel-like leaves and pendulous clusters of fragrant, yellow flowers. They need to be grown in a good, moist but well-drained, lime-free soil. Frost damage is possible, so they are best planted in a sheltered site within the garden.

Pruning is not normally necessary; however, to restrict growth or to remove dead or damaged wood, branches can be removed after flowering has finished.

Corylopsis pauciflora
This is the most popular species of the genus, and develops into a bushy, spreading shrub with leaves that are bronze when they first open, but then turn bright green. The small, but profusely borne, nodding clusters of pale yellow, fragrant flowers open in early to mid-spring.

Native range: Japan, Taiwan
Height: 5 ft (1.5 m)
Spread: 6 ft (2 m)
Hardiness: Zone 6

Corylopsis spicata
A rounded-to-spreading, deciduous shrub with blue-green leaves, bronze-purple in color when young, and bluish white beneath. Drooping spikes of fragrant yellow flowers tipped with orange open on the bare shoots in early spring.

Native range: Japan
Height: 10 ft (3 m)
Spread: 10 ft (3 m)
Hardiness: Zone 5

Corylus
Corylaceae

The hazels comprise some ten species of Northern-Hemisphere deciduous shrubs and trees. They bear separate male and female flowers on the same plant—the males in drooping catkins. They are grown as specimen shrubs and as trees for their foliage, early catkins, and edible fruits. They are suitable for any well-drained soil. Forms with colored foliage do best in a sunny position.

Corylus avellana
A large, deciduous shrub or small tree with broad, roughly hairy leaves. The pendulous, pale yellow male catkins are a familiar sight in late winter and early spring, while the tiny, red female flowers give rise to edible hazelnuts. It is mainly grown in gardens as one of the cultivars listed below.

Common name: European hazel
Native range: Europe, North Africa, W Asia
Height: 16 ft (5 m)
Spread: 16 ft (5 m)
Hardiness: Zone 4
Variants: 'Aurea' has bright yellow young foliage, turning yellow-green. 'Contorta' (corkscrew hazel, Harry Lauder's walking stick) has contorted shoots and makes a striking winter feature plant.

Corylus colurna
This is a medium-sized, vigorously growing deciduous tree with a compact, conical head and dark green, coarsely toothed leaves that sometimes turn yellow in the autumn. The male flowers are borne in small, pale yellow, pendulous catkins in the late winter, while the nuts, which ripen as the leaves are falling, are surrounded by a husk that is deeply divided into numerous slender, rigid lobes.

Corylus avellana 'Contorta'

Corylus maxima 'Purpurea'

Common name: Turkish filbert
Native range: SE Europe, W Asia
Height: 65 ft (20 m)
Spread: 33 ft (10 m)
Hardiness: Zone 4

Corylus maxima

A large, vigorous deciduous shrub—
sometimes treelike in habit—with
broad, dark green leaves. Pendulous
male catkins open on the bare shoots
in late winter. The large, edible nuts
are enclosed in a long, tubular husk.

Common name: Filbert
Native range: SE Europe, W Asia

Cotinus 'Grace'

Height: 20 ft (6 m)
Spread: 16 ft (5 m)
Hardiness: Zone 4
Variants: The most commonly grown
form is 'Purpurea', which has deep
red-purple leaves and fruit husks.
The catkins are also tinged with
purple. Other forms are also grown
for their edible, autumn-ripening
fruits.

Cotinus
Anacardiaceae

This small genus of plants consisting
of three species of deciduous shrubs
and trees has produced some striking
and extremely popular additions to
the garden, which are grown
principally for their attractive foliage
and conspicuous autumn color.
Individually the flowers are tiny, but
as the small fruits ripen they develop
into large, plumelike clusters, which
can then remain attractive well into
the winter season.

The trees and shrubs of this genus
are all suitable for any reasonably
good, well-drained soil, as long as it is
not too dry, but the foliage color is
seen at its best only in full sun. They

can be grown in the border or
positioned together as a group
specimen planting.

If it proves necessary to restrict
their size, they can be cut back, hard
if required, in the early spring,
before the new season's growth
commences.

Cotinus coggygria
This bushy, deciduous shrub grows
vigorously and its smooth,
untoothed, blue-green leaves turn
to shades of yellow to orange-red in
autumn. The large and persistent,
conical fruit clusters range in color
from pale brown to pink.

Common name: Smoke tree
Native range: S Europe to China
Height: 16 ft (5 m)
Spread: 16 ft (5 m)
Hardiness: Zone 4
Variants: There are several selected
forms of this species with deep red-
purple foliage turning red in autumn,
as well as purple-pink fruit clusters.
Notable examples include 'Notcutt's
Variety' and 'Velvet Cloak'.

Cotinus coggygria

Cotinus obovatus

Cotinus 'Flame'

This is a garden hybrid that makes a large, vigorous, treelike deciduous shrub with scaly bark and pale blue-green leaves. Foliage turns a brilliant orange-red in autumn. Its conspicuously large fruiting clusters are purple-pink in color.

Height: 20 ft (6 m)
Spread: 16 ft (5 m)
Hardiness: Zone 4

Cotinus 'Grace'

This is a vigorous, deciduous, garden hybrid that develops into a large shrub, sometimes treelike in habit, with attractive, scaly bark and bold, deep red-purple leaves that turn a bright red in autumn. It bears large, conical-shaped, purple-pink fruit clusters in autumn.

Height: 20 ft (6 m)
Spread: 16 ft (5 m)
Hardiness: Zone 4

Cotinus obovatus

A deciduous, upright tree with striking, scaly bark when mature. The bold, thin, untoothed leaves are bronze at first, becoming blue-green and then shades of orange, yellow, red, and purple in autumn.

Common name: American smoketree
Native range: C and S United States of America
Height: 33 ft (10 m)
Spread: 26 ft (8 m)
Hardiness: Zone 4

Cotoneaster
Rosaceae

This is a very large genus, made up of several hundred species of deciduous and evergreen trees and shrubs that are widely distributed throughout Europe, Asia, and North Africa. By far the largest number of species is found in China.

All species have small, white or pink-tinged flowers and they usually bear red fruits in autumn. The larger examples of the genus can be used as specimen shrubs, while smaller ones make an attractive addition to the garden when grown in a shrub border. Some sorts are used for hedging, while dwarf species are useful either in the rock garden or for ground cover.

Cotoneaster atropurpureus 'Variegatus'

Cotoneaster 'Cornubia'

Cotoneaster atropurpureus

This is a low, spreading, deciduous shrub that makes a broad, dense mound with small, rounded, glossy dark green leaves that turn deep red-purple in autumn. Small, white flowers, flushed with red, are borne singly on the shoots, and these are followed by small orange-red fruits.

Native range: China
Height: 30 in (75 cm)
Spread: 6 ft (2 m)
Hardiness: Zone 4
Variant: 'Variegatus' (*C. horizontalis* 'Variegatus') has leaves that are edged with white.

Cotoneaster bullatus

This is a large, deciduous shrub with bold, dark green, conspicuously and deeply veined leaves turning red in the autumn. Small clusters of white flowers, tinged with pink in early summer, are followed by showy, glossy, bright red fruits.

Native range: China
Height: 13 ft (4 m)
Spread: 10 ft (3 m)
Hardiness: Zone 5

Cotoneaster congestus

This is a dense, creeping, evergreen shrub forming a wide mound with tiny, deep matt-green leaves. The small, white flowers that appear in early summer are followed by bright red fruits. It makes good ground cover in a rock garden.

Native range: Himalayas
Height: 12 in (30 cm)
Spread: 6 ft (2m) or more
Hardiness: Zone 6

Cotoneaster conspicuus

This is an evergreen shrub with a compact, rounded habit with stiff, arching shoots and small, glossy, dark green leaves. Small, white flowers are borne singly or in clusters in early summer, and these are followed by bright orange-red fruits in autumn. These attractive fruits can persist for several months. It is most commonly grown under the name *C. conspicuus* 'Decorus'. Apart from removing unwanted, dead, or damaged branches in spring, pruning is not usually necessary.

Native range: SE Tibet
Height: 6 ft (2 m)

Cotoneaster bullatus

Cotoneaster sternianus

Spread: 8 ft (2.5 m)
Hardiness: Zone 6

Cotoneaster 'Cornubia'
A garden-raised hybrid making a vigorous, large semi-evergreen shrub with arching branches and bold, dark green leaves. Foliage can turn bronze-purple in winter. Clusters of white flowers in summer are followed by profuse, bright red fruits.

Height: 16 ft (5 m)
Spread: 20 ft (6 m)
Hardiness: Zone 6

Cotoneaster dammeri
This creeping, evergreen shrub has glossy, dark green leaves that sometimes turn bronze-purple in cold weather. Small, white flowers in early summer are followed by bright red fruits. This is an excellent and vigorous species for ground cover.

Native range: China
Height: 8 in (20 cm)
Spread: 8 ft (2.5 m) or more

Hardiness: Zone 5
Variants: 'Major' is a commonly grown form producing large leaves.

Cotoneaster franchetii
This is a vigorous, evergreen shrub with arching shoots bearing attractive, gray-green leaves. The leaves later turn glossy and dark green, with the undersurfaces becoming white with hairs. Clusters of white flowers, tinged with pink in early summer, are followed by fruits turning orange-red. *C. sternianus* has larger leaves and fruit.

Native range: China
Height: 10 ft (3 m)
Spread: 10 ft (3 m)
Hardiness: Zone 6

Cotoneaster horizontalis
This wide-spreading, deciduous shrub develops with a characteristic flattened, "herring-bone" pattern of branches, growing largely horizontal with the ground and bearing rounded, glossy, dark green leaves

Cotoneaster horizontalis

,that turn red-purple in autumn. The small, white and pink-tinged flowers stud the branches in late spring and these are followed by bright red fruits.

Native range: China
Height: 3 ft (1 m)
Spread: 6 ft (2 m)
Hardiness: Zone 5

Cotoneaster 'Hybridus Pendulus'

This garden-raised hybrid is usually grafted on top of a stem to make a small, weeping, semi-evergreen tree with branches arching gracefully to the ground and deep matt-green leaves. Clusters of small, white flowers in early summer are followed by a profusion of bright red fruits. Apart from the removal of dead, damaged, or crossing wood, pruning is not usually required.

Height: 6 ft (2 m)
Spread: 10 ft (3 m)
Hardiness: Zone 6

Cotoneaster integrifolius

A rigidly branched, mound-forming, evergreen shrub with small, narrow, glossy, dark green leaves. The white flowers are borne singly on the shoots in early summer and these are followed by deep pink fruits in autumn. This species is commonly grown as *C. microphyllus*.

Native range: Himalayas
Height: 3 ft (1 m)
Spread: 6 ft (2 m)
Hardiness: Zone 5

Cotoneaster lacteus

This is a compact, evergreen shrub popular for its handsome foliage, flowers, and fruits. The arching branches bear dark green, deeply veined leaves, while conspicuous clusters of creamy white flowers in summer are followed by long-lasting, red fruits.

Native range: China
Height: 8 ft (2.5 m)
Spread: 13 ft (4 m)
Hardiness: Zone 6

Cotoneaster x *suecicus* 'Erlinda'

Cotoneaster salicifolius

This is a wide-spreading, evergreen shrub with arching branches and long, slender, dark green, and deeply veined leaves. The large clusters of white flowers that appear in the early summer are followed by glossy, red-colored fruits.

Native range: China
Height: 16 ft (5 m)
Spread: 16 ft (5 m)
Hardiness: Zone 6
Variants: 'Exburiensis' has yellow fruits. 'Gnom' is low-growing, to a height of about 12 in (30 cm), and makes good ground cover. 'Rothschildianus' is notable for its creamy yellow fruits.

Cotoneaster simonsii

This vigorous, upright, deciduous or semi-evergreen shrub is often used for hedging, and its glossy, dark green leaves turn red in the autumn. Small clusters of white, pink-tinged flowers in early summer are followed by glossy, orange-red fruits.

Native range: Himalayas
Height: 10 ft (3 m)
Spread: 6 ft (2 m)
Hardiness: Zone 5

Cotoneaster x *suecicus*

A group of garden-raised hybrids between *C. conspicuus* and *C. dammeri* making evergreen, creeping, or mound-forming shrubs. They have glossy, green leaves and white flowers in late spring, followed by orange-red to red fruits.

Height: Variable
Spread: 6 ft (2 m) or more
Hardiness: Zone 5
Variants: 'Coral Beauty' makes a mound, up to 3 ft (1 m) high, with orange-red fruits. 'Erlinda' has leaves edged with creamy white and is usually top-grafted to make a small, weeping standard.

Crataegus crus-galli

Crataegus
Rosaceae

The hawthorns comprise a large genus of about 200 species of mainly deciduous, often spiny trees and shrubs that are widely distributed in the Northern Hemisphere.

These plants bear clustered, usually white, flowers, which are sometimes followed by edible fruits varying in color from yellow and red to blue, purple, or black.

Hawthorns are adaptable and will grow in most soils. They are generally very tough trees, standing up to exposed positions. They can be grow as specimen trees or for hedging.

Crataegus crus-galli
This is a spreading, flat-topped, deciduous tree featuring distinctly curved thorns. The glossy, dark green leaves turn attractive shades of orange and red in the autumn. Clusters of white flowers in early summer are followed by long-persistent, glossy, red fruits.

Common name: Cockspur thorn
Native range: E United States of America
Height: 26 ft (8 m)
Spread: 33 ft (10 m)
Hardiness: Zone 4

Crataegus laevigata
This densely branched, deciduous tree has a rounded habit with spiny shoots and shallowly lobed and toothed, glossy, dark green leaves. Clusters of white flowers in late spring are followed by small, glossy, red fruits. It is normally seen in cultivation as one of the selected forms listed below.

Synonym: *Crataegus oxyacantha*
Common name: English hawthorn
Native range: Europe, North Africa
Height: 33 ft (10 m)
Spread: 33 ft (10 m)

Crataegus laevigata 'Rosea Flore Pleno'

Hardiness: Zone 4
Variants: 'Crimson Cloud' has large, deep pink flowers, white in the center. 'Paul's Scarlet' has deep pink, double flowers. 'Plena' has white double flowers turning pink. 'Rosea Flore Pleno' has pink double flowers.

Crataegus x *lavallei* 'Carrièrei'

This popular garden-raised hybrid between *C. crus-galli* and *C. mexicana* is interesting for its late-ripening fruits, which are ornamental during winter. It makes a spreading, deciduous tree with bold, glossy, dark green, long-persistent leaves, which turn red in late autumn and winter. Clusters of white flowers appear in early summer and these are followed by bright orange-red fruits ripening in late autumn.

Height: 33 ft (10 m)
Spread: 33 ft (10 m)
Hardiness: Zone 4

Crataegus monogyna

This is a deciduous tree, rounded-to-spreading in habit, with thorny shoots and deeply lobed and toothed, glossy, dark green leaves. Clusters of fragrant, white flowers in late spring are followed by small, glossy, red-colored fruits. This species is often used for hedging.

Common names: Quickthorn, single seed hawthorn
Native range: Europe
Height: 33 ft (10 m)
Spread: 33 ft (10 m)
Hardiness: Zone 4
Variant: 'Biflora' (Glastonbury thorn) has two periods of interest: it comes into leaf and flower during winter and again in spring.

Crataegus x *persimilis* 'Prunifolia'

This garden hybrid makes a deciduous tree with a rounded habit. It has thorny shoots and glossy, dark green, sharply toothed leaves that turn brilliant orange and red in autumn. Clusters of white flowers in early summer are followed by bright red fruits.

Synonym: *Crataegus* x *prunifolia*
Height: 20 ft (6 m)
Spread: 26 ft (8 m)
Hardiness: Zone 4

Crataegus viridis

This is a rounded, deciduous tree of dense habit with spiny shoots and glossy, dark green, sharply toothed, and shallowly lobed leaves that sometimes turn red and purple in the autumn. Clusters of white flowers appear in late spring and these are followed by persistent bright red fruits.

Native range: E United States of America
Height: 33 ft (10 m)
Spread: 33 ft (10 m)
Hardiness: Zone 4
Variants: 'Winter King' has particularly large, long-persistent fruits.

Crinodendron hookerianum

Crinodendron
Elaeocarpaceae

This is a small genus comprising just two species of evergreen trees or shrubs. They are native of Chile and are grown for their unusual flowers.

The following species is the most commonly seen in garden cultivation and it requires a moist, well-drained, acidic soil enriched with abundant organic matter. It does best when planted in regions that experience cool, moist summers and mild winters.

Crinodendron hookerianum
This evergreen shrub has an upright habit, sometimes treelike, with narrow, dark green leaves. The striking, pendulous, lantern-like, deep pink flowers open in late spring and early summer from buds formed in the previous year.

Common name: Lantern tree
Native range: Chile
Height: 20 ft (6 m)
Spread: 13 ft (4 m)
Hardiness: Zone 8

Cydonia
Rosaceae

The single species in this small genus is a deciduous tree, native to Central and Southwest Asia, and is grown for its attractive flowers and edible fruits.

The tree will grow in any fertile, well-drained soil, but requires a position in full sun. In cooler regions it can be grown near to a warm, sun-facing wall for protection, or it can be fan-trained against it.

Cydonia oblonga
A wide-spreading, deciduous tree with dark green leaves, gray with down beneath. Pale pink or white flowers open singly in late spring, followed by fragrant, pear-shaped, edible yellow fruits.

Common name: Quince
Native range: C and SW Asia
Height: 20 ft (6 m)
Spread: 20 ft (6 m)
Hardiness: Zone 4
Variant: 'Vranja' is the most popular of several fruiting selections in garden cultivation. It bears very fragrant, golden yellow fruits.

Cytisus battandieri

Cytisus
Leguminosae

Grown for their foliage and also popular for their usually yellow, pealike flowers, the brooms are a genus of some 35 species of widely distributed, deciduous and evergreen shrubs and, more rarely, trees. The brooms are natives of Europe, North Africa, and West Asia.

The brooms are suitable for the shrub border, while the dwarf sorts make excellent additions to a rock garden. They prefer a not-too-rich, even poor or starved, well-drained soil. They also do best when planted in a position where they will receive full sun.

Prune lightly after flowering has finished to encourage a compact habit. The stems that have borne flowers can be cut back to about half their original length, but care must be taken not to cut into the old wood, since it will not produce new growing stems.

Cytisus battandieri

This is a vigorous, deciduous shrub of upright, treelike habit and has bold, silvery-gray leaves that are divided into three leaflets. The pineapple-scented, yellow flowers open in dense cylindrical clusters during summer.

Common name: Pineapple broom
Native range: Morocco
Height: 13 ft (4 m)
Spread: 13 ft (4 m)
Hardiness: Zone 7

Cytisus x *beanii*

Making a low, spreading, deciduous shrub, this garden-raised hybrid between *C. ardoinoi* and *C. purgans* produces slender, green, arching shoots and small, downy leaves that are divided into three leaflets. It produces profusely borne, small clusters of bright yellow, pealike flowers in the late spring or early summer on the previous year's growth. Prune lightly after flowering to maintain its shape.

Height: 18 in (45 cm)
Spread: 3 ft (1 m)
Hardiness: Zone 5

Cytisus x kewensis

This garden-raised hybrid between *C. ardoinoi* and *C. multiflorus* is suitable for a large rock garden or a sloping site. It makes a low-growing, spreading, deciduous shrub with slender, arching shoots and small, downy leaves that are divided into three very small leaflets. Small clusters of pale, creamy yellow to white, pealike flowers open in late spring. It is fully hardy and should be pruned lightly after flowering to maintain its shape.

Height: 12 in (30 cm)
Spread: 3 ft (1 m)
Hardiness: Zone 6
Variant: 'Niki' has golden yellow flowers.

Cytisus x praecox

This garden-raised hybrid between *C. multiflorus* and *C. purgans* makes a deciduous shrub with a dense, mound-forming habit. It has slender, upright, later arching, green shoots bearing small, gray-green leaves that are divided into three leaflets. Creamy yellow flowers are profusely borne in small clusters from mid- to late spring. It is normally grown as selected forms listed below.

Height: 4 ft (1.2 m)
Spread: 5 ft (1.5 m)
Hardiness: Zone 5
Variants: 'Albus' has white flowers. 'Allgold' has golden yellow flowers. 'Warminster' (Warminster broom) is sometimes grown as *Cytisus x praecox* and has creamy yellow flowers. Hybrids of this include 'Hollandia', which has cream and deep pink flowers, and 'Zeelandia', which has lilac-pink flowers flushed with cream.

Cytisus x praecox 'Allgold'

Cytisus x beanii

Cytisus scoparius

This is a deciduous shrub that produces slender, green, arching shoots and small leaves that are divided into three leaflets. Clusters of showy, deep yellow, pealike flowers open in late spring. This species, together with its many forms and hybrids, is not at its best if grown on shallow, chalky soils.

Common name: Scotch broom
Native range: Europe
Height: 5 ft (1.5 m)
Spread: 5 ft (1.5 m)
Hardiness: Zone 5
Variants: There are numerous selections and hybrids in garden cultivation with variously colored flowers. These include f. *andreanus*, which has dark green leaves and yellow flowers marked with red; 'Burkwoodii', with deep crimson and yellow flowers; and 'Lena', which is compact and has deep yellow flowers marked with red.

Daboecia cantabrica 'Alba'

Daboecia
Ericaceae

A genus of a single species—an evergreen shrub—related to the heathers. Native of western Europe and popular for its variously colored, urn-shaped flowers, it is suitable for the heather garden or a similar situation. It needs a neutral to acidic soil and does best in full sun. Cut back lightly before growth starts in spring to retain a compact habit.

Daboecia cantabrica

A heathlike, evergreen shrub with small, glossy, green, pointed leaves. The nodding, urn-shaped flowers, which are usually purple-pink, open in long, upright, spikelike clusters over a long period during summer and autumn.

Daboecia cantabrica 'William Buchanan'

Common names: Connemara heath, St. Dabeoc's heath
Native range: W Europe (W Ireland to Portugal), Azores
Height: 18 in (45 cm)
Spread: 24 in (60 cm)

Hardiness: Zone 6
Variants: 'Alba' has white flowers. 'Atropurpurea' has deep purple-pink flowers. 'Praegerae' has rich pink flowers. 'William Buchanan' has crimson-purple flowers.

Daphne bholua 'Jacqueline Postill'

Danae
Ruscaceae

The single species that comprises
this genus is a remarkable evergreen
plant, related to the butcher's broom,
and sends up new shoots from the
base each year.

The species is easy to grow in
either sun or shade and it is suitable
for any not-too-dry, well-drained soil.
The apparent leaves are really
flattened stems.

Any dead shoots can be cut back to
the base in spring.

Danae racemosa
An evergreen shrub forming a clump
of upright, later arching, green stems
with glossy, dark green "leaves."
Sprays of small, pale green flowers in
early summer are followed by red
berries.

Common name: Alexandrian laurel
Native range: Turkey, N Iran
Height: 3 ft (1 m)
Spread: 4 ft (1.2 m)
Hardiness: Zone 7

Daphne
Thymelaeaceae

This is a remarkable genus
comprising about 50 species of both
deciduous and evergreen shrubs
widely distributed throughout
Europe, North Africa, and Asia. They
are popular in gardens for their often
very fragrant, four-lobed flowers.

They can be grown in a good, moist
but well-drained soil in a sunny
position: the smaller sorts are
suitable for a rock garden. *D. bholua*,
D. laureola, and *D. pontica* are very
shade-tolerant plants and will thrive
in woodland conditions. They are all
extremely poisonous if eaten.

Daphne bholua
This is a very beautiful, deciduous or
evergreen shrub of upright growth
with dark green leaves. Clusters of
extremely fragrant, usually pink and
white flowers open at the ends of the
shoots during late winter and early
spring. Apart from removing dead or
damaged wood after flowering,
pruning is not usually recommended.

Daphne cneorum

Native range: Himalayas
Height: 8 ft (2.5 m)
Spread: 5 ft (1.5 m)
Hardiness: Zone 8
Variants: 'Gurkha' is deciduous with purple-pink and white flowers. 'Jacqueline Postill' is evergreen or semi-evergreen with particularly large, deep purple-pink and white-colored flowers.

Daphne blagayana

This low-growing, evergreen shrub has long, trailing shoots with dark green, leathery leaves growing mainly at the tips. In spring, the clusters of richly fragrant, creamy flowers open mainly at the ends of the shoots, and these are sometimes followed by fleshy white fruits. *D. blagayana* is equally successful in a semi-shaded woodland situation or in a scree bed.

Native range: SE Europe
Height: 18 in (45 cm)
Spread: 3 ft (1 m)
Hardiness: Zone 5

Daphne x burkwoodii

This popular, garden-raised hybrid between *D. caucasica* and *D. cneorum* makes an upright, semi-evergreen shrub, becoming more rounded as it matures, with bright green foliage. The dense clusters of extremely fragrant, pink flowers, fading to white, open over a long

Daphne mezereum

Daphne odora 'Aureomarginata'

Daphne laureola subsp. *philippi*

period during spring, and often there is a repeat flowering in autumn.

Height: 3 ft (1 m)
Spread: 3 ft (1 m)
Hardiness: Zone 4
Variants: Forms include 'Albert Burkwood' and the more upright 'Somerset'. Variegated forms include 'Carol Mackie', with yellow-edged leaves later turning creamy white.

Daphne caucasica

This is a rounded, deciduous shrub with slender, pale green leaves. The fragrant, white flowers open in dense clusters during late spring and early summer, and often there is a repeat flowering in the autumn.

Native range: Caucasus, W Asia
Height: 5 ft (1.5 m)
Spread: 5 ft (1.5 m)
Hardiness: Zone 5

Daphne cneorum

This dwarf-growing, evergreen shrub makes a low mound of spreading shoots with densely arranged, narrow, dark green leaves. Thick clusters of very fragrant, pink flowers open at the ends of the shoots in spring, and often there is a repeat flowering in the summer.

Common name: Rose daphne
Native range: Europe
Height: 8 in (20 cm)
Spread: 3 ft (1 m)
Hardiness: Zone 4
Variants: 'Eximia' produces deep pink-colored flowers and 'Variegata' has leaves that are edged with cream.

Daphne laureola

This is an evergreen shrub with stout shoots and glossy, dark green, leathery leaves. Pale green, slightly fragrant flowers open during the late winter and early spring in dense clusters under the leaves, followed by glossy, black fruits. Suitable for planting in sun or shade.

Common name: Spurge laurel
Native range: S and W Europe, N Africa
Height: 4 ft (1.2 m)
Spread: 5 ft (1.5 m)
Hardiness: Zone 7
Variant: subsp. *philippi* from the Pyrenees region makes a compact mound, up to 24 in (60 cm) tall.

Daphne mezereum

This deciduous shrub has an open habit with upright shoots and slender, gray-green leaves. The fragrant, deep pink flowers are borne profusely clustered on the bare shoots in the late winter and early spring, either before or as the leaves emerge. The flowers are followed by red fruits.

Common name: February daphne
Native range: Europe, W Asia
Height: 3 ft (1 m)
Spread: 3 ft (1 m)
Hardiness: Zone 4

Daphne odora

A dense, rounded, evergreen shrub with glossy, dark green, leathery leaves. The large, dense heads of very fragrant, purple-pink flowers open at the ends of the shoots in late winter and early spring, and these are sometimes followed by red fruits.

Native range: China, Japan
Height: 4 ft (1.2 m)
Spread: 4 ft (1.2 m)
Hardiness: Zone 7
Variants: f. *alba* produces white-colored flowers, while 'Aureomarginata' has leaf margins that are edged with yellow.

Daphne pontica

An evergreen shrub that makes a wide, spreading mound with glossy, dark green leaves. Its slightly fragrant, pale yellow-green flowers open in clusters during the spring, and these are followed by glossy, black fruits. Does well in shade

Native range: SE Europe, Caucasus, N Turkey
Height: 3 ft (1 m)
Spread: 5 ft (1.5 m)
Hardiness: Zone 6

Daphne tangutica

This is a handsome and an adaptable species that is suitable for growing either in a border or in a rock garden. It produces matt-green, leathery leaves and develops into a rounded, evergreen shrub. Clusters of fragrant, pink-colored flowers flushed with white open in the late spring and early summer, and these are followed by orange-red fruits.

Native range: China
Height: 3 ft (1 m)
Spread: 3 ft (1 m)
Hardiness: Zone 6

Davidia
Cornaceae

The single species that makes up this genus is a deciduous tree native to China. It has very distinctive, large, white bracts surrounding the flowerheads.

It prefers a good, moist, and well-drained soil and it is ideally suited to a position among other trees, where it can receive some protection from strong winds.

Davidia involucrata

A deciduous tree, conical when young but later spreading, with broadly heart-shaped leaves ending in a tapered point. Leaves are bright green above, densely covered in soft hairs beneath on mature trees. The rounded heads of small flowers in late spring have purple anthers and are surrounded by two large and conspicuous, unequal white bracts.

Common names: Dove tree, ghost tree, handkerchief tree
Native range: China

Davidia involucrata

Height: 50 ft (15 m)
Spread: 40 ft (12 m)
Hardiness: Zone 6
Variant: var. *vilmoriniana* is the most
commonly seen form, differing only
in having leaves that have smooth
undersurfaces.

Decaisnea
Lardizabalaceae

The two species in this genus are
deciduous shrubs, natives of the
Himalayas and China, with leaves
divided into many leaflets and
unusual flowers and fruits.

The following species is the only
example that is commonly found in
cultivation and does best when
planted in well-drained, not-too-dry
soil in a position where it is sheltered
by trees or other large shrubs.

Decaisnea fargesii
This is a vigorous, deciduous shrub
that has stout, sparsely branched,
upright shoots and bold, dark green
leaves. The leaves are colored blue-
green beneath and are divided up
into as many as 25 individual leaflets.
The drooping, pale green, bell-shaped
flowers open in large, pendulous
sprays in late spring to early summer,
and these are followed by large blue
fruits covered in a white bloom.
These fruits are filled with a thick
white pulp that contains the seeds.

Native range: W China
Height: 16 ft (5 m)
Spread: 16 ft (5 m)
Hardiness: Zone 5

Desfontainia spinosa

Desfontainia
Loganiaceae

The single species that makes up this genus is a South American evergreen shrub with foliage very similar to that of a holly, except that the leaves are borne opposite on the shoots. It requires a moist, peaty, lime-free soil, and is suitable for a sunny position. In dry areas, however, it needs more shade. Pruning is rarely necessary.

Desfontainia spinosa
An evergreen shrub of a dense, upright habit with spiny toothed, glossy, dark green, opposite-growing leaves. The showy, tubular flowers are bright red and tipped with orange-yellow. The flowers open during summer and early autumn.

Native range: Andes of South America
Height: 6 ft (2 m)
Spread: 5 ft (1.5 m)
Hardiness: Zone 7

Deutzia
Hydrangeaceae

A genus of about 60 species of mainly deciduous shrubs with opposite leaves and white to pink, starry flowers, native from the Himalayas to East Asia.

These plants are suitable for a shrub border, but old plants can become rather leggy and look best if they are regularly pruned. Either cut them back lightly after flowering or cut some of the older shoots right down to the base. Old plants can be rejuvenated by cutting them back to the base in early spring, before the new season's growth starts, but that year's flowers will then be lost.

Deutzia x elegantissima
This group of garden-raised hybrids makes upright to rounded deciduous shrubs with matt-green, toothed leaves that are rough to the touch. The rounded heads of pink or white flowers open during the late spring and early summer.

Height: 5 ft (1.5 m)
Spread: 5 ft (1.5 m)
Hardiness: Zone 6
Variants: 'Fasciculata' has bright rose-pink flowers. 'Rosealind' has deep carmine-pink flowers.

Deutzia gracilis
A mound-forming, deciduous shrub of spreading habit with slender shoots and bright green, toothed leaves. Small, slightly fragrant, white flowers open in clusters during late spring and early summer.

Native range: Japan
Height: 4 ft (1.2 m)
Spread: 4 ft (1.2 m)
Hardiness: Zone 4
Variant: 'Nikko' is a compact, dwarf form that makes a low, dense mound only 24 in (60 cm) tall.

Deutzia x *rosea* 'Carminea'

Deutzia x *hybrida*

Garden-raised hybrids between
D. *discolor* and D. *longifolia* making
deciduous, upright shrubs with dark
green, toothed leaves that are slightly
rough to the touch. Large sprays of
starry shaped flowers in various
shades of pink are produced in the
early summer period. Normally
grown as selected forms.

Height: 5 ft (1.5 m)
Spread: 5 ft (1.5 m)
Hardiness: Zone 6
Variants: 'Mont Rose' has profuse,
rose-pink flowers. 'Magicien' has
large, pink flowers that are banded
deep purple-pink on the outside.

Deutzia x *rosea* 'Carminea'

Deutzia x *rosea*

These are garden-raised, deciduous
hybrids between D. *gracilis* and
D. *purpurascens* with a compact,
rounded habit. They all have arching
shoots and dark green leaves. The
open, bell-shaped, white flowers,
flushed pink outside, are borne in
large clusters in the late spring and
early summer.

Height: 4 ft (1.2 m)
Spread: 5 ft (1.5 m)
Hardiness: Zone 5
Variant: 'Carminea' produces
attractive flowers that are carmine-
pink on the outside.

Diervilla x splendens

humus-rich, acid soil somewhere in a shady or partially shaded position.

These plants grow at their best in regions that experience mild winter temperatures and cool, moist summers. Dead fronds need to be regularly removed.

Dicksonia antarctica

This impressively large, treelike, evergreen or semi-evergreen fern has a sturdy, trunklike, unbranched rhizome that is densely covered in fibrous roots. The large, arching, palmlike fronds are deeply divided and dark green in color when mature. In areas that experience cold winters, *D. antarctica* may lose its foliage.

Common name: Soft tree fern
Native range: E Australia, Tasmania
Height: 16 ft (5 m)
Spread: 13 ft (4 m)
Hardiness: Zone 9

Diervilla
Caprifoliaceae

The three species of deciduous shrubs that make up this genus are all natives of North America. They are related to Weigela and are grown for their dense habit and autumn color, as well as for their attractive yellow flowers. They will grow in any good soil and are suitable for either a sunny or a shady shrub border.

These shrubs can be cut back hard in spring before the new season's growth starts in order to improve vigor and maintain a compact habit.

Deutzia scabra

This is a vigorous, deciduous shrub of a dense, upright habit, with pale brown, peeling bark and deep matt-green leaves that are rough to the touch on both sides. Large, conical clusters of white or pink-tinged flowers open in early summer.

Native range: Japan
Height: 10 ft (3 m)
Spread: 8 ft (2.5 m)
Hardiness: Zone 5
Variants: 'Candidissima' has double, white flowers. 'Plena' has double, white flowers that are flushed purple-pink outside. 'Pride of Rochester' has double, white flowers that are pink outside.

Dicksonia
Dicksoniaceae

This is a genus consisting of some 25 species of widely distributed evergreen or semi-evergreen ferns that are native to Australasia, the Pacific Islands, Southeast Asia, and South America. These treelike ferns have creeping or upright rhizomes and large fronds. They are often used to provide a variety of heights in a fern bed. When grown outside, the following species needs a moist,

Diervilla x *splendens*

This garden-raised, deciduous hybrid between *D. lonicera* and *D. sessilifolia* develops into a thicket-forming shrub. It has glossy, dark green, taper-pointed leaves that are bronze when young, red-purple in autumn. Slender, tubular, pale yellow flowers open in small clusters during summer.

Dipelta floribunda

Height: 5 ft (1.5 m)
Spread: 5 ft (1.5 m)
Hardiness: Zone 4

Dipelta
Caprifoliaceae

Four species of deciduous shrubs, natives of China and all with opposite leaves, make up this genus. Species are grown for their large flowers. The following is the most commonly grown species and is suitable for any well-drained soil. It can be planted either in a shrub border or as a specimen among trees and other large shrubs.

Dipelta floribunda
This is a large, vigorous, deciduous shrub with stout, upright shoots and bold, taper-pointed leaves with, on mature plants, pale brown, peeling bark. The large, funnel-shaped, fragrant flowers are white flushed with pink and marked with yellow in the throat. Flowers open in clusters during the late spring and early

summer. As the flowers fade, large, pale green, later brown, persistent bracts expand around them.

Native range: China
Height: 13 ft (4 m)
Spread: 10 ft (3 m)
Hardiness: Zone 6

Drimys
Winteraceae

This genus, which is composed of about 30 species of evergreen trees and shrubs, is native to Central and South America, Australasia, and Southeast Asia. The following species are grown for their foliage and flower interest and require a moist, well-drained soil.

They do best when planted in woodland conditions, and they require more shade and shelter in cooler, drier areas.

Drimys lanceolata
A conical, evergreen, aromatic shrub, sometimes treelike, of upright habit

Drimys winteri

Drimys lanceolata

and with red-purple shoots and deep green, leathery leaves, bronze when young. Clusters of small, greenish-white flowers open during late spring and early summer.

Common name: Mountain pepper
Native range: SE Australia, Tasmania
Height: 10 ft (3 m)
Spread: 6 ft (2 m)
Hardiness: Zone 8

Drimys winteri

An evergreen tree of upright, conical habit, often with several stems, with smooth, aromatic bark and glossy, dark green, aromatic leaves. Large clusters of white, many-petalled, fragrant flowers open in spring and early summer.

Common name: Winter's bark drimys
Native range: Mexico, South America
Height: 50 ft (15 m)
Spread: 26 ft (8 m)
Hardiness: Zone 8

Dryas
Rosaceae

This is a genus of three species of sun-loving, evergreen shrubs with attractive foliage and flowers, widely distributed in Arctic and high mountain regions of the Northern Hemisphere.

Dryas octopetala

This is a prostrate, evergreen shrub with creeping stems that are densely clothed with glossy, dark green leaves edged with rounded teeth. The creamy white flowers, each with a center of yellow stamens, are borne on slender, upright stalks in spring and early summer, and these are then followed by attractive silky seed heads.

Common name: Mount Washington dryas
Native range: N Europe, N Asia, North America
Height: 4 in (10 cm)
Spread: 5 ft (1.5 m)
Hardiness: Zone 2

Elaeagnus
Elaeagnaceae

About 45 species of deciduous and evergreen shrubs, sometimes trees, natives of Asia, Europe, and North America, make up this genus. Fast-growing and tough, they are cultivated for their foliage and small but fragrant flowers. The variegated sorts sometimes produce reverting shoots, which should be promptly removed. They make excellent specimen shrubs or they can be used for hedging. *E. angustifolia* is best in full sun.

Elaeagnus pungens 'Maculata'

Elaeagnus pungens 'Frederici'

Elaeagnus angustifolia
A vigorous, deciduous, often spiny shrub or tree of conical-to-spreading habit, with slender, dark green leaves covered in silvery scales beneath. Small, pale yellow, fragrant flowers open in clusters in late spring to early summer, followed by edible, yellow fruits covered in silvery scales.

Common names: Oleaster, Russian olive
Native range: W Asia
Height: 16 ft (5 m)
Spread: 16 ft (5 m)
Hardiness: Zone 2

Elaeagnus x ebbingei
This garden-raised hybrid between *E. macrophylla* and *E. pungens* makes a vigorous and dense evergreen shrub with glossy, dark green, leathery leaves, the undersides of which are covered in silvery scales. The small, creamy white, and very fragrant flowers open during autumn.

Height: 10 ft (3 m)
Spread: 13 ft (4 m)
Hardiness: Zone 6
Variants: 'Gilt Edge' has leaves that are broadly margined with yellow. 'Limelight' has leaves that are blotched in the center with deep yellow and pale green.

Elaeagnus pungens
This is a dense, evergreen shrub that has spiny shoots and glossy, dark green leaves, white beneath, with brownish scales. Clusters of white, fragrant flowers appear in the autumn and these are followed by red, scaly fruits.

Native range: Japan
Height: 10 ft (3 m)
Spread: 13 ft (4 m)
Hardiness: Zone 6
Variants: 'Dicksonii' has leaves that are broadly margined with golden yellow. 'Frederici' is slow-growing sort with creamy yellow leaves that are narrowly edged with green. 'Maculata' has leaves that feature a conspicuous deep yellow blotch in the center.

Elaeagnus 'Quicksilver'
This is a garden-raised hybrid between *E. angustifolia* and *E. commutata*. It is a deciduous shrub with slender, very silvery leaves. Clusters of pale yellow, fragrant flowers open during the late spring and early summer.

Height: 10 ft (3 m)
Spread: 16 ft (5 m)
Hardiness: Zone 2

Elaeagnus umbellata

Elaeagnus umbellata

This is a vigorous and large-growing, deciduous shrub with a spreading habit. It has silvery, sometimes spiny shoots and often wavy-edged, bright green leaves that are densely covered with silvery scales on their undersurfaces. The small, fragrant, white flowers open in late spring to early summer and these are followed by red, pea-sized fruits dotted with silvery scales.

Native range: China, Korea, Japan
Height: 16 ft (5 m)
Spread: 20 ft (6 m)
Hardiness: Zone 4

Elsholtzia
Labiatae

This genus is made up of about 35 species of annual and perennial herbs, shrubs, and subshrubs, all of which are native to Asia. They have opposite, aromatic leaves and small, two-lipped flowers that are borne in dense spikes.

They are suitable plants for growing in a border in any well-drained soil, but they do best if given a sunny position in the garden. They can be cut back hard to suitable buds just as the new growth starts to appear in the spring.

Elsholtzia stauntonii

This is a deciduous subshrub, which tends to spread with age, and it has taper-pointed and sharply toothed, bright green, mint-scented leaves. It produces upright spikes of attractive purple-pink flowers that open during the late summer and autumn period.

Native range: China
Height: 5 ft (1.5 m)
Spread: 5 ft (1.5 m)
Hardiness: Zone 5

Embothrium
Proteaceae

This is a genus comprising some eight species of evergreen or semi-evergreen trees and shrubs, natives mainly of the Andes of South America, reaching sea level in the south.

Only the following species is in garden cultivation, primarily for its striking flowers. To do well, it requires a moist but well-drained, lime-free soil. It is suitable for a woodland setting, where the surrounding trees can protect it from strong winds.

Enkianthus campanulatus 'Albiflorus'

Embothrium coccineum

This is a vigorous, evergreen or semi-evergreen tree with an upright habit and with narrow, glossy, dark green to blue-green leaves. Dense clusters of striking, bright orange-red, tubular-shaped flowers open during late spring and early summer. The plant prefers a semishaded position.

Common name: Chilean firebush
Native range: Chile, Argentina
Height: 30 ft (9 m)
Spread: 16 ft (5 m)
Hardiness: Zone 8

Enkianthus
Ericaceae

The ten species that make up this genus of deciduous and evergreen shrubs or small trees are all natives of the Himalayas and East Asia.

The cultivated members make charming garden additions, and they are grown both for their small drooping flowers, which vary in color from white to red, as well as for their autumn color, which can be a spectacular display of brilliant yellows and reds. They require a moist but well-drained, lime-free soil and do best in a bright but semi-shaded position.

Pruning is not usually required, but dead, damaged, or unwanted wood can be removed after flowering has finsihed.

Enkianthus campanulatus

This is a deciduous shrub with a spreading habit that becomes more treelike as it matures. Its dark green leaves, which are clustered at the ends of the shoots, turn orange, red, and yellow in autumn. The small, pendulous, bell-shaped flowers are creamy yellow, veined variously with pink, and open in drooping clusters during the late spring to early summer.

Native range: Japan
Height: 16 ft (5 m)
Spread: 16 ft (5 m)
Hardiness: Zone 5
Variants: 'Albiflorus' has creamy white flowers. 'Red Bells' is upright in

habit and its flowers are conspicuously veined with deep pink.

Enkianthus cernuus f. rubens

This deciduous, bushy shrub has a rounded habit with bright green leaves that turn deep red-purple in autumn. Its slender, pendulous clusters of small, deep red flowers are fringed at the mouth, and open in the late spring and early summer.

Native range: Japan
Height: 10 ft (3 m)
Spread: 10 ft (3 m)
Hardiness: Zone 5

Erica
Ericaceae

This is a large genus of more than 700 species of evergreen shrubs, sometimes small trees, that are natives mainly of South Africa, but are also found in Europe, North and East Africa, and Turkey. They are invaluable in a heather garden, where they can be combined with forms of *Calluna vulgaris* and *Daboecia cantabrica* to create a patchwork of flower and foliage that is attractive throughout the year. *E. arborea* and *E. cinerea* require a lime-free soil, and all do best in full sun.

Erica arborea

This is a vigorous, upright shrub with short, slender, dark green leaves that are densely arranged on plumelike shoots. In early spring, clusters of small, white, fragrant flowers densely cover the shoots.

Common name: Tree heath
Native range: S Europe, N and E Africa, SW Asia
Height: 8 ft (2.5 m)
Spread: 10 ft (3 m)
Hardiness: Zone 7
Variants: 'Albert's Gold' produces bright yellow young foliage, while

Erica arborea

var. *alpina* is a particularly hardy form and flowers profusely.

Erica carnea

This is a low, mound-forming, evergreen shrub with a spreading habit and has slender, needle-like, bright green leaves. The upright spikes of tubular or bell-shaped flowers vary in color from white to deep pink and they open during the winter and early spring.

Common name: Spring heath
Native range: Europe
Height: 10 in (25 cm)
Spread: 24 in (60 cm)
Hardiness: Zone 5
Variants: 'Ann Sparkes' has golden yellow foliage and purple-pink flowers. 'Foxhollow' has yellow foliage, tinged with red in winter, and pale pink flowers. 'Myretoun Ruby' has deep rose-pink flowers. 'Springwood White' bears a profusion of white flowers. 'Vivellii' has bronze-purple winter foliage and deep purple-pink flowers.

Erica carnea 'Ann Sparkes'

Erica tetralix 'Pink Star'

Erica cinerea

This is a mat-forming shrub that has slender, upright shoots densely clothed in narrow, dark green leaves. Urn-shaped flowers, varying in color from white to pink or red-purple, open in clusters during summer and early autumn.

Common name: Twisted heath
Native range: Europe
Height: 12 in (30 cm)
Spread: 30 in (75 cm)
Hardiness: Zone 6
Variants: 'CD Eason' has rich, deep pink flowers, while 'Pink Ice' is compact in form with bright green foliage and pale pink flowers.

Erica x darleyensis

This garden-raised hybrid between *E. carnea* and *E. erigena* makes a mound-forming shrub with a spreading habit and narrow, dark green leaves. The upright spikes of flowers, varying from white to deep pink, open in the late winter and early spring period.

Height: 24 in (60 cm)
Spread: 35 in (90 cm)
Hardiness: Zone 6
Variants: 'Arthur Johnson' produces long sprays of magenta-colored flowers. 'Darley Dale' bears a profusion of pale pink flowers over a

Erica tetralix 'Alba Mollis'

long period. 'Ghost Hills' has bright green foliage that is tipped with cream in spring and pink flowers, deeper at the tips. 'Jack H Brummage' has yellow foliage, red-tinged in winter, and deep pink flowers. 'Kramer's Rote' has bronze-green foliage and magenta-pink flowers. 'Silberschmelze' produces a profusion of white flowers.

Erica erigena

This is a compact shrub with an essentially upright habit and with dark green, needle-like foliage. Fragrant, deep pink flowers open over a long period during the spring months.

Erica x darleyensis 'Arthur Johnson'

Synonym: *Erica mediterranea*
Common name: Irish heath
Native range: W Ireland, SW Europe,
N Africa
Height: 24 in (60 cm)
Spread: 18 in (45 cm)
Hardiness: Zone 8
Variants: 'Brightness' has blue-green
foliage that turns bronze-green in
winter and rose-pink flowers. 'Irish
Dusk' is compact in habit with deep
green foliage and rose-pink flowers.
'WT Rackliff' produces pure white
flowers.

Erica tetralix

This dwarf shrub has a spreading
habit with softly hairy, gray-green
foliage. Nodding, urn-shaped flowers,
varying in color from white to pink,
open in dense clusters at the ends of
the shoots in the summer and
autumn.

Common name: Cross-leaved heath
Native range: N and W Europe

Height: 10 in (25 cm)
Spread: 24 in (60 cm)
Hardiness: Zone 3
Variants: 'Alba Mollis' has gray foliage
and white flowers. 'Con Underwood'
has crimson flowers. 'Pink Star' has
upright, lilac-pink flowers.

Erica vagans

This is a mound-forming shrub of
dense habit and dark green foliage.
White to pink or red flowers open in
long, conical clusters from
midsummer to mid-autumn.

Common name: Cornish heath
Native range: W Europe
Height: 20 in (50 cm) or more
Spread: 35 in (90 cm)
Hardiness: Zone 5
Variants: 'Lyonesse' has white
flowers. 'Mrs DF Maxwell' has deep
cerise-pink flowers. 'Valerie Proudley'
is low and compact, up to 6 in
(15 cm) high, with bright yellow
foliage and white flowers.

Eriobotrya japonica

Eriobotrya
Rosaceae

The 30 species or so of this genus of evergreen trees and shrubs are natives of the Himalayas and East Asia. The following is the most commonly grown species, due to its bold foliage and attractive flowers. It also produces edible fruits, but only in warm climates. It is suitable for any well-drained soil and prefers a sunny position sheltered from strong winds. It is at its best in warm climates; in cooler areas it can be grown against a sunny wall.

Eriobotrya japonica
This is a vigorous, stoutly branched, often multi-stemmed tree or large shrub of spreading habit with large, leathery, and prominently veined leaves that are glossy and dark green. Clusters of fragrant, white, five-petalled flowers open in late autumn or winter and these are followed by edible pear-shaped, yellow-colored fruits. It is frost-hardy, but appreciates the protection of a sun-facing wall.

Common name: Loquat
Native range: China, Japan
Height: 20 ft (6 m)
Spread: 20 ft (6 m)
Hardiness: Zone 8

Escallonia
Escalloniaceae

This genus is made up of some 40 species of evergreen shrubs and trees native to South America and popular for their bushy habit, foliage, and flowers. They are easy to cultivate in any well-drained soil and are excellent for shelter and hedging in mild localities. They are also popular for coastal gardens.

Prune lightly after flowering, if necessary to retain a compact habit or to restrict growth; cut back hard to rejuvenate old plants.

Escallonia 'CF Ball'
This is a vigorous, large, evergreen shrub of dense habit with bold, aromatic, glossy, dark green leaves. Clusters of showy, rich red flowers open over a long period during the summer months.

Height: 10 ft (3 m)
Spread: 13 ft (4 m)
Hardiness: Zone 8

Escallonia 'Edinensis'
A garden-raised hybrid making a compact evergreen shrub of bushy, spreading habit, with small, glossy, dark green leaves. Pink flowers from carmine-colored buds in summer.

Escallonia rubra

Height: 8 ft (2.5 m)
Spread: 10 ft (3 m)
Hardiness: Zone 8

Escallonia laevis

This is a vigorous and stoutly
branched evergreen shrub that has
slightly sticky shoots and glossy,
dark green, aromatic leaves. Tubular,
deep pink flowers open in the late
summer and early autumn period.
The shrub is mainly seen as the forms
listed below.

Native range: Brazil
Height: 5 ft (1.5 m)
Spread: 5 ft (1.5 m)
Hardiness: Zone 8
Variants: 'Gold Brian' has golden-
colored young foliage that turns dark
green as the seasons progress. 'Gold
Ellen' has dark green leaves that are
margined with yellow.

Escallonia 'Peach Blossom'

This garden-raised hybrid makes a
bushy, evergreen shrub with arching
shoots and glossy, dark green leaves.
It bears clear peach-pink and white
flowers that open in clusters during
summer.

Height: 5 ft (1.5 m)
Spread: 5 ft (1.5 m)
Hardiness: Zone 8

Escallonia 'Edinensis'

Escallonia rubra

This is an evergreen shrub with a
compact and vigorous habit and with
aromatic, glossy, dark green leaves.
Clusters of tubular, deep pink to red
flowers open during the summer
months.

Native range: Chile, Argentina
Height: 13 ft (4 m)
Spread: 16 ft (5 m)
Hardiness: Zone 8
Variants: var. *macrantha* has larger
leaves and larger, bright red flowers.
'Crimson Spire' is a very vigorous
form of this, with deep red flowers,
and is recommended for hedging.

Eucalyptus coccifera

Eucalyptus
Myrtaceae

This is a large genus with some 700 species of evergreen trees, sometimes shrubs, that are mainly natives of Australia. Young plants have opposite, usually rounded leaves, while on mature trees they are alternate, narrow, and drooping. The following sorts have white flowers without petals but with numerous stamens.

Valued in gardens for their very rapid growth, their ornamental bark, and their foliage, they are suitable for any well-drained, lime-free soil in a sunny position. Cut back hard to the base in spring if juvenile foliage is to be retained.

Eucalyptus coccifera
This is a vigorous, spreading tree that has smooth, gray and white, peeling bark and aromatic foliage. Juvenile leaves are blue-gray in color and rounded, while adult leaves are blue-green with a distinctly hooked tip. The white flowers open in clusters of three to seven in the early summer period.

Common name: Mount Wellington peppermint
Native range: Tasmania
Height: 50 ft (15 m)
Spread: 33 ft (10 m)
Hardiness: Zone 7

Eucalyptus dalrympleana
This is a large, evergreen tree of vigorous, upright growth and features gray-brown and cream, peeling bark. Foliage is blue-green—juveniles leaves are rounded in shape, while the adult leaves slender and pointed. White flowers are borne in clusters of

three during the late spring and summer period.

Common name: Mountain gum
Native range: SE Australia, Tasmania
Height: 80 ft (25 m)
Spread: 33 ft (10 m)
Hardiness: Zone 7

Eucalyptus gunnii

This is a fast-growing, evergreen tree that has very attractive gray and green, flaking bark and striking, silvery blue, rounded, juvenile leaves. The adult leaves are narrow and pointed and gray-green in color. White flowers open in clusters of three throughout the summer period.

Common name: Cider gum
Native range: Tasmania
Height: 65 ft (20 m)
Spread: 33 ft (10 m)
Hardiness: Zone 7

Eucalyptus pauciflora

This spreading, evergreen tree, often with several stems, has gray and white, peeling bark. Its juvenile leaves are leathery and oval to rounded, while on adult plants the leaves are glossy green, narrow, and curved, opening from red shoots. Flowers are white and open in clusters of up to 12 blooms in summer.

Common name: Snow gum
Native range: SE Australia, Tasmania
Height: 50 ft (15 m)
Spread: 50 ft (15 m)
Hardiness: Zone 7
Variant: The subsp. *niphophila* (*E. niphophila*) is a particularly hardy form with bloomy shoots and fewer flowers in each cluster.

Eucalyptus perriniana

This is a fast-growing, evergreen tree with gray and brown, peeling bark. Juvenile leaves are joined around the stem, remaining attached and

Eucalyptus pauciflora subsp. *niphophila*

spinning around the stem with age. Adult leaves are deep blue-green, taper-pointed and drooping. White flowers are borne in small clusters during summer.

Common name: Spinning gum
Native range: SE Australia, Tasmania
Height: 26 ft (8 m)
Spread: 23 ft (7 m)
Hardiness: Zone 7

Eucryphia
Eucryphiaceae

This is a small genus of some seven species of evergreen and deciduous trees, all with opposite leaves and showy, white flowers.

Natives of Australia and South America, they require a moist but well-drained, lime-free soil and should be planted where the base of the tree remains in cool shade.

Eucryphia glutinosa

This is a deciduous or semi-evergreen tree of upright habit. Its glossy, dark green leaves, which turn orange-red in autumn, are divided up into three to five leaflets. Large, white, four-

Eucryphia x nymansensis 'Nymansay'

petalled, fragrant flowers, with centers of numerous pink-tipped stamens, open during the late summer period.

Native range: Chile
Height: 33 ft (10 m)
Spread: 16 ft (5 m)
Hardiness: Zone 8

Eucryphia x intermedia 'Rostrevor'

This is a garden-raised hybrid between *E. glutinosa* and *E. lucida* that makes a bushy-headed, evergreen tree with undivided and divided leaves on the same tree. Leaves are glossy, dark green above, gray-green beneath. Large, white flowers with pink-tipped stamens open in late summer and autumn.

Height: 33 ft (10 m)
Spread: 20 ft (6 m)
Hardiness: Zone 8

Eucryphia lucida

This is an evergreen tree of narrow, upright growth, with slender, glossy, dark green leaves, blue-white beneath. Fragrant four-petalled flowers with pink-tipped stamens open during late summer.

Native range: Tasmania
Height: 23 ft (7 m)
Spread: 10 ft (3 m)
Hardiness: Zone 8

Eucryphia milliganii

A narrowly upright, evergreen tree, sometimes shrubby with several branches from the base, and tiny, glossy, dark green leaves, blue-white beneath. Small, white, cupped flowers with pink-tipped stamens open during late summer and autumn.

Native range: Tasmania
Height: 20 ft (6 m)
Spread: 5 ft (1.5 m)
Hardiness: Zone 8

Eucryphia x nymansensis 'Nymansay'

A vigorous, garden-raised hybrid between *E. cordifolia* and *E. glutinosa* making a columnar evergreen tree. Leaves are glossy and dark green above, paler beneath, either

Eucryphia x intermedia 'Rostrevor'

Euonymus alatus 'Compactus'

undivided or with up to three leaflets. The large, white, fragrant flowers have centers of numerous pink-tipped stamens and open during the late summer and autumn.

Height: 50 ft (15 m)
Spread: 20 ft (6 m)
Hardiness: Zone 8

Euonymus
Celastraceae

This is a large genus of about 175 species of deciduous and evergreen trees, shrubs, and climbers widely distributed throughout the world, but mainly in Asia. They have opposite leaves and small, usually greenish flowers. The lobed fruits split to release the often attractively colored seeds. This genus provides a wide range of popular ornamentals suitable for the shrub border, specimen planting, hedging, or for ground cover. Species can be grown in any well-drained soil.

Euonymus alatus
The shoots of this vigorous and densely branched deciduous shrub are edged with broad, corky wings. Dark green leaves turn bright red early in autumn. Tiny, green flowers in late spring to early summer are followed by small, red fruits, which open to reveal orange-coated seeds.

Native range: China, Japan
Height: 8 ft (2.5 m)
Spread: 10 ft (3 m)
Hardiness: Zone 4
Variant: 'Compactus' is a more compact form.

Euonymus europaeus
This large, deciduous shrub or small tree has a spreading habit with dark green leaves turning red in autumn. Clusters of small, greenish flowers in late spring to early summer are followed by pink, four-lobed fruits, which split to reveal bright orange-coated seeds. Some plants may be mostly male or female.

Euonymus europaeus

Euonymus fortunei 'Silver Queen'

Common name: European spindle tree
Native range: Europe, W Asia
Height: 20 ft (6 m)
Spread: 20 ft (6 m)
Hardiness: Zone 4
Variant: 'Red Cascade' has arching branches, leaves that turn deep red in autumn, and profusely borne fruits.

Euonymus fortunei

This is a variable, evergreen shrub—prostrate in the juvenile form and climbing by aerial roots if provided with suitable support, such as that from a wall or tree. Juvenile plants that are allowed to climb will eventually reach the bushy adult stage and will then produce small, green flowers in summer. The flowers are later followed by white or pinkish fruits, which open to reveal orange-coated seeds. The juvenile forms of *E. fortunei* make excellent ground cover plants.

Native range: China
Height: 12 in (30 cm) and more, but can climb to 33 ft (10 m) or more
Spread: 10 ft (3 m) or more
Hardiness: Zone 5
Variants: 'Coloratus' is a juvenile form with leaves that turn deep red-purple in winter. 'Emerald Gaiety' is a bushy adult form with leaves that are broadly margined with white.

'Emerald 'n' Gold' is a juvenile form, and its leaves have golden yellow margins. 'Kewensis' is a creeping juvenile form with tiny leaves. 'Silver Queen' is a bushy adult form of upright growth and with white-edged leaves. 'Sunspot' is a juvenile form and its leaves are blotched in their centers with yellow and are borne on yellow shoots.

Euonymus japonicus

This is a bushy and evergreen shrub with a dense, upright habit that often makes it treelike in appearance. It has glossy, dark green leaves and bears clusters of greenish flowers in summer. The flowers are followed by pinkish-white fruits, which split to reveal orange-coated seeds.
E. japonicus responds well to pruning, so it is useful as a hedging plant, even in shady places, and is also suitable for coastal sites. Cut it back in spring to encourage a compact habit. Variegated plants sometimes produce shoots with all green or all yellow leaves—these should be removed as soon as they appear.

Common name: Evergreen euonymus
Native range: China, Japan
Height: 13 ft (4 m)
Spread: 10 ft (3 m)
Hardiness: Zone 7

Euonymus planipes

Variants: 'Aureus' has leaves that are blotched with golden yellow, but it often reverts. 'Latifolius Albomarginatus' ('Macrophyllus Albus') has broad, gray-green leaves that are edged with creamy white. 'Microphyllus Albovariegatus' is a dwarf form and is upright in habit, with small leaves edged with white. 'Ovatus Aureus' has leaves broadly edged with golden yellow.

Euonymus kiautschovicus

This semi-evergreen shrub grows vigorously and has a wide-spreading habit. Its dark green leaves turn orange or red in the autumn and clusters of small, green flowers open in summer. The flowers are followed by pink fruits, which split to show orange-red seeds.

Native range: China
Height: 8 ft (2.5 m)
Spread: 13 ft (4 m)
Hardiness: Zone 5

Euonymus planipes

This vigorous, deciduous shrub is among the most showy of the genus. *E. planipes* is particularly valued for its attractive fruit as well as for its

Euryops pectinatus

dark green leaves, which turn a brilliant red color in the autumn. Clusters of small, green flowers appear in summer and mature into large, slender-stalked, red fruits, which open to reveal bright orange-coated seeds. It has often been grown as *E. sachalinensis*.

Native range: China, Korea, Japan
Height: 10 ft (3 m)
Spread: 10 ft (3 m)
Hardiness: Zone 4

Euryops
Compositae

This is a large genus consisting of approximately 100 or so species of evergreen shrubs and perennial and annual herbs. They are popular in the garden for their attractive foliage and daisy-like flowers, and they are ideal for a border situation or a rock garden. These plants are natives mainly of South Africa, but their natural range also extends to northeast Africa and Arabia.

Species will grow in any moist but well-drained soil, and they prefer a position where they receive full sun. Once they have been planted, however, they are best not moved, since they do not respond well to having their roots disturbed.

Some species are fully hardy, but the following is frost-tender and so is suitable only for gardens situated in more mild locations.

Euryops pectinatus
This is a small, evergreen shrub of upright growth with deeply cut, downy gray shoots and gray-green leaves. Large, rich yellow, daisy-like flowerheads are produced on long, slender stalks during the late spring and early summer period. Often there is a repeat flowering in winter.

Native range: South Africa
Height: 3 ft (1 m)
Spread: 3 ft (1 m)
Hardiness: Zone 8

Exochorda x *macrantha* 'The Bride'

Exochorda
Rosaceae

The four species in this small genus are all deciduous shrubs native to Central and East Asia. The following species is now the most commonly seen, and it is grown for its attractive habit and profuse flowers. Grow in any well-drained soil and in a sunny position for best flowering. However, it may become chlorotic on shallow chalky soils.

Exochorda x *macrantha* 'The Bride'
This is a garden-raised hybrid between E. *korolkowii* and E. *racemosa* that makes a deciduous shrub of a dense, spreading habit. The clusters of large and showy white flowers densely wreathe the pendulous shoots in late spring and early summer.

Height: 6 ft (2 m)
Spread: 10 ft (3 m)
Hardiness: Zone 5

Fabiana
Solanaceae

This genus is made up of some 25 species of heathlike, evergreen shrubs, natives mainly of the temperate regions of South America. Only the following is commonly grown, however. It requires a well-drained and not-too-rich soil in full sun and may become chlorotic if planted in very shallow, chalk soils.

If necessary, it can be cut back lightly in spring before the new season's growth begins.

Fabiana imbricata
This loosely branched, upright, evergreen shrub has plume-shoots that are densely covered in tiny, scalelike leaves. The branches are wreathed in white, tubular flowers during early summer.

Native range: Chile
Height: 8 ft (2.5 m)
Spread: 6 ft (2 m)
Hardiness: Zone 8

Fagus sylvatica 'Pendula'

Variants: 'Prostrata' makes a low, dense mound to 35 in (90 cm), while f. *violacea* has mauve flowers.

Fagus
Fagaceae

A genus of ten species of deciduous trees widely distributed in north temperate regions. The following is grown for its handsome stature and foliage as a specimen or for hedging. It is suitable for any well-drained soil.

Fagus sylvatica
A large, handsome tree with smooth, gray bark and glossy, dark green leaves that are pale and silkily hairy when young, turning yellow in autumn. Male and female flowers occur separately on the same tree—the male flowers in yellow-brown, tassel-like clusters in spring as the leaves emerge, and the females are followed by brown fruits covered in dense bristles.

Common name: European beech
Native range: Europe
Height: 80 ft (25 m) or more
Spread: 65 ft (20 m)
Hardiness: Zone 4
Variants: 'Aspleniifolia' has narrow, slender-pointed, and deeply lobed leaves. 'Atropurpurea' (purple beech) has bronze to purple leaves. 'Dawyck' is a conical form with upright branches, growing up to 26 ft (8 m) across. 'Dawyck Gold' is similar to 'Dawyck' except that it is columnar in habit, with foliage that is yellow when young and later turns green. 'Dawyck Purple' is a conical tree with deep red-purple foliage. 'Pendula' (weeping beech) has pendulous branches, often drooping to the ground. 'Purple Fountain' develops into a slender tree with pendulous branches and deep red-purple foliage. 'Purpurea Pendula' is a weeping tree, growing up to 13 ft (4 m) tall, with pendulous branches and red-purple foliage. 'Riversii' has deep red-purple foliage. 'Zlatia' has golden yellow young foliage, later green.

Fagus sylvatica 'Dawyck Gold'

Fagus sylvatica 'Dawyck Purple'

Fagus sylvatica

Fargesia
Gramineae

This is a genus of four species of evergreen bamboos that are natives of the Himalayas and China. Grown for their elegant habit, they are suitable for any good, though not-too-dry, soil and ideally should be positioned away from strong winds.

The following are not invasive and make excellent specimen plants.

Fargesia murieliae
This is a vigorous, evergreen bamboo that forms dense clumps of arching, yellow-green culms, bloomy when young. It bears masses of slender, bright green, taper-pointed leaves. It has also been grown as *Thamnocalamus spathaceus*.

Synonym: *Arundinaria murieliae*
Native range: China
Height: 13 ft (4 m)
Spread: 16 ft (5 m)
Hardiness: Zone 7

Fargesia nitida
A dense, clump-forming, evergreen bamboo of elegant habit with upright, later arching, purple-flushed culms. Very slender, deep green leaves tapering to a fine point weigh down the ends of the shoots. Excellent as a specimen or container plant.

Synonyms: *Arundinaria nitida*, *Sinarundinaria nitida*
Native range: China
Height: 13 ft (4 m)
Spread: 10 ft (3 m)
Hardiness: Zone 8

x *Fatshedera lizei*
Araliaceae

An unusual, evergreen, garden-raised hybrid shrub, which can be scrambling if given support. The glossy, dark green leaves are divided into five or seven lobes, and rounded

Fatsia japonica

heads of small white flowers open in clusters in autumn. Suitable plants for any good, well-drained soil.

Height: 6 ft (2 m)
Spread: 10 ft (3 m)
Hardiness: Zone 8
Variants: 'Annemieke' has leaves boldly blotched in the center with bright yellow-green. 'Variegata' has the leaves edged with creamy white.

Fatsia
Araliaceae

A genus of three species of evergreen shrubs, natives of Japan and Taiwan. The following is grown for its bold leaves and white flowers. It is a shrub of architectural qualities and will grow in any good, not-too-dry soil. In cold areas, it needs protection from strong winds. Flowering and fruiting is best if it is planted in full sun.

Fatsia japonica
This is a vigorous and stoutly branched evergreen shrub with large, deeply lobed, glossy, dark green leaves. The long-stalked, rounded heads of small, white flowers open in large clusters in autumn, and these are followed by numerous green fruits, later turning black.

Common name: Japan fatsia
Native range: Japan
Height: 8 ft (2.5 m)
Spread: 10 ft (3 m)
Hardiness: Zone 8
Variant: 'Variegata' has leaf lobes that are prominently tipped with creamy white.

Ficus
Moraceae

The figs make up a very large genus of more than 800 species of deciduous and evergreen trees, shrubs, and climbers. They all bear inconspicuous flowers and the species are widely distributed—mainly in the tropical and subtropical regions of the world.

Ficus carica requires a warm and sunny position in the garden, and it grows well against a wall. F. pumila prefers a moist but well-drained soil and does best if grown in warm, humid areas. Given the appropriate conditions, it is an excellent plant for covering walls.

Ficus carica
This is a spreading, deciduous tree that has stout branches and large, bold, glossy, green leaves that turn yellow in autumn. The large, edible, and fleshy green fruits, later turning brown or purple, ripen in the autumn.

Common name: Common fig
Native range: SW Asia
Height: 16 ft (5 m)
Spread: 16 ft (5 m)
Hardiness: Zone 7

Ficus pumila
This is a slender-stemmed, creeping, evergreen shrub that produces small, dark green, and rather puckered-looking leaves. In warm climates it climbs vigorously, clinging firmly to any available support by sending out aerial roots. Mature plants reach the

Ficus pumila

adult stage, producing large leaves and, possibly, small, red fruits in the autumn.

Common name: Creeping fig
Native range: E and SE Asia
Height: Prostrate to 33 ft (10 m) or more
Spread: 10 ft (3 m) or more
Hardiness: Zone 8

Fontanesia
Oleaceae

The single species in this genus is a deciduous shrub that is related to the privets (Ligustrum). Although it is little known in garden cultivation, the species is very hardy and can be used for screening as well as for hedges.

The shrub is suitable for any well-drained soil, and although it prefers a sunny position, it will also tolerate a position in light shade. A little light pruning in the spring will help to promote a good, compact habit.

Forsythia suspensa

Fontanesia phillyreoides

This is a vigorous, deciduous or semi-evergreen shrub that has upright branches and slender, drooping shoots bearing narrow, dark green, pointed leaves. Inconspicuous, greenish-white flowers appear in the early summer period and the flowers are followed by small, winged fruits.

Native range: SW Asia
Height: 16 ft (5 m)
Spread: 13 ft (4 m)
Hardiness: Zone 4
Variant: subsp. *fortunei* (*F. fortunei*) is also sometimes found in garden cultivation. It is similar in appearance and occurs naturally in China.

Forsythia
Oleaceae

This genus contains some seven species of deciduous shrubs, natives of southeast Europe and East Asia, with opposite leaves that are sometimes divided into three leaflets. These plants are popular for their four-lobed yellow flowers that open in early spring. They are suitable for any well-drained soil and flower best in a sunny position. To restrict growth or retain a compact habit they can be cut back—hard, if necessary—once flowering has finished.

Forsythia 'Arnold Dwarf'

This is a garden-raised hybrid that makes a low, wide-spreading

deciduous shrub with bright green,
sharply toothed leaves on creeping
shoots. The yellow-green flowers that
open in early spring are usually
sparse, but the shrub makes good
ground cover.

Height: 3 ft (1 m)
Spread: 6 ft (2 m)
Hardiness: Zone 5

Forsythia x intermedia

A group of garden-raised hybrids
between *F. suspensa* and *F. viridissima*
making vigorous, deciduous shrubs
and containing some of the most
popular plants in the entire genus.
The sharply toothed, dark green
leaves are sometimes divided into
three leaflets and can turn yellow,
or occasionally purple, in autumn.
Bright yellow flowers wreathe the
shoots in early to mid-spring.

Height: 10 ft (3 m)
Spread: 10 ft (3 m)
Hardiness: Zone 6
Variants: 'Lynwood' has profuse, deep
yellow flowers. 'Minigold' is compact
and upright in habit with profuse,
small, deep yellow flowers.

Forsythia ovata

This is a spreading, bushy, deciduous
shrub with a compact habit. It
produces stiff shoots bearing dark
green, sharply toothed leaves. The
bright yellow, four-lobed flowers of
F. ovata open very early in the spring,
and it is among the earliest flowering
of all the forsythias.

Native range: Korea
Height: 5 ft (1.5 m)
Spread: 8 ft (2.5 m)
Hardiness: Zone 4

Forsythia suspensa

This is a vigorous, deciduous shrub
that has slender, drooping shoots
bearing dark green, sharply toothed
leaves that are sometimes divided

Forsythia x intermedia 'Minigold'

into three leaflets. Yellow, trumpet-
shaped flowers open in clusters on
the bare, arching shoots in early to
mid-spring. This species can also be
trained to grow against a wall.

Native range: China
Height: 10 ft (3 m)
Spread: 10 ft (3 m)
Hardiness: Zone 5

Forsythia viridissima

This is a deciduous or sometimes
semi-evergreen shrub that has rigid,
upright shoots bearing dark green,
toothed or untoothed leaves growing
from green shoots. Bright yellow
flowers open singly or in small
clusters on the shoots in the early to
mid-spring period.

Native range: China
Height: 8 ft (2.5 m)
Spread: 6 ft (2 m)
Hardiness: Zone 5
Variant: 'Bronxensis' is a low,
compact, densely growing form with
a spreading habit and reaches a
height of up to 12 in (30 cm) with a
spread of about 30 in (75 cm). It has
small, bright green leaves and
primrose-yellow flowers.

Fothergilla major

Fothergilla
Hamamelidaceae

The witch alders make up a small
genus of just two species of
deciduous shrubs, both natives of
the southeast of the United States
of America. These plants are grown
primarily for their autumn color and
their unusual, fragrant, spring flower
clusters, the showy parts of which
are the long stamens rather than
the outer petals.

   The witch alders require a good,
lime-free soil rich in organic matter.
The flowers are borne more profusely,
and the autumn color is more
pronounced, if they are grown in a
sunny position.

Fothergilla gardenii
This is a compact and densely
growing, deciduous shrub with a
spreading, sometimes suckering,

Fothergilla gardenii

habit. The shrub produces dark green to blue-green leaves that turn colors of brilliant orange, yellow, and red in autumn. The dense, cylindrical, bottlebrush-like spikes of fragrant, white flowers open in the late spring, before or as the young leaves begin to emerge.

Common name: Dwarf fothergilla
Native range: SE United States of America
Height: 3 ft (1 m)
Spread: 5 ft (1.5 m)
Hardiness: Zone 5
Variant: 'Blue Mist' is a form that has attractive blue-green foliage, but it produces less striking autumn color.

Fothergilla major

This is a deciduous shrub of usually upright habit with dark green leaves, whitish beneath, turning yellow, orange, and red in autumn. Its dense, bottlebrush-like spikes of fragrant, white flowers open in the late spring to early summer.

Common name: Large fothergilla
Native range: SE United States of America
Height: 8 ft (2.5 m)
Spread: 6 ft (2 m)
Hardiness: Zone 4

Fraxinus
Oleaceae

This genus is made up of some 65 species of mainly deciduous trees and, sometimes, shrubs. Species of ash are usually fast-growing and are widely distributed throughout the Northern Hemisphere. They have opposite leaves divided into several leaflets. The individual flowers are small and usually undistinguished and mostly without petals, although in some species white petals are present. They will grow in any well-drained soil, as long as it is not too dry, and they do particularly well in alkaline soils.

Ash will tolerate both wind and salt, making this genus suitable for coastal locations. Leaves do not change color on all species before dropping in autumn, and the large root system associated with ash trees makes them difficult to accommodate in anything other than a very large area.

Fraxinus americana

A vigorous, deciduous tree of broad, columnar habit, the leaves of which are composed of up to nine dark green leaflets, blue-green beneath and turning yellow to red-purple in autumn. The tiny flowers lack petals and open in spring, males and females on separate plants. Female trees bear drooping clusters of small, slender, winged fruits, known as keys. Pruning is not usually necessary, though dead, damaged, or crossing wood can be removed as necessary.

Common name: White ash
Native range: E North America
Height: 80 ft (25 m)
Spread: 50 ft (15 m)
Hardiness: Zone 4
Variant: 'Autumn Purple' is a selection with good, red-purple autumn color.

Fraxinus angustifolia

This elegant, deciduous tree has a rounded to spreading habit, and its leaves are borne in whorls of three, with up to 13 narrow, slender-pointed leaflets. Bright and glossy green in summer, leaves turn yellow in autumn. It bears tiny flowers in the spring, and these are followed by slender, winged fruits.

Synonym: Fraxinus oxycarpa
Common name: Narrow-leaved ash
Native range: S Europe, North Africa
Height: 80 ft (25 m)
Spread: 50 ft (15 m)
Hardiness: Zone 5
Variant: 'Raywood' is broadly upright in habit with red-purple autumn color.

Fraxinus angustifolia 'Raywood'

Fraxinus excelsior

A vigorous, deciduous tree with a domed-to-rounded head and dark green leaves with up to 13 toothed leaflets turning yellow in autumn. Tiny flowers open from black buds in spring, followed by dense clusters of slender, winged fruits.

Common name: European ash
Native range: Europe
Height: 100 ft (30 m)
Spread: 80 ft (25 m)
Hardiness: Zone 5
Variants: 'Jaspidea' has yellow young leaves, turning bright yellow in autumn, and yellow winter shoots contrasting with black buds. 'Pendula' (weeping ash) is a weeping tree with pendulous branches.

Fraxinus ornus

This is a deciduous tree that has a dense, rounded head and produces dark matt-green leaves divided up into nine leaflets, turning red-purple in autumn. Flowers with white petals, fragrantly scented, open in dense, fluffy heads in the late spring to early summer, and these are followed by clusters of slender, winged fruits.

Common name: Flowering ash
Native range: S Europe, SW Asia
Height: 65 ft (20 m)
Spread: 50 ft (15 m)
Hardiness: Zone 6

Fraxinus pennsylvanica

This vigorous, deciduous tree has a broadly oval to spreading head. It bears dark green leaves, often velvety on their undersurfaces, divided up into as many as nine taper-pointed leaflets. Leaves turn yellow in the autumn. The tiny, insignificant flowers open in clusters during the

Fraxinus ornus

spring, male and female flowers on separate plants. Female trees bear clusters of slender, winged fruits in autumn.

Common name: Green ash
Native range: North America
Height: 65 ft (20 m)
Spread: 50 ft (15 m)
Hardiness: Zone 3
Variant: 'Summit' is conical with glossy foliage.

Fremontodendron
Sterculiaceae

The flannel bushes make up a genus of just two species of evergreen shrub, natives of California and northern Mexico, grown for their displays of showy flowers. Although in warm climates they will grow as free-standing plants, in cooler areas they are normally grown against a

Fraxinus pennsylvanica 'Summit'

Fremontodendron 'California Glory'

Fuchsia magellanica 'Sharpitor'

sunny wall. They need well-drained soil and a sunny position in order to thrive.

The hairs that cover these plants can be an irritant, so care should be taken, especially when pruning. They can be cut back lightly after flowering, if necessary. However, once planted they should not be moved, since they do not tolerate any disturbance to their roots.

Fremontodendron 'California Glory'

A garden-raised hybrid between *F. californicum* and *F. mexicanum* making a vigorous, evergreen shrub with bold, glossy, dark green, five-lobed leaves. The large, deep yellow flowers open over a long period during summer and autumn.

Height: 26 ft (8 m)
Spread: 20 ft (6 m)
Hardiness: Zone 8

Fuchsia
Onagraceae

This genus is made up of some 100 species of deciduous and evergreen shrubs with opposite leaves, sometimes in whorls of three, native from Mexico to South America and

New Zealand. The prominent, showy flowers, which are nearly always pendulous, are produced over a long period during the summer and autumn months. The flowers have colored petals in the center and colored, sometimes contrasting, sepals joined into a slender, colored tube at the base. Upright forms can make dense shrubs, while trailing forms are suitable for planting in hanging baskets.

They will grow in any good, well-drained soil, and they can be cut back to the base in spring.

Fuchsia x *bacillaris*

A vigorous, naturally occurring hybrid between *F. microphylla* and *F. thymifolia* of spreading habit, with small, dark green leaves. Flowers are small but numerous, with red sepals and petals.

Native range: Mexico
Height: 3 ft (1 m)
Spread: 4 ft (1.2 m)
Hardiness: Zone 9

Fuchsia excorticata

This is a large, deciduous shrub, sometimes treelike in form, with pale brown, peeling bark. It is unusual in the genus as its dark green leaves,

Fuchsia magellanica var. *gracilis*

which are silvery white beneath, are alternate. The drooping flowers have pale green sepals that become flushed red-purple with age, and deep purple petals.

Common name: Tree fuchsia
Native range: New Zealand
Height: 10 ft (3 m) or more
Spread: 10 ft (3 m) or more
Hardiness: Zone 9

Fuchsia magellanica

This spreading, deciduous shrub has bright green to dark green leaves, usually arranged in threes, and pale brown, peeling bark on older shoots. The pendulous flowers have red sepals and violet-purple petals. *F. magellanica* can make an effective hedge in mild areas.

Native range: Chile, Argentina
Height: 6 ft (2 m) or more

Spread: 10 ft (3 m)
Hardiness: Zone 6
Variants: 'Aurea' has bright yellow foliage; var. *gracilis* produces slender flowers and its leaves usually grow in pairs; var. *molinae* produces white flowers that are tinged pale mauve. 'Sharpitor' is similar to var. *molinae* except that it has gray-green leaves edged with white. 'Variegata' has leaves that are edged with cream and pink. 'Versicolor' produces gray-green leaves edged with white, but they are pink-flushed when young.

Fuchsia procumbens

This low-growing, creeping plant, sometimes scrambling into small shrubs, has very slender shoots and small, rounded, bright green leaves. The small, upright flowers are densely borne on the shoots, and they have green, sharply reflexed sepals that are deep purple at the tip and no

Fuchsia magellanica var. molinae

petals. The flowers are often followed by large, deep red fruits.

Native range: New Zealand
Height: 4 in (10 cm)
Spread: 3 ft (1 m)
Hardiness: Zone 8

Garden hybrids

There are thousands of *Fuchsia* garden hybrids from which to choose, though many are suitable only for frost-free conditions. The following sorts can be grown outside except in the coldest of areas. They are normally evergreen until they are cut back by the first frost.

Fuchsia 'Alice Hoffman'

This attractive, garden-raised hybrid makes a small shrub of compact, bushy habit with densely clustered leaves tinged bronze-purple. Flowers are small and semidouble, with deep pink sepals and white petals veined with pink.

Height: 24 in (60 cm)
Spread: 24 in (60 cm)
Hardiness: Zone 8

Fuchsia 'Brutus'

This is a free-flowering shrub of essentially upright growth. The flowers are single with cerise sepals and purple petals, shading to carmine at the base.

Height: 30 in (75 cm)
Spread: 30 in (75 cm)
Hardiness: Zone 8

Fuchsia 'Chillerton Beauty'

This spreading shrub has thick, sea-green, purple-stalked leaves. Flowers are single but are profusely borne, and have pale rose-pink sepals and violet-purple petals.

Height: 3 ft (1 m)
Spread: 4 ft (1.2 m)
Hardiness: Zone 8

Fuchsia 'Corallina'

This distinct and vigorous, spreading shrub has graceful, arching shoots and dark green leaves, flushed purple beneath, that are sometimes borne in threes or fours on the shoots. The flowers are single with scarlet sepals and purple-red petals.

Height: 24 in (60 cm)
Spread: 3 ft (1 m)
Hardiness: Zone 8

Fuchsia 'Display'

This vigorous, garden-raised hybrid has an upright habit and bears dark green leaves. The large, single flowers have carmine-colored sepals and deep rose-pink petals.

Height: 30 in (75 cm)
Spread: 30 in (75 cm)
Hardiness: Zone 8

Fuchsia 'Dollar Princess'

This plant makes a strongly growing shrub with a bushy habit. The double flowers have cerise-colored sepals and deep purple petals.

Fuchsia 'Corallina'

Height: 20 in (50 cm)
Spread: 20 in (50 cm)
Hardiness: Zone 8

Fuchsia 'Garden News'

This is a vigorously growing shrub
with an upright habit. The flowers are
double and compactly formed, with
pale pink sepals and tube, and deep
magenta-pink petals.

Height: 35 in (90 cm)
Spread: 3 ft (1 m)
Hardiness: Zone 8

Fuchsia 'Genii'

Fuchsia 'Genii'

This bushy, upright shrub has young
foliage that is pale yellow, becoming
yellow-green. Shoots are red. Flowers
are single with cerise tubes and
sepals, and deep violet petals.

Height: 30 in (75 cm)
Spread: 30 in (75 cm)
Hardiness: Zone 8

Fuchsia 'Lady Thumb'

This is a compact, bushy shrub of
upright habit. Flowers are small but
profusely borne, semidouble, with
light carmine tubes and sepals and
white petals veined with carmine.

Height: 18 in (45 cm)
Spread: 18 in (45 cm)
Hardiness: Zone 8

Fuchsia 'Prosperity'

Fuchsia 'Lena'
This vigorously growing shrub has a spreading habit. Its flowers are large and semidouble with very pale pink tubes and sepals, and deep rose-purple petals.

Height: 24 in (60 cm)
Spread: 30 in (75 cm)
Hardiness: Zone 8

Fuchsia 'Margaret'
This is a vigorous and bushy shrub with an upright habit. Its flowers are double and are profusely borne, and they have deep rose-pink sepals and violet-purple petals.

Height: 3 ft (1 m)
Spread: 3 ft (1 m)
Hardiness: Zone 8

Fuchsia 'Margaret Brown'
This shrub grows vigorously and has profusely borne, single flowers. The flower sepals and the slender tubes are colored pink, and the petals are a deep rose-pink.

Height: 3 ft (1 m)
Spread: 3 ft (1 m)
Hardiness: Zone 8

Fuchsia 'Mrs Popple'
This is a vigorous and spreading bushy shrub with dark green foliage. Its flowers are single and have scarlet-colored tubes and sepals, and deep violet-purple petals.

Height: 3 ft (1 m)
Spread: 4 ft (1.2 m)
Hardiness: Zone 8

Fuchsia 'Phyllis'

This is a very strongly growing shrub with an upright habit. Its flowers are semidouble and small, but they are profusely borne, with rose-red sepals and tubes, and deep rose-colored petals.

Height: 4 ft (1.2 m)
Spread: 3 ft (1 m)
Hardiness: Zone 8

Fuchsia 'Prosperity'

This is a vigorous shrub of strong, upright growth. Its flowers are very large and double, its sepals are deep rose-pink, and its petals white flushed with pink. An extremely attractive and hardy hybrid.

Height: 4 ft (1.2 m)
Spread: 35 in (90 cm)
Hardiness: Zone 8

Fuchsia 'Riccartonii'

This vigorous and upright shrub has arching branches and dark green, bronze-tinged leaves, sometimes borne in threes, on red shoots. Its flowers are small and single, with scarlet tubes and sepals, and broad, violet petals.

Height: 5 ft (1.5 m)
Spread: 5 ft (1.5 m)
Hardiness: Zone 6

Fuchsia 'Tom Thumb'

This is a compact, dwarf shrub of bushy, upright habit. The flowers are small but profusely borne, with carmine-pink tubes and sepals, and violet-purple petals.

Height: 24 in (60 cm)
Spread: 24 in (60 cm)
Hardiness: Zone 8

Garrya elliptica

Garrya
Garryaceae

A genus of about 13 species of evergreen shrubs with opposite leaves, natives of the western United States of America, Mexico, and the West Indies. The following is the most commonly grown, for its winter catkins. The individual flowers are small—males and females on separate plants.

It is suitable for any good, well-drained soil, and can be grown in the border or as a specimen shrub. In cold areas it should be given protection from strong winds, such as that provided by a sun-facing wall. It can be lightly pruned if necessary after flowering has finished.

Garrya elliptica
This is a vigorous, evergreen shrub that has glossy, dark green, wavy-edged, leathery leaves. The male is the most commonly grown form. It produces long, slender, gray catkins, from which yellow anthers protrude. The catkins open in the winter and early spring period.

Common name: Silk-tassel bush
Native range: W United States of America
Height: 13 ft (4 m)
Spread: 10 ft (3 m)
Hardiness: Zone 8
Variant: 'James Roof' is a male form with very long catkins.

Gaultheria
Ericaceae

This genus contains about 170 species of evergreen shrubs, often spreading by suckers, and is widely distributed in the New World, as well as from the Himalayas to East Asia and Australasia.

Grown for their small, usually white flowers and often ornamental fruits, they require a moist, peaty, lime-free soil and do best in shade or semishade.

Gaultheria cuneata
This low, spreading shrub has a compact habit and small, pointed, glossy leaves. Small clusters of nodding, urn-shaped, white flowers open during late spring and early summer, and these are followed by ivory-white fruits.

Native range: China
Height: 12 in (30 cm)
Spread: 35 in (90 cm)
Hardiness: Zone 6

Gaultheria mucronata
This is a vigorously growing, thicket-forming, and stiffly branched shrub with glossy, dark green, sharply pointed, and leathery leaves. Small, nodding, white flowers open in the late spring to early summer, and these are followed by showy, marble-like fruits. The fruits range in color from white to pink and red.

Gaultheria procumbens

Gaultheria shallon

Synonym: *Pernettya mucronata*
Native range: Chile, Argentina
Height: 3 ft (1 m)
Spread: 5 ft (1.5 m)
Hardiness: Zone 6
Variants: 'Bell's Seedling' produces large, deep red fruits. 'Crimsonia' has very large, crimson-colored fruits. 'Parelmoer' ('Mother of Pearl') has pale pink fruits. 'Signaal' has very large, persistent, cherry-red fruits. 'Sneeuwwitje' ('Snow White') produces white fruits that are spotted with pink.

Gaultheria procumbens
This low, creeping shrub, bearing glossy, dark green, aromatic leaves, forms dense mats and is an excellent candidate for ground cover. Small, nodding, urn-shaped, white or pale pink flowers appear in summer, and these are followed by long-persistent, aromatic, red fruits.

Common names: Checkerberry, wintergreen

Native range: E North America
Height: 4 in (10 cm)
Spread: 3 ft (1 m) or more
Hardiness: Zone 4

Gaultheria shallon
This is an extremely vigorous and thicket-forming shrub. It spreads strongly by suckers and its leaves are leathery, appearing from red shoots. Slender, arching clusters of small, pink-tinged, white flowers open at the ends of the shoots in mid- to late spring, and the flowers are followed by deep purple-colored fruits.

Common name: Salal
Native range: W North America
Height: 4 ft (1.2 m)
Spread: 10 ft (3 m) or more
Hardiness: Zone 5

Gaultheria x wisleyensis
This vigorous, garden-raised hybrid between *G. mucronata* and *G. shallon* develops into a dense, thicket-like

Genista aetnensis

shrub. It spreads by sending out suckers and has dark green leaves. It produces clusters of small, white, urn-shaped flowers opening during the late spring and early summer. It is usually grown as named forms.

Synonym: x *Gaulnettya wisleyensis*
Height: 4 ft (1.2 m)
Spread: 6 ft (2 m) or more
Hardiness: Zone 5
Variants: 'Pink Pixie' has pink-tinged flowers and purple-red fruits. 'Wisley Pearl' has deep ox-blood red fruits.

Genista
Leguminosae

This widely distributed genus is made up of about 80 species of deciduous and evergreen, often sparsely leafy, shrubs and trees, natives of Europe, North Africa, and West Asia. Grown for their yellow, pealike flowers, several species are popular plants for the shrub border and rock garden, while *G. aetnensis* is probably best as a specimen tree.

These plants do best if they are grown in a not-too-rich, well-drained soil in full sun. If necessary, they can be pruned after flowering, but take care not to cut into the old wood.

Genista aetnensis
This deciduous, rounded tree, sometimes shrubby on more than one trunk, has slender, bright green shoots and small, sparse leaves, which fall early. The fragrant, golden yellow, pealike flowers are profusely borne in mid- to late summer.

Common name: Mount Etna broom
Native range: Sardinia, Sicily
Height: 33 ft (10 m)
Spread: 26 ft (8 m)
Hardiness: Zone 8

Genista pilosa

Genista hispanica

This is a deciduous shrub that makes a dense mound with deep green, very spiny shoots. The small, slender leaves are borne only on the flowering shoots, each of which ends in a dense cluster of bright golden yellow, pealike flowers. It makes an excellent shrub for a large rock garden.

Common name: Spanish gorse
Native range: SW Europe
Height: 24 in (60 cm)
Spread: 3 ft (1 m)
Hardiness: Zone 7

Genista lydia

Genista lydia

A deciduous shrub of compact habit with slender, green, arching shoots and sparsely borne, small, blue-green leaves. Small clusters of bright yellow, pealike flowers open during late spring and early summer. Good in a dry border or rock garden.

Native range: SE Europe, SW Asia
Height: 24 in (60 cm)
Spread: 3 ft (1 m)
Hardiness: Zone 6

Genista pilosa

This is a dwarf, deciduous shrub of dense, spreading habit that forms a low-growing mat. It produces slender shoots and small, narrow leaves. The small, bright yellow, pealike flowers are densely borne along the shoots during the late spring and early summer period. It makes an excellent ground cover plant for a dry, sunny site and in a large rock garden.

Native range: Europe
Height: 18 in (45 cm)
Spread: 5 ft (1.5 m)
Hardiness: Zone 5
Variants: There are several good selections, including 'Goldilocks', which grows up to about 24 in (60 cm) tall, and 'Vancouver Gold,' which bears very profuse, golden yellow flowers and reaches up to 12 in (30 cm) in height.

Gleditsia triacanthos 'Sunburst'

Genista tinctoria

A deciduous shrub that varies from low and spreading to upright, with green shoots and small, slender, dark green leaves. Upright clusters of bright yellow flowers open during the summer.

Common name: Dyer's greenweed
Native range: Europe, Turkey
Height: 24 in (60 cm)
Spread: 35 in (90 cm)
Hardiness: Zone 4
Variants: 'Flore Pleno' is dwarf and spreading, up to 12 in (30 cm) tall, with double flowers, and does best in a rock garden. 'Royal Gold' is vigorous and upright, up to 3 ft (1 m), with large flower clusters.

Gleditsia
Leguminosae

This is a small genus made up of only about 12 species of deciduous, often very spiny, graceful trees. The leaves, which appear late in the season, are distinct in that they are divided up into numerous leaflets.

The species in this genus are grown principally for their habit and their foliage—the flowers themselves are inconspicuous, but they are followed by often large, striking pods. They are suitable for any good, fertile, well-drained soil and they do best if they are provided with a sunny position. When mature, trees are fully hardy, but young specimens may succumb to frost damage in cold areas. Pruning is not usually required, but dead,

Grevillea rosmarinifolia

Gleditsia triacanthos

damaged, or crossing wood can be removed in the spring. Wind damage is not unusual as branches tend to be quite brittle.

Gleditsia triacanthos

This is a large-growing, deciduous tree of columnar-to-spreading habit, with a trunk and shoots that are often very spiny. Its glossy, bright green, fernlike leaves are divided into numerous leaflets, turning yellow in autumn. Spikes of small, yellow-green flowers open in early summer, and these are followed by long, often twisted pods.

Common name: Common honey locust
Native range: North America
Height: 100 ft (30 m)
Spread: 50 ft (15 m)
Hardiness: Zone 4
Variants: 'Rubylace' has deep red-purple young leaves that turn dark green as it matures, but it is viciously spiny. 'Sunburst' is a smaller, spineless tree, growing up to 40 ft (12 m) tall, its bright yellow young foliage contrasting attractively with the dark green of its older leaves.

Grevillea
Proteaceae

This is a large genus made up of approximately 250 species of evergreen shrubs and trees, natives mainly of Australia. They are grown for their striking and unusual flowers, which have long, projecting styles, and they need a well-drained, lime-free soil in a sunny position.

Suitable for the shrub border or a dry garden, these trees and shrubs should be provided with a sheltered position or be planted against a wall in cool areas.

Grevillea juniperina f. *sulphurea*

A stoutly branched, evergreen shrub of spreading habit with arching shoots and slender, pointed, bright green leaves. The dense clusters of pale yellow flowers open at the ends of the shoots in late spring and early summer.

Native range: New South Wales (Australia)
Height: 6 ft (2 m)
Spread: 6 ft (2 m)
Hardiness: Zone 8

Grevillea rosmarinifolia

This is a spreading, evergreen shrub of vigorous growth with rosemary-like foliage. Its shoots are covered with slender, gray-green leaves that are silvery beneath. Clusters of deep red flowers open over a long period from winter to summer.

Native range: Australia (New South Wales)
Height: 5 ft (1.5 m)
Spread: 8 ft (2.5 m)
Hardiness: Zone 8

Griselinia
Griseliniaceae

The six species of evergreen shrubs and trees that make up this small genus are natives of New Zealand and South America.

A handsome foliage plant, the following will grow in any well-drained soil, in sun or shade. In mild areas it is suitable for shelter and hedging and does particularly well in coastal areas. In order to restrict growth, plant can be pruned back in the spring.

Griselinia littoralis

This vigorous, dense, evergreen shrub has bright apple-green, leathery foliage. Small clusters of pale green flowers open in late spring, males and females on separate plants. In very mild areas it can reach a height of 33 ft (10 m) or more.

Native range: New Zealand
Height: 16 ft (5 m) or more
Spread: 10 ft (3 m) or more
Hardiness: Zone 8
Variant: 'Variegata' is slower-growing and smaller in size, with leaves edged with creamy white.

Gymnocladus
Leguminosae

This is a small genus consisting of about five species of deciduous tree that are natives of East Asia and North America. Only the following, however, is commonly seen in garden cultivation, where it is grown for its bold foliage.

In order to do well, it requires a good, moist but well-drained site. It is fully hardy, but is at its best if planted in a sunny position. The flowers and fruits will probably be produced only in regions that experience reliably hot summers.

Gymnocladus dioica

This is a slow-growing, deciduous tree with stout shoots and very large leaves that are divided into four to seven pairs of dark green leaflets. Leaves are bronze when they are young, often turning yellow in autumn. Conical clusters of fragrant, greenish-white, star-shaped flowers open in late spring to early summer, the males and females usually on separate plants, and the flowers are followed by leathery, persistent, red-brown pods.

Common name: Kentucky coffee tree
Native range: C and E United States of America
Height: 65 ft (20 m)
Spread: 50 ft (15 m)
Hardiness: Zone 4
Variant: 'Variegata' has leaves that are blotched with creamy white.

Gymnocladus dioica 'Variegata'

Halesia
Styracaceae

This is a small genus of plants that encompasses some five species of attractive, spring-flowering deciduous trees or shrubs that are natives of the southeast region of the United States of America and also of East China.

They are grown for their beautiful white or pinkish, snowdrop-like flowers, which are followed by winged fruits. They need a good, moist but well-drained, lime-free soil that is rich in organic matter, and they are ideal for planting among other trees or in woodland situations.

Halesia carolina

This is a broadly conical to spreading, deciduous tree with bright green, taper-pointed leaves that turn yellow in the autumn. Prolific clusters of white or pink-flushed, bell-shaped flowers open in mid- to late spring on bare branches before the young leaves emerge, and these are followed by four-winged, green-colored fruits that turn a pale brown color in autumn.

Halesia monticola

Halesia monticola var. *vestita*

Synonym: *Halesia tetraptera*
Common name: Carolina silverbell
Native range: SE United States of
America
Height: 33 ft (10 m)
Spread: 26 ft (8 m)
Hardiness: Zone 4

Halesia monticola

This is a fast-growing, deciduous tree
that is very similar to *H. carolina*,
except that it produces larger and
showier flowers and reaches a greater
height and spread.

Common name: Mountain silverbell
Native range: SE United States of
America
Height: 50 ft (15 m)
Spread: 33 ft (10 m)
Hardiness: Zone 5
Variant: var. *vestita* produces large,
white flowers flushed with pink.

x *Halimiocistus*
Cistaceae

These garden-raised hybrids between *Cistus* and *Halimium* are evergreen shrubs with opposite leaves grown for their showy flowers. They require essentially similar treatment to *Cistus*, and so are best in a well-drained soil, not too rich, in a warm, sunny position and with shelter from cold winds.

x *Halimiocistus wintonensis*
A low-growing, evergreen shrub of spreading habit with gray-green leaves that are covered in white hairs when young. The white flowers in late spring and early summer are heavily marked with a ring of deep red blotches. They also have a contrasting yellow center and yellow marks at the base.

Height: 18 in (45 cm)
Spread: 30 in (75 cm)
Hardiness: Zone 8
Variant: 'Merristwood Cream' has creamy yellow flowers with red blotches.

Halimium
Cistaceae

This is a small genus made up of about ten species of evergreen shrubs with opposite leaves. They are natives of the Mediterranean region as well as Southwest Asia, and are grown for their attractive, conspicuous flowers.
   Related to *Cistus* and to *Helianthemum*, these species are suitable for coastal gardens and require well-drained soil that is not too rich. They do best in a sunny position, while in cold regions they need protection from winds.

Halimium lasianthum
This is a low, evergreen shrub of spreading habit and with arching shoots covered in gray-hairy leaves.

The bright yellow, saucer-shaped flowers, each marked with red blotches near the bases of the petals, open during the late spring and early summer.

Native range: S Spain, S Portugal
Height: 24 in (60 cm)
Spread: 3 ft (1 m)
Hardiness: Zone 8

Halimium 'Susan'
A garden-raised hybrid that makes an evergreen shrub of upright growth, later spreading, with small, gray-green leaves. Profusely borne, deep yellow flowers, blotched with maroon in the center, open in early summer.

Height: 18 in (45 cm)
Spread: 24 in (60 cm)
Hardiness: Zone 8

Hamamelis
Hamamelidaceae

The witch hazels are a small genus of five species, providing gardens with some of the best known winter-flowering, deciduous shrubs. In addition, they produce a good autumn color display.
   Natives of China, Japan, and North America, they require a good, deep, lime-free soil. No pruning is usually needed, but it may be necessary to remove suckers from the base, as plants are sometimes produced on grafted root stock.

Hamamelis x *intermedia*
This group of garden-raised hybrids between *H. japonica* and *H. mollis* produces deciduous shrubs of usually vase-shaped habit with bold, dark green, hazel-like leaves turning from yellow to orange, red, and purple in autumn. The four-petalled, spidery, fragrant flowers open on the bare shoots during the mid- and late winter period, when color in the garden is usually at a premium. It is

Hamamelis x intermedia 'Diane'

normally grown only as selected forms. Its autumn color is yellow unless otherwise stated.

Height: 16 ft (5 m)
Spread: 16 ft (5 m)
Hardiness: Zone 5
Variants: There are now numerous named forms available for planting, including 'Arnold Promise', which has large, yellow flowers in late winter and early spring. 'Diane' produces deep red-colored flowers and purple-red autumn foliage color. 'Jelena' is upright in habit, with deep orange flowers opening early, and orange-red autumn color. 'Pallida' (*H. mollis* 'Pallida') has very profuse, large yellow flowers.

Hamamelis mollis

This is a large, deciduous shrub with an upright-to-spreading habit and bears bold, hazel-like leaves, felted beneath, that turn yellow in autumn. The four-petalled, deep yellow, spidery flowers, each petal stained with red at the base, are very fragrant and open on the bare shoots in mid- to late winter.

Common name: Chinese witch hazel
Native range: China
Height: 16 ft (5 m)
Spread: 13 ft (4 m)
Hardiness: Zone 5

Hamamelis vernalis

This is a deciduous shrub of upright habit that becomes rounded to spreading with age. It has dark green leaves, often bronze when young and usually turning yellow in autumn. The small, yellow to orange or sometimes reddish, fragrant flowers open in the late winter to early spring period.

Common name: Vernal witch hazel
Native range: SC United States of America
Height: 13 ft (4 m)
Spread: 16 ft (5 m)
Hardiness: Zone 4
Variant: 'Sandra' is an upright and open shrub, producing deep bronze-purple young foliage, which later turns to shades of orange, yellow, red, and purple in autumn. The flowers are fragrant, small, and deep yellow in color.

Hebe albicans

Hebe
Scrophulariaceae

This is a large genus containing more than 100 species of plants. Found mainly in New Zealand, but also naturally occurring in Australia and the south of South America, the shrubby veronicas, as they are sometimes known, are evergreen shrubs, occasionally trees, with opposite leaves.

Grown principally for their flowers, which, although individually small, are usually borne in dense, showy, often spikelike clusters (or racemes), as well as their foliage, larger species make ideal specimens for the border while the smaller types are suitable for a rock garden. In addition, some of the denser-growing species can be used for hedging—particularly in mild regions.

Hebes can be grown successfully in any well-drained soil, as long as it is not too rich. In general, they prefer a position in full sun but they will also tolerate partial shade. Pruning is not usually necessary, although the more vigorous, larger-growing sorts can be cut back lightly in spring, before new growth starts. Leggy plants will also benefit from light pruning in spring, and any frost-damaged branches should be removed at the same time.

Hebe albicans

This is a compact, bushy shrub that forms a wide mound with densely arranged, blue-gray leaves. Small, white flowers with purple anthers open in very dense clusters in early to midsummer.

Native range: New Zealand
Height: 24 in (60 cm)
Spread: 3 ft (1 m)
Hardiness: Zone 8

Hebe 'Autumn Glory'

This is a popularly grown, garden-raised hybrid. It makes an evergreen, upright shrub that becomes more spreading with age. It bears rounded, dark green leaves, attractively edged with red-purple, that open from purple buds. Dense clusters of deep violet flowers with white tubes open over a long period from midsummer to autumn.

Hebe albicans

Hebe cupressoides 'Boughton Dome'

Height: 30 in (75 cm)
Spread: 3 ft (1 m)
Hardiness: Zone 8

Hebe 'Baby Marie'

This attractive hybrid shrub has been grown incorrectly as *H. buxifolia* 'Nana'. It makes a compact, dwarf mound of bright green foliage composed of small, thick leaves. Suitable for a rock garden, the plant is covered in clusters of pale lilac flowers during mid- to late spring.

Height: 12 in (30 cm)
Spread: 18 in (45 cm)
Hardiness: Zone 8

Hebe cupressoides

This unusual-looking shrub is one of a group known as the whipcord hebes, plants that have shoots that are densely covered in tiny, scalelike leaves. *H. cupressoides* is an upright shrub, developing a more rounded, conifer-like appearance as it develops. It has blue-green foliage and, on mature plants, tiny, pale lilac flowers that open during the period from early to midsummer.

Native range: New Zealand
Height: 5 ft (1.5 m)

Spread: 5 ft (1.5 m)
Hardiness: Zone 6
Variant: 'Boughton Dome' makes a compact, rounded bush, growing to a height of about 30 in (75 cm), with bright green foliage. This is strictly a foliage plant, however, since it does not bear flowers.

Hebe 'Emerald Green'

Found as a naturally occurring hybrid in New Zealand, this dwarf-growing shrub makes a low, spreading mound of foliage. The densely arranged, upright shoots are covered in small, glossy, green, scalelike leaves. It is grown principally as a foliage plant, since it rarely flowers.

Height: 12 in (30 cm)
Spread: 18 in (45 cm)
Hardiness: Zone 7

Hebe x franciscana

This is a popular, garden-raised hybrid and is commonly found in cultivation in mild areas, and since it will tolerate salt-laden air it is particularly suitable for coastal gardens, where it is often seen planted up as bedding and hedging. It makes a compact bush with a spreading habit and it has densely

Hebe 'Midsummer Beauty'

arranged, rather thick, dark green leaves. It bears dense, showy spikes of lilac-colored flowers over a long period during the summer and autumn seasons.

Height: 3 ft (1 m)
Spread: 5 ft (1.5 m)
Hardiness: Zone 8
Variants: 'Blue Gem' has densely growing, mid-green leaves and bears spikes of individually small, pale mauve flowers between midsummer and early winter. 'Variegata' has leaves edged with creamy white.

Hebe hulkeana

This is a very distinct and attractive species that makes a spreading, evergreen bush with an open habit. The shrub produces oval-shaped, glossy, bright green, toothed leaves narrowly edged with red. The tiny, white or lilac-colored flowers are borne in prolific, large, open clusters in late spring and early summer.

Common name: New Zealand lilac
Native range: New Zealand
Height: 18 in (45 cm)
Spread: 30 in (75 cm)
Hardiness: Zone 8
Variant: 'Lilac Hint' is a much larger-growing shrub, up to about 5 ft

(1.5 m) in height and with a similar spread. It has glossy, pale green leaves, and bears a profusion of pale lilac flowers in spring and early summer.

Hebe 'Midsummer Beauty'

This is a vigorous and popularly grown, garden-raised hybrid that makes a rounded bush with purple-tinged shoots and long, slender, bright green leaves, which are flushed with purple on their undersurfaces. Small, violet-purple flowers, which fade to white as they age, are borne in long, slender clusters during the summer and autumn seasons.

Height: 5 ft (1.5 m)
Spread: 5 ft (1.5 m)
Hardiness: Zone 8

Hebe 'Mrs Winder'

This is a garden-raised hybrid that makes a dense, rounded bush with upright, purple shoots bearing narrow, densely arranged, dark green leaves that are purple-colored when young. Dense clusters of small, violet-blue flowers open in the late summer and autumn.

Hebe x *franciscana* 'Variegata'

Height: 3 ft (1 m)
Spread: 5 ft (1.5 m)
Hardiness: Zone 8

Hebe ochracea

This very distinctive and popular,
slow-growing, whipcord hebe has an
upright habit and produces slender,
arching shoots that are densely
covered in small, ocher-colored
leaves. Tiny, white flowers are borne
along the shoots in the late spring
and early summer. It is sometimes
grown in gardens under the name
H. armstrongii.

Native range: New Zealand
Height: 4 ft (1.2 m)
Spread: 5 ft (1.5 m)
Hardiness: Zone 6
Variant: 'James Stirling' is a dwarf
form with a compact and flat-topped
habit that reaches a height of about
16 in (40 cm).

Hebe rakaiensis

Hebe 'Pewter Dome'

This garden-raised hybrid makes a
compact, spreading mound with
densely arranged, gray-green leaves.
Short, dense spikes of small, white
flowers open during the summer.

Hebe pinguifolia

This is a very variable and low-growing shrub that has a spreading, rounded, or upright habit. It produces small, thick, blue-green leaves, which appear on often purple-tinged shoots. Small, dense clusters of white flowers open during the late spring and early summer period.

Native range: New Zealand
Height: 18 in (45 cm)
Spread: 24 in (60 cm)
Hardiness: Zone 6
Variants: 'Pagei' is probably the most commonly seen form in garden cultivation. It is a low-growing shrub with a spreading habit, reaching a height of only about 8 in (20 cm), but with a spread of about 3 ft (1 m). It has blue-gray, slightly cup-shaped leaves and makes excellent ground cover. Spikes of small, white flowers appear in spring or early summer. 'Sutherlandii' has a compact and rounded habit, growing to a height of about 18 in (45 cm), and it bears attractive, gray-green foliage.

Height: 35 in (90 cm)
Spread: 5 ft (1.5 m)
Hardiness: Zone 8

Hebe pimeleoides

This very variable species is grown in several forms, differing in habit and leaf size. Leaves are usually gray-green to blue-green in color, often with red margins, rather thick, and they emerge from purple shoots. The flowers range from pale lilac to blue-purple and are borne in small clusters during the summer season.

Native range: New Zealand
Height: 16 in (40 cm)
Spread: 24 in (60 cm)
Hardiness: Zone 7
Variant: 'Quicksilver' is a wide-spreading shrub with very deep purple shoots and tiny silvery leaves. Its flowers are violet-blue and are borne in small clusters.

Hebe rakaiensis

This popular, evergreen species develops into a dense mound of purple-tinged shoots and bright, glossy, green leaves. Its dense spikes of small, white flowers open during early to midsummer. This versatile shrub works well in a border or it can also be used as ground cover.

Native range: New Zealand
Height: 30 in (75 cm)
Spread: 5 ft (1.5 m)
Hardiness: Zone 6

Hebe 'Red Edge'

This garden-raised hybrid grows into a low, sprawling mound. Its gray-green leaves have a distinct red margin and those at the ends of the shoots are red in winter. Clusters of pale violet-blue flowers open in mid- to late summer.

Hebe ochracea 'James Stirling'

Height: 24 in (60 cm)
Spread: 3 ft (1 m)
Hardiness: Zone 8

Hebe topiaria

This is a compact, dome-shaped bush with a neat habit and densely arranged, small and thick, gray-green leaves. Dense clusters of small, white flowers open during the summer season.

Native range: New Zealand
Height: 32 in (80 cm)
Spread: 5 ft (1.5 m)
Hardiness: Zone 8

Hebe vernicosa

This is a low-growing, spreading shrub with a compact habit. Its green shoots are purple at the leaf bases. The leaves themselves are small, oval-shaped, and leathery, and are glossy and bright green. Dense and prolific spikes of small, white flowers open from mid-spring to early summer.

Native range: New Zealand
Height: 20 in (50 cm)
Spread: 3 ft (1 m)
Hardiness: Zone 7

Hebe 'Youngii'

This attractive and popular, garden-raised hybrid has a low, spreading habit with dark, nearly black shoots and glossy green, red-edged leaves. Short spikes of violet-blue flowers open during mid- to late summer, fading to white as they age.

Synonym: *Hebe* 'Carl Teschner'
Height: 8 in (20 cm)
Spread: 24 in (60 cm)
Hardiness: Zone 8

Helianthemum
Cistaceae

The rock roses are a genus of more than 100 species of usually dwarf, evergreen shrubs. They are mainly found in the Mediterranean region, but they are also widely distributed throughout Europe, western Asia, North Africa, and both North and South America.

These plants are grown for their flowers, which occur in a wide range of colors, and they make excellent flowering shrubs for the rock garden, provided they are given well-drained soil and a position in full sun. Individual flowers are short-lived, but are borne in profusion. They can be cut back lightly after flowering to retain a compact habit and to promote further flowering. Removing spent blooms also helps to promote flower growth.

Helianthemum nummularium

This dwarf, spreading shrub forms mats of bright green foliage, gray-green beneath. The bright yellow, occasionally white or pink, flowers open during the late spring and early summer period.

Native range: Europe, SW Asia
Height: 4 in (10 cm) or more
Spread: 18 in (45 cm)
Hardiness: Zone 5
Variants: The most common rock

Helianthemum 'The Bride'

Helianthemum 'Mrs CW Earle'

roses in garden cultivation are forms or hybrids of this and other species. Recommended types are: 'Amy Baring', which is deep yellow with orange in the center; 'Ben Afflick' has bronze-orange with copper centers; 'Ben Fhada' is golden yellow with orange centers and gray-green foliage; 'Ben Ledi' is bright pink; 'Ben More' is rich orange, deeper colored in the center; 'Boughton Double Primrose', a double, primrose yellow with deeper-colored centers; 'Cerise Queen', which is double and colored scarlet; 'Chocolate Blotch' is pale buff, blotched chocolate-brown in the center; 'Fire Dragon' has bright orange-red flowers and gray-green foliage; 'Georgeham' has flowers that are large and pink with paler pink centers; 'Jubilee' has double, nodding, primrose yellow flowers with deeper-colored centers; 'Mrs CW Earle' is double, scarlet, with yellow centers; 'Raspberry Ripple' is white with deep pink centers and gray-green foliage; 'Rhodanthe Carneum' is pale pink with yellow centers and silver-gray foliage; 'The Bride' is creamy white with yellow centers and silver-gray foliage; 'Wisley Primrose' has primrose yellow flowers with deep yellow centers and gray-green foliage.

Helichrysum
Compositae

This is a large genus made up of some 500 species of annual and perennial herbs and evergreen shrubs and subshrubs. These summer- and autumn-flowering plants are widely distributed, particularly in Australia and South Africa.

As well as their showy flowers, many species of *Helichrysum* make valuable additions to the garden because of their attractive gray- or silver-colored foliage. Flower arrangers also sometimes use these plants in their arrangements, since they are very long-lasting once the blooms have been dried.

Helichrysum need to be planted in very well-drained soil in order to grow and thrive, and they also require a position in full sun. The following sorts are suitable for a garden border or a rock garden.

Pruning is not usually essential, but in order to retain a compact habit, plants can be cut back lightly after flowering has finished, and dead or damaged wood should be removed as necessary.

Helichrysum italicum

This is a compact and bushy, evergreen subshrub with upright, gray-hairy shoots that bear slender, silver-gray, aromatic leaves. Sometimes grown under the name *H. angustifolium*, it produces clusters of small, golden yellow flowerheads, which open over a long period during the summer and autumn seasons.

Native range: S Europe
Height: 24 in (60 cm)
Spread: 24 in (60 cm)
Hardiness: Zone 8
Variant: The subsp. *serotinum* (curry plant) makes a more compact plant, growing to a height of only about 16 in (40 cm). Its foliage is intensely aromatic and distinctly curry-scented.

Helichrysum splendidum

This compact and evergreen shrub grows with a dense, bushy, upright habit. Its shoots are covered in white, woolly hairs and they produce small, silver-gray leaves. *H. splendidum* eventually forms a spreading mound of a size suitable for a large border. Dense clusters of small, deep yellow-colored flowerheads open over a long period during the summer and autumn seasons, sometimes extending into winter.

Native range: South Africa
Height: 3 ft (1 m)
Spread: 4 ft (1.2 m)
Hardiness: Zone 7

Hibiscus
Malvaceae

This genus is made up of about 200 species of deciduous and evergreen shrubs, trees, and herbaceous plants widely distributed in mainly tropical regions. They are grown for their very showy flowers that have centers of long clusters of prominent stamens.

The following example is the most commonly seen hardy species in garden cultivation. It is suitable for a shrub border as long as it receives full sun and is provided with good, well-drained soil. *H. rosa-sinensis* is an evergreen species commonly grown in warm regions and, in colder parts of the world, under glass.

Pruning is not usually required. However, any dead, damaged, crossing, or straggly growth can be cut back in spring.

Hibiscus syriacus

This deciduous shrub has an upright habit with dark green, variously three-lobed leaves. A succession of large, widely funnel-shaped flowers opens over a long period from late summer through to the autumn. It is normally grown as selected forms, with flowers that vary in color from white to pink, mauve or blue, with

Hibiscus syriacus 'Woodbridge'

Hibiscus syriacus 'Hamabo'

deeper blotches at the bases of the petals. Pruning is not usually necessary.

Native range: E Asia
Height: 13 ft (4 m)
Spread: 10 ft (3 m)
Hardiness: Zone 5
Variants: 'Diana' has large, pure white flowers. 'Hamabo' has very pale pink

flowers with deep crimson central blotches. 'Oiseau Bleu' ('Blue Bird') has deep violet-blue flowers that are blotched red in their centers. 'Pink Giant' has very large, rich pink flowers that are deep red in their centers. 'Woodbridge' has large, deep pink flowers with red centers.

Hippophae
Elaeagnaceae

This small genus is made up of just three species of deciduous shrubs and trees widely distributed across Europe and Asia. The following is the most commonly grown and is principally cultivated for its foliage and persistent fruits.

Suitable for a wide range of soils, except those that are very dry, it can be grown in the border or to provide shelter, and it is excellent for exposed coastal positions. Male and female flowers are borne on separate plants

Hippophae rhamnoides

so both types need to be present in order to produce fruit.

Hippophae rhamnoides

This is a thicket-forming, spiny, deciduous shrub, sometimes a tree, with slender, gray-green leaves that are white beneath. Inconspicuous flowers appear in spring, followed, on female plants, by striking, bright orange, long-persistent fruits.

Common name: Common sea buckthorn
Native range: Europe, Asia
Height: 16 ft (5 m) or more
Spread: 13 ft (4 m) or more
Hardiness: Zone 4

Hoheria
Malvaceae

The members of this small genus of five species of deciduous and evergreen trees and shrubs are natives of New Zealand. Grown for their white flowers, they are suitable for any well-drained soil and can be planted in the shrub border or in woodland conditions. Evergreen species should be given protection from cold winds, and in cooler areas they can be grown against a wall.

Hoheria angustifolia

This compact and relatively hardy, evergreen tree of columnar habit has small, glossy, dark green leaves. In midsummer the plant is covered in masses of small, white flowers. It makes an excellent, small specimen tree for the garden.

Native range: New Zealand
Height: 26 ft (8 m)
Spread: 10 ft (3 m)
Hardiness: Zone 8

Hoheria glabrata

A broadly conical-to-spreading, deciduous tree, sometimes shrubby, with dark green, taper-pointed,

Hoheria glabrata

sharply toothed leaves that turn yellow in autumn. Clusters of white flowers open during summer.

Common name: Mountain ribbonwood
Native range: New Zealand
Height: 33 ft (10 m)
Spread: 26 ft (8 m)
Hardiness: Zone 8

Hoheria 'Glory of Amlych'

This garden-raised hybrid between *H. glabrata* and *H. sexstylosa* makes a small, semi-evergreen tree with slender-pointed, toothed, glossy, green leaves. Profuse white flowers open in clusters in summer.

Height: 26 ft (8 m)
Spread: 23 ft (7 m)
Hardiness: Zone 8

Hoheria lyallii

This is a broadly conical to spreading, deciduous tree with taper-pointed

Hoheria sexstylosa

and sharply toothed, gray-green, downy leaves. Clusters of white flowers open during the summer season.

Common name: Mountain ribbonwood
Native range: New Zealand
Height: 20 ft (6 m)

Spread: 20 ft (6 m)
Hardiness: Zone 8

Hoheria sexstylosa

A vigorous, evergreen tree of broad,
columnar habit with upright
branches bearing glossy, dark green,
sharply toothed and taper-pointed
leaves. Clusters of small, white
flowers open during summer.

Common name: Lace-bark
Native range: New Zealand
Height: 26 ft (8 m)
Spread: 16 ft (5 m)
Hardiness: Zone 8
Variant: 'Stardust' is a selection of
compact, upright habit with profusely
borne flowers.

Hydrangea
Hydrangeaceae

This genus is made up of some 23
species of deciduous and evergreen
shrubs and climbers with opposite
leaves that are natives of East Asia
and North and South America. They
are grown principally for their
flowers, which, although they are
individually small, are borne in
showy, prominent clusters. A feature
of many species of plants of the
genus is the presence of sterile
flowers, which consist of large,
sometimes colored, sepals.

They require a good, humus-rich,
moist but well-drained soil and they
are an excellent choice for the shrub
border or a woodland setting. The
flower color of *H. macrophylla* forms
is influenced by soil pH values: pink
on alkaline soils; blue on acidic soils.
Proprietary bluing agents are
available to change flower color.

Hydrangea arborescens

This clump-forming, rounded,
deciduous shrub has slender shoots
and broad, heart-shaped, dark green
leaves. Domed heads of white flowers
containing scattered, sterile flowers

open during summer. To rejuvenate,
cut back hard in spring. Cutting back
after flowering may promote further
flowers in late summer or autumn.

Native range: E United States of
America
Height: 5 ft (1.5 m)
Spread: 6 ft (2 m)
Hardiness: Zone 4
Variants: 'Annabelle' has very large
heads of mainly sterile, white flowers.
'Grandiflora' has dense heads of large,
white, sterile flowers.

Hydrangea aspera

This sparsely branched, deciduous
shrub has an upright habit and bears
bold, dark green leaves. It is also
notable for its peeling bark. The
broad, flattened flowerheads that
appear in late summer and autumn
contain small, pink to blue-purple,
fertile flowers that are surrounded by
a ring of conspicuous, white to pink
or purple-colored, sterile flowers.

Native range: Himalayas to China
and Taiwan
Height: 13 ft (4 m)
Spread: 10 ft (3 m)
Hardiness: Zone 7
Variants: The subsp. *sargentiana* (*H.
sargentiana*) has densely bristly
shoots. Villosa Group (*H. villosa*) has
narrower leaves and, usually, smaller
flowerheads.

Hydrangea involucrata

This is a low-growing, deciduous
shrub with a spreading, open habit
and has bristly, dark green, heart-
shaped leaves. The open flower heads
of blue, fertile flowers, which are
produced in late summer, are
surrounded by blue to pink sterile
flowers.

Native range: Japan, Taiwan
Height: 35 in (90 cm)
Spread: 5 ft (1.5 m)
Hardiness: Zone 7
Variant: 'Hortensis' is the most

Hydrangea arborescens 'Annabelle'

Hydrangea aspera subsp. *sargentiana*

Hydrangea involucrata 'Hortensis'

commonly seen form in garden cultivation, with profuse, pink and white, sterile, double flowers.

Hydrangea macrophylla

This is a vigorous, dome-shaped bush with bold, glossy, dark green leaves on shoots that are often distinctly spotted. Two types are cultivated: the hortensias, which bear dense, hemispherical heads of mainly sterile flowers; and the more delicate-looking lacecaps, which have flattened heads of pink or blue fertile flowers edged with a ring of large, sterile flowers. These shrubs are susceptible to late frosts in cold areas and can be cut back hard in early spring if necessary.

Native range: Japan
Height: 6 ft (2 m) or more
Spread: 10 ft (3 m) or more
Hardiness: Zone 6
Variants: 'Alpenglühen', hortensia type with large, crimson-colored flowerheads. 'Ami Pasquier' is a compact hortensia with deep crimson to purple-blue flowerheads. 'Europa', hortensia type with large, deep pink to blue-purple flowerheads.

'Générale Vicomtesse de Vibraye', hortensia type with large heads of pale pink or blue flowers. 'Hamburg', hortensia with large heads of deep pink or blue flowers with large, sterile flowers. 'King George', hortensia with large heads of pink or blue flowers. 'Lanarth White', lacecap with white, sterile flowers. 'Mariesii Perfecta' ('Blue Wave'), lacecap with large, sterile flowers—either pink or blue. 'Nigra', hortensia type with pink or blue flowerheads and dark, nearly black stems. 'Pia', compact hortensia, up to 24 in (60 cm) high, with purple-red flowerheads. 'Quadricolor', lacecap with leaves variegated with dark and pale green and cream and yellow, and pale pink, sterile flowers. 'Veitchii', lacecap with white, sterile flowers turning pink. 'White Wave', lacecap with large, white, sterile flowers.

Hydrangea paniculata

This is a large, vigorous and very hardy, deciduous shrub with an upright habit. The branches are often arching, bearing bold, dark green leaves. Large, conical clusters of white flowers open in the late

Hydrangea paniculata 'Tardiva'

summer and autumn, the blooms containing varying amounts of cream-colored, sterile flowers, which often turn pink as they age. Pruning of this species is unusual in that it can be cut back hard in spring to encourage the production of large flowerheads. Pruning may also be needed in order to restrict growth.

Native range: E Asia
Height: 16 ft (5 m)
Spread: 10 ft (3 m)
Hardiness: Zone 3
Variants: 'Grandiflora' has large, dense heads of mainly sterile flowers that turn from white to pink as they age. 'Kyushu' is a vigorous and upright shrub, with glossy, bright green foliage and heads of mixed fertile and sterile flowers. 'Tardiva' produces large flowerheads with both sterile and fertile flowers, opening in autumn. 'Unique' has huge flowerheads of mainly sterile flowers produced over a long period, turning from white to deep pink with age.

Hydrangea 'Preziosa'
This is a garden-raised hybrid between *H. macrophylla* and *H. serrata*. It makes a small, deciduous shrub of upright growth with attractive, purple-red stems and glossy, green leaves that are bronze when young. The domed heads of sterile flowers open white and turn to pink, red, mauve, or blue.

Height: 5 ft (1.5 m)
Spread: 3 ft (1 m)
Hardiness: Zone 6

Hydrangea quercifolia
This is a very distinct, late-deciduous shrub that makes a spreading mound.

Hydrangea macrophylla 'Quadricolor'

Hydrangea serrata 'Grayswood'

Its branches usually arch to the ground and the bark tends to peel on the older shoots. The bold, deeply lobed, oaklike leaves are dark green, turning to orange, red, and purple in late autumn and winter. White flowers open in the summer and early autumn. These are borne in large, usually arching or drooping, conical clusters, with the sterile flowers turning pink.

Common name: Oak-leaved hydrangea
Native range: SE United States of America
Height: 6 ft (2 m)
Spread: 10 ft (3 m)
Hardiness: Zone 5
Variants: Several selections are grown, including 'Snow Flake', with double, sterile flowers, and 'Snow Queen', with large, upright flower clusters.

Hydrangea serrata

This small, deciduous shrub has an upright habit, similar to that of *H. macrophylla* but differing in its smaller size, leaves, and flowerheads.

Native range: Korea, Japan
Height: 5 ft (1.5 m)
Spread: 4 ft (1.2 m)

Hardiness: Zone 6
Variants: 'Bluebird', lacecap, produces pale blue to pink, sterile flowers. 'Grayswood', lacecap, has white, sterile flowers that turn to a deep red color as they age. 'Rosalba', lacecap, has white, sterile flowers that become blotched with red as the season progresses.

Hypericum
Guttiferae

This is a large genus of about 400 species of annual and perennial herbs, as well as deciduous and evergreen subshrubs and shrubs, occasionally trees, with opposite leaves. Species of this genus are widely distributed throughout the world.

The cultivated species are grown principally for their prominent, yellow flowers, which are usually borne over a long part of the year. The flowers are made even more conspicuous by their centers of long, yellow stamens.

Although many species are suitable for growing in a shrub border, others can be planted in a rock garden or used for ground cover. These are generally easy plants to grow and will do well in any well-drained soil.

Hypericum androsaemum

Where they find conditions to their liking, *H. androsaemum* and the very tough *H. calycinum* will grow well in shade, while *H. olympicum* prefers a position in full sun.

Low-growing types can be cut back hard in spring, almost to soil level, to encourage dense new stems, while the taller-growing varieties should have their branches reduced in length only by about a third, again in the spring.

Hypericum androsaemum

This clump-forming, deciduous or semi-evergreen shrub has sparsely branched, upright shoots bearing dark green leaves that turn orange and red in autumn. Clusters of small, yellow flowers open in summer and these are followed by fleshy, black fruits that are initially red.

Common name: Tutsan St John's wort
Native range: Europe, W Asia, North Africa
Height: 3 ft (1 m)
Spread: 3 ft (1 m)
Hardiness: Zone 6
Variant: 'Albury Purple' has attractive, purple-flushed leaves.

Hypericum calycinum

This is a low, compact, evergreen shrub that spreads by underground stems. It bears dark green leaves and its large, bright yellow flowers are produced over a long period between summer and autumn. It makes good, dense ground cover and is suitable for either sun or shade.

Common names: Aaron's beard, rose of Sharon

Hypericum 'Hidcote'

Native range: Bulgaria, Turkey
Height: 18 in (45 cm)
Spread: 6 ft (2 m) or more
Hardiness: Zone 5

Hypericum frondosum

This is a stoutly branched and low-growing, deciduous shrub. It has an essentially rounded habit with pale brown, peeling bark and blue-green, oblong-shaped leaves. It bears bright yellow flowers, opening in summer, and each bloom has a central mass of conspicuous, long, yellow stamens.

Common name: Golden St John's wort
Native range: SE United States of America
Height: 3 ft (1 m)
Spread: 3 ft (1 m)
Hardiness: Zone 5

Hypericum 'Hidcote'

This is a very commonly grown, garden-raised hybrid. It makes a vigorous evergreen or semi-evergreen shrub of dense, rounded habit and it bears dark green leaves. The large, golden yellow flowers are borne over a long period from the summer to the early autumn. Flowers are very open in shape and the shrub makes an ideal specimen for a large border.

Height: 5 ft (1.5 m)
Spread: 6 ft (2 m)
Hardiness: Zone 6

Hypericum x moserianum

This garden-raised hybrid between *H. calycinum* and *H. patulum* makes a dwarf, clump-forming, evergreen shrub with arching, red shoots and dark green leaves. Suitable for a rock garden, this shrub produces small, golden yellow flowers with prominent clusters of stamens that are tipped with conspicuous, reddish-colored anthers. The bowl-shaped flowers are borne over a long period from midsummer to autumn.

Height: 18 in (45 cm)
Spread: 35 in (90 cm)

Hypericum x moserianum

Hypericum olympicum

Hardiness: Zone 7

Variants: With its attractive, three-colored foliage, 'Tricolor' is by far the most commonly found form of *H. x moserianum* in garden cultivation. Its name derives from its striking foliage—its green leaves are conspicuously edged with cream and pink. It is less vigorous and a little less hardy than most other hypericums, so it may benefit from being grown in a more sheltered position in the garden.

Hypericum olympicum

This is a dwarf, mound-forming, deciduous shrub with slender, upright shoots that are densely clothed with small, oval-shaped, gray-green leaves. The shrub's relatively large, deep yellow flowers open in

Ilex x *altaclerensis* 'Hendersonii'

clusters at the ends of the shoots throughout the summer season. *H. olympicum* makes an excellent shrub for the rock garden.

Native range: SE Europe, Turkey
Height: 12 in (30 cm)
Spread: 18 in (45 cm)
Hardiness: Zone 6

Ilex
Aquifoliaceae

This is a large, widely distributed genus of about 400 species of deciduous and evergreen trees, shrubs and, more rarely, climbers. The leaves of holly are very variable, and on evergreen species they are sometimes spiny. The distinct male and female flowers are usually white and are borne on separate plants. Both types need to be present for the females to produce fruit, which takes the form of red, or sometimes black, berries.

Hollies are suitable for any good, well-drained soil, either in sun or shade, and they can be planted in the shrub border or used as specimens. *I. aquifolium* is suitable for use as

hedging. Prune (or cut) hedges in the early spring, before the new season's growth starts. Specimen shrubs should be trimmed in the summer. Cut out any single-color reversions on variegated plants as soon as they appear. If necessary, hollies can be cut back hard without causing them any lasting damage.

Ilex x altaclerensis

This is a garden-raised hybrid between I. *aquifolium* and I. *perado*. It makes a vigorous evergreen tree of conical, later columnar, habit with broad, dark green, and often spiny leaves. Small, white flowers, often flushed on the outside with purple, are borne in clusters in spring and these are followed, on female plants, by bright red berries. This tree is suitable for planting in exposed sites and also for growing in coastal regions. It is normally grown only as selected forms.

Common name: Altaclera holly
Height: 65 ft (20 m)
Spread: 50 ft (15 m)
Hardiness: Zone 7
Variants: The following are all female

Ilex aquifolium 'Amber'

Ilex aquifolium 'Pyramidalis Fructu Luteo'

the plants develop, however, adult foliage begins to appear, and on mature trees leaves are spineless. White flowers, often tinged with purple, open in the spring, and these are are followed, on female plants, by red berries.

Common name: English holly
Native range: Europe, W Asia, N Africa
Height: 65 ft (20 m)
Spread: 33 ft (10 m)
Hardiness: Zone 6
Variants: 'Amber' is a female form with orange berries. 'Argentea Marginata' is female with leaves edged with creamy white. 'Argentea Marginata Pendula' (Perry's silver weeping holly) is female with weeping shoots and grows to about 10 ft (3 m) tall. 'Bacciflava' is a female form and bears yellow berries. 'Ferox Argentea' is male and slow-growing, eventually reaching about 26 ft (8 m) in height. Its leaves are edged with creamy white and they are very spiny, both on the surface as well as around the margin. 'Golden van Tol' is female with leaves that are broadly margined with yellow. 'Handsworth New Silver' is female with purple shoots and white-margined leaves. 'Madame Briot' is female with leaves that are edged with golden yellow. 'Pyramidalis Fructu Luteo' is a conical, female form with nearly spineless leaves and bears a profusion of yellow berries.

Ilex cornuta

This is a dense, rounded evergreen shrub that is sometimes treelike, with glossy, dark green, rigidly spiny leaves. Clusters of small, white flowers open in the spring and these are followed by large, persistent, red berries on the female plants.

Common name: Chinese holly
Native range: China, Korea
Height: 16 ft (5 m)
Spread: 13 ft (4 m)
Hardiness: Zone 7

selections and bear red berries. 'Belgica Aurea' has nearly spineless leaves that are edged with yellow when young but later turn cream. 'Camelliifolia' produces nearly spineless leaves that are purple when young. 'Golden King' has leaves that are boldly margined with yellow. 'Hendersonii' has matt-green, spineless or sparsely spined leaves and goes on to produce deep red berries. 'Lawsoniana' has leaves that are boldly blotched with yellow and pale green.

Ilex aquifolium

This is an evergreen tree that is conical when young, later becoming columnar. The glossy dark green leaves are spiny on young plants. As

Ilex aquifolium 'Madame Briot'

Variants: 'Burfordii' is a female form with usually spineless leaves and profuse, very long-persistent berries. 'Rotunda' is female and makes a low, compact mound, about 3 ft (1 m) or more tall, with very spiny leaves. It bears few fruits.

Ilex crenata

This is a variable, bushy, evergreen shrub, sometimes treelike, with small, glossy, dark green leaves. Clusters of small, greenish-white flowers open in late spring to early summer, and these are followed, on female plants, by glossy, black berries. It can be used for hedging and is very tolerant of heavy pruning.

Common name: Japanese holly
Native range: Japan, Sakhalin, Korea
Height: 16 ft (5 m) or more
Spread: 13 ft (4 m)
Hardiness: Zone 5
Variants: 'Convexa' is a female form that makes a dense, rounded bush, growing up to about 6 ft (2 m) or more in height, and with convex leaves. 'Fastigiata' is narrowly upright in habit. 'Golden Gem' is slow-growing, eventually reaching up to

about 3 ft (1 m) in height, with young foliage that is golden yellow in color. It does best in full sun and although it is a female form, it bears few fruits. 'Helleri' has a compact and spreading habit, reaching up to about 3 ft (1 m) in height. It is an excellent choice where ground cover is required. Although it is female, it rarely fruits. 'Mariesii' is female, slow-growing, and has stout, upright shoots and small, rounded leaves.

Ilex × meserveae

This group of garden-raised hybrids between *I. aquifolium* and *I. rugosa* makes large, evergreen, upright to rounded shrubs, spreading by suckers when mature, with purple shoots and glossy, dark blue-green, spine-toothed leaves. Clusters of white flowers open in spring and these are followed, on female plants, by bright red berries. It is normally grown only as selected forms.

Common name: Meserve holly
Height: 10 ft (3 m) or more
Spread: 10 ft (3 m)
Hardiness: Zone 5
Variants: 'Blue Angel' is a compact,

Ilex crenata 'Golden Gem'

female form that bears large, glossy, red berries. 'Blue Prince' is a compact, conical male form that has very glossy foliage and is a good pollinator. 'Blue Princess' is a female form that produces a profusion of deep red fruits.

Ilex opaca

This compact, evergreen tree has a conical habit with deep matt-green to yellow-green, spine-edged leaves. Clusters of small, white flowers open in late spring, and these are followed, on female plants, by red berries. There are numerous selected forms, varying in the glossiness of their foliage, vigor, habit, and fruit color— some bearing orange- or yellow-colored berries.

Common name: American holly
Native range: E United States of America
Height: 33 ft (10 m)
Spread: 20 ft (6 m)
Hardiness: Zone 5

Ilex 'Sparkleberry'

A splendid, garden-raised hybrid between *I. serrata* and *I. verticillata* making a vigorous, large, deciduous shrub, sometimes treelike, with dark green leaves attractively flushed with deep bronze-purple when young. Clusters of white flowers in spring are followed by small, glossy berries that are bright red, very profuse, and long-persistent. It needs a suitable male to pollinate it, such as the similar plant 'Apollo' or a male *I. verticillata*.

Height: 16 ft (5 m)
Spread: 13 ft (4 m)
Hardiness: Zone 4

Ilex verticillata

A spreading, deciduous shrub with dark green leaves, sometimes turning yellow in autumn. Clusters of small, white flowers in spring are followed, on females, by persistent, bright red berries. A suitable pollinator is required for berries, such as a male *I. verticillata*.

Common name: Winterberry
Native range: E North America
Height: 10 ft (3 m)
Spread: 13 ft (4 m)
Hardiness: Zone 3
Variants: There are several selections, some dwarf, some with either orange or yellow fruits. 'Winter Red' has very profuse, bright red fruits that persist throughout winter.

Indigofera
Leguminosae

This is a large and widely distributed, mainly tropical, genus made up of some 700 species of herbaceous perennials and deciduous and evergreen trees and shrubs. The cultivated species have leaves divided into several small leaflets and bear spikes of small, pealike flowers.

They can be grown in any good, well-drained soil, and are suitable for

Indigofera heterantha

a shrub border. In cold regions they can be trained against a wall.

They can be pruned as necessary in spring before the new season's growth starts and they respond well to being cut back to the base.

Indigofera amblyantha

This is a deciduous shrub of upright habit with arching shoots bearing deep green leaves divided into seven to eleven small leaflets. Slender, upright spikes of small, pink, pealike flowers open over a long period during the summer and early autumn.

Native range: China
Height: 6 ft (2 m)
Spread: 6 ft (2 m)
Hardiness: Zone 6

Indigofera heterantha

A vigorous, deciduous shrub of spreading habit, with arching branches bearing deep gray-green leaves divided into numerous small leaflets. The dense spikes of deep purple-pink flowers open over a long period from summer to early autumn.

Native range: NW Himalayas
Height: 6 ft (2 m)
Spread: 10 ft (3 m)
Hardiness: Zone 7

Itea
Escalloniaceae

This genus is made up of ten species of deciduous and evergreen shrubs, natives of the Himalayas and East and Southeast Asia, with just one species native in the east of the United States of America.

Cultivated for their foliage and flowers, the two most commonly grown species are very different in general appearance. *I. ilicifolia* requires a well-drained soil and is suitable for the shrub border or

Itea virginica

woodland, or for growing against a wall. *I. virginica* requires a moist, lime-free soil and is best planted in full sun. Plants can be pruned after flowering if necessary.

Itea ilicifolia

A spreading, evergreen shrub with glossy, dark green, holly-like leaves edged with small teeth. The long, pendulous, and slender, catkin-like clusters of small, greenish-white flowers remain attractive over a long period during summer.

Native range: China
Height: 13 ft (4 m)
Spread: 16 ft (5 m)
Hardiness: Zone 8

Itea virginica

This deciduous, thicket-forming shrub spreads by suckers. It has upright, later arching, shoots bearing dark green, long-persistent leaves, which sometimes turn yellow, red, or purple in autumn. Dense, upright spikes of slightly fragrant, white flowers open during the summer.

Common name: Virginia sweetspire
Native range: E United States of America
Height: 5 ft (1.5 m) or more
Spread: 6 ft (2 m) or more
Hardiness: Zone 5
Variant: 'Henry's Garnet' has rich red-purple autumn color.

Jasminum
Oleaceae

The jasmines make up a very widely distributed genus of 200 or more species of deciduous and evergreen shrubs and woody stemmed climbers with opposite or alternate leaves. These plants are natives of Africa and Asia to the Pacific Islands and Australia, as well as being found throughout Europe. The shrubby species all have yellow flowers. However, unlike many of the climbing species of jasmine, the shrubs are not strongly fragrant.

The following species all require good, well-drained soil in order to thrive, and all do best if they are planted in full sun. They can be pruned by cutting back to suitable buds after flowering. On mature plants, some of the older shoots can be cut to the base in order to encourage new growth. (*See also chapter on Climbers.*)

Jasminum humile

This is a vigorous, semi-evergreen, bushy shrub with graceful, green shoots and alternate leaves. The leaves are usually divided up into seven dark green leaflets. Clusters of bright yellow, slightly fragrant flowers open from summer through to autumn, and these are followed by glossy black berries.

Common name: Italian jasmine
Native range: Himalayas to China
Height: 8 ft (2.5 m)

Spread: 10 ft (3 m)
Hardiness: Zone 8
Variants: This is an extremely variable
species with several forms.
Particularly popular in garden
cultivation is 'Revolutum', an
evergreen that has large leaves and
large, more fragrant, tubular-shaped
flowers.

Jasminum mesnyi

This is a very vigorous, evergreen or
semi-evergreen shrub. It produces
upright, later arching, green shoots
bearing opposite leaves that are
divided into three dark green leaflets.
The attractive, bright yellow, double
flowers open during the late spring
and summer period, but the blooms
fade to white as they age. The woody
stems of this species allow it to be
effectively trained as a climber
against a wall or some other suitable
support.

Common name: Primrose jasmine
Native range: China
Height: 13 ft (4 m)
Spread: 10 ft (3 m)
Hardiness: Zone 8

Jasmimum nudiflorum

Jasminum nudiflorum

This is a deciduous shrub that
produces long, arching, green shoots
bearing opposite, glossy, dark green
leaves that are divided up into three
oval-shaped leaflets. Its bright yellow
flowers open on the bare shoots
during late winter and early spring,
making it a valuable addition in the
garden. Although it is not strictly a
climber, this species is nearly always
grown trained against a wall. Such
plants are best cut back after
flowering. This is an easy to grow
plant that does well in any well-
drained soil.

Common name: Winter jasmine
Native range: China
Height: 13 ft (4 m)
Spread: 13 ft (4 m)
Hardiness: Zone 6

Jasmimum mesnyi

Jovellana violacea

Jovellana
Scrophulariaceae

This is a small genus made up of just six species of Southern-Hemisphere, herbaceous perennials and subshrubs, all of which are native to Chile and New Zealand.

Grown for its showy flowers, the following species is suitable for any good, well-drained soil, and it will do best if provided with a position in full sun. In mild areas it can be grown in the shrub border, but in cooler regions it often requires the protection of being grown against a wall. Light pruning in spring helps to maintain a compact habit.

Jovellana violacea
This evergreen or semi-evergreen subshrub has upright shoots and dark green leaves edged with large teeth. The clusters of unusual, pale violet flowers that open during summer are blotched yellow inside and have purple spots.

Native range: Chile
Height: 3 ft (1 m)
Spread: 3 ft (1 m)
Hardiness: Zone 9

Juglans
Juglandaceae

The walnuts comprise a small genus of some 15 species of deciduous trees that are natives of southeast Europe, Asia, and North and South America. All have bold leaves divided into several leaflets. Male and female flowers are borne separately on the same tree—the males in pendulous

Juglans regia

catkins. Several species of this genus produce edible nuts.

Walnuts require a good, deep, well-drained soil and a sunny position. They should be planted when small, rather than as well-grown specimens.

Juglans nigra

This fast-growing, deciduous tree of spreading habit has large, dark green, aromatic leaves with up to 23 taper-pointed leaflets. The pendulous, green, male catkins open in late spring to early summer, while the small, female flowers develop into rounded, edible nuts enclosed in a green husk.

Common name: Eastern black walnut
Native range: E United States of America
Height: 80 ft (25 m) or more
Spread: 50 ft (15 m)
Hardiness: Zone 4

Juglans regia

This is a large, deciduous tree with distinctive, pale gray bark and large, aromatic leaves, bronze-colored when young, divided up into five to nine glossy green leaflets. Green male flowers open in pendulous catkins in late spring to early summer period, and the female flowers ripen to edible nuts confined in a green husk. Selected forms are often grown for their nuts.

Common name: English walnut
Native range: SE Europe to China
Height: 100 ft (30 m)
Spread: 65 ft (20 m)
Hardiness: Zone 6

Kalmia angustifolia f. *rubra*

Kalmia
Ericaceae

The seven species that comprise this genus are mainly natives of North America, with one occurring in Cuba. They are mainly evergreen shrubs, with alternate or opposite leaves, and they are popular in garden cultivation for their attractive clusters of ornamental flowers, which are pink or, sometimes, white.

To do well, they require a moist, acid soil that is rich in organic matter, and they do best if given a sunny position in the garden—as long as the soil is not too dry.

Kalmia angustifolia
This is an extremely hardy, evergreen shrub of compact habit that makes a low, spreading mound with deep blue-green, opposite or whorled leaves. Clusters of small, pink to purple-pink flowers are borne during the early to midsummer period.

Common names: Lambkill, sheep laurel
Native range: E North America
Height: 24 in (60 cm)
Spread: 5 ft (1.5 m)
Hardiness: Zone 1
Variants: The flowers are variable in color—white in f. *candida* and deep red-purple in f. *rubra*.

Kalmia latifolia
This is a compact and evergreen shrub of rounded habit with alternate, glossy, dark green leaves. The pale to deep pink, sometimes white, flowers, which are often attractively spotted or banded on the inside, open from distinctively crimped buds in the late spring and

Kalmia latifolia

early summer. Both the size and coloring of the flowers are extremely variable.

Common name: Mountain laurel
Native range: E North America
Height: 6 ft (2 m) or more
Spread: 10 ft (3 m) or more
Hardiness: Zone 4
Variants: 'Carousel' has white flowers that are heavily marked with deep red inside. 'Freckles' has pink buds opening to a creamy white color, spotted with purple. 'Little Linda' is a compact, dwarf form up to 3 ft (1 m) tall, with deep pink-colored flowers opening from red buds. 'Minuet' is compact and dwarf, up to 3 ft (1 m) tall, with small leaves and white flowers that are banded with deep red. 'Olympic Fire' has large, red buds opening to pink-colored flowers. 'Ostbo Red' has bright red buds opening to pale pink flowers.

Kerria
Rosaceae

The single species in this genus is an invaluable garden plant that is grown in several forms for its bright, early-opening flowers. Easy to grow in any well-drained soil, it is particularly suitable for the shrub border. The double form, 'Plena', is extremely vigorous and should be used with care in small gardens.

Pruning can be carried out in spring if necessary. On mature plants, some of the older shoots can be cut back right to the base.

Kerria japonica

A vigorous, deciduous shrub spreading by suckers, with arching, green shoots bearing alternate, bright green, sharply toothed, and taper-pointed leaves, sometimes turning

Kerria japonica 'Picta'

Kerria japonica 'Pleniflora'

yellow in autumn. The buttercup-like, golden yellow flowers open early in the year, in mid- to late spring or sometimes earlier.

Native range: China
Height: 6 ft (2 m)
Spread: 10 ft (3 m)
Hardiness: Zone 5
Variants: 'Golden Guinea' is notable for its very large flowers. 'Picta' ('Variegata') is smaller, growing up to 4 ft (1.2 m) tall, with leaves that are edged with white. 'Pleniflora' ('Plena') is an extremely vigorous and upright plant, forming dense thickets of foliage and bearing large, fully double flowers.

Koelreuteria
Sapindaceae

A genus of three species of deciduous trees native to East Asia, with leaves divided into numerous leaflets. The following is a useful small tree, grown not only for its elegant foliage but also its flowers and fruits.

Suitable for any good, well-drained soil, it flowers and fruits best if grown in full sun.

Koelreuteria paniculata
This spreading, deciduous tree has fernlike, bright green leaves, bronze-colored when young, that turn yellow in autumn. Each leaf is divided up into about 15 leaflets, which themselves are further divided, lobed, or toothed. The large clusters of small, bright yellow flowers, marked with red in the center, open in mid- to late summer, followed by green, bladder-like fruits ripening to pale brown, or pink in some forms.

Common name: Golden rain tree
Native range: China, Korea
Height: 33 ft (10 m)
Spread: 33 ft (10 m)
Hardiness: Zone 5

Kolkwitzia
Caprifoliaceae

The single species that makes up this small genus develops into a splendid, large shrub that is valued in gardens for its display of profusely borne flowers. Suitable for planting in a shrub border or for growing as a specimen plant, it will grow in any good, well-drained soil. It does best if

Koelreuteria paniculata

Kolkwitzia amabilis 'Pink Cloud'

positioned in full sun, since it may become leggy if it is given too much shade.

Ideally, it should be left uncut in order to attain full size, but can be pruned if necessary by trimming it back lightly after flowering. Damaged wood should also be removed at this time. On mature plants, some of the older shoots can be cut right back to the base.

Kolkwitzia amabilis

This is a vigorous, deciduous shrub with opposite, dark green, taper-pointed leaves borne on arching shoots. On older wood, the bark develops a tendency to peel. The beautiful, bell-shaped, usually pale pink flowers, colored yellow in the throat, are profusely borne in arching clusters during the late spring and early summer. The small fruits are densely covered in long bristles.

Common name: Beauty bush
Native range: China
Height: 13 ft (4 m)
Spread: 16 ft (5 m)
Hardiness: Zone 5
Variant: 'Pink Cloud' is a deciduous

shrub bearing masses of bright pink flowers in mid-spring.

+ *Laburnocytisus*
Leguminosae

The plant listed here is known as a "graft hybrid." This means it is not a true hybrid but originated when a purple broom was grafted onto a *Laburnum*. The tissues of the two plants combined to produce a completely new, third plant.

The plant will grow in any well-drained soil and prefers a sunny position in the garden.

+ *Laburnocytisus* 'Adamii'

This is a graft hybrid between *Laburnum anagyroides* and *Chamaecytisus purpureus*. It develops into a small, deciduous tree with spreading branches bearing dark green leaves that are divided into three leaflets. The short, pendulous clusters of pink, pea-shaped flowers flushed with yellow open from late spring to early summer. The tree usually also carries long, pendulous clusters of yellow laburnum flowers,

Laburnum x watereri 'Vossii'

in addition to the purple-pink flowers of purple broom.

Height: 20 ft (6 m)
Spread: 20 ft (6 m)
Hardiness: Zone 5

Laburnum
Leguminosae

This is a small genus comprising of just two species of deciduous trees that are popular in garden cultivation for their flowers. Their size makes them suitable for small gardens and they are also easy to grow in any reasonably good, well-drained soil. Take note that all parts of the trees are poisonous.

Laburnun alpinum
This deciduous, spreading tree, which is sometimes shrubby and with several branches coming from the base, has dark green leaves composed of three leaflets. The long, slender chains of small, bright yellow, pealike flowers open in the early summer. This species is less frequently seen than the other laburnums described here, and it is most commonly grown in the weeping form listed below.

Common name: Scotch laburnum
Native range: C and S Europe
Height: 26 ft (8 m)
Spread: 20 ft (6 m)
Hardiness: Zone 4
Variant: 'Pendulum' is shorter, with pendulous shoots weeping right to the ground.

Laburnum anagyroides

This spreading, deciduous tree has dark green leaves divided up into three leaflets, gray with hairs on their undersurfaces. The dense, pendulous chains of yellow flowers open in the late spring. The flowers are larger than those of L. alpinum, although its flowering period is shorter. This was once the most commonly found laburnum in cultivation, but it has now been largely superseded by the hybrid L. x *watereri*.

Common name: Golden chain
Native range: C and S Europe
Height: 26 ft (8 m)
Spread: 20 ft (6 m)
Hardiness: Zone 5

Laburnum x watereri

This is a popularly grown, vigorous hybrid between L. *alpinum* and

Laburnum anagyroides

L. anagyroides, and it makes a spreading, deciduous tree with dark green leaves. This attractive tree combines the best characteristics of both its parents—the long chains of *L. alpinum* and the larger flowers of *L. anagyroides*, which open in the late spring to early summer period. It has been raised in gardens and it also occurs naturally.

Native range: Austria, Switzerland
Height: 26 ft (8 m)
Spread: 20 ft (6 m)
Hardiness: Zone 5
Variant: 'Vossii' is the form commonly grown and it has very long flower clusters.

Laurus
Lauraceae

The two species that make up this small genus are evergreen trees or shrubs, natives of the Mediterranean region. Only the following, however, is commonly grown in gardens, where it is valued for its very aromatic foliage. It makes an excellent specimen shrub or tree, but it is also suitable for growing in containers and for hedging.

Plant in any good, well-drained soil; in colder areas it will benefit from the protection afforded by a wall. Prune trees if necessary in spring, while hedges should be cut and pot-grown specimens trimmed in the summer. Both male and female trees are needed to obtain fruit.

Laurus nobilis

Laurus nobilis

This is a dense evergreen tree with an upright, conical habit, often suckering at the base. It produces glossy, dark green, very aromatic foliage, and the leaves are often wavy-edged. Small clusters of yellow-green flowers open in the spring —males and females on separate plants. The flowers are then followed by fleshy berries that ripen from green to black throughout the season.

Common names: Laurel, sweet bay
Native range: Mediterranean region
Height: 50 ft (15 m)
Spread: 33 ft (10 m)
Hardiness: Zone 8
Variants: 'Angustifolia' is a form with very narrow leaves. 'Aurea' has golden yellow foliage.

Lavandula
Labiatae

The lavenders make up a genus comprising some 25 species of evergreen shrubs, all with opposite leaves, that are distributed from the Mediterranean region right through to India.

Lavenders are popular in gardens for their gray or gray-green, very aromatic foliage and for their dense clusters of fragrant flowers. They require a not-too-rich, very well-drained soil and a position in full sun in order to thrive. They can be used effectively to create low hedges or garden divisions.

They are best pruned lightly but regularly in spring to encourage a compact growth habit.

Lavandula angustifolia 'Hidcote'

Lavandula angustifolia

This is a bushy, rounded shrub with a compact habit and slender, aromatic, gray-green leaves. The dense, long-stalked clusters of small, pale to deep purple flowers open during mid- to late summer.

Common name: True lavender
Native range: Mediterranean region
Height: 3 ft (1 m)
Spread: 5 ft (1.5 m)
Hardiness: Zone 5
Variants: 'Alba' has white flowers. 'Folgate' makes compact shrub with lavender blue flowers. 'Hidcote' is very compact, up to 24 in (60 cm) tall, with silvery foliage and deep purple flowers. 'Hidcote Pink' resembles 'Hidcote', but has pale pink-colored flowers. 'Loddon Pink' has soft pink flowers. 'Nana Alba' is a dense, dwarf form, growing only up to about 12 in (30 cm) high, and bearing white flowers.

Lavandula x *intermedia*

These garden-raised hybrids between *L. angustifolia* and *L. latifolia* make vigorous and robust, rounded, evergreen shrubs with aromatic, gray-green foliage. In summer, they bear long-stalked clusters of blue to purple-colored flowers.

Lavandula stoechas subsp. *pedunculata*

Height: 3 ft (1 m)
Spread: 5 ft (1.5 m)
Hardiness: Zone 5
Variant: The flower color of
'Grappenhall' is blue-purple.

Lavandula stoechas

This compact, evergreen shrub has
upright shoots and slender, gray-
green, aromatic leaves. The short-
stalked clusters of small, purple
flowers, which open in late spring
and summer, are topped with
conspicuous purple bracts.

Common name: French lavender
Native range: Mediterranean region

Height: 24 in (60 cm)
Spread: 24 in (60 cm)
Hardiness: Zone 8
Variants: f. *leucantha* has white
flowers and bracts, while subsp.
pedunculata has flower clusters
growing on long stalks.

Lavatera
Malvaceae

The 25 species in this genus are all
herbaceous annuals and perennials,
natives of Europe and Asia, with
some species found in Australia and
California. The cultivated woody
members are mainly garden-raised

Lavatera 'Rosea'

Lavatera 'Barnsley'

hybrids between *L. olbia* and
L. thuringiaca, making vigorous,
semi-evergreen shrubs with lobed,
gray-green leaves. The large and
showy mallow-like flowers are borne
over a long period in summer. They
will grow in any well-drained soil and
prefer a position in full sun.

They are best cut back hard to a
woody base in spring before the new
season's growth starts.

Height: 6 ft (2 m)
Spread: 6 ft (2 m)
Hardiness: Zone 8
Variants: 'Barnsley' has white flowers
with red centers and they turn to pale
pink with age. It occasionally reverts
to 'Rosea', of which it is a sport.
'Blushing Bride' is very similar to
'Barnsley' but is more compact in
habit and does not revert. 'Bredon
Springs' has deep dusky pink flowers.
'Burgundy Wine' has deep purple-
pink flowers. 'Candy Floss' has very
pale pink flowers. 'Kew Rose' has
purple shoots and large, bright pink
flowers. 'Rosea' produces deep pink-
colored flowers.

Leptospermum
Myrtaceae

The 80 or so species in this genus of
evergreen shrubs and trees are largely
natives of Australia, with a few
occurring in New Zealand and
Southeast Asia. The cultivated
species are grown for their attractive
foliage and small, starry flowers. They
prefer a not-too-rich soil in a sunny
position. The less hardy species can
be grown with wall protection.
Pruning is rarely required.

Leptospermum lanigerum
This vigorous, treelike, evergreen
shrub has upright growth with silver-
gray, aromatic foliage. Profusely
borne, small, white flowers open
during the late spring and early
summer.

Common name: Woolly tea tree
Native range: SE Australia, Tasmania
Height: 16 ft (5 m)
Spread: 8 ft (2.5 m)
Hardiness: Zone 8

Leptospermum rupestre
This is a compact, spreading,
evergreen shrub developing into a
low mound with arching branches
densely covered in small, glossy, dark
green leaves. The leaves turn bronze-
purple in winter. The whole plant is
studded with numerous small, white
flowers in the late spring and early
summer period.

Synonym: *Leptospermum humifusum*
Native range: Tasmania
Height: 3 ft (1 m)
Spread: 16 ft (5 m)
Hardiness: Zone 8

Leptospermum scoparium

A graceful, evergreen shrub with
arching shoots and aromatic, dark
green, sharply pointed leaves.
Flowers, usually white but pink in
some forms, are profusely borne in
late spring and early summer.

Common name: Tea tree
Native range: New Zealand
Height: 8 ft (2.5 m) or more
Spread: 10 ft (3 m)
Hardiness: Zone 8
Variants: 'Chapmanii' is compact and
upright with bronze foliage and bright
pink flowers. 'Kiwi' is a compact,
dwarf form, to 3 ft (1 m) tall, with
bronze foliage and deep pink flowers.
'Nicholsii' has bronze foliage and
carmine-red flowers. 'Red Damask'
has deep red, double flowers.

Leptospermum lanigerum

Lespedeza
Leguminosae

This is a genus of about 40 species of
herbaceous annuals and perennials,
and deciduous shrubs, with leaves
divided into three leaflets and small
pealike flowers. They are natives of
North America, Asia, and Australia.
   The following is the most
commonly grown and makes an
excellent border shrub for its late and
showy flowers. In cold areas it often
behaves like a herbaceous plant, and
the old shoots should be cut to the
ground in spring.

Lespedeza thunbergii

This vigorous, deciduous shrub or
subshrub has long, arching shoots
bearing blue-green leaves divided
into three leaflets. The plant has
large clusters of deep rose-purple,
pealike flowers that open at the ends

of the shoots in late summer and
early autumn.

Native range: China, Japan
Height: 5 ft (1.5 m)
Spread: 10 ft (3 m)
Hardiness: Zone 5

Leucothoe
Ericaceae

This is a genus made up of
approximately 45 species of
deciduous, evergreen, and semi-
evergreen shrubs that are natives of
North and South America, East Asia,
and Madagascar.
   The following species is grown for
its attractive foliage and for its small,
white flowers, and is also useful for
growing in shady places. In order to
thrive, it requires a moist, but well-
drained, lime-free soil that is rich in
organic matter, and it prefers a
shaded or partially shaded site.

Leycesteria formosa

Little pruning is usually required. However, with established plants some of the old shoots can be cut back hard right to the base in spring in order to encourage new growth.

Leucothoe fontanesiana

This vigorous, evergreen shrub has long, arching shoots, which are red when young, and glossy, deep green, leathery, taper-pointed leaves that are sometimes bronze when young. The leaves also turn bronze in the autumn. The small, slightly fragrant, white, urn-shaped flowers hang in attractive clusters along the shoots in late spring.

Native range: SE United States of America
Height: 5 ft (1.5 m)
Spread: 8 ft (2.5 m)
Hardiness: Zone 5
Variants: 'Rainbow' has leaves mottled with cream and pink. 'Scarletta' has red-purple young foliage that turns bronze-red in autumn and winter.

Leycesteria
Caprifoliaceae

The six species that make up this genus are deciduous shrubs, with opposite leaves, and all are natives of the Himalayas and China.

The following species is popular in gardens due to its vigorous habit and long period of interest in flowers and fruit. It is suitable for any good, well-drained soil, and it does best if given a sunny position, although it will tolerate semishade. Some of the old stems should be cut back right to the ground each year.

Leycesteria formosa

This is a vigorous, deciduous shrub that forms dense clumps and spreads by sending out suckers. It produces upright, blue-green, hollow shoots that bear taper-pointed, dark green leaves. In summer and autumn, drooping clusters of white flowers mixed with deep red-purple bracts, ripen to glossy red-purple berries.

Leucothoe fontanesiana 'Rainbow'

Ligustrum lucidum 'Excelsum Superbum'

Common name: Himalayan
honeysuckle
Native range: Himalayas, W China
Height: 6 ft (2 m)
Spread: 6 ft (2 m)
Hardiness: Zone 7

Ligustrum
Oleaceae

The privets are a widely distributed
genus that is composed of some
40 species of deciduous and
evergreen shrubs and trees with
opposite leaves. They are natives of
Europe, North Africa, and West Asia
and from the Himalayas to East Asia
and Australia.

The privets are grown principally
for their foliage: *L. ovalifolium* is
used most often for hedging, while
L. lucidum can be planted as a
specimen tree. They can be grown in
any well-drained soil and will often
do well in either full sun or in shade.

Hedges can be cut as necessary to
keep them in shape during the late
spring and summer period.

Specimen trees and shrubs do not
usually require any pruning.
However, any damaged, straggly, or
unwanted branches can be removed
in spring.

Ligustrum japonicum

This vigorous, evergreen shrub,
which is sometimes treelike in form,
has an upright habit with arching
shoots and glossy, dark green,
leathery leaves. Dense, conical
clusters of small, white, rather
unpleasantly scented flowers open at
the ends of the shoots in summer,
and these are followed by black fruits
covered in a white bloom. It thrives
best in areas with hot summers.

Common name: Japanese privet
Native range: China, Korea, Japan
Height: 10 ft (3 m)
Spread: 6 ft (2 m)
Hardiness: Zone 7
Variants: 'Rotundifolium' is a very
compact and slow-growing shrub, to
5 ft (1.5 m), with a congested habit
and thick, rounded, black-green
leaves. 'Silver Star' has leaves edged
with white.

Ligustrum lucidum

This is a vigorous, evergreen tree—
upright when young, later
spreading—with bold, dark green
leaves. The large, conical clusters of
white flowers are attractive over a
long period during late summer and
autumn, and these are followed by
blue-black fruits, which are most

Liquidambar styraciflua

profusely borne in areas that
experience hot summers.

Common name: Glossy privet
Native range: China
Height: 33 ft (10 m)
Spread: 33 ft (10 m)
Hardiness: Zone 8
Variants: 'Excelsum Superbum' has
leaves with a yellow edge, turning to
creamy white. 'Tricolor' has young
leaves that are flushed with pink,
later becoming edged with white.

Ligustrum ovalifolium

This vigorous, semi-evergreen or
deciduous shrub has upright growth,
with glossy, green leaves that are
sometimes purple-flushed in late
autumn or winter. Dense clusters of
rather unpleasantly scented, small,
white flowers open during summer at
the ends of the shoots, and these are
followed by small, glossy, black fruits.
It is most frequently used as a
hedging plant.

Common name: Californian privet
Native range: Japan
Height: 16 ft (5 m)
Spread: 10 ft (3 m)
Hardiness: Zone 5

Variants: 'Argenteum' has leaves that
are edged with white. 'Aureum'
(golden privet) has leaves that are
broadly edged with yellow. Any
reverting shoots producing all-yellow
leaves should be cut out at once.

Liquidambar
Hamamelidaceae

This small genus of four species of
deciduous trees, natives of North
America, Turkey, and East Asia,
provides gardens with valuable
autumn color. The following is the
most commonly grown species, and
it does best in a good, deep, moist but
well-drained, lime-free soil, coloring
best in full sun.

Liquidambar styraciflua

This is a deciduous tree of conical
habit, whose shoots often have
conspicuous, corky wings and bear
bold and glossy, green, deeply lobed,
maple-like leaves, each normally with
five pointed lobes. The leaves turn to
brilliant shades of orange, yellow, red,
and purple over a long period in
autumn. The inconspicuous, yellow-
green flowers open in late spring and

Liriodendron tulipifera 'Fastigiatum'

these are followed by spherical, pendulous fruit clusters. It flowers and fruits freely only in regions that experience hot summers.

Common name: Sweet gum
Native range: E United States of America, Mexico
Height: 80 ft (25 m)
Spread: 50 ft (15 m)
Hardiness: Zone 5
Variants: Numerous forms have been selected, mainly for their autumn color. 'Golden Treasure' is slow-growing and has leaves that are broadly edged with deep yellow, the center turning deep purple in autumn. 'Lane Roberts' has deep red-purple autumn coloring, starting early in the season. 'Silver King' has leaves that are edged with creamy yellow, later turning white. 'Variegata' has leaves that are blotched with yellow and pale green. 'Worplesdon' has deeply lobed leaves that turn purple and then orange and yellow in autumn.

Liriodendron
Magnoliaceae

The two similar species of deciduous tree that make up this small genus

Liriodendron tulipifera

are both found in North America and in China.

With leaves of a unique shape, the North American species is the more commonly grown—usually as a specimen tree in large gardens and parks—for its flowers, foliage, and its attractive autumn color. It does best in a good, moist but well-drained, slightly acidic soil.

Apart from the removal of any dead, damaged, or crossing wood, no pruning is required.

Liriodendron tulipifera

This is a vigorous, large-growing, deciduous tree of broadly columnar habit, with bold, dark green leaves that turn yellow in autumn. The unusually shaped leaves have two lobes at the truncated tip, and two more at the base. Cup-shaped, tulip-like flowers, which are orange at the base and banded with green toward the tip, open in early to midsummer.

Trees may take as long as ten years, or even longer, to flower if planted from seed.

Common name: Tulip tree
Native range: E North America
Height: 100 ft (30 m)
Spread: 65 ft (20 m)
Hardiness: Zone 4
Variants: 'Aureomarginatum' has leaves broadly margined with golden yellow, eventually turning to green. 'Fastigiatum' ('Arnold') is a form with a narrow, conical habit and bears upright branches.

Lithodora
Boraginaceae

This is a genus made up of seven species of evergreen shrub that are natives of southern Europe and North Africa. The most popular species is a delightful, rock garden plant, which is grown for its blue

Lithodora diffusa 'Heavenly Blue'

flowers, and requires a well-drained, acidic soil and a sunny position.

Pruning is not usually necessary, but it can be trimmed back lightly after flowering.

Lithodora diffusa

This sprawling, evergreen shrub, which forms dense ground cover, has slender, bristly shoots and narrow, dark green leaves. The five-lobed flowers have a tubular base and are bright blue. They open in profusion during the late spring and early summer seasons.

Synonym: *Lithospermum diffusum*
Native range: SW Europe
Height: 12 in (30 cm)
Spread: 5 ft (1.5 m)
Hardiness: Zone 7
Variants: 'Alba' produces white flowers. 'Cambridge Blue' has pale blue flowers. 'Heavenly Blue' has azure-blue flowers.

Lonicera
Caprifoliaceae

This is a genus composed of some 200 species of deciduous and evergreen shrubs and climbers, with opposite leaves. They are widely distributed mainly in the temperate regions of the Northern Hemisphere.

The shrubby species are grown either for their sometimes fragrant flowers or their foliage. Most are suitable for the shrub border, while *L. nitida* and its forms are useful for hedging and *L. pileata* makes an excellent groundcover plant. It can be grown in any well-drained soil, and the winter-flowering sorts do best if given a position in full sun.

Prune hedges of *L. nitida* as necessary in summer. Winter-flowering sorts can be cut back after flowering, if required. (*See also chapter on Climbers.*)

Lonicera fragrantissima

Lonicera nitida 'Baggesen's Gold'

Lonicera fragrantissima

This is a spreading, late-deciduous or semi-evergreen shrub with arching shoots bearing dark green leaves. Very fragrant, white flowers open in pairs during winter and early spring and these are sometimes followed by red berries in summer. It flowers best in areas with hot summers, or when grown against a warm wall.

Native range: China
Height: 6 ft (2 m)
Spread: 8 ft (2.5 m)
Hardiness: Zone 4

Lonicera nitida

This vigorous and densely bushy evergreen shrub has small, dark green leaves. Its small, creamy white flowers open in spring, sometimes followed by violet-purple berries. Its vigorous growth, dense habit, and ability to withstand clipping make *L. nitida* very useful as a hedging plant.

Native range: China
Height: 10 ft (3 m)
Spread: 13 ft (4 m)
Hardiness: Zone 7
Variants: 'Baggesen's Gold' has bright yellow foliage. 'Lemon Beauty' has leaves broadly edged with creamy white. 'Maigrün' is low and spreading, making dense ground cover. 'Red Tips' has deep red-purple young leaves. 'Silver Beauty' has leaves edged with silvery white.

Lonicera pileata

This low-growing shrub has a dense, spreading habit and small, dark green, leathery leaves. Pairs of small, creamy white flowers open in late

Lonicera x purpusii

spring, followed by violet-colored
berries. It is a useful plant for ground
cover in either sun or shade.

Native range: China
Height: 30 in (75 cm)
Spread: 6 ft (2 m)
Hardiness: Zone 6
Variant: 'Silver Lining' has leaves that
are narrowly edged with white.

Lonicera x *purpusii*

This garden-raised hybrid between
L. fragrantissima and *L. standishii* has
dark green leaves remaining late into
the season. Creamy white and very
fragrant flowers, with yellow anthers,
open during winter, and these are
sometimes followed by small, red
berries in summer.

Height: 6 ft (2 m)
Spread: 10 ft (3 m)
Hardiness: Zone 5
Variant: 'Winter Beauty' flowers very
profusely over a long period, from
early winter to mid-spring.

Lonicera syringantha

This bushy, spreading, deciduous
shrub has a graceful habit, with
slender, arching shoots bearing blue-
green leaves often arranged in whorls
of three. The soft pink, bell-shaped,
fragrant flowers open in drooping

pairs during the late spring and early
summer, most profusely if growing in
a sunny position.

Native range: China
Height: 5 ft (1.5 m)
Spread: 10 ft (3 m)
Hardiness: Zone 4

Luma
Myrtaceae

The two South American species of
evergreen trees or shrubs that make
up this small genus are sometimes
found listed under the name *Myrtus*,
a genus to which they are closely
related. They are natives of Chile
and Argentina and have opposite-
growing, aromatic leaves. They bear
white flowers that have conspicuous
stamens.

   The following species is the most
commonly seen in garden cultivation,
and it is best grown as a specimen
tree or shrub in an open position.
However, if it is grown in cold
regions, it will benefit from the
protection afforded by a wall.

Luma apiculata

This is a fast-growing, evergreen
shrub or tree, often with several
stems from the base. Mature stems
bear cinnamon-brown bark, which
peels to reveal striking, creamy white
patches. The glossy, dark green leaves
are aromatic when crushed and white
flowers with numerous, protruding,
white stamens open over a long
period during summer and autumn.
These are followed by red and then
purple-black, fleshy, edible fruits.

Synonym: *Myrtus luma*
Native range: Argentina, Chile
Height: 33 ft (10 m)
Spread: 33 ft (10 m)
Hardiness: Zone 8
Variant: 'Glanleam Gold' is slower-
sgrowing and shrubby, with pink-
tinged young leaves that become dark
green edged with creamy yellow.

Magnolia campbellii

Magnolia
Magnoliaceae

The 120 or so species of deciduous and evergreen trees and shrubs that make up this genus are widely distributed in North, Central, and South America, as well as from the Himalayas to Southeast Asia. Because of their strikingly attractive, often highly fragrant flowers, some of the trees and shrubs in this genus should ideally be grown as specimens.

In order to do best, magnolias require a good, humus-rich, moist but well-drained soil that is acidic or neutral. They also benefit from the application of mulch around the base. They are usually best grown in a sheltered position, among other trees and shrubs. However, *M. grandiflora* flowers best in full sun. All species may bear fruit clusters in autumn from which glossy, red-coated seeds emerge. The flowers of early-flowering sorts can be damaged by late frosts.

Magnolia campbellii
This is a vigorous, deciduous tree of broadly conical habit that produces large, dark green leaves that are bronze when young. The very large, fragrant, pink-colored flowers, with a characteristic "cup-and-saucer" shape, open in late winter and early

spring before the leaves emerge. Young trees of this species may take many years to produce flowers.

Native range: Himalayas, China
Height: 65 ft (20 m) or more
Spread: 50 ft (15 m)
Hardiness: Zone 8
Variants: There are several selected grafted forms that produce flowers at an earlier age than seedlings. 'Alba' has white flowers; 'Charles Raffill' purple-pink flowers; and 'Lanarth' deep lilac-purple flowers.

Magnolia denudata

This deciduous shrub or small tree is conical when young, but as it

matures it takes on more of a spreading or rounded habit. The large, fragrant, pure white, cup-shaped flowers open in spring on the bare shoots, before the new season's leaves start to emerge.

Common name: Yulan magnolia
Native range: China
Height: 26 ft (8 m)
Spread: 33 ft (10 m)
Hardiness: Zone 5

Magnolia grandiflora

This is an evergreen tree with a conical habit. It produces bold, glossy, dark green leaves that are pale to bronzy green beneath or with a

Magnolia denudata

dense layer of rust-colored hairs. The very large and extremely fragrant, creamy white, cup-shaped flowers open during the summer and autumn seasons. *M. grandiflora* flowers best and grows to a greater size in regions that experience hot summers, while in cool areas it can be grown or trained against a sunny wall. It is an adaptable species that is also suitable for alkaline soils.

Common name: Southern magnolia
Native range: SE United States of America
Height: 33–65 ft (10–20 m) or more
Spread: 33 ft (10 m)
Hardiness: Zone 7
Variants: Numerous selections have been made. These include 'Bracken's Brown Beauty', which is a compact and very hardy, conical form with extremely glossy, dark green, wavy-edged leaves that are covered with rust-colored hairs on their undersurfaces. 'Exmouth' is a very hardy form with leaves that are pale green beneath. 'Goliath' produces very large flowers and has rather wavy-edged leaves. 'Little Gem' is compact and upright in habit, up to 16 ft (5 m) in height, with smaller, very dark green leaves, covered in brown hairs beneath, and smaller flowers. 'Victoria' is an extremely hardy form with leaves that are covered in rust-colored hairs beneath.

Magnolia 'Heaven Scent'

This is a very vigorous, garden-raised hybrid between *M. liliiflora* 'Nigra' and *M.* x *veitchii*. It makes a small, spreading, attractive, deciduous tree with dark green, taper-pointed leaves. The upright, vase-shaped, and fragrant flowers are pale pink in color, shading to deep pink at the flower base. The blooms open during the spring and early summer, either before or just as the young leaves start to emerge.

Height: 33 ft (10 m)
Spread: 33 ft (10 m)
Hardiness: Zone 7

Magnolia kobus

This is a strong-growing, deciduous tree with a broadly conical habit that bears dark green leaves on aromatic shoots. The slightly fragrant, creamy white flowers, measuring about 4 in (10 cm) across, are often tinged pink

Magnolia liliiflora 'Nigra'

at the base and are held horizontally. The flowers open in early to mid-spring before the leaves emerge. This species is also suitable for growing on alkaline soils.

Native range: Japan, South Korea
Height: 33 ft (10 m)
Spread: 26 ft (8 m)
Hardiness: Zone 4

Magnolia liliiflora

A deciduous shrub of compact, bushy habit with dark green leaves. The slightly fragrant, upright, vase-shaped flowers are red-purple outside and white inside. They start to open in spring with the young leaves and continue well into summer.

Native range: China
Height: 10 ft (3 m)
Spread: 10 ft (3 m)
Hardiness: Zone 5
Variant: 'Nigra' has very deep red-purple flowers opening over a long period into late summer.

Magnolia x loebneri

This is a group of garden-raised hybrids between *M. kobus* and

Magnolia 'Heaven Scent'

M. stellata and it combines some of the best features from both parents. The group is made up of deciduous shrubs or small trees of upright to spreading habits, with dark green leaves that are bronze-colored when young. The striking, fragrant flowers open in the early to mid-spring period and they vary in color from white to pink.

Height: 26 ft (8 m)
Spread: 20 ft (6 m)
Hardiness: Zone 5
Variants: 'Leonard Messel' is

Magnolia x *loebneri* 'Merrill'

Magnolia x *soulangeana* 'Rustica Rubra'

Common name: Anise magnolia
Native range: Japan
Height: 40 ft (12 m)
Spread: 23 ft (7 m)
Hardiness: Zone 4
Variant: 'Wada's Memory' is a very
floriferous selection, with red-purple
young leaves and large, profusely
borne flowers.

Magnolia x *soulangeana*

This group of garden-raised hybrids
between *M. denudata* and *M. liliiflora*
contains some of the most popular of
all the cultivated magnolias. They
generally make rounded to spreading,
deciduous trees that are often multi-
stemmed and shrubby in habit, and
have broad, dark green leaves. The
prominent, upright, goblet-shaped
flowers are white, streaked with
purple-pink toward their bases. The
flowers, which are large and fragrant,
begin to open before the young leaves
appear and continue as the leaves
break in late spring to early summer.

Height: 26 ft (8 m)
Spread: 26 ft (8 m)
Hardiness: Zone 4
Variants: Popular forms of *M.* x

spreading and graceful, with lilac-
pink flowers with drooping petals
that are deeper in bud. 'Merrill' is
vigorous and upright, with profusely
borne, white flowers that are pale
pink in bud.

Magnolia salicifolia

This is a deciduous tree of conical
habit with slender, aromatic shoots
and dark green leaves, bronzy when
young. The leaves are blue-green in
color beneath. The fragrant, pure
white flowers are held horizontally,
and are about 4 in (10 cm) across.
Flowers open in spring before the
leaves appear.

Magnolia salicifolia 'Wada's Memory'

soulangeana include 'Alba', which has pure white flowers; 'Lennei', which produces large, purple-pink flowers; and 'Rustica Rubra', which has large, deep red-purple flowers.

Magnolia stellata

This is a very popular garden selection due to its relatively small size and profusely borne flowers. *M. stellata* makes a dense, bushy, rounded, deciduous shrub with dark green, narrow leaves. The fragrant, white, starlike flowers are composed of numerous slender petals and open on the bare branches from distinctly furry buds in the early to mid-spring period before the new season's leaves emerge.

Common name: Star magnolia
Native range: Japan
Height: 8 ft (2.5 m)
Spread: 10 ft (3 m)
Hardiness: Zone 4
Variants: There are several selections, including 'Rosea', which has pale pink flowers that are deeper colored in bud, and 'Royal Star', which produces large, white flowers from pink-colored buds.

Magnolia wilsonii

Magnolia stellata

Magnolia virginiana

This is a deciduous to semi-evergreen or evergreen tree of conical habit, sometimes shrubby and multi-stemmed, with glossy, green leaves that are silvery white beneath. The lemon-scented, creamy white flowers open during summer. This species flowers and grows best in regions with hot summer, where it will grow in wet soils.

Common name: Sweet bay magnolia
Native range: E United States of America
Height: 26 ft (8 m)
Spread: 20 ft (6 m)
Hardiness: Zone 5

Magnolia wilsonii

This is a spreading, deciduous shrub, often tree-like, with dark green leaves that are velvety beneath. The white, pendulous, cup-shaped flowers, up to 4 in (10 cm) across, have conspicuous centers of red-purple stamens and open with the young leaves in late spring and early summer.

Native range: China
Height: 23 ft (7 m)
Spread: 23 ft (7 m)
Hardiness: Zone 6

Mahonia
Berberidaceae

The 70 or so species in this genus are evergreen shrubs found in western North America, Central America, and in the Himalayas and East Asia. They are grown for their foliage and flowers and often have bold leaves divided into several to numerous leaflets, and small, but usually densely clustered, sometimes fragrant, flowers, usually yellow in color. Suitable for a border, the larger sorts make impressive specimen shrubs while the lower-growing ones make good ground cover. They will grow in any well-drained soil that is not too dry.

To prune, cut back lightly after flowering, if necessary. Leggy plants of *M. aquifolium* can have their older shoots cut back right to ground level.

Mahonia japonica

Mahonia aquifolium
This is a variable, evergreen shrub that is thicket-forming and spreads by underground stems. The glossy, bright green leaves have up to nine leaflets edged with spiny teeth, and often turn bronzy in winter. Dense, upright clusters of bright yellow flowers open at the ends of the shoots in spring, and these are followed by blue-black berries.

Common name: Oregon holly-grape
Native range: W North America
Height: 3 ft (1 m)
Spread: 6 ft (2 m)
Hardiness: Zone 5
Variants: 'Apollo' is low and spreading, with large clusters of bright yellow flowers. 'Atropurpurea' has leaves turning deep red-purple in winter. 'Smaragd' is compact and upright with handsome, glossy foliage and dense flower clusters.

Mahonia japonica
This is a sparsely branched evergreen, shrub with stout shoots bearing bold, dark green leaves. The leaves are divided up into a maximum of 19 very spiny leaflets. Slender spikes of fragrant, rather pale yellow flowers open in clusters at the ends of the shoots in late autumn and winter, and these are followed by deep blue-purple berries.

Native range: China
Height: 6 ft (2 m)
Spread: 8 ft (2.5 m)
Hardiness: Zone 6

Mahonia x *media*
These vigorous, evergreen shrubs of upright habit are garden-raised hybrids between *M. japonica* and *M. lomariifolia*. Their stout shoots have deeply ridged bark when mature and they bear large, glossy, green leaves with up to 21 sharply toothed leaflets. In the late autumn and winter the long, clustered spikes of yellow flowers open at the ends of the shoots.

Height: 13 ft (4 m)
Spread: 16 ft (5 m)
Hardiness: Zone 7
Variants: This hybrid is grown normally only as selected forms, which include 'Buckland', with long, spreading flower spikes; 'Charity', with dense clusters of upright, then spreading flower spikes; and 'Winter Sun' with dense, upright spikes.

Malus floribunda

Malus
Rosaceae

The crab apples are a genus of about 35 species of deciduous trees and shrubs found in temperate regions of the Northern Hemisphere.

Grown for their flowers, fruit, and sometimes their ornamental foliage, they provide some very tough and easy-to-grow trees that are particularly useful for small gardens. They are suitable for any good, well-drained soil and do best in full sun.

Malus floribunda
This popular crab apple is a hybrid of Japanese origin. It makes a bushy-headed, small tree of dense, spreading habit with dark green,

taper-pointed leaves opening from arching shoots. Masses of small, white flowers, pale pink at first, open from deep red buds in mid-spring, and these are followed by small, yellow fruits.

Common name: Japanese flowering crab apple
Height: 20 ft (6 m)
Spread: 26 ft (8 m)
Hardiness: Zone 4

Malus 'Golden Hornet'
This vigorous, garden-raised hybrid makes a rounded tree, upright when young, with bright green, sharply toothed leaves. The white flowers in late spring are 1½ in (4 cm) across and open from deep pink buds. They

Malus hupehensis

are followed by profuse, spherical,
deep yellow fruits 1 in (2.5 cm)
across.

Height: 33 ft (10 m)
Spread: 26 ft (8 m)
Hardiness: Zone 4

Malus hupehensis

This strong-growing tree develops a
dense, spreading habit. It has flaking,
purple-brown bark and dark green,
taper-pointed, and finely toothed
leaves. Clusters of white, fragrant
flowers open in mid-spring from pink
buds, and these are followed in
autumn by pea-sized, deep red fruits.

Native range: China
Height: 40 ft (12 m)

Malus 'Golden Hornet'

Spread: 40 ft (12 m)
Hardiness: Zone 4

Malus 'John Downie'

The upright branches of this garden-raised hybrid give it a characteristically narrow crown with bright green foliage, making it useful in confined spaces. Clusters of white flowers open from soft pink buds in late spring, and these are followed by egg-shaped, orange-yellow fruits flushed with red.

Height: 30 ft (9 m)
Spread: 16 ft (5 m)
Hardiness: Zone 4

Malus 'Royalty'

This is one of the best of all the purple-leaved crab apples. It is a garden-raised hybrid that develops into a small, spreading tree with arching shoots bearing glossy red-purple leaves that are sometimes lobed. The leaves retain their color right throughout the summer until they turn red in the autumn. Deep red-purple flowers open from prominent red buds in mid- to late spring, and these are followed by deep purple-colored fruits.

Height: 20 ft (6 m)
Spread: 26 ft (8 m)
Hardiness: Zone 4

Malus tschonoskii

Popular for its narrow habit and good autumn color, this crab apple is frequently seen as a street-planted tree, but it can also make a useful addition to a small garden. It develops a broadly conical habit with upright branches bearing glossy, green leaves, gray and hairy when young and turning to bright red, yellow, and purple in autumn. Clusters of white flowers, flushed with pink, open in late spring, and these are followed by yellow-green fruits flushed with red.

Native range: Japan
Height: 50 ft (15 m)
Spread: 26 ft (8 m)
Hardiness: Zone 4

Mespilus
Rosaceae

The single species in this genus is a small tree or shrub grown for its picturesque habit, its flowers, and its unusual, edible fruits. It is suitable for any reasonably good, well-drained soil, and prefers a sunny position. It is usually grown as forms selected for the quality and size of its fruits, which are edible only after the first frosts.

Mespilus germanica

This is a deciduous tree with a spreading habit, sometimes having spiny shoots, and, on mature plants, flaking bark. The bold leaves are dark green in color, turning yellow-brown in autumn. Large, white flowers, 2 in (5 cm) across, open singly at the ends of the shoots in late spring and early summer, and sometimes there is a repeat flowering in late summer. The russet-brown fruits, with sunken tips and conspicuous, projecting sepals, ripen in late autumn and early winter.

Common name: Medlar
Native range: SW Asia, SE Europe
Height: 20 ft (6 m)
Spread: 26 ft (8 m)
Hardiness: Zone 5
Variants: Selections recommended for their fruit include 'Dutch' and 'Nottingham'.

Mitraria
Gesneriaceae

This small genus is made up of just a single species—an evergreen shrub with opposite leaves that is grown for its attractive and showy flowers.

It requires a cool, moist but well-drained, lime-free soil, and it does best if provided with a bright

Mespilus germanica 'Nottingham'

position. In drier regions, however, it may require a more shaded spot in which to grow. In areas that experience mild winters and cool, moist summers, it can sometimes climb vigorously.

Apart from the removal of any dead, damaged, or unwanted wood, little in the way of pruning is usually necessary, but it can be trimmed back lightly before the new season's growth starts in spring if required.

Mitraria coccinea

This is an evergreen shrub with trailing shoots that will often climb over low shrubs if it finds the conditions favorable. It bears toothed, glossy, dark green leaves. The long-stalked, bright red, tubular-shaped flowers have protruding yellow anthers and open in late spring and early summer and, intermittently, until autumn.

Native range: Chile, Argentina
Height: 5 ft (1.5 m) or more
Spread: 6 ft (2 m)
Hardiness: Zone 8

Mitraria coccinea

Morus nigra

Morus
Moraceae

The mulberries are a small, widely distributed genus made up of some ten species of deciduous trees and shrubs, natives of North and South America, Africa, southern Europe, and Asia. The individual flowers are small, but are borne in profuse clusters, the males and females on the same or separate plants, and these are followed by dense clusters of edible fruits.

They are grown for their attractive foliage as well as their fruits, and are suitable for any reasonably good, well-drained soil. They do best if provided with a position in full sun.

Morus alba

This is a spreading, deciduous tree with smooth, glossy, bright green, toothed, and taper-pointed leaves that turn yellow in autumn. The small, dense, drooping clusters of tiny, greenish flowers open in early summer, and these are followed by cylindrical, white to pink or red, edible fruits.

Common name: White mulberry
Native range: China
Height: 33 ft (10 m)
Spread: 40 ft (12 m)
Hardiness: Zone 5
Variant: 'Pendula' is a smaller-growing selection, weeping in habit and reaching up to about 10 ft (3 m) in

Morus nigra

height, with shoots hanging right down to the ground.

Morus nigra

This is a spreading, deciduous tree that bears broad, heart-shaped, dark green leaves that are roughly hairy on both sides and edged with numerous teeth. Small, pendulous clusters of greenish-colored flowers open in the early summer, and these are followed by dense, edible, blackish-red fruits. This is the best species to grow for edible fruits.

Common name: Black mulberry
Native range: Uncertain, but probably SW Asia

Height: 33 ft (10 m)
Spread: 40 ft (12 m)
Hardiness: Zone 5

Myrtus
Myrtaceae

This is a small genus made up of two species of evergreen, aromatic shrubs, with opposite leaves, natives of the Mediterranean region and Southwest Asia. Only the following is commonly cultivated. It has handsome foliage and flowers and is suitable for any well-drained soil in a sunny position. It can be used as a specimen or grown in a border. In areas where it is not fully hardy, it

Myrtus communis

does best when grown against a sunny wall. Prune in spring before growth starts.

Myrtus communis

This is a vigorous and bushy, evergreen shrub with glossy, dark green, pointed leaves that are very aromatic when crushed. The attractive, fragrant, white flowers, with their dense central clusters of white stamens, are borne on slender stalks during the summer period, and the flowers are followed by fleshy, purple-black berries.

Common name: Myrtle
Native range: Mediterranean region
Height: 10 ft (3 m)
Spread: 13 ft (4 m)
Hardiness: Zone 8
Variants: The subsp. *tarentina* (Tarentum myrtle) is a compact form and produces small leaves, pink-flushed flowers, and white fruits. 'Variegata' has leaves that are edged with creamy white.

Myrtus communis subsp. *tarentina*

Nandina domestica 'Fire Power'

Nandina
Berberidaceae

The single species to be found in this small genus is an evergreen shrub that is grown for its attractive foliage as well as for its flowers and fruits.

It is suitable for any well-drained soil, and shows the best foliage color, as well as flowering and fruiting more reliably, in a sunny position, rather than in the shade. It is an ideal candidate for a sunny border or for growing against a wall. The low-growing, compact forms make good groundcover plants.

Cutting back lightly in spring will encourage the maintenance of a compact habit.

Nandina domestica
This is an evergreen shrub with upright shoots bearing bold leaves divided into numerous slender, blue-green leaflets. Leaves are bronzy when young and they often turn red-purple in winter. Conical panicles of small, white flowers in summer are followed by bright red berries that persist through winter. It flowers and fruits best in areas that experience hot summers.

Common name: Nandina
Native range: China, Japan
Height: 6 ft (2 m)
Spread: 5 ft (1.5 m)
Hardiness: Zone 6
Variant: 'Fire Power' is one of several dwarf selections, reaching up to 24 in (60 cm) in height, with bright red winter foliage.

Neillia
Rosaceae

The ten species that make up this genus are thicket-forming, deciduous shrubs with lobed leaves. They are natives of the Himalayas and East Asia and are grown for their clusters of small, pink flowers.

They are easy to grow in any reasonably good, well-drained soil,

Nothofagus obliqua

and they are particularly suitable for the shrub border.

Cut back some of the older shoots to the base after flowering.

Neillia thibetica

This vigorous, deciduous shrub forms dense clumps of arching shoots with peeling bark and has dark green, sharply toothed, and lobed leaves. Large clusters of small, bell-shaped, pink flowers open in late spring and early summer.

Native range: China
Height: 6 ft (2 m)
Spread: 6 ft (2 m)
Hardiness: Zone 5

Nothofagus
Fagaceae

The 34 species that comprise this genus include both deciduous and evergreen trees. They have a wide distribution in the Southern Hemisphere, stretching from South America to Australia, New Zealand, New Caledonia, and New Guinea. They provide gardens with some splendid foliage trees, while the deciduous species give good autumn color as well.

Grow plants in a good, moist but well-drained, lime-free soil, in a site that is sheltered from strong winds—perhaps among other trees for the added protection they give.

Nothofagus alpina

This is a vigorous, deciduous tree with a broadly conical habit. It bears deep green leaves, up to 4 in (10 cm) long, with conspicuous veins in numerous parallel pairs. Bronze when young, the leaves turn to orange and yellow in autumn. Separate, inconspicuous, male and female flowers open on the same tree in late spring.

Synonyms: *Nothofagus nervosa*, *Nothofagus procera*
Common name: Southern beech
Native range: Chile, Argentina
Height: 80 ft (25 m)
Spread: 40 ft (12 m)
Hardiness: Zone 7

Nothofagus antarctica

This is a deciduous tree with a conical habit, often shrubby and branching low down. It has glossy, dark green leaves that turn yellow in the autumn. The attractive leaves are shallowly lobed and wavy edged with fine teeth at their margins. Small flower clusters—the males and females being borne separately but on the same tree—open in the late spring.

Common name: Antarctic beech
Native range: S Chile, S Argentina
Height: 50 ft (15 m)
Spread: 26 ft (8 m)
Hardiness: Zone 7

Nothofagus antarctica

Nyssa sylvatica

Nyssa
Cornaceae

This is a small genus made up of five species of deciduous tree from the east of North America and China. The following species are grown for their striking autumn color. The tiny, green flowers are borne in long-stalked clusters, males and females separate but on the same tree, and these are followed by small, bluish-colored fruits.

These trees require a moist, lime-free soil and color best in a sunny position. Nyssas should always be planted when small. Remove dead or damaged wood in autumn.

Nyssa sinensis
This medium-sized, deciduous tree has a broad to spreading habit, often with several stems and branching from low down. The narrow, taper-pointed, deep green leaves are up to 8 in (20 cm) long. These attractive leaves are bronze when young and then turn to brilliant shades of orange, red, and yellow in autumn.

Common name: Chinese sour gum
Native range: China
Height: 33 ft (10 m)
Spread: 40 ft (12 m)
Hardiness: Zone 6

Nyssa sylvatica
This is a slow-growing, deciduous tree of conical-to-columnar habit, the lower branches often drooping. The variable leaves are up to 6 in (15 cm) long and end in a short point. Glossy and dark green above, blue-green beneath, leaves turn orange,

red, and yellow colours in autumn.
Inconspicuous flowers are followed
by blue-black berries.

Common names: Black gum, black
tupelo
Native range: E North America
Height: 50 ft (15 m) or more
Spread: 40 ft (12 m) or more
Hardiness: Zone 4

Olearia
Compositae

The 130 or so species in this genus
are evergreen shrubs, occasionally
trees, or herbaceous perennials, from
New Zealand and Australia. Grown
for their foliage and their daisy-like,
usually white flowerheads, they are
ideal for the shrub border, or the
larger ones for specimen planting.
   They require a well-drained soil in
a sunny position, while in colder
regions they need shelter from strong
winds. In mild, coastal areas O. x
haastii and *O. macrodonta* can be
used for hedging. To restrict their
growth, prune in spring as the new
growth starts to emerge.

Olearia avicenniifolia
This vigorous, evergreen shrub has
white-hairy shoots and deep gray-
green leaves, to 4 in (10 cm) long,
densely covered with white hairs
beneath. The small, fragrant, white,
daisy-like flowerheads are borne in
broad clusters during summer.

Native range: New Zealand
Height: 13 ft (4 m)
Spread: 10 ft (3 m)
Hardiness: Zone 8

Olearia x haastii
A naturally occurring hybrid between
O. avicenniifolia and *O. moschata*
that makes a dense, bushy, evergreen
shrub. Its white shoots are densely
covered with small, leathery, glossy,
green leaves, which are also white

Olearia x haastii

beneath. Clusters of white, daisy-like
flowerheads, yellow in the center,
open in mid- to late summer.

Native range: New Zealand
Height: 6 ft (2 m)
Spread: 8 ft (2.5 m)
Hardiness: Zone 8

Olearia macrodonta
This vigorous, evergreen shrub,
sometimes tree-like, has flaking bark
and leathery, dark gray-green,
aromatic, holly-like leaves—white
beneath and edged with pointed
teeth. Broad clusters of fragrant,
white, daisy-like flowerheads with
small, reddish centers open in the
early summer period.

Common name: New Zealand holly
Native range: New Zealand
Height: 16 ft (5 m)
Spread: 13 ft (4 m)
Hardiness: Zone 8

Olearia nummulariifolia
This is a densely branched, evergreen
shrub with a rounded habit. The
plant has stout, upright shoots
bearing small, leathery, dark green
leaves. The white undersides of the
leaves are partly hidden by the

Olearia phlogopappa Splendens Group

Olearia macrodonta

recurved leaf edges. The small, daisy-like, white flowerheads, which have yellowish centers, are attractively fragrant and open in midsummer.

Native range: New Zealand
Height: 6 ft (2 m)
Spread: 8 ft (2.5 m)
Hardiness: Zone 8

Olearia phlogopappa

This evergreen shrub has upright, white-felted shoots and gray-green, wavy edged leaves. The undersurfaces of the oblong-shaped leaves are covered in white hairs. Large and showy clusters of usually white, daisy-like flowerheads, yellow in the center, open in profusion in mid- to late spring.

Native range: SE Australia, Tasmania
Height: 8 ft (2.5 m)
Spread: 6 ft (2 m)
Hardiness: Zone 8
Variants: Forms of *O. phlogopappa* that have colored flowerheads are known as Splendens Group. These include 'Comber's Blue', which produces heads of blue flowers, and 'Comber's Pink', which bears pink-colored flowerheads.

Olearia x scilloniensis

This is an attractive garden-raised hybrid between *O. lirata* and *O. phlogopappa*. It makes a vigorous, evergreen shrub, upright at first, later becoming more rounded in habit, with slender, gray-green, wavy-edged leaves that have white undersurfaces. The extremely profuse and showy, daisy-like, white-colored flowerheads, yellow in the center, open in large clusters in the late spring. This shrub does best if it is cut back lightly after the flowers have finished.

Height: 8 ft (2.5 m)
Spread: 6 ft (2 m)
Hardiness: Zone 8

Osmanthus
Oleaceae

This is a genus made up of about 30 species of evergreen shrubs and trees with opposite leaves, natives of the

Osmanthus x burkwoodii

southeast of the United States of America, East Asia, and the Pacific Islands. Often of holly-like appearance, these shrubs and trees are grown principally for their foliage and fragrant flowers. They make suitable subjects for the shrub border or they can be grown as specimens among other trees and plants.

They can be grown in any reasonably good, well-drained soil, but they will require some shelter from strong wind in cold regions. *O. x burkwoodii* and *O. heterophyllus* can be used for hedging.

Pruning is not usually required, apart from the removal of dead, damaged, or diseased wood. If it does become necessary, prune spring-flowering species after flowering, *O. heterophyllus* in spring. Cut hedges as necessary during the summer.

Osmanthus x burkwoodii

This is an attractive, garden-raised hybrid between *O. delavayi* and *O. decorus*. It makes a dense and bushy shrub with a rounded habit and bears leathery, dark green, tooth-edged leaves. Clusters of white, tubular, very fragrant flowers open in the mid- to late spring period.

Height: 10 ft (3 m)
Spread: 13 ft (4 m)
Hardiness: Zone 6

Osmanthus delavayi

This is a rather slow-growing, rigidly branched, evergreen shrub with a spreading habit, and it bears small, glossy, dark green, leathery leaves edged with small teeth. Clusters of pure white and very fragrant, tubular-shaped flowers open in mid- to late spring, and these are sometimes followed by small, blue-black, egg-shaped fruits. This species is suitable for growing against a wall.

Native range: China
Height: 6 ft (2 m) or more
Spread: 10 ft (3 m)
Hardiness: Zone 7

Osmanthus x fortunei

This is a vigorous, garden-raised hybrid between *O. fragrans* and *O. heterophyllus* making a large

Osmanthus delavayi

evergreen shrub, sometimes treelike.
The bold, glossy, dark green, holly-
like leaves are sharply toothed on
young plants, but they become
untoothed toward the tops of mature
plants. Clusters of small, white, very
fragrant flowers open in the autumn.

Height: 16 ft (5 m)
Spread: 13 ft (4 m)
Hardiness: Zone 7

Osmanthus heterophyllus

This is an evergreen, holly-like shrub
with a dense, upright to rounded
habit, sometimes treelike in stature.
O. heterophyllus has glossy, dark
green leaves edged with spiny teeth,
but becoming spineless toward the
tops of mature plants. Small, white,
fragrant flowers open during the
autumn.

Native range: Japan
Height: 16 ft (5 m) or more
Spread: 13 ft (4 m)
Hardiness: Zone 6
Variants: 'Aureomarginatus' has

attractively yellow-edged leaves.
'Goshiki' ('Tricolor') has leaves that
are mottled with yellow, bronze when
young. 'Purpureus' has glossy, deep
purple-colored young foliage.
'Variegatus' has leaves that are edged
with creamy white.

Oxydendrum
Ericaceae

The single species in this genus is
grown for its late flowers and its
autumn color. It requires a moist but
well-drained, acidic, and humus-rich
soil. Although shade-tolerant, it
flowers and produces its best autumn
color in a sunny position.

Oxydendrum arboreum

This is a deciduous tree of conical
habit, sometimes shrubby, with
deeply furrowed bark when mature.
Its bold, dark green, finely toothed
leaves, up to 8 in (20 cm) long, turn
to shades of orange, red, and purple
in autumn. Small, urn-shaped,

fragrant, white flowers open in large clusters at the ends of the shoots in autumn, or in summer in hot regions.

Common names: Sorrel tree, sour wood
Native range: E North America
Height: 33 ft (10 m)
Spread: 20 ft (6 m)
Hardiness: Zone 5

Ozothamnus
Compositae

A genus of 50 species of evergreen shrubs related to *Helichrysum* and grown for their attractive, sometimes aromatic foliage and their small, but usually clustered flowerheads. The following species require well-drained soil and a sunny position sheltered from strong winds. They can be pruned in spring if necessary.

Ozothamnus ledifolius
This is a strongly aromatic, small, rounded shrub that has a dense

habit, and with yellowish shoots and small, dark green leaves, yellow beneath. Dense clusters of small, white flowerheads open in the early summer period.

Common name: Kerosene bush
Native range: Tasmania
Height: 4 ft (1.2 m)
Spread: 5 ft (1.5 m)
Hardiness: Zone 8

Ozothamnus rosmarinifolius
This is a vigorous, evergreen shrub with upright shoots that are covered in white hairs, and densely arranged, narrow, dark green, rosemary-like leaves that are white beneath. Dense clusters of small, fragrant, white-colored flowerheads open from striking red buds in the early summer.

Native range: SE Australia, Tasmania
Height: 10 ft (3 m)
Spread: 6 ft (2 m)
Hardiness: Zone 8

Pachysandra terminalis

Pachysandra
Buxaceae

The four or five species that make up this small genus are evergreen or semi-evergreen subshrubs and herbaceous perennials from China, Japan, and the southeast of the United States of America.

The following species makes a useful groundcover plant in a shady position in the garden, and it is popular both for its foliage and its flowers. It should be planted in a shaded or partially shaded site in a moist but well-drained soil rich in organic matter.

Pachysandra terminalis
This evergreen subshrub spreads vigorously by underground stems. It has glossy, dark green, leathery leaves concentrated toward the ends of short, upright shoots. Clusters of small, white flowers open at the ends of the shoots during the spring and early summer.

Native range: China, Japan
Height: 10 in (25 cm)
Spread: 10 ft (3 m) or more
Hardiness: Zone 4
Variants: 'Green Carpet' is a very compact form, good for ground cover. 'Variegata' is less vigorous and its leaves are edged with white.

Paeonia
Paeoniaceae

The peonies are a genus of some 30 species of mainly herbaceous perennials, natives of East Asia and the west of North America. The shrubby species, which are often referred to as tree peonies, are deciduous, sparsely branched plants that spread by suckers, and they are grown for their showy flowers and bold, deeply cut leaves.

Paeonia delavayi

Suitable for any good, well-drained soil, they make excellent border plants. Little pruning is necessary, but wayward branches on vigorous plants can be cut back in early spring before growth starts. Foliage, particularly of forms of *P. suffruticosa*, can emerge very early in the year and is then subject to damage by late frosts should they occur.

Paeonia delavayi

This is an upright, deciduous shrub with large, dark green leaves, blue-green on their undersides, deeply cut into slender, pointed segments. The nodding, cup-shaped flowers, which open in early summer, are colored deep red and have conspicuous centers composed of golden anthers.

Native range: China
Height: 6 ft (2 m)
Spread: 6 ft (2 m)
Hardiness: Zone 6

Paeonia lutea var. ludlowii

This vigorous, deciduous shrub has stout shoots and deep green leaves that are deeply cut into slender-pointed lobes. Large, yellow, cup-shaped flowers, 5 in (12 cm) across, open in late spring.

Common name: Tibetan peony
Native range: Tibet
Height: 8 ft (2.5 m)
Spread: 13 ft (4 m)
Hardiness: Zone 6

Paeonia suffruticosa

A sparsely branched, deciduous shrub with stout, upright shoots bearing large, deep green leaves. The leaves are bronze when they are young and are cut into pointed lobes. The very large flowers, sometimes growing up to 12 in (30 cm) across, can be single to semidouble or double. Flowers vary in color, from white to pink and red.

Parahebe cattaractae

Common name: Tree peony
Native range: China
Height: 6 ft (2 m)
Spread: 6 ft (2 m)
Hardiness: Zone 7

Parahebe
Scrophulariaceae

This Southern Hemisphere genus is made up of about 30 species of evergreen subshrubs and herbaceous perennials. All plants are natives of Australasia and have opposite leaves. They are closely related to Hebe and Veronica.

Grown for their small flowers, they are suitable for any well-drained soil in a sunny position. They make excellent rock garden plants.

Parahebe cattaractae
This is an evergreen or semi-evergreen subshrub with a sprawling habit, and with slender, upright, purple shoots and glossy, green, oval-shaped, and toothed leaves. The small, funnel-shaped flowers, which bloom in upright, open clusters during the summer, vary in color from white to pink or blue. The flowers are often prominently veined with pink or purple.

Native range: New Zealand
Height: 12 in (30 cm)
Spread: 24 in (60 cm)
Hardiness: Zone 8
Variant: The form 'Delight' bears blue-colored, summer-opening flowers.

Parahebe perfoliata
This is an evergreen, clump-forming subshrub, which is sometimes known as *Veronica perfoliata*. It produces attractively arching and usually unbranched shoots bearing rounded, blue-green leaves with overlapping bases. The slender, branched spikes of deep blue flowers open in the late summer period.

Common name: Digger's speedwell
Native range: SE Australia
Height: 24 in (60 cm)
Spread: 3 ft (1 m)
Hardiness: Zone 8

Parrotia
Hamamelidaceae

The single species in this genus is a deciduous tree grown for its handsome foliage, which colors well in autumn, as well as for its bark and unusual winter flowers. Suitable for growing as a specimen tree in woodland conditions, the species requires a moist but well-drained, preferably lime-free soil.

Parrotia persica
This is a deciduous tree with a spreading habit, often branching low down, with gray-brown bark flaking

Parrotia persica

on mature plants to leave creamy white patches. Its glossy, green leaves, which are often edged with red when they are young, turn to brilliant shades of orange, yellow, red, and purple in the autumn. Small, red flower clusters open on the bare shoots during the winter and early spring.

Common name: Persian parrotia
Native range: Caucasus, N Iran
Height: 33 ft (10 m)
Spread: 40 ft (12 m)
Hardiness: Zone 5

Paulownia
Scrophulariaceae

The six species that make up this small genus are all deciduous trees. They have stout shoots and bold, opposite leaves, and are grown principally for their flowers.

The following species makes an excellent contribution as a specimen tree and it does best in a good, deep, well-drained soil in a sunny position, preferably sheltered from strong winds among other trees.

By cutting it back annually in the early spring, the tree can be grown as a foliage plant, producing leaves of an enormous size.

Paulownia tomentosa

This vigorous, deciduous tree bears bold, angled, dark green leaves up to 12 in (30 cm) long. The large, foxglove-like, pale purple flowers, marked with yellow on the insides, are borne in large, upright clusters before the leaves emerge. Many plants grown as *P. fargesii* are, in fact, *P. tomentosa*.

Common names: Empress tree, royal paulownia
Native range: China
Height: 50 ft (15 m)
Spread: 33 ft (10 m)
Hardiness: Zone 6

Perovskia
Labiatae

The seven species in this genus are all deciduous subshrubs with opposite, aromatic leaves, and are native from Southwest Asia to the Himalayas.

The following is grown for its attractive foliage and small, profusely borne flowers. It is ideal for planting in groups in a dry border or against a sunny wall. It is suitable for any not-too-rich, well-drained soil in full sun.

Cut back to just above the base in spring, just as the new foliage starts to emerge.

Perovskia atriplicifolia

This deciduous subshrub has upright shoots densely covered in white hairs, and bearing toothed, gray-green, aromatic leaves. Large, open clusters of deep violet-blue flowers open in the late summer and early autumn.

Native range: W Himalayas
Height: 5 ft (1.5 m)
Spread: 3 ft (1 m)
Hardiness: Zone 5
Variant: 'Blue Spire' has deeply cut leaves and very large flower clusters.

Philadelphus
Hydrangeaceae

The mock oranges include about 65 species of deciduous shrubs with opposite leaves, from eastern Europe, Asia, and North and Central America. They are grown for their often very fragrant, white or pink-blotched flowers, double in some forms, and they make ideal border or specimen plants.

They are suitable for any good, well-drained soil. They mainly benefit from regular pruning—cut back some of the older shoots to ground level in spring before growth starts, leaving the younger shoots to flower. To renovate old plants, cut all of the shoots right back to the base,

Perovskia atriplicifolia 'Blue Spire'

but the plant will then not flower until the following year.

Philadelphus 'Beauclerk'

This vigorous, garden-raised hybrid is a deciduous shrub with arching shoots bearing dark green leaves. Large, single, white flowers, up to 3 in (7.5 cm) across, flushed pink at the base of the petals, open in clusters in early to midsummer.

Height: 6 ft (2 m)
Spread: 8 ft (2.5 m)
Hardiness: Zone 5

Philadelphus 'Belle Etoile'

A compact, deciduous shrub with arching shoots bearing dark green, toothed or untoothed leaves. The very fragrant, white flowers in late spring and early summer are cupped at first, later opening more widely, and are conspicuously blotched with red-purple in their centers.

Height: 5 ft (1.5 m)
Spread: 6 ft (2 m)
Hardiness: Zone 5

Philadelphus coronarius

A large, deciduous shrub with upright shoots, dark green, toothed leaves, and peeling bark on the older branches. Creamy white, fragrant flowers, 1 in (2.5 cm) across, open in clusters at the ends of the shoots in early summer. In its typical form, this species has largely been replaced by hybrids and it is now most commonly seen in the forms listed below.

Philadelphus coronarius 'Aureus'

Native range: SE Europe, SW Asia
Height: 11–12 ft (3.5 m)
Spread: 8 ft (2.5 m)
Hardiness: Zone 4
Variants: 'Aureus' produces golden
yellow-colored foliage that may
scorch in full sun. 'Variegatus' is
slower growing and has creamy
white-edged leaves.

Philadelphus 'Innocence'

A garden-raised hybrid making a
deciduous shrub with upright, later
arching, shoots and bright green
leaves blotched and mottled with
yellow. Clusters of very fragrant, cup-
shaped, white flowers, 1½ in (4 cm)
across, open in early to midsummer.

Height: 8 ft (2.5 m)
Spread: 8 ft (2.5 m)
Hardiness: Zone 5

Philadelphus 'Manteau d'Hermine'

This garden-raised hybrid is a dwarf,
deciduous shrub with small, dark
green leaves. The double, fragrant,
creamy white flowers are produced
in small clusters during the early to
midsummer period.

Height: 3 ft (1 m)
Spread: 4 ft (1.2 m)
Hardiness: Zone 5

Philadelphus microphyllus

This is a very distinct species that
makes a dense bush with slender,
upright shoots bearing small,
untoothed, bright green leaves. The
leaves are gray with hairs beneath.
The small, very fragrant flowers, only
about 1 in (2.5 cm) across, are borne
singly on the shoots, but only in
profusion if the shrub is grown in a
hot, sunny position.

Native range: SW United States of
America
Height: 3 ft (1 m)
Spread: 5 ft (1.5 m)
Hardiness: Zone 6

Philadelphus 'Sybille'

A popular garden-raised hybrid that
makes a graceful, deciduous shrub
with arching, pink shoots and dark
green, nearly untoothed leaves. The
showy, white, and very fragrant,
saucer-shaped flowers, about 2 in
(5 cm) across, are marked with deep
purple-pink at the base of the petals
and are profusely borne during early
to midsummer.

Height: 4 ft (1.2 m)
Spread: 5 ft (1.5 m)
Hardiness: Zone 5

Philadelphus 'Virginal'

This is a very vigorous, deciduous
shrub of upright habit, with sharply
toothed to nearly untoothed leaves.
The large, white, double or

Philadelphus 'Virginal'

semidouble, fragrant flowers, 2 in (5 cm) across, open in clusters in midsummer.

Height: 10 ft (3 m) or more
Spread: 8 ft (2.5 m)
Hardiness: Zone 5

Phlomis
Labiatae

This is a genus of some 100 species of shrubs and herbaceous perennials with opposite leaves, natives of Europe, Asia, and North Africa. The following species are not only attractive foliage plants, but they are also grown for their whorled, two-lipped flowers.

Suitable for a border or for growing against a wall, they require well-drained soil in full sun. Little pruning is usually required, but stray branches may occasionally need removing. To rejuvenate old plants, cut back hard in spring.

Phlomis fruticosa
This compact, mound-forming evergreen shrub has stout, upright shoots densely covered in gray hairs and sagelike, gray-green, deeply

Philadelphus 'Manteau d'Hermine'

veined leaves. Large, deep yellow flowers open in dense whorls along the shoots in summer.

Common name: Jerusalem sage
Native range: E Mediterranean region
Height: 4 ft (1.2 m)
Spread: 5 ft (1.5 m)
Hardiness: Zone 7

Phlomis italica

This is an evergreen shrub with upright shoots covered in white, woolly hairs and slender, gray-white, woolly leaves. Whorls of pale lilac-pink flowers open along the shoots in summer.

Native range: Balearic Islands
Height: 24 in (60 cm)
Spread: 18 in (45 cm)
Hardiness: Zone 8

Photinia
Rosaceae

The 40 species in this genus are deciduous and evergreen trees and shrubs, native from the Himalayas to East and Southeast Asia.

The evergreen species are mainly grown for their often attractively colored young foliage, with forms of *P. x fraseri* being useful for hedging. *P. villosa* is grown for its fruits and autumn color. Grow in any well-drained soil, although P. villosa needs lime-free soil. Cut hedges as necessary.

Photinia davidiana

This is a vigorous, evergreen tree or treelike shrub, with dark green, leathery leaves that usually turn red before they fall. Broad clusters of small, white flowers in summer are followed by small, long-persistent, crimson-colored fruits.

Synonym: *Stranvaesia davidiana*
Native range: China
Height: 20 ft (6 m)
Spread: 16 ft (5 m)
Hardiness: Zone 6
Variants: 'Palette' is smaller in size and slower-growing, up to about 10 ft (3 m), with leaves that are variously blotched with creamy white.

Photinia x fraseri

This garden-raised hybrid between *P. glabra* and *P. serratifolia* makes a small evergreen tree or large shrub, with bright red young foliage maturing to dark green. Small, white flowers open in flattened heads during the spring, sometimes followed by small, red fruits. On mature plants, the young foliage is bronze rather than bright red.

Height: 20 ft (6 m)
Spread: 16 ft (5 m)
Hardiness: Zone 7
Variants: 'Birmingham', 'Red Robin', and 'Robusta' are recommended forms.

Photinia villosa

A spreading, deciduous tree with finely toothed, taper-pointed, dark green leaves, often bronze or bronze-edged when young, turning to bright orange and red in autumn. Small, white flowers in late spring are followed by egg-shaped, red berries.

Native range: China, Japan, Korea
Height: 16 ft (5 m)
Spread: 20 ft (6 m)
Hardiness: Zone 4

Phygelius
Scrophulariaceae

The two species that make up this genus are both evergreen shrubs with opposite leaves, and are natives of South Africa.

Grown for their showy, tubular flowers, they require a well-drained but moist, light soil and they do best if given a sunny position. In good conditions they can spread extensively by suckers. In cold areas they may be deciduous or herbaceous, dying down to ground level during winter. Shrubs usually grow taller if they are planted against a sunny wall.

Unpruned plants can become tall and leggy and grow best if they are cut back hard in spring as the young growth emerges. Removing spent flowerheads will often prolong the flowering period.

Phygelius x *rectus* 'Salmon Leap'

Phygelius aequalis

This is a suckering shrub with upright, angled shoots and dark green leaves. One-sided spikes of tubular flowers, up to 2½ in (6 cm) long, red to pink outside, yellow in the throat, open during summer and early autumn.

Native range: South Africa
Height: 3 ft (1 m)
Spread: 3 ft (1 m)
Hardiness: Zone 8
Variants: 'Sensation' ('Sani Pass') bears deep magenta-purple flowers. 'Trewidden Pink' has dusky pink flowers. 'Yellow Trumpet' produces pale yellow flowers.

Phygelius capensis

This vigorous shrub has angled, upright shoots and glossy, dark green

Phygelius x *rectus* 'Moonraker'

Phyllostachys aurea

leaves. The long, upright spikes of orange-red, tubular flowers, yellow in the throat, open on all sides of the spike over a long period during the summer and early autumn.

Common name: Cape fuchsia
Native range: South Africa
Height: 4 ft (1.2 m)
Spread: 3 ft (1 m)
Hardiness: Zone 8

Phygelius x *rectus*
These garden-raised hybrids between *P. aequalis* and *P. capensis* make suckering shrubs with upright shoots with dark green leaves and spikes of tubular-shaped flowers. It is mainly grown as the selected forms listed below, with flowers varying in color from yellow to orange, pink, or red.

Height: 3–4 ft (1–1.2 m)
Spread: 3 ft (1 m)
Hardiness: Zone 8
Variants: 'African Queen' produces pale red flowers. 'Devil's Tears' has deep pinkish-red flowers. 'Moonraker' has pale yellow flowers. 'Salmon Leap' has orange flowers. 'Sunshine' has yellow-flushed foliage and dusky reddish-pink flowers. 'Winchester Fanfare' has dusky reddish-pink flowers.

Phyllostachys
Gramineae

A genus of some 80 species of clump-forming or spreading evergreen bamboos, native from the Himalayas to East Asia. Characterized by their canes, which are distinctly grooved on one side, they do best in a good, moist but well-drained soil, and should be sheltered from strong winds, particularly in colder areas.

Phyllostachys aurea
This vigorous, evergreen bamboo has stout, erect, yellow-green canes, the

Physocarpus opulifolius 'Dart's Gold'

joints crowded together at the base. It is a lush and strongly spreading species bearing masses of dark green, taper-pointed leaves, up to 6 in (15 cm) long, which are blue-green in color beneath.

Common name: Fishpole bamboo
Native range: China
Height: 26 ft (8 m) or more
Spread: 16 ft (5 m) or more
Hardiness: Zone 6

Phyllostachys nigra
This is an elegant and vigorous, evergreen bamboo that forms a dense clump of slender, arching canes, green at first but eventually becoming shiny black. The rather glossy, dark green leaves, blue-green beneath and up to 5 in (12 cm) long, end in tapered points.

Common name: Black bamboo
Native range: China
Height: 20 ft (6 m)

Spread: 20 ft (6 m)
Hardiness: Zone 7
Variants: It is a variable species with selected forms, including 'Boryana' with green to yellow-green canes that are blotched with purple.

Physocarpus
Rosaceae

The ten species in this genus are deciduous shrubs, natives of North America and East Asia. Grown for their lobed leaves, colored in some forms, and their densely clustered flowers, they are suitable for any well-drained soil—except shallow chalk. To prune, cut them back lightly or remove some of the older shoots after they have flowered.

Physocarpus opulifolius
This is a vigorous, deciduous shrub, the bark of older stems peeling, with sharply toothed, usually three-lobed

leaves. Dense, hemispherical heads of small, white flowers tinged with pink in early summer are followed by clusters of small, inflated pods that turn red-purple when they are ripe.

Common name: Eastern ninebark
Native range: E North America
Height: 8 ft (2.5 m)
Spread: 10 ft (3 m)
Hardiness: Zone 2
Variants: 'Dart's Gold' is a compact form with conspicuous, bright yellow foliage. 'Diabolo' produces striking, deep red-purple foliage. 'Luteus' has leaves that are yellow when young, turning green in summer.

Pieris
Ericaceae

The seven species of evergreen shrub within this genus are natives of North America, the Himalayas, and East Asia. They provide a range of valuable, garden evergreens that are grown for their small, profusely borne flowers, which are usually white and are often ornamental in bud before they open, and attractive foliage, which is often strikingly colored when the leaves are young.

They can be grown in moist but well-drained, lime-free soil that is rich in organic matter. They may come into growth early and, as a result, young foliage can be damaged by any late frosts.

Little pruning is usually needed apart from the removal of damaged or unwanted branches, but they do benefit from being dead-headed after flowering.

Pieris 'Flaming Silver'
This is a sport of 'Forest Flame' that makes an evergreen shrub with slender-pointed leaves. The leaves are bright red when they first emerge and later turn to dark green with a silvery white margin. Drooping clusters of small, white flowers open in spring.

Height: 5 ft (1.5 m)
Spread: 4 ft (1.2 m)
Hardiness: Zone 5

Pieris 'Forest Flame'
This is a vigorous, garden-raised hybrid between P. formosa and P. japonica with slender-pointed, glossy, dark green leaves that emerge bright red in spring, before turning to pink, creamy white, and eventually green. Large, drooping clusters of small, white flowers open in spring.

Height: 16 ft (5 m)
Spread: 8 ft (2.5 m)
Hardiness: Zone 5

Pieris formosa
This vigorous, evergreen shrub, often spreading by suckers, has bold, glossy, dark green, leathery leaves that are bronze to red when young. The large, conical clusters of nodding, white flowers open at the ends of the shoots in spring. It is mainly cultivated as the forms listed below.

Native range: Himalayas, China
Height: 16 ft (5 m)
Spread: 16 ft (5 m)
Hardiness: Zone 8
Variants: 'Jermyns' has deep red-purple young foliage and white flowers emerging from red buds; buds are conspicuous during winter. 'Wakehurst' produces brilliant red young foliage.

Pieris japonica
This is a compact and bushy, evergreen shrub with an essentially rounded habit. It has glossy, dark green leaves that vary in color from pale green to bronze when young. Large clusters of white flowers open at the ends of the shoots in early to mid-spring. There are now numerous selections commonly available, varying in habit and foliage, as well as in flower color.

Pieris formosa 'Wakehurst'

Native range: Japan, China, Taiwan
Height: 10 ft (3 m) or more
Spread: 13 ft (4 m) or more
Hardiness: Zone 5
Variants: 'Blush' produces white flowers flushed with pink that emerge from deep pink buds. 'Little Heath' is a dwarf and compact form, up to 24 in (60 cm) in height, with leaves edged in creamy white. 'Little Heath Green' is similar to 'Little Heath' but with green leaves, bronze when young. 'Purity' is a compact and rounded form, growing up to 3 ft (1 m) tall, with pale green young foliage. 'Valley Rose' has deep pink buds that open as rose-pink and then fade to white. 'Valley Valentine' produces large clusters of deep dusky red flowers. 'Variegata' is a compact form, up to 5 ft (1.5 m) tall, with leaves edged with creamy white.

Pieris 'Flaming Silver'

Piptanthus
Leguminosae

The two species in this genus are deciduous or semi-evergreen shrubs, natives of the Himalayas and China. Only the following, however, is commonly grown in the garden, where it is valued for its fine foliage and showy flowers.

Suitable for any well-drained soil, the species can be grown in the border or trained against a wall. In cold areas it should be given protection from the effects of the wind. Little pruning is usually necessary, but some of the older shoots can be cut back right to the base in spring.

Piptanthus nepalensis
This is a vigorous, deciduous or semi-evergreen shrub with upright shoots and leaves composed of three blue-green leaflets that are whitish beneath. Dense, upright clusters of large, bright yellow, pealike flowers open at the ends of the shoots in late spring, and these are followed by pendulous, flattened pods up to 5 in (12 cm) in length.

Synonym: *Piptanthus laburnifolius*
Common name: Nepalese laburnum
Native range: Himalayas, China
Height: 10 ft (3 m)
Spread: 10 ft (3 m)
Hardiness: Zone 8

Pittosporum
Pittosporaceae

This is a large genus of some 200 species of evergreen shrubs and trees, natives of Australia and New Zealand, with some species in South Africa, the Pacific Islands, and East Asia. The cultivated species provide gardens with valuable ornamentals, grown for their foliage and their often fragrant flowers. They are suitable for use in the shrub border, as specimen plants, or—as with *P. tenuifolium*—

for hedging, and they can be grown in any well-drained soil.

Provide protection from winds in cold areas by growing them against a wall or among other trees and shrubs. Pruning is not essential, but trim them in spring as growth starts for a compact habit, and cut hedges again in summer, if necessary.

Pittosporum 'Garnettii'
This is a garden-raised hybrid between *P. ralphii* and *P. tenuifolium* and makes an evergreen tree or large shrub of columnar habit. The gray-green leaves are edged with an irregular border of creamy white, which turns more pink-tinged in cold weather. Small, deep red-purple, fragrant flowers open in late spring and early summer.

Height: 20 ft (6 m)
Spread: 10 ft (3 m)
Hardiness: Zone 8

Pittosporum tenuifolium
This vigorous, evergreen tree of columnar habit, sometimes shrubby, has deep purple-black shoots and glossy, bright green, wavy-edged leaves. The small, red-purple flowers open in late spring and early summer and are strongly scented of honey, especially in the evening.

Common name: Tawhiwhi
Native range: New Zealand
Height: 33 ft (10 m)
Spread: 16 ft (5 m)
Hardiness: Zone 8
Variants: 'Abbotsbury Gold' has young leaves blotched in the center with yellow-green. 'Irene Paterson' is slower-growing, to 10 ft (3 m), with nearly white young leaves becoming mottled with dark green. 'Purpureum' has glossy red-purple foliage, pale green when young. 'Silver Queen' has gray-green leaves edged with white. 'Tom Thumb' is a compact, rounded, dwarf bush with red-purple foliage, pale green when young. 'Warnham

Platanus x hispanica

Gold' has pale green foliage turning yellow in winter.

Pittosporum tobira

This bushy, evergreen shrub has a dense, spreading habit and leathery, glossy, dark green-colored leaves. The extremely fragrant, white flowers that open during the spring season in dense clusters at the ends of the shoots turn yellow with age. It does best in regions that experience hot summers, where it will thrive in sun or shade.

Native range: China, Japan, Taiwan
Height: 16 ft (5 m)
Spread: 16 ft (5 m)
Hardiness: Zone 8
Variant: 'Variegatum' is a slower-growing form and is less hardy. It has gray-green leaves that are edged with creamy white.

Platanus
Platanaceae

The planes are a small genus of six species of large, deciduous trees found in North America and Mexico, the southeast of Europe, and Southeast Asia. The following are grown for their bold, maple-like leaves, their stately habit, and their attractive, peeling bark. The tiny, inconspicuous flowers are borne in clusters in the spring and are followed by rounded fruit clusters, which can persist on the trees throughout the entire winter season.

These trees are suitable for planting in any well-drained soil and they prefer a sunny position. However, due to their mature size, they are ideal only in parks or large gardens. They should never be planted close to buildings.

Platanus x hispanica

This vigorous, garden-raised hybrid between *P. occidentalis* and *P. orientalis* makes a large, deciduous tree. The trunk is gray and brown and features cream-colored, flaking bark. The large, bright and glossy, green leaves can be up to 10 in (25 cm) across and are divided into three to five toothed lobes.

Synonym: *Platanus x acerifolia*
Common name: London plane tree
Height: 100 ft (30 m)
Spread: 80 ft (25 m)
Hardiness: Zone 5
Variant: 'Suttneri' has leaves mottled with white.

Platanus occidentalis

This is a large, vigorous, deciduous tree, usually taller than it is broad, with mottled, flaking bark and large, dark green, usually three-lobed leaves up to 8 in (20 cm) or more across. This tree needs hot summers and succeeds only in continental climates, such as those in mainland Europe or in North America.

Common name: Buttonwood
Native range: E North America
Height: 100 ft (30 m) or more
Spread: 80 ft (25 m)
Hardiness: Zone 4

Platanus orientalis

A large, deciduous tree, broadly columnar in habit, or often low and wide-spreading, with a flaking patchwork of gray and cream bark. The broad and glossy, green leaves, up to 10 in (25 cm) across, are deeply cut into five, sometimes seven, lobes.

Pleioblastus auricomus

Common name: Oriental plane tree
Native range: SE Europe
Height: 100 ft (30 m)
Spread: 80 ft (25 m)
Hardiness: Zone 7

Pleioblastus
Gramineae

A genus with a narrow distribution comprising 20 species of clump-forming or spreading, evergreen bamboos. They have slender, upright, usually hollow, canes and are natives of China and Japan.

Grown for their graceful canes and foliage, which is sometimes variegated, they are suitable for any moist but well-drained soil that is rich in organic matter. The following

species can be grown in open positions among other shrubs or in containers.

Pleioblastus auricomus

This is an evergreen bamboo that forms small clumps and spreads slowly by sending out underground shoots. The upright, slender, purple-green canes bear slender, pointed leaves, up to about 8 in (20 cm) long, that are striped with bright yellow and green.

Synonyms: *Arundinaria auricoma*, *Arundinaria viridistriata*
Native range: Japan
Height: 5 ft (1.5 m)
Spread: 6 ft (2 m)
Hardiness: Zone 7

Pleioblastus pygmaeus

This is a dwarf-growing, evergreen species of bamboo that forms dense clumps of slender, upright canes and spreads by sending out underground stems. The dark green, densely arranged leaves are up to 4 in (10 cm) long. It is useful for ground cover, and it does best in a sunny position. It is taller growing in shady garden conditions.

Synonym: *Arundinaria pygmaea*
Native range: Japan
Height: 8 in (20 cm)
Spread: 5 ft (1.5 m)
Hardiness: Zone 6
Variant: var. *distichus* (*Arundinaria disticha*) is taller and more vigorous and has larger leaves.

Pleioblastus variegatus

This is a vigorous, evergreen bamboo that forms dense clumps of slender, upright, pale green canes. The narrow leaves, up to 8 in (20 cm) long, are dark green and conspicuously striped with creamy white. It is an excellent specimen plant for the garden or container.

Synonyms: *Arundinaria fortunei*, *Arundinaria variegata*
Native range: Japan
Height: 5 ft (1.5 m)
Spread: 5 ft (1.5 m)
Hardiness: Zone 7

Polygala
Polygalaceae

This very large genus of some 500 species of annual and perennial herbaceous plants and evergreen shrubs is widely distributed throughout the world. The following is grown for its unusual flowers and it requires a mois,t well-drained, lime-free soil. It prefers a sunny position, ideally in a peat or rock garden.

Polygala chamaebuxus

This dwarf, evergreen shrub has a low, spreading habit with slender, creeping stems and narrow, dark green leaves. The small, rather pealike flowers, which open in late spring to early summer, are creamy white and tipped with bright yellow.

Native range: Europe
Height: 4 in (10 cm)
Spread: 12 in (30 cm)
Hardiness: Zone 6
Variant: var. *grandiflora* (var. *rhodoptera*) has purple-pink flowers that are tipped with yellow.

Populus
Salicaceae

The 35 species that make up this genus are mainly deciduous trees and are widely distributed in Europe, Asia, North Africa, and North America.

Most species are grown only in plantations for timber, while others can be useful as fast-growing screens. Even the few species grown in gardens are vigorous trees with invasive roots systems and should not be planted anywhere close to buildings. Flowers are borne in catkins—males and females on separate plants.

Populus alba

This is a deciduous tree with a broadly upright to spreading habit. The young shoots are densely covered with white wool. The leaves, which are covered in white hairs, becoming dark green above, are five-lobed and maple-like on vigorous shoots, while on other shoots they are oval and only shallowly lobed.

Common name: White poplar
Native range: Europe, C and W Asia, North Africa
Height: 80 ft (25 m)
Spread: 50 ft (15 m)
Hardiness: Zone 3
Variants: 'Racket' is a fast-growing form with a conical habit. 'Richardii' produces golden yellow foliage.

Populus x jackii

This naturally occurring hybrid between *P. balsamifera* and *P. deltoides* makes a vigorous, broadly columnar, deciduous tree with dark green, heart-shaped leaves that are whitish beneath. The female form is most commonly grown, bearing green, pendulous catkins in early spring. It is most commonly seen as the form listed below.

Synonym: *Populus x candicans*
Common name: Balm of Gilead
Native range: E North America
Height: 50 ft (15 m)
Spread: 26 ft (8 m)
Hardiness: Zone 2

Populus nigra

Potentilla fruticosa 'Elizabeth'

Variant: 'Aurora' has leaves that are conspicuously mottled with creamy yellow, and are flushed with pink when young.

Populus nigra

This is a vigorous, deciduous tree with a spreading habit when mature, and with nearly triangular, glossy, dark green leaves ending in a fine, tapered point. The leaves are bronze-colored when they are young and turn shades of yellow in the autumn. In garden cultivation, *P. nigra* is most frequently seen as the form listed below.

Common name: Black poplar
Native range: Europe, W Asia
Height: 100 ft (30 m)
Spread: 80 ft (25 m)
Hardiness: Zone 3
Variant: 'Italica' (Lombardy poplar) is a male form of narrow habit and with upright branches.

Populus tremula

This spreading, deciduous tree has long-stalked, gray-green leaves edged with small, rounded teeth. Foliage is bronze when young and turns yellow in the autumn. The flattened leaf stalks cause the leaves to flutter in the wind. Male plants have pendulous, red catkins in early spring before the leaves emerge.

Common name: Aspen
Native range: Europe, North Africa, Asia
Height: 65 ft (20 m)
Spread: 50 ft (15 m)
Hardiness: Zone 2
Variants: 'Erecta' is a slender tree with upright branches. 'Pendula' is a weeping form.

Potentilla
Rosaceae

This large genus of some 500 species of mainly herbaceous perennials and shrubs provides gardens with numerous ornamental plants. The following is the most commonly grown shrubby species.

Variable and of wide distribution, it has given rise to many different garden forms. It is suitable for any well-drained soil in a sunny position, and it can be used for ground cover; the more vigorous forms are ideal for hedging. They benefit from regular pruning and should be cut back lightly after flowering to maintain a compact habit.

Potentilla fruticosa

This is a bushy, deciduous shrub of a spreading to rounded or upright habit. Its small, dark green to blue-green leaves are usually divided into five or seven leaflets. The saucer-shaped flowers vary in color from yellow to orange, red, pink, and white, and open over a long period from late spring to autumn. Those with orange, red, or pink flowers tend to fade in hot sun.

Common name: Bush cinquefoil
Native range: Europe, N Asia, North America
Height: up to 5 ft (1.5 m)
Spread: up to 3 ft (1 m)
Hardiness: Zone 2
Variants: 'Abbotswood', up to 30 in (75 cm), with white flowers. 'Abbotswood Silver' is similar but with leaflets edged with white, often reverting. 'Beesii' is compact, to 24 in (60 cm), with silvery foliage and yellow-colored flowers. 'Elizabeth' is spreading, up to 3 ft (1 m), with golden yellow flowers. 'Goldfinger' is compact, to 35 in (90 cm), with large, rich yellow flowers. 'Katherine Dykes' is spreading, to 5 ft (1.5 m), with gray-green foliage and primrose yellow flowers. Marion Red Robin ('Marrob', Red Robin) is low and spreading with red flowers. 'Princess' ('Blink'), to 24 in (60 cm), has pale pink flowers. 'Red Ace', spreading, to 30 in (75 cm), has vermilion flowers. 'Sunset' has orange-colored flowers. 'Tangerine' is spreading, to 3 ft (1 m), with coppery yellow flowers. 'Tilford Cream' is compact and spreading, to 24 in (60 cm), with creamy white flowers. 'Vilmoriniana' is vigorous and upright, to 4 ft (1.2 m), with silvery foliage and creamy flowers.

Prostanthera
Labiatae

The mint bushes are a genus of about 50 species of aromatic evergreen shrubs with opposite leaves, natives of Australia and Tasmania. Grown in gardens for their neat habit, attractive foliage, and their small, two-lipped flowers, they are suitable for a sheltered garden border or for growing against a sunny wall in well-drained soil. Prune lightly after flowering if necessary.

Prostanthera cuneata
This compact and rounded, bushy evergreen shrub has very densely arranged, small, thick, glossy, dark green, and very aromatic leaves, only about ¼ in (5 mm) long. Clusters of tubular, two-lipped flowers, blotched inside with yellow and purple, open during the summer.

Common name: Alpine mint bush
Native range: SE Australia, Tasmania
Height: 24 in (60 cm)
Spread: 35 in (90 cm)
Hardiness: Zone 9

Prostanthera rotundifolia
This is an evergreen shrub with a bushy, spreading habit and slender, gray-hairy shoots. Its small, aromatic, dark green, rounded leaves have only a few shallow teeth. Dense clusters of purple, bell-shaped flowers open at the ends of the shoots in the spring.

Common name: Round-leaved mint bush
Native range: SE Australia, Tasmania
Height: 6 ft (2 m)
Spread: 10 ft (3 m)
Hardiness: Zone 9
Variant: 'Rosea' has pink flowers.

Prunus
Rosaceae

This is a large and varied genus of some 200 species of deciduous and evergreen trees and shrubs, widely distributed mainly in the temperate regions of the Northern Hemisphere and extending to South America.

It provides a wide range of ornamental flowering shrubs and trees, many of which are of a size suitable for smaller gardens, including the Japanese cherries. Several, such as P. x cistena, P. spinosa, P. laurocerasus, and P. lusitanica, can be used for hedging. Prune deciduous hedges after flowering; evergreens in spring.

Prunus 'Accolade'
This garden-raised hybrid between P. sargentii and P. x subhirtella makes

Prunus 'Accolade'

a spreading tree with dark green, taper-pointed, and sharply toothed leaves. In early spring, deep pink-colored buds open to pale pink, semidouble flowers, up to about 1½ in (4 cm) across, with yellow anthers in their centers.

Height: 26 ft (8 m)
Spread: 26 ft (8 m)
Hardiness: Zone 4

Prunus 'Amanogawa'

This popular Japanese cherry makes a small, deciduous tree of narrow habit with upright branches and dark green, sharply toothed leaves. Foliage is bronze-colored when young, turning red and orange in autumn. Upright clusters of semidouble, fragrant, pale pink flowers open in late spring.

Height: 26 ft (8 m)
Spread: 10 ft (3 m)
Hardiness: Zone 5

Prunus avium

A vigorous, deciduous tree with red-brown bark peeling in horizontal bands. Taper-pointed and sharply toothed leaves, bronze when young, turn deep green, then red and yellow. Clusters of white flowers open in mid-spring before or as the leaves emerge, followed by edible, red fruits.

Common name: Mazzard cherry
Native range: Europe, W Asia
Height: 65 ft (20 m)
Spread: 50 ft (15 m)
Hardiness: Zone 3
Variant: The form 'Plena' has double flowers.

Prunus cerasifera

This is a small, vigorous, spreading tree or thicket-forming shrub of garden origin with glossy, dark green leaves. Small, white flowers are profusely borne on the bare shoots before the leaves emerge in early spring, and these are followed by red, edible, plumlike fruits.

Prunus avium 'Plena'

Prunus cerasifera 'Nigra'

Prunus glandulosa 'Alba Plena'

Common name: Myrobalan plum
Height: 26 ft (8 m)
Spread: 26 ft (8 m)
Hardiness: Zone 5
Variants: 'Nigra' has deep red-purple
foliage and pink flowers. 'Pissardii'
has deep red-purple foliage and
white flowers.

Prunus x cistena

This is a garden-raised hybrid
between *P. cerasifera* 'Pissardii' and
P. pumila that makes a deciduous
shrub with slender, upright shoots
bearing glossy, red-purple leaves.
Small, fragrant, pink flowers open
singly on the shoots in late spring
after the leaves have emerged, and
these are sometimes followed by
deep red-purple, cherry-like fruits.

Common name: Purple-leaved sand
cherry
Height: 10 ft (3 m)
Spread: 6 ft (2 m)
Hardiness: Zone 4

Prunus dulcis

This spreading, deciduous tree has
slender, glossy and green, taper-
pointed and finely toothed leaves.
Large, white or pink flowers, 2 in
(5 cm) across, open singly or in small
clusters on the bare shoots before
the leaves emerge in early spring.
The velvety green fruits, about 2½ in
(6 cm) long with a dry flesh, contain
the familiar edible nuts.

Common name: Almond
Native range: North Africa, SW and
C Asia
Height: 26 ft (8 m)
Spread: 26 ft (8 m)
Hardiness: Zone 7
Variant: 'Roseoplena' has double pink
flowers.

Prunus glandulosa

This is a spreading, deciduous shrub
with slender, arching shoots and
taper-pointed, finely toothed leaves.
Small, white or pink flowers are
borne in mid-spring, sometimes
followed by small, bright red fruits. It
is nearly always grown as one of the
double-flowered forms listed below.

Native range: N China, Korea, Japan
Height: 5 ft (1.5 m)
Spread: 6 ft (2 m)
Hardiness: Zone 4
Variants: 'Alba Plena' has double,
white flowers. 'Sinensis' ('Rosea
Plena') has double, pink flowers.

Prunus incisa

This is a small, bushy, spreading tree,
often shrubby, with small, dark green,
sharply toothed leaves. Foliage is
bronze when young and turns red and
yellow in autumn. White or pale pink
flowers, ¾ in (2 cm) across, are borne
in small clusters of two or three in
mid-spring before the leaves emerge,
and these are sometimes followed by
small, purple-black cherries.

Common name: Fuji cherry
Native range: Japan

Prunus 'Kanzan'

Height: 26 ft (8 m)
Spread: 33 ft (10 m)
Hardiness: Zone 5
Variants: 'February Pink' has pale
pink flowers throughout winter.
'Kojo-no-mai' has zigzag shoots and
pale pink flowers. 'Praecox' has white
flowers opening from pink buds in
early winter.

Prunus 'Kanzan'

This is one of the most popular of the
Japanese cherries. This vigorous,
deciduous tree is vase-shaped when
young with upright branches that
later spread more widely. The sharply
toothed leaves end in a fine, tapered
point and are deep bronze-colored
when young. Clusters of large,
purple-pink, double flowers, 2 in
(5 cm) across, open in spring as the
young leaves emerge.

Height: 33 ft (10 m)
Spread: 33 ft (10 m)
Hardiness: Zone 5

Prunus 'Kiku-shidare-zakura'

This Japanese cherry has a very
distinct habit and is normally grafted
on the top of a stem to make a small,
weeping tree. The hanging branches
often reach right to the ground. The
taper-pointed leaves are bronze when
young, and fully double, rich pink
flowers open as the young leaves
emerge in mid- to late spring.

Synonym: *Prunus* 'Cheal's Weeping'
Height: 8 ft (2.5 m)
Spread: 10 ft (3 m)
Hardiness: Zone 5

Prunus laurocerasus

This large, vigorous, evergreen shrub,
sometimes treelike, bears bold,
leathery, glossy, dark green leaves, to
8 in (20 cm) long, on short, stout
stalks. Upright spikes of small, white
flowers start to emerge early in the
year. The flowers open in mid-spring
and are followed by green, then red

Prunus laurocerasus 'Otto Luyken'

and finally glossy, black fruits. It is very variable in size and is normally grown as garden selections.

Common name: Cherry laurel
Native range: E Europe, SW Asia
Height: 20 ft (6 m) or more
Spread: 26 ft (8 m)
Hardiness: Zone 6
Variants: 'Castlewellan' ('Marbled White') has foliage heavily mottled in white. 'Otto Luyken' makes a dense mound of narrow, dark green leaves, up to 3 ft (1 m) tall. 'Rotundifolia' is compact and upright, and is the best form for growing as hedges. 'Zabeliana' is wide-spreading form, growing up to 5 ft (1.5 m), with slender leaves.

Prunus lusitanica

This vigorous, evergreen shrub or tree has very dark and glossy, green leaves on slender, red stalks. Slender, spreading spikes, up to 10 in (25 cm) long, of small, white flowers open in midsummer, followed by small, glossy, black fruits.

Common name: Portugal cherry laurel
Native range: SW Europe
Height: 33 ft (10 m) or more
Spread: 33 ft (10 m)
Hardiness: Zone 7

Prunus maackii

A broadly conical, deciduous tree notable for its striking, glossy, yellow-brown, peeling bark. Finely toothed and taper-pointed, dark green leaves turn yellow in autumn. Small, fragrant, white flowers open in dense, short clusters as the leaves emerge in mid-spring, followed by small, glossy, black fruits.

Common name: Amur chokeberry
Native range: NE Asia
Height: 40 ft (12 m)
Spread: 26 ft (8 m)
Hardiness: Zone 3

Prunus 'Okame'

This is a garden-raised hybrid between *P. campanulata* and *P. incisa*

Prunus maackii

Prunus padus 'Colorata'

that makes a small deciduous tree. The tree is upright when young, becoming rounded in habit as it matures, with sharply toothed, dark green leaves that turn orange-red in autumn. Small clusters of bright pink flowers, up to about 1 in (2.5 cm) across, open in the early spring.

Height: 26 ft (8 m)
Spread: 20 ft (6 m)
Hardiness: Zone 6

Prunus padus

This fast-growing, deciduous tree has a spreading habit and dark, matt-green, taper-pointed, and finely toothed leaves. Small, fragrant, white flowers open in slender, upright, spreading or drooping spikes in mid-to late spring, and these are followed by glossy, black fruits.

Common name: European bird cherry
Native range: Europe, N Asia
Height: 50 ft (15 m)
Spread: 40 ft (12 m)
Hardiness: Zone 3

Variants: 'Colorata' has deep red-purple leaves, becoming dark green, and pink flowers. 'Watereri' produces very long flower spikes.

Prunus 'Pink Perfection'

This spreading, deciduous tree has taper-pointed, dark green leaves that are bronze as they emerge. Drooping clusters of large, pink, double flowers open in late spring.

Height: 26 ft (8 m)
Spread: 26 ft (8 m)
Hardiness: Zone 5

Prunus sargentii

This is one of the most striking of all the cherries. It is a spreading, deciduous tree with glossy, green leaves ending in long, tapered points. Deep bronze-red when young, the leaves turn to brilliant shades of orange, red, and yellow in autumn. Pale pink-colored flowers, up to 1½ in (4 cm) across, open in clusters in mid-spring.

Prunus 'Pink Perfection'

Prunus serrula

Native range: Japan
Height: 50 ft (15 m)
Spread: 50 ft (15 m)
Hardiness: Zone 4

Prunus serrula

Grown primarily for its smooth, strikingly colored, glossy, red-brown bark, which peels in long, horizontal strips, this medium-sized *Prunus* species makes a spreading, deciduous tree with slender, taper-pointed, dark green leaves, which turn yellow in autumn. Nodding, five-petalled, white flowers open singly or in small clusters as the young leaves first emerge in spring, and these are followed by small red fruits.

Native range: China
Height: 33 ft (10 m)
Spread: 33 ft (10 m)
Hardiness: Zone 5

Prunus 'Shirofugen'

Among the best of the Japanese cherries, this spreading tree produces dark green leaves that emerge bronze-colored and turn to shades of orange and red in the autumn. The large, double flowers are pink in bud, turning white as they open in the late spring, before turning pink again before they fall.

Height: 33 ft (10 m)
Spread: 33 ft (10 m)
Hardiness: Zone 5

Prunus 'Shirotae'

This is a small, deciduous tree with spreading and slightly drooping branches bearing dark green leaves. The leaves—which end in long, tapered points—are pale green when young and turn orange and red in autumn. Pendulous clusters of large, semi-double, white flowers, up to 2 in (5 cm) across, open in mid-spring.

Synonym: *Prunus* 'Mount Fuji'
Height: 20 ft (6 m)
Spread: 26 ft (8 m)
Hardiness: Zone 5

Prunus sargentii

Prunus spinosa

This is a dense, spiny, deciduous shrub, sometimes a tree, often spreading by suckers, with dark green, sharply toothed leaves. Profuse, small, white flowers open on the bare shoots before the leaves emerge in the early spring, and these are followed by edible but bitter, blue-black fruits. It is a useful plant for hedging.

Common names: Blackthorn, sloe
Native range: Europe, W Asia
Height: 16 ft (5 m)
Spread: 13 ft (4 m)
Hardiness: Zone 4
Variants: 'Plena' produces double, rosette-like, white flowers. 'Purpurea' has purple leaves and pink flowers.

Prunus x subhirtella

This is a naturally occurring hybrid between *P. incisa* and *P. pendula*. It makes a small, deciduous tree of spreading habit with taper-pointed and sharply toothed, deep green leaves. The leaves are bronze when young and turn yellow in autumn. Small clusters of pink or white flowers, up to about ¾ in (2 cm) across, open in the early spring before or as the young leaves emerge. *P. x subhirtella* is most commonly grown as the two forms listed below.

Common name: Higan cherry
Native range: Japan
Height: 26 ft (8 m)
Spread: 20 ft (6 m)
Hardiness: Zone 5
Variants: 'Autumnalis' produces semidouble, white flowers that open from pink buds over a long period from late autumn through to early spring. 'Autumnalis Rosea' is similar, except that it bears pink flowers.

Prunus tenella

This small, deciduous shrub spreads by suckers and has slender, upright shoots bearing glossy, dark green, sharply toothed leaves. Pink flowers, about 1 in (2–3 cm) across, open along the shoots in mid-spring. It prefers a warm, sunny position and

Prunus tenella 'Fire Hill'

old plants can be rejuvenated by cutting them back hard after they have flowered.

Common name: Russian almond
Native range: C and E Europe, W Asia
Height: 5 ft (1.5 m)
Spread: 5 ft (1.5 m)
Hardiness: Zone 2
Variant: 'Fire Hill' produces deep pink flowers.

Prunus 'Ukon'

This is a very distinct, Japanese cherry that makes a vigorous, deciduous tree. The branches, which are upright at first, later spreading, bear dark green, taper-pointed, and finely toothed leaves that are bronze when young. The unusual double flowers, up to 1½ in (4 cm) across, are pale yellow-green. The flowers are flushed with pink at first, but later turn to white.

Height: 26 ft (8 m)
Spread: 33 ft (10 m)
Hardiness: Zone 5

Prunus x *yedoensis*

A naturally occurring hybrid between *P. pendula* and *P. speciosa* making a spreading deciduous tree with widely

Pseudosasa japonica

arching branches bearing glossy, green, sharply toothed leaves. Masses of pale pink flowers, fading to white, open in clusters along the bare shoots in the early spring, and these are followed by small, red fruits that ripen to black.

Common name: Yoshino cherry
Native range: Japan
Height: 33 ft (10 m)
Spread: 40 ft (12 m)
Hardiness: Zone 5

Pseudosasa
Gramineae

This is a small genus made up of six species of evergreen bamboos that spread by sending out underground stems, and are natives of Japan, Taiwan, and Korea.

The following species is best grown as a specimen plant or it can also be used to form an effective barrier or screen. It is suitable for any reasonably good, moist but well-drained soil. The size of clumps can be controlled by cutting out unwanted canes.

Pseudosasa japonica

This is a vigorous and evergreen bamboo with upright, green canes that later turn yellow-brown. It makes dense clumps and spreads by underground stems. The large, dark green, taper-pointed leaves, which are blue-green beneath, can grow up to about 14 in (35 cm) long. Flowers are rarely produced.

Synonym: *Arundinaria japonica*
Common name: Metake
Native range: Japan
Height: 16 ft (5 m)
Spread: 26 ft (8 m) or more
Hardiness: Zone 6

Ptelea trifoliata 'Aurea'

Ptelea
Rutaceae

This is a small genus comprising about ten species of deciduous shrubs and small trees, all natives of North America. Grown for their aromatic foliage, they have leaves that are divided up into three leaflets. Small flowers are followed by winged fruits in autumn.

The following is the most commonly seen species in garden cultivation. It is suitable for any well-drained soil, but requires a sunny position in order to thrive.

Ptelea trifoliata
This is a vigorous, though small-growing, deciduous tree with a spreading habit. The leaves, which are very aromatic when crushed, are composed of three, glossy, dark green leaflets that turn yellow in the autumn. Rounded clusters of small, yellow-green flowers at the ends of the shoots appear in the summer, and these are followed by pale green fruits, which turn pale brown later in the year. The fruits are surrounded by a broad, circular wing.

Common name: Common hop tree
Native range: E North America
Height: 20 ft (6 m)
Spread: 20 ft (6 m)
Hardiness: Zone 3
Variant: 'Aurea' produces foliage that is bright yellow when young.

Pterocarya
Juglandaceae

This small genus, made up of ten species of vigorous, deciduous trees, is related to the walnuts. The trees produce large leaves that are divided into numerous leaflets, and the flowers are borne in catkins—males and females separate but on the

Pterostyrax hispida

same tree. Male catkins are pendulous, while females develop into long, hanging clusters of small, winged fruits.

Popular in garden cultivation principally for their foliage and fruits, they are suitable for any good, moist but well-drained soil. They do best if given a position in full sun.

Pterocarya fraxinifolia

This vigorous, large-growing and spreading, deciduous tree, often branching low down, bears bold, glossy dark green leaves that turn yellow in the autumn. The leaves grow up to about 16 in (40 cm) in length, and are divided up into as many as 23 or more individual leaflets. The tree bears pendulous male catkins, up to about 5 in (12 cm) long, in the spring and slender, drooping clusters, up to about 6 in (15 cm) long, of winged fruits in the autumn.

Common name: Caucasian wingnut
Native range: Caucasus, N Iran
Height: 80 ft (25 m) or more
Spread: 65 ft (20 m)
Hardiness: Zone 6

Pterostyrax
Styracaceae

The four species that make up this small genus of hardy deciduous shrubs and trees are all natives of East Asia.

The following is the most commonly seen species in garden cultivation and it is grown for its bold foliage as well as for its fragrant flowers. It can be grown as a specimen tree or planted out in more of a woodland situation.

It requires a good depth of well-drained soil and a sunny position in order to thrive.

Pyracantha 'Dart's Red'

Pterostyrax hispida

This is a deciduous tree—upright when young, but adopting more of a spreading habit as it grows and develops. It has bold, bright green leaves, growing up to about 8 in (20 cm) long, that are gray-green beneath. The pendulous clusters of small, fragrant, white flowers reach a length of up to about 8 in (20 cm) and open in early to midsummer. The flowers are followed by small, persistent, bristly fruits.

Common name: Fragrant epaulette tree
Native range: China, Japan
Height: 33 ft (10 m)
Spread: 33 ft (10 m)
Hardiness: Zone 5

Punica
Punicaceae

The two species of shrubs or trees that make up this small genus are both natives of West Asia. However, only the following species is commonly seen in garden cultivation, principally for its showy flowers and its edible fruits.

In gardens situated in warm regions, it makes a handsome specimen shrub, where it is also useful for screening or shelter. In regions where the winters are cooler, it can be grown in a sheltered border or against a wall.

It is suitable for any well-drained soil if given a position in full sun, and it can be cut back in spring if necessary to restrict growth.

Punica granatum

This vigorous, deciduous or semi-evergreen shrub, sometimes a tree (evergreen in warm climates), has glossy, dark green leaves that are bronze-colored when young. Striking, bright orange-red flowers open over a long period during the summer and early autumn seasons, and these are followed by edible fruits in warm climates.

Common name: Pomegranate
Native range: W Asia
Height: 16 ft (5 m)
Spread: 13 ft (4 m)
Hardiness: Zone 8
Variants: var. *nana* is a dwarf form of compact habit, up to 3 ft (1 m) high, with smaller leaves, flowers, and fruits. 'Plena' has double flowers.

Pyracantha
Rosaceae

The firethorns make up a small genus of seven species of spiny, evergreen shrubs that are natives of southeast Europe, West Asia, the Himalayas, and East Asia.

Grown for their dense habit, as well as for their flowers and their showy fruits, they are ideal for the shrub border, for hedging and screening, or for training against a wall or fence.

Suitable for any well-drained soil, they flower and fruit best when positioned in full sun. Although pruning is not essential, they can be cut back in spring to restrict growth. Cut hedges in spring and, as necessary, during the summer.

Pyracantha 'Soleil d'Or'

Pyracantha angustifolia

This dense and bushy, evergreen shrub has spiny shoots covered in gray hairs when young. The narrow-shaped leaves are dark green above with a thick, gray felt beneath. Clusters of small, white flowers open in midsummer, and these are followed by long-persistent, orange-yellow berries.

Native range: China
Height: 10 ft (3 m)
Spread: 10 ft (3 m)
Hardiness: Zone 7

Pyracantha coccinea

This vigorous, evergreen shrub has a dense, rounded habit with spiny shoots and glossy, dark green leaves. Clusters of small, white flowers open in early summer followed by orange-red berries.

Native range: SE Europe, W Asia
Height: 10 ft (3 m)
Spread: 13 ft (4 m)

Hardiness: Zone 5
Variants: 'Lalandei' is a very vigorous shrub and fruits profusely. 'Red Column' is upright in habit and has bright red fruits.

Pyracantha rogersiana

This is a vigorous and compact, evergreen shrub with arching, spiny shoots, red when young, and slender, glossy, dark green leaves. Dense clusters of white flowers appear in late spring, and these are followed by orange-red berries.

Native range: China
Height: 10 ft (3 m)
Spread: 13 ft (4 m)
Hardiness: Zone 7
Variant: 'Flava' produces yellow berries.

Pyracantha hybrids

Numerous hybrids between the various species have been raised in gardens, varying in habit and fruit

Pyrus calleryana 'Chanticleer'

color. These include 'Dart's Red'—vigorous with red berries; 'Golden Charmer'—vigorous, to 10 ft (3 m), with arching shoots and bright orange berries; 'Mohave'—vigorous and upright, to 13 ft (4 m), with broad, glossy, green leaves and profuse, bright red berries; 'Orange Glow'—upright with arching branches and profuse, long-persistent, bright orange-red berries, good for growing against a wall; 'Soleil d'Or'—large clusters of golden yellow berries;

'Teton'—compact and upright, with small, glossy, green leaves and orange-yellow berries.

Pyrus
Rosaceae

The pears comprise a genus of about 20 species of deciduous trees and shrubs from Europe, North Africa, and Asia. Well-known for providing the edible pear, the ornamental

Pyrus salicifolia 'Pendula'

species are grown for their habit, foliage, and flowers. Although they do best on good, well-drained soils, they are very tough trees and also perform well in moist and dry conditions. They prefer a sunny position.

Pyrus calleryana

This vigorous, usually broadly conical, deciduous tree produces glossy, green leaves that remain late into autumn or early winter, when they turn red-purple in color. Clusters of small, white flowers with pink anthers open in the spring followed by rounded to pear-shaped, russet-colored fruits. It is mainly grown as selected forms below.

Native range: China
Height: 50 ft (15 m)
Spread: 33 ft (10 m)
Hardiness: Zone 5

Variants: There are many forms selected mainly for their habit and autumn color, the most common of which are: 'Bradford' (United States of America), which is broadly conical but spreading, and often splitting with age; and 'Chanticleer' (Britain), narrowly conical even in old trees.

Pyrus salicifolia

Only commonly seen as the following form, this small, deciduous tree has slender, gray-green leaves that are silvery gray when young. Small, creamy white flowers with pink anthers open in dense clusters as the young foliage emerges, and the flowers are followed by small, green fruits.

Common name: Willow-leaved pear
Native range: Caucasus, NE Turkey
Height: 33 ft (10 m)

Quercus cerris 'Argenteovariegata'

Spread: 26 ft (8 m)
Hardiness: Zone 4
Variant: 'Pendula' is the form seen in gardens. It makes a dense, strongly weeping, small-sized tree, reaching up to about 20 ft (6 m) in height.

Quercus
Fagaceae

The oaks are a large genus consisting of approximately 500 species of deciduous and evergreen trees and shrubs widely distributed throughout the temperate and tropical regions of the Northern Hemisphere.

Flowers are borne in catkins in spring: males flowers are pendulous and usually yellow-green; the small, female flowers ripening to form the acorns. The cultivated species are grown principally for their habit and their foliage.

Preferring a good, deep, well-drained soil, the following species can make large trees and are suitable only for sizable gardens. Some require a lime-free soil.

Quercus alba

This is a spreading tree of rounded habit with bold, shallowly to deeply lobed leaves. The leaves are pink-tinged as they open, turning blue-green, then bright green, and finally red-purple in the autumn. This species prefers areas that experience hot summers and is most commonly grown in North America. It requires a lime-free soil.

Common name: White oak
Native range: E North America
Height: 80 ft (25 m) or more
Spread: 100 ft (30 m)
Hardiness: Zone 4

Quercus cerris 'Argenteovariegata'

Quercus coccinea

Quercus robur

Quercus cerris

This is a large, fast-growing, deciduous tree with deeply ridged bark. The glossy, dark green leaves, up to 5 in (12 cm) long, are edged with up to six, usually rounded, lobes on each side, turning yellow to yellow-brown in autumn. Large acorns, up to 1 in (2.5 cm) long, ripen in 18 months and are borne in a cup densely covered with slender scales. This tree is the alternate host to the knopper gall wasp, which causes deformed acorns on English oak

(*Q. robur*). In North America, the common name of turkey oak is also applied to a different species (*Q. laevis*).

Common name: Turkey oak
Native range: Europe, SW Asia
Height: 100 ft (30 m)
Spread: 80 ft (25 m)
Hardiness: Zone 5
Variants: 'Argenteovariegata', also known as 'Variegata', has leaves with a creamy yellow margin when young, turning creamy white with age. It is a smaller tree—about 33 ft (10 m) tall and across.

Quercus coccinea

This vigorous, deciduous tree is spreading to broadly columnar in habit. The glossy, dark green leaves, up to 6 in (15 cm) long, are deeply cut into lobes ending in bristle-tipped teeth, and they turn bright red in autumn. It needs a lime-free soil.

Common name: Scarlet oak
Native range: E North America
Height: 80 ft (25 m)
Spread: 65 ft (20m)
Hardiness: Zone 4
Variant: 'Splendens' is a form selected for its excellent deep red, autumn color.

Quercus frainetto

This is a vigorous, deciduous tree with a broadly upright-to-spreading habit. Among the finest species for general planting, the bold, dark green leaves, up to 8 in (20 cm) long, are deeply and conspicuously cut into numerous, often notched, lobes. The leaves turn yellow in autumn.

Common name: Hungarian oak
Native range: SE Europe
Height: 100 ft (30 m)
Spread: 80 ft (25 m)
Hardiness: Zone 5
Variant: 'Hungarian Crown' is a selection with a compact, broadly upright habit.

Quercus ilex

This is an evergreen tree, typically with a dense, rounded habit. The leathery, taper-pointed leaves are untoothed, or nearly so, on mature plants, but on younger leaves and shoots from the base of old trees can be spiny edged. Emerging gray and hairy, they become glossy, dark green on their upper surfaces. The yellow, male catkins are conspicuous as the leaves emerge in early summer.

Common name: Holm oak
Native region: Mediterranean region
Height: 65 ft (20 m)
Spread: 65 ft (20 m)
Hardiness: Zone 7

Quercus imbricaria

This deciduous tree is upright when young, wide-spreading with age, and with lower branches that often droop. The untoothed leaves, up to 6 in (15 cm) long, end in small, bristle-tipped points. Pale green to bronze when young, leaves turn and glossy dark green, then yellow-green or red-brown in the autumn. It requires a lime-free soil.

Common name: Shingle oak
Native range: C and E United States of America
Height: 65 ft (20 m) or more
Spread: 65 ft (20 m)
Hardiness: Zone 4

Quercus palustris

A vigorous, deciduous tree with a characteristic broadly conical habit, with the lower branches wide-spreading and drooping. The glossy, dark green leaves are cut into deep lobes, ending in bristle-tipped teeth, and turn red in autumn. This species requires a lime-free soil.

Common name: Pin oak
Native range: E North America
Height: 65 ft (20 m)
Spread: 50 ft (15 m)
Hardiness: Zone 4

Quercus rubra

Quercus phellos

This is a vigorous, deciduous tree that is conical when young, but becoming dense and rounded as it matures. The distinct willow-like leaves are slender and without teeth, ending in small, bristle-like points. Pale green to bronze when young, the leaves mature to a dark green color and usually turn yellow to yellow-brown in the autumn.

Common name: Willow oak
Native range: E United States of America
Height: 65 ft (20 m) or more
Spread: 50 ft (15 m) or more
Hardiness: Zone 5

Quercus robur

A wide-spreading, deciduous tree of rounded habit. The dark green leaves are blue-green beneath and have three to six rounded lobes on each side. Borne on very short stalks, the leaves usually turn yellow-brown in autumn. There are many selected forms varying in habit and leaf shape.

Common name: English oak
Native range: Europe
Height: 80 ft (25 m) or more
Spread: 65 ft (20 m) or more
Hardiness: Zone 4
Variants: 'Concordia' has bright yellow young foliage. 'Fastigiata' (Cypress oak) is a narrow tree.

Quercus rubra

This very fast-growing, deciduous tree has a rounded, spreading habit. The bold leaves are shallowly cut into several lobes, each ending in a bristle-tipped tooth. Dark matt-green above and usually rather blue-green beneath, they turn yellow-brown in autumn, or red on young trees.

Common name: Red oak
Native range: E North America
Height: 80 ft (25 m)
Spread: 65 ft (20 m)
Hardiness: Zone 4

Variant: 'Aurea' has bright yellow young foliage and does best in a partially shaded position.

Rhamnus
Rhamnaceae

This is a large genus comprising some 150 species of deciduous and evergreen trees and shrubs, with alternate or opposite leaves. Species are widely distributed, mainly in the Northern Hemisphere but also extending through to South Africa and South America.

The buckthorns have rather inconspicuous flowers and are grown principally for their attractive foliage and fruits. The following species are suitable for any well-drained soil, while R. frangula will tolerate wet soil. Apart from the removal of dead, damaged, or unwanted wood, no pruning is usually necessary.

Rhamnus alaternus

This is a variable, evergreen shrub or small tree with alternate, leathery, glossy, dark green leaves. Tiny, yellow-green flowers open in clusters in late spring and early summer, and these are followed by small, red fruits, which ripen to black. It is most commonly grown as the form listed below.

Common name: Italian buckthorn
Native range: Mediterranean region
Height: 16 ft (5 m)
Spread: 16 ft (5 m)
Hardiness: Zone 8
Variant: 'Argenteovariegata' produces leaves that are edged with white.

Rhamnus frangula

This vigorous and bushy, often spiny, deciduous shrub or small tree has glossy, dark green, alternate leaves that turn red in autumn. Clusters of tiny, yellow-green, pink-tinged flowers open during summer, and these are followed by red, later black,

Rhaphiolepis umbellata

fruits. This species can be used successfully for hedging.

Synonym: *Frangula alnus*
Common name: Alder buckthorn
Native range: Europe, W Asia, North Africa
Height: 16 ft (5 m)
Spread: 16 ft (5 m)
Hardiness: Zone 3

Rhaphiolepis
Rosaceae

This is a small, narrowly distributed genus comprising about 15 species of evergreen shrubs, sometimes trees. All are natives of East Asia.

The following species are cultivated for their foliage, flowers, and fruits. In warm areas they can be used as specimen shrubs, for ground cover, or for hedging. In cooler regions, however, they generally require more of a sheltered site. They

do best in well-drained soil and when given a position in full sun.

Rhaphiolepis x *delacourii*

This garden-raised hybrid between *R. indica* and *R. umbellata* makes a rounded, evergreen shrub with glossy, dark green leaves that are often bronze when young. Clusters of pink flowers open over a long period during the spring and summer.

Height: 3 ft (1 m)
Spread: 5 ft (1.5 m)
Hardiness: Zone 8
Variants: 'Coates' Crimson' has deep pink flowers. 'Enchantress' is a compact form with large clusters of rose-pink flowers.

Rhaphiolepis umbellata

A stiffly branched, evergreen shrub with very thick and leathery, glossy, dark green leaves, usually clustered at

Rhamnus alaternus 'Argenteovariegata'

the ends of the shoots. Dense clusters of white-colored flowers open in late spring to early summer, and these are followed by long-persistent, blue-black fruits.

Native range: Japan, Korea
Height: 5 ft (1.5 m)
Spread: 5 ft (1.5 m)
Hardiness: Zone 8

Rhododendron
Ericaceae

The 700 or more evergreen, semi-evergreen, and deciduous species that make up this large genus range from dwarf shrubs of no more than 3 ft (1 m) in height to sizable, treelike shrubs. Species are widely distributed, mainly in the Northern Hemisphere but also extending to Australasia.
The great variation in the genus gives them many uses in the garden. While the larger species are suitable for woodland situations, the dwarf species are ideal for the peat garden, or the rock garden where summers are not too dry. Those known as hardy hybrids can withstand exposure and make good hedges.

Rhododendrons need a moist but well-drained, lime-free soil, and any yellowing of the leaves is usually an indication of poor drainage or incorrect soil chemistry.
Plants benefit from dead-heading and leggy stems can be cut back hard in the spring.

Rhododendron augustinii
This vigorous, evergreen shrub of bushy, upright habit has scaly young shoots and dark green, taper-pointed leaves, scaly beneath, to 4 in (10 cm) long. Wide funnel-shaped flowers, in various shades of blue, sometimes pink or white, 2½ in (6 cm) across, open in small clusters in the mid- to late spring.

Native range: China
Height: 13 ft (4 m)
Spread: 10 ft (3 m)
Hardiness: Zone 6

Rhododendron 'Blue Diamond'
This is garden-raised hybrid between *R. augustinii* and *R.* 'Intrifast' making a compact, upright, evergreen shrub with small leaves. The funnel-shaped flowers, up to 2 in (5 cm) long, are deep violet-blue in color and open in small clusters in the mid- to late spring season.

Height: 6 ft (2 m)
Spread: 5 ft (1.5 m)
Hardiness: Zone 6

Rhododendron 'Blue Tit'
A garden-raised hybrid between *R. augustinii* and *R. impeditum* making a dense, dwarf, evergreen shrub with small, light green leaves to 1 in (2.5 cm) long. Small clusters of funnel-shaped, pale lavender blue flowers open in early to mid-spring.

Height: 4 ft (1.2 m)
Spread: 6 ft (2 m)
Hardiness: Zone 6

Rhododendron augustinii

Rhododendron 'Blue Tit'

Rhododendron 'Blue Diamond'

Rhododendron 'Bow Bells'

This charming, garden-raised hybrid is between R. 'Corona' and R. *williamsianum* and it makes a dome-shaped, evergreen shrub of compact habit with nearly rounded, purple-stalked leaves, which are bronze when young. Profuse clusters of pale pink, wide bell-shaped flowers, 2½ in (6 cm) across, open from deep pink buds in late spring.

Height: 6 ft (2 m)
Spread: 6 ft (2 m)
Hardiness: Zone 7

Rhododendron 'Britannia'

This popular, hardy hybrid makes a compact, spreading, evergreen shrub with light green leaves. Large clusters of broadly bell-shaped, scarlet flowers, up to about 2¾ in (7 cm) long, open in the late spring.

Height: 5 ft (1.5 m)
Spread: 6 ft (2 m)
Hardiness: Zone 6

Rhododendron calostrotum

This low-growing and compact, evergreen shrub has scaly young shoots and small, rather rounded, blue-green leaves, up to about 1 in (3 cm) long, covered with brown scales beneath. Purple-pink flowers, often with deeper spots, open in the late spring.

Native range: N Burma (Myanmar), NE India, SE Tibet, SW China
Height: 3 ft (1 m)
Spread: 4 ft (1.2 m)

Rhododendron 'Britannia'

Rhododendron 'Cynthia'

Hardiness: Zone 6
Variants: 'Gigha' has red flowers. The
subsp. *keleticum* is dwarf and
spreading, up to 12 in (30 cm) tall,
with red-purple flowers.

Rhododendron 'Carmen'

This garden-raised hybrid between
R. forrestii and *R. sanguineum* subsp.
didymum makes a dwarf, spreading,
evergreen shrub producing dark
green leaves up to about 2 in (5 cm)
long. Clusters of conspicuous, bell-
shaped, blood-red flowers, growing
up to 1½ in (4 cm) across, open in
mid- to late spring.

Height: 24 in (60 cm)
Spread: 3 ft (1 m)
Hardiness: Zone 5

Rhododendron 'Chikor'

This is a compact, dwarf-growing,
evergreen shrub and is a garden-
raised hybrid of *R. rupicola* var.
chryseum and *R. ludlowii*. It produces
small, dark green leaves, up to 2 in
(5 cm) long, that turn bronze in cold
weather. Clusters of pale yellow-
colored flowers, up to about 1½ in
(4 cm) across, open in the mid- to
late spring season.

Height: 24 in (60 cm)
Spread: 35 in (90 cm)
Hardiness: Zone 6

Rhododendron 'Cunningham's White'

This compact, hardy hybrid has dark
green leaves up to 4 in (10 cm) long.
The white, funnel-shaped flowers,
2 in (5 cm) across, are pale mauve as
they open, and have yellow-brown
spots in the throat. Reasonably lime-
tolerant if the soil is not too dry.

Height: 8 ft (2.5 m)
Spread: 10 ft (3 m)
Hardiness: Zone 5

Rhododendron 'Cynthia'

This is a large-growing and vigorous,
hardy hybrid making a dome-shaped,
evergreen shrub with dark green
leaves reaching up to 6 in (15 cm) in
length. Large, funnel-shaped, deep
pink flowers, up to about 2¾ in
(7 cm) across, and with darker spots
inside, are borne in dense, conical
clusters in the late spring.

Height: 16 ft (5 m) or more
Spread: 16 ft (5 m)
Hardiness: Zone 5

Rhododendron 'Fastuosum Flore Pleno'

Rhododendron 'Ginny Gee'

Rhododendron 'Dopey'

This is a garden-raised hybrid involving R. yakushimanum and it makes a compact, evergreen shrub with an upright habit. Dense, rounded clusters of bell-shaped, bright orange-red flowers with wavy-edged lobes open in the late spring.

Height: 6 ft (2 m)
Spread: 6 ft (2 m)
Hardiness: Zone 6

Rhododendron 'Egret'

This is a compact, garden-raised hybrid between R. racemosum 'White Lace' and R. campylogynum. It makes a free-flowering, dwarf shrub of neat habit with glossy, dark green leaves growing up to about 1 in (2.5 cm) long. Broad funnel-shaped, white-colored flowers, up to about ¾ in (2 cm) across, tinged with green, open in clusters 2¾ in (7 cm) across in the late spring.

Height: 24 in (60 cm)
Spread: 3 ft (1 m)
Hardiness: Zone 6

Rhododendron 'Elizabeth'

This is a popular, garden-raised hybrid between R. forrestii and R. griersonianum and ir makes a dense, spreading, evergreen shrub bearing small, red-stalked leaves up to about 3 in (8 cm) long. Clusters of bright red, funnel-shaped flowers open in mid-spring.

Height: 3 ft (1 m)
Spread: 6 ft (2 m)
Hardiness: Zone 6

Rhododendron 'Fastuosum Flore Pleno'

This is a compact, hardy hybrid that makes a large, evergreen shrub with dark matt-green leaves growing up to about 5 in (12 cm) long. Mauve-blue, funnel-shaped, double flowers, up to about 2¾ in (7 cm) across, flushed with yellow-brown inside, open in dense clusters in the late-spring to early-summer period.

Height: 13 ft (4 m)
Spread: 16 ft (5 m)
Hardiness: Zone 5

Rhododendron 'Fragrantissimum'

This is an attractive garden-raised hybrid between R. edgeworthii and R. formosum, making an open-branched, evergreen shrub with veined leaves. Large and extremely fragrant, funnel-shaped, white flowers, up to 4 in (10 cm) across, with a conspicuous, yellow flare inside, open in mid-spring. Suitable for a conservatory where it cannot be grown outdoors.

Height: 6 ft (2 m)
Spread: 6 ft (2 m)
Hardiness: Zone 8

Rhododendron 'Ginny Gee'

A dwarf, garden-raised hybrid between R. keiskei 'Yaku Fairy' and R. racemosum making a spreading, evergreen shrub with small, dark green leaves. The wide funnel-shaped, pale pink flowers, 1 in (2.5 cm) long, are deeper in bud, opening in mid-spring and fading to nearly white, edged with pink.

Height: 24 in (60 cm)
Spread: 35 in (90 cm)
Hardiness: Zone 5

Rhododendron 'Gomer Waterer'

A vigorous, tough, hardy hybrid making a compact, evergreen shrub with dark green leaves up to 5 in (12 cm) long. Funnel-shaped, white flowers, 3 in (8 cm) across, edged with mauve-pink and flushed yellow-brown in the center, open from mauve buds in dense, rounded clusters in early summer.

Height: 6 ft (2 m)
Spread: 8 ft (2.5 m)
Hardiness: Zone 5

Rhododendron 'Grumpy'

A garden-raised hybrid of
R. yakushimanum making a
spreading, evergreen shrub with dark
green leaves up to 3 in (8 cm) long.
The funnel-shaped flowers, 2 in (5
cm) across, cream flushed with pale
pink at the edges and spotted orange-
yellow, open in rounded clusters in
mid-spring.

Height: 3 ft (1 m)
Spread: 5 ft (1.5 m)
Hardiness: Zone 6

Rhododendron impeditum

A dwarf, evergreen shrub of compact,
upright habit with very small, blue-
green leaves up to about ⅓ in (1 cm)
long. The wide funnel-shaped, blue-
purple flowers, up to 1 in (2.5 cm)
across, open in small clusters in mid-
to late spring.

Native range: China
Height: 24 in (60 cm)
Spread: 24 in (60 cm)
Hardiness: Zone 4

Rhododendron 'Loderi King George'

This magnificent, garden-raised
hybrid between R. fortunei and
R. griffithianum makes a large,
evergreen shrub of open habit with
bold leaves up to 12 in (30 cm) long.
The white, funnel-shaped, fragrant
flowers, up to 6 in (15 cm) across,
open from pink buds in late springr.

Height: 13 ft (4 m)
Spread: 16 ft (5 m)
Hardiness: Zone 7

Rhododendron lutescens

This is a vigorous, evergreen shrub
with upright shoots and slender-
pointed, dark green leaves, bronze
when young, scaly beneath. Broad
funnel-shaped, pale yellow flowers,
up to 1 in (2.5 cm) across, open in
early to mid-spring.

Native range: China
Height: 10 ft (3 m)
Spread: 13 ft (4 m)
Hardiness: Zone 7

Rhododendron macabeanum

This is a large, evergreen, stoutly
branched shrub, sometimes treelike
in stature, and bears bold, glossy,
dark green leaves, up to about 12 in
(30 cm) long, densely covered with
pale brown hairs beneath. Clusters
of bell-shaped, pale to deep yellow
flowers, about 2¾ in (7 cm) long, and
blotched red-purple inside at the
base, open in the early to mid-spring
period.

Native range: NE India
Height: 20 ft (6 m) or more
Spread: 20 ft (6 m)
Hardiness: Zone 8

Rhododendron 'Morning Cloud'

This is a garden-raised hybrid of
R. yakushimanum that makes a
compact, evergreen shrub bearing
narrow, dark green leaves densely
covered in brown hairs beneath.
Dense clusters of white flowers,
flushed with pink, open from the late
spring to early summer.

Height: 5 ft (1.5 m)
Spread: 6 ft (2 m)
Hardiness: Zone 6

Rhododendron 'Mrs GW Leak'

This is a large-growing, compact and
vigorous, hardy hybrid with dark
matt-green leaves reaching up to 6 in
(15 cm) in length. The wide funnel-
shaped flowers are up to about 3 in

Rhododendron impeditum

(8 cm) across. Flowers are pale pink, flushed with deeper pink, and with a conspicuous flare of deep red-brown markings inside. They open in dense, conical clusters in late spring.

Height: 10 ft (3 m)
Spread: 13 ft (4 m)
Hardiness: Zone 7

Rhododendron 'Patty Bee'

This is a compact, garden-raised hybrid between R. *fletcherianum* and R. *keiskei* 'Yaku Fairy' that makes a vigorous, dwarf shrub with dark green leaves growing up to about 2 in (4.5 cm) long. The leaves turn bronze in winter. Pale yellow, funnel-shaped flowers, up to about 2 in (4.5 cm) across, with wavy margins, open in dense clusters in the early spring.

Height: 30 in (75 cm)
Spread: 3 ft (1 m)
Hardiness: Zone 6

Rhododendron 'Percy Wiseman'

This is a compact, garden-raised hybrid of R. *yakushimanum* that makes a small-growing, evergreen shrub bearing glossy dark green leaves up to about 3 in (7.5 cm) in length. The funnel-shaped flowers, up to about 2 in (5 cm) across, are cream, flushed with pink, and fade to creamy white. The flowers are borne in rounded clusters in mid- to late spring.

Height: 5 ft (1.5 m)
Spread: 6 ft (2 m)
Hardiness: Zone 6

Rhododendron 'Pink Pearl'

Rhododendron 'Pink Pearl'

This is an old and very popular, hardy hybrid that makes a strongly growing, evergreen shrub producing large, dark green leaves. The profusely borne, broad funnel-shaped, pink flowers, fading to nearly white, reaching up to about 4 in (10 cm) across, have wavy edges and open in large clusters in mid- to late spring.

Height: 10 ft (3 m)
Spread: 13 ft (4 m)
Hardiness: Zone 6

Rhododendron 'PJM'

This is a popular, garden-raised hybrid between *R. minus* and *R. dauricum*, valued in gardens for its great hardiness. It is a medium-sized, compact, evergreen shrub bearing dark green leaves that turn a bronze-purple color in winter. Clusters of bright, lavender pink, saucer-shaped flowers, up to 1½ in (4 cm) across, open in the early spring.

Height: 6 ft (2 m)
Spread: 5 ft (1.5 m)
Hardiness: Zone 4

Rhododendron ponticum

This species is largely represented in gardens by hybrids that make vigorous, large shrubs with dark green leaves up to about 8 in (20 cm) long. The large clusters of funnel-shaped, blue-purple flowers, marked with yellow-green spots, open in late spring and early summer.

Native range: S Spain, S Portugal, SW Asia
Height: 16 ft (5 m)
Spread: 16 ft (5 m)
Hardiness: Zone 5
Variant: 'Variegatum' is smaller, up to 10 ft (3 m) high, and has leaves edged with creamy white.

Rhododendron 'Praecox'

Valuable for its very early flowers, this semi-evergreen shrub is a garden-raised hybrid between *R. ciliatum* and *R. dauricum*. A compact and rather upright bush, it has glossy, dark green, aromatic leaves that are scaly beneath. Open, funnel-shaped, rose-purple flowers, up to about 2 in (5 cm) across, open in late winter and early spring.

Height: 5 ft (1.5 m)
Spread: 5 ft (1.5 m)
Hardiness: Zone 6

Rhododendron 'Princess Anne'

This is an evergreen, garden-raised hybrid between *R. hanceanum* and *R. keiskei* making a dense, spreading mound with light green leaves, 2½ in (6 cm) long, bronze when young. Funnel-shaped flowers, 1 in (3 cm) across, are green in bud but open pale yellow, and are faintly spotted with green.

Height: 24 in (60 cm)
Spread: 3 ft (1 m)
Hardiness: Zone 6

Rhododendron 'Ptarmigan'

This is a garden-raised hybrid between *R. leucaspis* and *R. orthocladum* var. *microleucum*

Rhododendron ponticum 'Variegatum'

forming a low-spreading, compact shrub with dark green, scaly leaves, ¾ in (1–2 cm) long. Pure white, saucer-shaped flowers, 1 in (3 cm) across, are profusely borne in small clusters in early to mid-spring.

Height: 24 in (60 cm)
Spread: 3 ft (1 m)
Hardiness: Zone 7

Rhododendron 'Purple Splendour'

This is an old and popular, vigorous, hardy hybrid making a compact shrub with dark green leaves to 6 in (15 cm) long. The wide funnel-shaped, wavy edged flowers, about 3 in (8 cm) across, are deep purple with conspicuous, nearly black, markings within, and open in late spring and early summer.

Height: 10 ft (3 m)
Spread: 13 ft (4 m)
Hardiness: Zone 6

Rhododendron 'Ramapo'

This is a very hardy, garden-raised hybrid between *R. fastigiatum* and *R. minus* that makes a dwarf, compact, evergreen shrub with blue-gray young foliage. Small, violet-blue flowers are profusely borne in small clusters in early to mid-spring.

Height: 24 in (60 cm)
Spread: 24 in (60 cm)
Hardiness: Zone 4

Rhododendron 'Sappho'

This is a vigorous, hardy hybrid that makes a large, dome-shaped, evergreen shrub with glossy, dark green leaves up to 7 in (18 cm) long. The wide funnel-shaped flowers, 3 in (8 cm) across, are mauve in bud, opening in mid-spring to pure white with a blotch of rich purple-black.

Height: 10 ft (3 m)
Spread: 10 ft (3 m)
Hardiness: Zone 6

Rhododendron 'Scarlet Wonder'

Rhododendron 'Scarlet Wonder'

A hardy, garden-raised hybrid between *R.* 'Essex Scarlet' and *R. forrestii* forming a compact mound of dense foliage, with glossy, green leaves up to 3 in (8 cm) long. Funnel-shaped, ruby-red flowers, 2 in (5 cm) long, with frilly edged lobes are borne in loose trusses at the ends of the shoots.

Height: 3 ft (1 m)
Spread: 5 ft (1.5 m)
Hardiness: Zone 6

Rhododendron 'Titian Beauty'

This is a garden-raised hybrid involving *R. yakushimanum* that makes a small evergreen shrub with a compact, rather upright habit. The dark green leaves have a thin layer of brown hairs on their undersurfaces. Clusters of waxy red, bell-shaped flowers open in the late spring and early summer.

Height: 6 ft (2 m)
Spread: 6 ft (2 m)
Hardiness: Zone 6

Rhododendron williamsianum

This dome-shaped, evergreen shrub has a dense habit with nearly rounded, dark green leaves, growing up to about 2 in (5 cm) in length. The leaves are blue-green beneath and bronze-colored when young. Open clusters of wide bell-shaped, pink or sometimes white-colored flowers, up to 2 in (5 cm) across, open in mid-spring.

Rhododendron williamsianum

Native range: China
Height: 4 ft (1.2 m)
Spread: 5 ft (1.5 m)
Hardiness: Zone 7

Rhododendron yakushimanum

This dense, evergreen shrub develops into a spreading dome-shaped specimen with thick, dark green leaves, white-felted when young, and covered beneath with a thick layer of pale brown hairs. Dense clusters of attractive white, funnel-shaped flowers, up to about 2 in (5 cm) across, open from deep pink buds in mid-spring.

Native range: Japan
Height: 4 ft (1.2 m)
Spread: 5 ft (1.5 m)
Hardiness: Zone 5

Rhododendron yakushimanum

Deciduous azaleas

The deciduous azaleas that make such striking shrubs generally reach about 6 ft (2 m) in height, with showy, usually fragrant flowers in spring and leaves often coloring in

Rhododendron 'Daviesii' (deciduous azalea)

Rhododendron 'Blaauw's Pink' (evergreen azalea)

Rhododendron 'Narcissiflorum'
(deciduous azalea)

Rhododendron 'Mother's Day'
(evergreen azalea)

autumn. They flower best in a bright position and can be grown in full sun. They are generally hardy to Zone 5.

R. **'Berryrose'** Bright salmon-pink flowers with a red tube, and young foliage that is bronze-colored.

R. **'Daviesii'** Large, very fragrant, white flowers, cream-colored and flushed with pink when they first open.

R. **'Gibraltar'** Large clusters of rich, orange-red, frilly edged flowers.

R. **'Homebush'** Dense, rounded clusters of bright pink, double flowers.

R. **'Klondyke'** Golden yellow flowers with a red flush, opening from yellow buds flushed red.

R. **luteum** Very fragrant, bright yellow flowers.

R. **'Narcissiflorum'** Pale yellow, very fragrant double flowers in dense clusters.

R. **'Silver Slipper'** Creamy white flowers flushed with yellow, pink-tinged in bud.

R. **'Strawberry Ice'** Pale pink flowers, flushed deep pink, with a yellow flare.

Evergreen azaleas

Generally of compact habit and growing to about 3 ft (1 m) tall, these are excellent for mass planting and prefer light shade, except where summers are cool. The foliage often turns bronze in winter.

R. **'Addy Wery'** Deep vermilion-red flowers.

R. **'Amoenum'** Bright rose-purple, double flowers.

R. **'Blaauw's Pink'** Salmon-pink flowers.

R. **'Blue Danube'** Large violet-purple flowers.

R. **'Hatsugiri'** Compact, with profusely borne, magenta-purple flowers.

R. **'Hino-crimson'** Profuse, bright red flowers.

R. **'Hinode-giri'** Clusters of bright crimson flowers.

R. **'Hinomayo'** Compact, with profusely borne, clear pink flowers.

R. **'Kirin'** Rich pink, double flowers, silvery pink on the outside.

R. **'Madame van Hecke'** Small, rose-pink flowers.

R. **'Mother's Day'** Deep crimson, often semi-double flowers.

R. **nakaharae** Dwarf and spreading, to 12 in (30 cm) tall, with orange-red to pink flowers. (Zone 7)

R. **'Orange Beauty'** Bushy, spreading habit with orange-red, frilly edged flowers.

R. **'Squirrel'** Dwarf and compact, with deep reddish-orange flowers.

R. **'Vuyk's Rosyred'** Large, deep rose pink flowers with a deeper flush in the center.

R. **'Vuyk's Scarlet'** Large, bright crimson flowers, and a low, spreading habit.

Rhus glabra

Rhodotypos
Rosaceae

The single species in this small genus is a deciduous shrub with opposite leaves, and is grown for its showy, white flowers, which can open very early in the year given a warm spring.

This species is suitable for the shrub border and will grow in any good, well-drained soil, and does best in a sunny position. Little pruning is generally needed, but some of the shoots that have flowered can be cut back after flowering.

Rhodotypos scandens
This deciduous shrub is upright at first and later develops arching shoots. The dark green and sharply toothed leaves are taper-pointed and have conspicuous, parallel veins. White, four-petalled flowers with yellow stamens in their centers, open at the ends of the shoots in late spring and early summer, sometimes earlier, followed by clusters of small, glossy black, persistent fruits.

Native range: China, Japan
Height: 6 ft (2 m)
Spread: 8 ft (2.5 m)
Hardiness: Zone 4

Rhus
Anacardiaceae

The sumacs are a large and widely distributed genus made up of deciduous and evergreen shrubs and trees, and occasionally climbers as well.

The following species are grown for their foliage, which colors up richly in autumn, and for their often conspicuous fruit clusters. They are suitable for any well-drained soil in full sun, but they are generally too invasive for the border—however, *R. glabra* and *R. typhina* are suitable as specimen plants. Planting them in a lawn that is cut regularly will prevent them spreading. Remove suckers as necessary, and cut back hard in spring to rejuvenate them or to encourage the production of large, showy leaves.

Rhus aromatica

This is a spreading, deciduous shrub with dark green to blue-green, aromatic foliage. The leaves are divided into three sharply toothed leaflets and turn orange-red in autumn. Upright spikes of small, yellow flowers open in spring, and these are followed by clusters of small, red fruits. It does best in regions with hot summers.

Common name: Fragrant sumac
Native range: E North America
Height: 5 ft (1.5 m)
Spread: 8 ft (2.5 m)
Hardiness: Zone 3

Rhus glabra

This is a vigorous, sturdily branched, and upright shrub with stout, bloomy shoots that spreads by suckers. It has dark green leaves with numerous, up to 31, sharply toothed leaflets that turn brilliant orange- to purple-red in autumn. Small, yellow-green flowers open in large, conical clusters at the ends of the shoots during summer and these are followed by red-ripening fruits.

Common name: Smooth sumac
Native range: North America
Height: 10 ft (3 m)
Spread: 10 ft (3 m)
Hardiness: Zone 3

Rhus typhina

This is a vigorous, thicket-forming, deciduous shrub, sometimes a tree, with stout, velvety shoots. The bold, dark green leaves are divided up into

Rhus typhina 'Dissecta'

as many as 27 leaflets, and leaves turn to brilliant shades of orange and red in autumn. Dense heads of small, yellow-green flowers in summer ripen to conical, long-persistent, matted clusters of red fruits.

Common name: Staghorn sumac
Native range: E North America
Height: 20 ft (6 m)
Spread: 16 ft (5 m)
Hardiness: Zone 4
Variants: 'Dissecta' is lower-growing with deeply lobed leaflets. It is sometimes known as 'Laciniata'.

Ribes
Grossulariaceae

The currants are a genus of some 150 species of deciduous and evergreen, sometimes spiny shrubs. They are widely distributed mainly in temperate regions of the Northern Hemisphere, with some species found in South America.

While the ornamental species are grown principally for their flowers, others (such as the gooseberry, redcurrant, and blackcurrant) have edible fruits. Suitable for any reasonably good, well-drained soil, they do best in general if given a position in full sun.

Ribes alpinum

Ribes alpinum

This compact, deciduous shrub has bright green, three- to five-lobed leaves. Tiny, yellow-green flowers are borne in dense clusters in spring, males and females usually on separate plants. Females bear small, glossy, red berries. This species will grow well in sun or shade.

Common name: Alpine currant
Native range: Europe
Height: 4 ft (1.2 m) or more
Spread: 5 ft (1.5 m)
Hardiness: Zone 2
Variant: 'Aureum' produces foliage that is bright yellow when young.

Ribes laurifolium

This is a low-growing and spreading, evergreen shrub bearing dark green, leathery leaves that grow up to 5 in (12 cm) long. Large, drooping clusters of pale greenish-white flowers open in late winter and early spring. The male and female flowers are borne on separate plants, the males distinguished by being more showy. It is an excellent groundcover plant, especially for shady places.

Native range: China
Height: 3 ft (1 m)

Spread: 10 ft (3 m)
Hardiness: Zone 8

Ribes odoratum

This is a clump-forming, deciduous shrub with upright shoots that become arching with age. The bright green, deeply lobed leaves turn to yellow, red, and purple in autumn. Drooping clusters of clove-scented, bright yellow flowers open in mid- to late spring.

Common name: Clove currant
Native range: C United States of America
Height: 6 ft (2 m)
Spread: 8 ft (2.5 m)
Hardiness: Zone 4

Ribes sanguineum

This is a vigorous, deciduous shrub of a dense, upright habit with aromatic, three- to five-lobed leaves, useful as a specimen shrub, in a border, or as a hedging plant. Drooping clusters of pink flowers open in spring, and these are followed by blue-black, bloomy berries. To prune, cut some of the older shoots to the base when flowering has finished.

Common name: Winter currant
Native range: W North America
Height: 8 ft (2.5 m)
Spread: 6 ft (2 m)
Hardiness: Zone 5
Variants: 'Brocklebankii' produces yellow foliage and pale pink flowers. 'King Edward VII' has a spreading habit and produces deep red-colored flowers. 'Pulborough Scarlet' is vigorous and upright, with deep red flowers. 'White Icicle' produces white-colored flowers.

Ribes speciosum

This vigorous, upright, deciduous shrub has red, bristly shoots and small, glossy green, three- to five-lobed leaves. Slender, pendulous, bright red, fuchsia-like flowers open

Ribes sanguineum 'Pulborough Scarlet'

in small clusters in mid- to late spring. It can be trained effectively against a sunny wall.

Common name: Fuchsia-flowered currant
Native range: California
Height: 8 ft (2.5 m) or more
Spread: 6 ft (2 m)
Hardiness: Zone 7

Robinia
Leguminosae

This is a small genus of only about ten species of deciduous trees and shrubs, all natives of North America. They have leaves divided into numerous leaflets and pendulous clusters of pealike flowers.

Species are suitable for any well-drained soil and they are particularly useful on dry soils. They all thrive in a sunny position. *R. pseudoacacia* can produce invasive suckers.

Robinia hispida

This is a deciduous shrub with an open habit that spreads by sending out suckers. The blue-green, bristly stalked leaves are divided up into as many as 13 leaflets, and leaves are borne on densely bristly shoots. Drooping clusters of large, pealike, deep pink flowers open in late spring and early summer. However, fruit is rarely produced.

Common name: Rose acacia
Native range: SE United States of America
Height: 10 ft (3 m)
Spread: 13 ft (4 m)
Hardiness: Zone 5

Robinia pseudoacacia 'Frisia'

Robinia hispida

Robinia pseudoacacia

This vigorous, deciduous tree of broadly columnar habit often has spiny branches and bears blue-green leaves divided up into as many as 21 leaflets. Drooping clusters of fragrant, white, pealike flowers, blotched yellow-green, hang from the shoots in early to midsummer, and these are followed later in the year by dark brown pods.

Common name: Black locust
Native range: SE United States of America
Height: 80 ft (25 m)
Spread: 50 ft (15 m)
Hardiness: Zone 4
Variants: 'Frisia' is a smaller tree with pale yellow foliage. 'Tortuosa' is a small, slow-growing tree with conspicuously twisted shoots.

Robinia x slavinii 'Hillieri'

This is a garden-raised hybrid of *R. pseudoacacia* and it makes a vigorous, rounded tree with spreading, slightly bristly shoots and dark green leaves bearing up to 19 leaflets. Drooping clusters of fragrant, lilac-pink flowers hang from the shoots in late spring.

Romneya coulteri 'White Cloud'

Height: 33 ft (10 m)
Spread: 33 ft (10 m)
Hardiness: Zone 5

Romneya
Papaveraceae

The single species in this genus is a subshrub grown for its strikingly large flowers. Suitable for a border, it may need restricting as it can spread vigorously by underground stems. In cold areas it can be grown against a sunny wall.

Grow in any good, well-drained soil in full sun. The old shoots can be cut back to the ground in spring.

Romneya coulteri

A vigorous, suckering subshrub with upright, bloomy shoots with deeply cut, blue-gray leaves. Large, white, poppy-like flowers, 5 in (12 cm) across, have petals with crinkled edges and a conspicuous central boss of golden yellow stamens. They open singly at the ends of the young shoots over a long period during summer.

Common name: Matilija poppy
Native range: California, N Mexico
Height: 6 ft (2 m)
Spread: 16 ft (5 m) or more
Hardiness: Zone 7
Variant: 'White Cloud' produces very large flowers and spreads vigorously.

Rosa
Rosaceae

The roses are some of the most widely grown of all woody plants. The 150 or so species are deciduous or sometimes evergreen shrubs, widely distributed in temperate regions of the Northern Hemisphere. With often spiny or bristly stems and leaves divided into several leaflets, the wild species have flowers with normally five petals, and these are often followed by ornamental fruits (hips). Most roses prefer a good, moist but well-drained soil rich in organic matter and a position in full sun.

The vast number of garden hybrids have given a diverse array of plants suitable for many purposes in the garden, from specimen shrubs, hedging, or bedding, or growing up a wall, over a pergola, or into trees. Others are suitable for ground cover or for growing in containers.

The species roses and their immediate hybrids are often left unpruned, but they can be cut back as necessary in late summer after flowering, or in late winter if they continue flowering into the autumn. Most other roses benefit from regular pruning. The various methods are discussed below under the different groups to which roses are assigned.

All roses that are planted when they are dormant, with the exception of climbers, should be pruned hard immediately to ensure that the subsequent growth breaks from the base.

Some roses are offered under selling names or trademarks. These are shown without quotation marks. If the plant also has a cultivar name, then this is given afterwards in parentheses.

Alba

These old hybrids are vigorous and hardy, usually sparsely spiny shrubs with gray-green foliage and white to pink, usually fully double, fragrant flowers. Useful as specimens or for hedging. Prune in late summer after flowering by cutting old shoots back by about one-third. Any long shoots can also be cut back in autumn. To renovate, after flowering or in spring, cut all the old shoots to the base, and cut back vigorous young shoots by one-third.

Bourbon

A group of old hybrids making vigorous, sometimes climbing, shrubs. The usually double flowers are borne in summer through to autumn, so they should be pruned in the dormant season. Prune as for Alba roses, but in late winter, when any thin and overcrowded shoots should also be removed.

Centifolia

These are old hybrids involving the Alba roses that make open shrubs with thorny stems and large, usually double, fragrant flowers. Prune immediately after flowering, as for Alba roses.

Climbers

These are vigorous shrubs with long, thorny shoots useful for training against a wall or onto a pergola. Do not cut back on planting. Provide a support of wires and tie in lateral shoots to these as they develop. When established, prune as necessary to restrict growth. Cut some older stems back to young, developing shoots. When mature, the oldest stems can be cut back to the ground.

Cluster-flowered (Floribunda)

Vigorous, upright shrubs with single to double, clustered flowers borne over a long period from summer to autumn. Useful for bedding and for a border. Cut out any dead or diseased wood during the growing season and dead-head regularly. Prune in late winter by cutting out any weak or dead shoots and reducing other shoots to about 12 in (30 cm). Some have climbing forms.

Damask

This group of old hybrids makes open shrubs with thorny stems and semidouble or double, white to pink flowers. Prune as for Alba roses.

Gallica

This is an old group of hybrids deriving from R. gallica, with single to fully double, white to pink flowers. Prune as for Alba roses.

Ground cover

These are low-growing shrubs, all with a spreading to trailing habit, and with long, prickly shoots and profuse, single to double flowers. They are shrubs ideal for trailing over low walls and banks. Prune as necessary in late winter to restrict growth.

Hybrid Musk

This is a group of vigorous hybrids with clustered, usually fragrant flowers produced from summer through to autumn. They are useful for hedging. Prune in late winter by removing any dead or weak shoots and by cutting some of the oldest shoots back to the base. Reduce the remaining shoots by about one-third.

Large-flowered (Hybrid Tea)

These are vigorous, upright shrubs with large, usually double, and fragrant flowers. The flowers are borne singly or in small clusters in summer and autumn. They are mainly used for bedding. Prune in late winter as for cluster-flowered roses, cutting stems back to 8 in (20 cm). Some have climbing forms.

Pimpinellifolia hybrid

Also known as Burnet or Scotch roses, these hybrids make vigorous, suckering shrubs deriving from R. pimpinellifolia, with small leaves that often color well in autumn. Flowers are single to semidouble, white to pink or red-purple in color, sometimes yellow. To prune, cut the stems back lightly after flowering. They are suitable for bedding or for planting in a shrub border.

Polyantha

These are compact, free-flowering shrubs suitable for bedding or growing in containers, producing clustered, single to double flowers. Prune shrubs in late winter, as for large-flowered roses.

Rambler

These vigorous shrubs have long, thorny shoots bearing profuse clusters of small, usually unscented flowers. Useful for growing on walls, fences, or into trees and as weeping standards. Given space, they can be left to grow freely. Prune on planting by cutting back to about 16 in (40 cm). Cut back after flowering to restrict growth, and remove some of the old shoots by cutting back to

Rosa 'Albéric Barbier'

ground level to encourage new growth from the base.

Rugosa hybrid

These vigorous hybrids of *R. rugosa* have distinctive and prominently veined leaves that often color up well in autumn. The usually large, single to semi-double flowers are often followed by conspicuous fruits. After flowering, cut some of the older shoots right back to the base and reduce the length of the remaining shoots slightly by cutting out the tips.

Shrub

These are vigorous, modern hybrids with single to semidouble flowers. The flowers open in summer and again usually in autumn. They are useful shrubs for the border, but they can also do service as bedding plants. Prune them after they have finished flowering by lightly cutting back shoots. Remove some of the older stems of any plants that have become congested, cutting them right back to the base.

Rosa 'Abraham Darby'

This is a vigorous and bushy shrub rose with large, double, fragrant, apricot-pink flowers growing up to about 4–5 in (11 cm) across. The flowers open from summer through to autumn.

Height: 5 ft (1.5 m)
Spread: 5 ft (1.5 m)
Hardiness: Zone 5

Rosa 'Albéric Barbier'

This is a strong-growing and popular rambler, a hybrid of *R. wichurana*, with handsome, glossy foliage. Double, fragrant, creamy white flowers, 3 in (8 cm) across, open in the summer.

Height: 16 ft (5 m)
Spread: 10 ft (3 m)
Hardiness: Zone 5

Rosa 'Albertine'

This is an extremely vigorous rambler—a hybrid of *R. wichurana*—with strongly growing, thorny shoots

and glossy, green foliage that is
bronze-colored when young. The
profuse and very fragrant, double,
pale pink flowers, up to 3 in (8 cm)
across, are flushed with orange when
they first open.

Height: 16 ft (5 m)
Spread: 10 ft (3 m)
Hardiness: Zone 5

Rosa 'American Pillar'

This is a vigorous rambler deriving
from R. wichurana with long, stout,
very thorny shoots and large, glossy,
green leaves. In summer, the shrub
bears large clusters of single, red
flowers, growing up to about 2 in
(5 cm) across. Flowers are white in
the center, fading to deep pink.

Height: 16 ft (5 m)
Spread: 10 ft (3 m)
Hardiness: Zone 5

Rosa 'Arthur Bell'

This cluster-flowered rose produces
glossy, green foliage. The semidouble,
yellow or creamy flowers, up to about
3 in (8 cm) across, are fragrant and
have a center of golden-colored
stamens. Flowers open from the
summer through to autumn.

Height: 3 ft (1 m)
Spread: 30 in (75 cm)
Hardiness: Zone 5

Rosa 'Ballerina'

This is a bushy Polyantha type rose
with a good, compact habit. The
shrub bears large sprays of
individually small, single, pink-
colored flowers, about 1 in (3 cm)
across, each with a white center. It is
a useful plant, equally suitable for
growing in containers or planted out
for bedding.

Height: 4 ft (1.2 m)
Spread: 3 ft (1 m)
Hardiness: Zone 5

Rosa banksiae

This is a vigorous, evergreen climber
with long, slender shoots and light
green leaves that are composed of up
to seven leaflets. A useful plant
where children may play, as its shoots
are thornless. Flowers, which may be
white or yellow, single or double,
open in late spring. It prefers a
Mediterranean climate and in colder
regions it benefits from being grown
up a sun-facing wall.

Native range: China
Height: 33 ft (10 m)
Spread: 20 ft (6 m)
Hardiness: Zone 7
Variant: 'Lutea' produces attractive,
double, yellow flowers.

Rosa 'Blanc Double de Coubert'

This is a vigorous, rugosa hybrid
with densely prickly shoots and
dark green, deeply veined leaves.
The large, loosely semidouble, pure
white, strongly fragrant flowers, up to
3 in (8 cm) across, have conspicuous
yellow stamens and open from
summer through to autumn. The
flowers are sometimes followed by
large, orange-red fruits.

Height: 5 ft (1.5 m)
Spread: 4 ft (1.2 m)
Hardiness: Zone 2

Rosa Blessings

This vigorous, large-flowered rose
produces dark green foliage, and
fragrant, double, salmon-pink flowers
that open from the summer through
to autumn.

Height: 3 ft (1 m)
Spread: 30 in (75 cm)
Hardiness: Zone 5

Rosa Blue Moon ('Tannacht')

This is a large-flowered rose with
dark green foliage. It bears fragrant,

double, lilac-colored flowers, up to 4 in (10 cm) across, from summer through to the autumn.

Height: 3 ft (1 m)
Spread: 30 in (75 cm)
Hardiness: Zone 5

Rosa 'Bobbie James'

This is a vigorous rambler with lush, bright green foliage, red when young. The white flowers, in large clusters of semidouble, very fragrant, blooms, up to 2 in (5 cm) across, have centers of white stamens and open in summer from cream buds.

Height: 33 ft (10 m)
Spread: 26 ft (8 m)
Hardiness: Zone 5

Rosa 'Boule de Neige'

This vigorous, upright, and sparsely thorny Bourbon rose has dark green, leathery leaves. The fully double and strongly fragrant flowers are globular in shape, opening white in summer and autumn from red-flushed buds.

Height: 4 ft (1.2 m)
Spread: 35 in (90 cm)
Hardiness: Zone 4

Rosa 'Buff Beauty'

This is an extremely beautiful Hybrid Musk rose with a spreading habit and arching shoots bearing dark green leaves that are bronze when young. Clusters of large, fully double, buff-yellow to apricot, fragrant flowers, up to about 3½ in (9 cm) across, open from summer to autumn.

Height: 5 ft (1.5 m)
Spread: 5 ft (1.5 m)
Hardiness: Zone 5

Rosa 'Cardinal de Richelieu'

This compact Gallica rose has slender, almost thornless shoots and dark green, occasionally purple-edged, foliage. The sweetly fragrant, fully double, rounded blooms have rich purple-red, velvety petals and the flowers open in clusters during the summer.

Height: 4 ft (1.2 m)
Spread: 35 in (90 cm)
Hardiness: Zone 4

Rosa 'Cécile Brünner'

This slender-stemmed, upright Polyantha rose produces small, dark green, rather sparse leaves. Pale pink, double, and delicately scented flowers, up to about 1½ in (4 cm) across, open in clusters, on long stalks, during summer and autumn. Another form, 'Climbing Cécile Brünner', is similar but is a vigorous climber.

Height: 4 ft (1.2 m)
Spread: 24 in (60 cm)
Hardiness: Zone 5

Rosa 'Céleste'

This dense and vigorous Alba rose has an upright habit with gray-green foliage and sparsely prickly shoots. Soft pink, loosely double, sweetly fragrant flowers, up to 3 in (8 cm) across, open in summer.

Height: 6 ft (2 m)
Spread: 4 ft (1.2 m)
Hardiness: Zone 5

Rosa x centifolia

The Centifolia roses are old, complex hybrids. The typical form makes a vigorous shrub with arching, spiny shoots and matt-green foliage. Fully double, fragrant, pink flowers, up to 3½ in (9 cm) across, and with incurved petals, open in summer.

Common name: Cabbage rose
Height: 5 ft (1.5 m)
Spread: 5 ft (1.5 m)
Hardiness: Zone 5

Rosa 'Blanc Double de Coubert'

Rosa x *centifolia* 'Muscosa'

Variants: 'Cristata' (crested moss rose) produces conspicuous, green, mosslike crests on its sepals. 'Muscosa' (moss rose) has shoots and sepals covered in mosslike bristles.

Rosa Chinatown

This is a vigorous, cluster-flowered rose of an upright habit that produces dark green leaves. The large, double, very fragrant flowers, growing up to about 4 in (10 cm) across, are yellow, sometimes flushed with pink or red, and open in the summer and autumn.

Height: 5 ft (1.5 m)
Spread: 3 ft (1 m)
Hardiness: Zone 5

Rosa Constance Spry

Height: 20 ft (6 m)
Spread: 10 ft (3 m)
Hardiness: Zone 5

Rosa 'Climbing Iceberg'

A climbing, cluster-flowered rose with glossy, light green foliage and almost thornless shoots. Pure white, double flowers, up to 3 in (8 cm) across, open over an extended period from summer to autumn.

Rosa Compassion

This is a climbing, large-flowered rose that produces glossy, dark green foliage. The large, double, fragrant flowers are salmon-pink flushed apricot and yellow, and they open from summer through to the autumn.

Height: 10 ft (3 m)
Spread: 6 ft (2 m)
Hardiness: Zone 5

Rosa 'Complicata'

This is a vigorous Gallica rose that has arching shoots and matt gray-green foliage. The large, single, bright pink flowers, up to about 4–5 in (11 cm) across, have paler centers and a dense cluster of yellow stamens. Flowers are borne in clusters in midsummer. It can be grown as a specimen or trained on a pillar or as a climber.

Height: 10 ft (3 m)
Spread: 6 ft (2 m)
Hardiness: Zone 5

Rosa Constance Spry ('Austance')

This is an extremely beautiful shrub rose with large, gray-green leaves produced on arching, thorny shoots. The large, slightly nodding, fragrant, double flowers, which grow up to about 5 in (12 cm) across, are a soft pink color and open in midsummer. It can be trained as a climber, if required.

Height: 6 ft (2 m) or more
Spread: 5 ft (1.5 m)
Hardiness: Zone 5

Rosa 'Cornelia'

This is a vigorous Hybrid Musk rose with glossy, dark green leaves that are bronze when young. Its small, double, and sweetly fragrant flowers, growing up to about 2 in (5 cm) across, are an apricot-pink color and are attractively flushed with shades of a deeper pink. The flowers are borne in small clusters during the summer and larger clusters of flowers are produced in the autumn.

Height: 5 ft (1.5 m)
Spread: 5 ft (1.5 m)
Hardiness: Zone 5

Rosa 'Crimson Shower'

This is a vigorous, rambling rose bearing glossy, bright green foliage. The small, scented, semidouble flowers, up to about 1 in (3 cm) across, are a deep crimson color that does not fade with age. The flowers open in large, pendulous clusters over a long period during the summer and autumn.

Height: 13 ft (4 m)
Spread: 10 ft (3 m)
Hardiness: Zone 5

Rosa Danse du Feu

This is a climbing rose producing lush, dark green foliage. Double, bright scarlet flowers, up to 3 in (8 cm) across are profusely borne, opening from the summer through to autumn.

Height: 13 ft (4 m)
Spread: 10 ft (3 m)
Hardiness: Zone 5

Rosa 'Deep Secret'

This is a vigorous, large-flowered rose with glossy, dark green foliage. The large, fully double, and fragrant flowers, up to 4 in (10 cm) across, are deep crimson in color and open from summer through to autumn.

Height: 3 ft (1 m)
Spread: 30 in (75 cm)
Hardiness: Zone 5

Rosa 'Dorothy Perkins'

This is a popular and well-known, vigorous rambler—a hybrid of R. wichurana—with glossy, dark green foliage. Small, double, clear pink, and slightly fragrant flowers, about ¼ in (2 cm) across, are profusely borne in large, drooping clusters in late summer.

Height: 10 ft (3 m)
Spread: 8 ft (2.5 m)
Hardiness: Zone 5

Rosa filipes 'Kiftsgate'

Rosa 'Fantin-Latour'

This is a vigorous Centifolia hybrid and it produces dark green-colored foliage. The large, soft pink, double flowers, growing up to about 4 in (10 cm) across, have strongly folded petals and a small, green center. The flowers, which open in the summer months, have the extra benefit of being richly scented.

Height: 5 ft (1.5 m)
Spread: 4 ft (1.2 m)
Hardiness: Zone 4

Rosa 'Felicia'

This vigorous Hybrid Musk rose is among the very best of its type, making a rounded bush with rich green foliage. The loosely double, sweetly fragrant flowers, up to about 3 in (8 cm) across, open a deep pink color, but this pales as the blooms age. Flowers open in large clusters in summer and autumn. It can be used for hedging.

Height: 5 ft (1.5 m)
Spread: 6 ft (2 m)
Hardiness: Zone 5

Rosa 'Félicité Perpetué'

This rambler, a hybrid involving *R. sempervirens*, has nearly evergreen, dark green leaves that emerge from sparsely thorny shoots. Double, creamy white-colored flowers, flushed pink, up to about 1½ in (4 cm) across, open in summer.

Height: 16 ft (5 m)
Spread: 10 ft (3 m)
Hardiness: Zone 6

Rosa filipes

This vigorous species is a strong-growing climber with glossy, rather pale green leaves on arching, thorny shoots. Fragrant, white flowers, 1 in (2.5 cm) across, open in clusters from cream buds in late summer, followed by orange, later scarlet, fruits.

Native range: China
Height: 33 ft (10 m)
Spread: 20 ft (6 m)
Hardiness: Zone 5
Variant: 'Kiftsgate' is the most popular form. It is extremely vigorous with large flower clusters.

Rosa Fragrant Cloud ('Tanduft')

This large-flowered rose produces dark green foliage. It flowers are double, growing up to 3 in (8 cm) across, deep scarlet in color and very fragrant. The flowers open from summer through to the autumn.

Height: 3 ft (1 m)
Spread: 30 in (75 cm)
Hardiness: Zone 5

Rosa 'Fru Dagmar Hastrup'

This dense and bushy Rugosa hybrid has densely prickly shoots and deeply veined leaves that turn yellow in autumn. The large and sweetly fragrant, clear, silvery pink flowers, up to about 3½ in (9 cm) across, have a center of yellow stamens and open in clusters during summer. The flowers are followed by conspicuous, bright red fruits.

Height: 4 ft (1.2 m)
Spread: 5 ft (1.5 m)
Hardiness: Zone 2

Rosa 'Frühlingsgold'

This vigorous Pimpinellifolia hybrid has arching, spiny shoots and small, dark green leaves. The semidouble flowers, up to 4 in (10 cm) across, are very fragrant and open a rich golden

Rosa 'Fru Dagmar Hastrup'

yellow in early summer, fading to creamy white with age.

Height: 6 ft (2 m)
Spread: 8 ft (2.5 m)
Hardiness: Zone 4

Rosa 'Frühlingsmorgen'

A Pimpinellifolia hybrid of open, upright habit and with dark gray-green leaves. The single, strongly fragrant flowers, 4 in (10 cm) across, are rich pink with a yellow center and maroon stamens. They open in early summer, often with a second flush in autumn, and are followed by red-purple fruits.

Height: 6 ft (2 m)
Spread: 5 ft (1.5 m)
Hardiness: Zone 4

Rosa gallica

This species makes a suckering shrub with slender, upright stems and leaves with up to seven leaflets. The single, deep pink to red, fragrant flowers, growing to about 3 in (8 cm) across, open singly or in small clusters in summer, and these are followed by red fruits. It is mainly represented in gardens by the forms listed below.

Rosa 'Geranium'

and have paler centers, each with a cluster of yellow stamens. The flowers open in small clusters in summer, and these are followed by rounded, red fruits.

Synonym: *Rosa rubrifolia*
Native range: Europe
Height: 8 ft (2.5 m)
Spread: 6 m (2 m)
Hardiness: Zone 2

Common name: French rose
Native range: Europe, W Asia
Height: 4 ft (1.2 m)
Spread: 3 ft (1 m)
Hardiness: Zone 5
Variants: 'Officinalis' (apothecaries' rose) is bushy and upright, with gray-green foliage and very fragrant, semidouble, deep pinkish-red flowers. 'Versicolor' ('Rosa Mundi') has pale pink, semidouble flowers streaked with red.

Rosa 'Geranium'

This hybrid of *R. moyesii* develops into a compact, bushy shrub with arching branches bearing bright green leaves. The single, bright red flowers, up to 2½ in (6 cm) across, have centers of golden stamens and open during summer. They are followed by bright orange-red, bottle-shaped fruits.

Height: 8 ft (2.5 m)
Spread: 8 ft (2.5 m)
Hardiness: Zone 5

Rosa glauca

This is a vigorous and upright shrub with arching, bloomy shoots and purple-gray leaves. The shrub produces single, deep pink flowers, reaching up to 1½ in (4 cm) across,

Rosa 'Gloire de Dijon'

This is an old and popular climbing rose of vigorous growth. It produces purple shoots bearing glossy, dark green leaves that are bronze when young. The large and very fragrant double flowers, reaching up to 4 in (10 cm) across, are pale apricot in color and open in summer. There is a repeat flowering in autumn.

Height: 13 ft (4 m)
Spread: 10 ft (3 m)
Hardiness: Zone 5

Rosa 'Golden Wings'

This is a popular and compact shrub rose of bushy, upright habit with light green foliage on prickly shoots. The large, single, sweetly fragrant, pale yellow flowers are deeper colored in the center and have golden stamens. They start to open in early summer and continue until autumn.

Height: 5 ft (1.5 m)
Spread: 5 ft (1.5 m)
Hardiness: Zone 5

Rosa 'Graham Thomas'

This vigorous shrub rose has arching shoots bearing bright green foliage. Its fully double, fragrant, rich yellow flowers are up to about 4–5 in (11 cm) across and open from summer through to the autumn.

Height: 4 ft (1.2 m)
Spread: 4 ft (1.2 m)
Hardiness: Zone 5

Rosa glauca

Rosa 'Grandpa Dickson'

This is a large-flowered rose with glossy, green foliage. The very large, clear yellow, double flowers, growing up to about 7 in (18 cm) across, are well-shaped with a high center and are richly fragrant. Flushed with pink on the outer petals, the flowers open freely during the summer and autumn season.

Height: 35 in (90 cm)
Spread: 24 in (60 cm)
Hardiness: Zone 5

Rosa Heritage ('Ausblush')

This is a bushy and vigorous shrub rose producing glossy, dark green foliage. The double, pale pink flowers, up to about 4–5 in (11 cm) across, are deeper colored in their centers and have a strong scent that is reminiscent of lemons. They are freely borne during the summer and into autumn.

Height: 4 ft (1.2 m)
Spread: 4 ft (1.2 m)
Hardiness: Zone 5

Rosa 'Louise Odier'

This vigorous Bourbon rose has slender, arching shoots and gray-green foliage. The double, bright pink, camellia-like flowers, about 3½ in (9 cm) across, are richly fragrant and are heavily borne in summer and autumn.

Height: 5 ft (1.5 m)
Spread: 4 ft (1.2 m)
Hardiness: Zone 4

Rosa 'Madame Alfred Carrière'

This is a climber producing light green-colored foliage from sparsely thorny shoots. The white, fully double flowers, flushed pale pink, are about 2½ in (6 cm) across, and open over a long period from summer through to autumn.

Height: 13 ft (4 m)
Spread: 10 ft (3 m)
Hardiness: Zone 5

Rosa 'Madame Grégoire Staechelin'

A vigorous climber with arching shoots and dark green foliage. The double, clear pink flowers, 5 in (12 cm) across, are flushed deep pink. Flowers open early summer, followed by orange-red fruits.

Height: 16 ft (5 m)
Spread: 10 ft (3 m)
Hardiness: Zone 5

Rosa 'Madame Hardy'

An old but popular Damask rose making a vigorous bush with bright green foliage. The pure white, fragrant, fully double flowers, 4 in (10 cm) across, have a green eye and open during summer.

Height: 5 ft (1.5 m)
Spread: 5 ft (1.5 m)
Hardiness: Zone 4

Rosa 'Madame Isaac Pereire'

This is a vigorous Bourbon rose with arching, sometimes climbing, shoots and dark green foliage. The very large and fully double, rich purple-pink flowers, reaching about 6 in (15 cm) across, are strongly fragrant and open from summer through to autumn.

Height: 8 ft (2.5 m)
Spread: 6 ft (2 m)
Hardiness: Zone 4

Rosa 'Maiden's Blush'

This vigorous Alba-type rose produces arching shoots bearing blue-gray foliage. The fully double, pale pink flowers, growing up to about 2¾ in (7 cm) across, are extremely fragrant and open in large clusters from creamy buds in the midsummer season.

Height: 5 ft (1.5 m)
Spread: 5 ft (1.5 m)
Hardiness: Zone 4

Rosa Margaret Merril ('Harkuly')

This is a cluster-flowered rose with a bushy, upright habit bearing dark green foliage. The pale pink to almost white, double flowers, reaching up to about 4 in (10 cm) across, are fragrant and open from silvery pink buds in clusters from summer through to the autumn.

Height: 4 ft (1.2 m)
Spread: 35 in (90 cm)
Hardiness: Zone 5

Rosa Mary Rose ('Ausmary')

This is a vigorous and bushy shrub rose with dense foliage. The deep pink-colored, double, highly fragrant flowers, growing up to about 3½ in (9 cm) across, open from summer through to autumn.

Height: 4 ft (1.2 m)
Spread: 4 ft (1.2 m)
Hardiness: Zone 5

Rosa 'Mermaid'

This beautiful, nearly evergreen climber, is a hybrid of *R. bracteata* and has strongly spiny, red-brown shoots and glossy, dark green foliage. The large, single, fragrant, yellow flowers, up to 4 in (10 cm) across, have centers of deep yellow stamens and open from summer to autumn. It is best grown against a sunny wall.

Height: 26 ft (8 m)
Spread: 20 ft (6 m)
Hardiness: Zone 7

Rosa moyesii

This vigorous species has arching, spiny shoots and dark green leaves that are blue-green beneath. Deep crimson flowers, up to 2½ in (6 cm) across, with centers of golden stamens, open during the summer, and these are followed by profusely borne, bright orange-red, bottle-shaped fruits.

Native range: China
Height: 10 ft (3 m)
Spread: 10 ft (3 m)
Hardiness: Zone 5

Rosa 'Nevada'

This is a very attractive shrub rose with a dense habit and arching, purple-brown, sparsely thorny shoots bearing light green foliage. The large, semidouble, fragrant, creamy white flowers, up to about 4 in (10 cm) across, have contrasting centers of golden stamens and are profusely borne, mainly during the summer season.

Height: 6 ft (2 m)
Spread: 8 ft (2.5 m)
Hardiness: Zone 5

Rosa 'New Dawn'

A vigorous climber with arching shoots and glossy, green foliage. The semidouble, pale blush pink, fragrant flowers, up to 3 in (8 cm) across, are freely borne over a long period from summer to autumn.

Height: 10 ft (3 m)
Spread: 8 ft (2.5 m)
Hardiness: Zone 5

Rosa 'Nozomi'

This miniature groundcover rose of compact habit has low, arching shoots and dark green foliage. Small, single, very pale pink flowers, about 1 in (2.5 cm) across, open in clusters along the shoots during the summer. It can be trained to grow as a weeping standard.

Height: 24 in (60 cm)
Spread: 6 ft (2 m)
Hardiness: Zone 5

Rosa x odorata 'Mutabilis'

This is a slender-stemmed, open shrub with purple, sparsely thorny shoots and glossy, dark green leaves that are purple when young. Single, fragrant flowers, up to 2½ in (6 cm) across, open buff yellow and then turn coppery pink followed by deep pink as they age. It is in almost continuous flower from spring to late autumn, and it can be trained as a climber against a wall.

Height: 8 ft (2.5 m)
Spread: 8 ft (2.5 m)
Hardiness: Zone 7

Rosa Pascali ('Lenip')

This is a large-flowered rose with dark green foliage. Double, white flowers, up to about 3½ in (9 cm) across, open from summer through to autumn.

Height: 30 in (75 cm)
Spread: 20 in (50 cm)
Hardiness: Zone 5

Rosa 'Paul's Himalayan Musk'

This very vigorous climber has glossy, dark green foliage, bronze-colored when young, and shoots bearing large, hooked thorns. Small, double, pale pink flowers, 1½ in (4 cm) across, are profusely borne in large, drooping clusters.

Height: 26 ft (8 m)
Spread: 20 ft (6 m)
Hardiness: Zone 5

Rosa pimpinellifolia 'Canary'

Rosa pimpinellifolia 'Bicolor'

Rosa 'Paul's Lemon Pillar'

This is a vigorously climbing, large-flowered rose with stout shoots and large, dark green leaves. The very large, fully double, and fragrant flowers, about 5 in (12 cm) across, are creamy white flushed with lemon yellow, and open in summer.

Height: 16 ft (5 m)
Spread: 10 ft (3 m)
Hardiness: Zone 5

Rosa 'Paul's Scarlet Climber'

This is a vigorous climbing rose producing dark green foliage borne on sparsely thorny, arching shoots. The double, bright scarlet flowers, reaching up to about 3 in (8 cm) across, open in clusters during the summer season.

Height: 10 ft (3 m)
Spread: 8 ft (2.5 m)
Hardiness: Zone 5

Rosa Peace ('Madame A Meilland')

One of the best known of all the roses, this classic, large-flowered plant is vigorous and upright with glossy, deep green foliage. The double, fragrant, and beautifully shaped flowers are 6 in (15 cm) across with a high center. Opening in summer to autumn, the flowers are creamy to golden yellow, the petals attractively edged with pink or red.

Height: 5 ft (1.5 m)
Spread: 3 ft (1 m)
Hardiness: Zone 5

Rosa 'Penelope'

This Hybrid Musk rose has a dense, bushy habit and dark green foliage flushed red. The large, semi-double, fragrant flowers, about 2¾ in (7 cm) across, are creamy pink with frilly edged petals and open in clusters from summer to autumn.

Height: 4 ft (1.2 m)
Spread: 5 ft (1.5 m)
Hardiness: Zone 5

Rosa pimpinellifolia

This is a low-growing, thicket-forming shrub that spreads by suckers. It has upright, spiny shoots and small, dark green leaves. Single, creamy white, sometimes pink, flowers, about 1½ in (4 cm) across, with centers of yellow stamens, open in late spring, and these are followed by glossy, black fruits.

Synonym: *Rosa spinosissima*
Common name: Scotch rose
Height: 3 ft (1 m)
Spread: 5 ft (1.5 m)
Hardiness: Zone 4
Variants: It is grown in several forms, with single or double, white or pink flowers. 'Dunwich Rose' is low-growing and spreading.

Rosa 'Pink Perpétué'

A climber with dark green foliage flushed purple. The double, fragrant, deep pink flowers, 3 in (8 cm) across, open from summer to autumn.

Height: 13 ft (4 m)
Spread: 10 ft (3 m)
Hardiness: Zone 5

Rosa 'Prosperity'

This Hybrid Musk rose has arching shoots and dark green foliage. Fully double, creamy white, fragrant flowers, 2 in (5 cm) across, open from creamy pink buds in clusters that weigh down the shoots in summer and autumn.

Height: 6 ft (2 m)
Spread: 5 ft (1.5 m)
Hardiness: Zone 5

Rosa 'Rambling Rector'

This old, vigorous rambling rose produces long, arching shoots bearing gray-green foliage. Fragrant, creamy white, semidouble flowers, up to about 1½ in (4 cm) across, with centers of golden stamens, open in clusters during the summer, and these are followed by profuse, rounded, red fruits.

Height: 20 ft (6 m)
Spread: 16 ft (5 m)
Hardiness: Zone 5

Rosa 'Reine Victoria'

This is a slender, upright Bourbon rose with elegant, light green foliage. The globular, silky, double flowers, about 3 in (8 cm) across, are fragrant and rich pink.

Height: 6 ft (2 m)
Spread: 4 ft (1.2 m)
Hardiness: Zone 4

Rosa 'Roseraie de l'Haÿ'

This is a vigorous Rugosa hybrid with a dense, bushy habit and very prickly shoots. The glossy, dark green, deeply veined leaves turn yellow in autumn. Large, semidouble, strongly scented, deep red-purple flowers, up to about 4–5 in (11 cm) across, open from summer to autumn.

Height: 6 ft (2 m)
Spread: 6 ft (2 m)
Hardiness: Zone 2

Rosa rubiginosa

This vigorous shrub rose has arching, prickly shoots and dark green leaves. Single, pale pink flowers, up to about 1 in (2.5 cm) across, open in summer, and these are followed by bright red, egg-shaped fruits.

Rosa 'Roseraie de l'Haÿ'

Synonym: *Rosa eglantaria*
Common name: Sweet brier
Native range: Europe, N Africa,
W Asia
Height: 8 ft (2.5 m)
Spread: 8 ft (2.5 m)
Hardiness: Zone 4

Rosa rugosa

This vigorous, thicket-forming shrub
has upright, densely prickly shoots
and dark green, deeply veined leaves
that turn yellow or red in autumn.
The fragrant, usually purple-pink
flowers, up to about 3½ in (9 cm)
across, open from summer to
autumn, followed by tomato-like,
bright red fruits.

Native range: NE Asia
Height: 6 ft (2 m)
Spread: 10 ft (3 m)
Hardiness: Zone 2
Variants: 'Alba' bears white flowers.
'Rubra' has deep crimson-purple

flowers. 'Scabrosa' has large, violet-
crimson flowers and large orange-red
fruits.

Rosa 'Sarah van Fleet'

A vigorous Rugosa hybrid of bushy,
upright habit with dark green, deeply
veined leaves, bronze when young.
Semidouble, fragrant, silvery pink
flowers, 3 in (8 cm) across, open from
summer to autumn.

Height: 8 ft (2.5m)
Spread: 5 ft (1.5 m)
Hardiness: Zone 2

Rosa 'Schneezwerg'

This is a Rugosa hybrid with an
upright habit and dark green,
wrinkled leaves. Fragrant,
semidouble, white flowers, up to 2 in
(5 cm) across, with centers of yellow
stamens, open in summer and
autumn, followed by orange-red fruit.

Rosa rugosa

Height: 5 ft (1.5 m)
Spread: 4 ft (1.2 m)
Hardiness: Zone 2

Rosa 'Seagull'

This is a vigorous rambler producing arching shoots bearing gray-green leaves. White, semidouble, very fragrant flowers, about 1 in (2.5 cm) across, with centers of yellow stamens, open in large clusters during summer.

Height: 20 ft (6 m)
Spread: 16 ft (5 m)
Hardiness: Zone 5

Rosa 'The Queen Elizabeth'

A vigorous and upright, cluster-flowered rose with large, dark green leaves. Semidouble, silvery pink, long-stalked flowers, 4 in (10 cm) across, open from pointed buds in summer and autumn.

Rosa rugosa 'Scabrosa'

Height: 6 ft (2 m)
Spread: 3 ft (1 m)
Hardiness: Zone 5

Rosa 'Veilchenblau'

This vigorous rambler has nearly thornless shoots and glossy bright green leaves. Semidouble, sweetly

Rosa xanthina 'Canary Bird'

scented flowers, about 1 in (3 cm) across, open violet-purple marked with white from crimson-purple buds, and fade to lilac-gray.

Height: 16 ft (5 m)
Spread: 13 ft (4 m)
Hardiness: Zone 5

Rosa Whisky Mac ('Tanky')

This is a large-flowered rose with very thorny shoots and dark green, bronze-tinged leaves. The double, fragrant, amber-yellow flowers, 4 in (10 cm) across, open from summer through to autumn.

Height: 35 in (90 cm)
Spread: 24 in (60 cm)
Hardiness: Zone 7

Rosa 'William Lobb'

A vigorous and upright Moss rose with small, dark green leaves and flower stems densely covered with pale green "moss." Large, semidouble flowers, 3 in (8 cm) across, open during summer, deep crimson-purple at first, fading to lavender-gray.

Height: 8 ft (2.5 m)
Spread: 5 ft (1.5 m)
Hardiness: Zone 3

Rosa xanthina 'Canary Bird'

This is a strong-growing shrub with a dense habit and arching, sparsely spiny shoots bearing dark green, fernlike leaves. The single, fragrant, rich yellow flowers, growing up to about 2 in (5 cm) across, are profusely borne in spring and sometimes there is a repeat-flowering later in the year.

Height: 10 ft (3 m)
Spread: 13 ft (4 m)
Hardiness: Zone 5

Rosa 'Zéphirine Drouhin'

This is a very popular Bourbon rose with foliage that is bronze when young, later turning gray-green, borne on thornless shoots. The fragrant, semidouble, deep cerise-pink flowers, up to about 3 in (8 cm) across, open over a long period from summer through to autumn. It can also be trained as a climber.

Height: 10 ft (3 m)
Spread: 6 ft (2 m)
Hardiness: Zone 4

Rosmarinus
Labiatae

This is a small genus of three species of evergreen shrubs, all with opposite leaves and natives of the Mediterranean. Only one species, however, is commonly found in garden cultivation, where it is valued for its flowers and aromatic foliage.

Suitable for any soil that is not too rich, this species needs a position in full sun, and it can be grown successfully in a border, dry garden, or against a wall. It can also be grown to form an effective hedge.

Cut plants back after flowering in order to restrict their growth; to renovate old plants, cut them back hard. Hedges can be cut after flowering and again as necessary during the summer.

Rosmarinus officinalis 'Roseus'

Rosmarinus officinalis

This is a vigorous, evergreen shrub with a dense, bushy habit and intensely aromatic, slender, dark green leaves that are white beneath. Clusters of small, violet-blue, two-lipped flowers open among the foliage at the ends of the shoots during spring, and sometimes again in the autumn.

Common name: Rosemary
Native range: Mediterranean region
Height: 6 ft (2 m)
Spread: 6 ft (2 m)
Hardiness: Zone 7
Variants: var. *albiflorus* produces white flowers. 'Benenden Blue' has rich blue flowers. 'Majorca Pink' is upright with lilac-pink flowers. 'Miss Jessopp's Upright' is a vigorous, upright form that is good for hedging. 'Prostratus' is low and spreading, but less hardy, and does well on a wall or in a rock garden. 'Roseus' has lilac-pink flowers. 'Severn Sea' is spreading and has arching shoots. 'Tuscan Blue' has deep blue flowers, often borne in the winter.

Rubus
Rosaceae

This widely distributed genus contains more than 250 species of often thorny, deciduous and evergreen shrubs, sometimes climbing, as well as herbaceous perennials. The ornamental species are grown for their flowers and foliage, and also sometimes for their attractive winter shoots.

These plants will grow in any well-drained soil. Those grown for their winter shoots do best if given a

Rubus thibetanus

Rubus 'Benenden'

Rubus 'Benenden'

This is a garden-raised hybrid between *R. deliciosus* and *R. trilobus* that makes a vigorous, thornless deciduous shrub. The arching branches are covered with pale brown, peeling bark and bear three-to five-lobed leaves. Its large, showy, white flowers, up to about 2¾ in (7 cm) across, have conspicuous centers of yellow stamens.

Height: 10 ft (3 m)
Spread: 13 ft (4 m)
Hardiness: Zone 5

Rubus cockburnianus

This is a vigorous, deciduous shrub that spreads by suckers and forms a dense thicket of spiny, white, bloomy shoots that look particularly striking in winter. The dark green leaves are white beneath and have prickly stalks and up to nine leaflets. Small, purple, relatively inconspicuous flowers open

position in full sun and any shoots that have flowered should be cut back, right to the ground, when flowering has finished. Other members of the genus are grown for their edible fruits.

in summer season, and these are followed by small, black fruits.

Common name: Ghost bramble
Native range: China
Height: 8 ft (2.5 m)
Spread: 16 ft (5 m) or more
Hardiness: Zone 6
Variant: 'Goldenvale' is less vigorous and lower-growing, to 3 ft (1 m), with equally white shoots.

Rubus spectabilis

This deciduous shrub has upright, sparsely prickly shoots and bold, glossy green leaves that are divided up into three sharply toothed leaflets. Small, fragrant, purple-pink flowers open in clusters at the ends of the shoots in mid-spring, and these are followed later in the year by orange-yellow fruits.

Common name: Salmonberry
Native range: W North America
Height: 6 ft (2 m)
Spread: 8 ft (2.5 m)
Hardiness: Zone 5
Variant: 'Olympic Double' has large, very showy, double flowers.

Rubus thibetanus

This deciduous shrub has upright, arching, prickly shoots covered in a conspicuous white bloom. The dark green leaves have up to 13 sharply toothed leaflets, white beneath. Clusters of small, purple flowers at the ends of the shoots in summer are sometimes followed by small, black-colored fruits.

Native range: China
Height: 6 ft (2 m)
Spread: 6 ft (2 m)
Hardiness: Zone 6

Rubus tricolor

A vigorous, sprawling, evergreen shrub with long shoots densely covered in red bristles. The glossy, dark green leaves are sharply toothed and sometimes shallowly lobed, white and bristly beneath. Clusters of white flowers at the ends of the shoots open in the summer, and these are followed by red, raspberry-like, edible fruits. It makes an excellent and quick-growing, ground-cover plant.

Native range: China
Height: 24 in (60 cm)
Spread: 16 ft (5 m) or more
Hardiness: Zone 7

Ruscus
Ruscaceae

This is a small, widely distributed genus of some six species of evergreen subshrubs, natives of Europe, North Africa, and West Asia. The apparent leaves are actually modified flattened shoots, on which the plant's rather inconspicuous flowers are borne.

   Grown for their foliage and fruits, they are suitable for any well-drained soil, and can be planted in either sun or shade. Most plants are male or female only and both are needed to produce fruit. Some forms of R. aculeatus have flowers that are both male and female. Cut any dead shoots back to the base in spring.

Ruscus aculeatus

This is a small, evergreen shrub that makes a dense clump of upright, green shoots and spreads by sending out underground stems. Glossy, dark green "leaves," which end in a sharp point, have small, greenish flowers on their surfaces in winter and spring, and these are followed—on female plants—by conspicuous and persistent, bright red berries.

Common name: Butcher's broom
Native range: Europe, North Africa, W Asia
Height: 35 in (90 cm)
Spread: 30 in (75 cm)
Hardiness: Zone 7

Ruta
Rutaceae

The eight species that make up this small genus are aromatic herbs and shrubs, natives of the Mediterranean region, North Africa, and Southwest Asia.

The following species is grown for its foliage, which is used as a flavoring, as well as its flowers. Suitable for a dry border or rock garden, it requires a well-drained soil in full sun in order to thrive. Prune by reducing shoots by one-half in spring.

Ruta graveolens
This is an evergreen shrub with upright shoots bearing blue-green, very aromatic leaves divided into numerous lobes. Clusters of small, four-petalled, mustard yellow flowers open at the ends of the shoots in summer, making an effective contrast with the foliage. All parts of the plant can be an irritant.

Common name: Common rue
Native range: SE Europe
Height: 35 in (90 cm)
Spread: 30 in (75 cm)
Hardiness: Zone 5
Variant: 'Jackman's Blue' is a compact form with vivid, blue-gray foliage.

Salix
Salicaceae

The 300 or more species of willows vary from dwarf shrubs to large trees and are widely distributed, mainly in the Northern Hemisphere. The flowers are borne in catkins, males and females on separate plants.

Grown in gardens for their habit, foliage, flowers, and sometimes their colored winter shoots, they prefer a moist but well-drained soil and a sunny position. The very dwarf willows do not need pruning, while shrubby species can have some of the older shoots removed after flowering or be cut back hard if renovation is required. Forms of *S. alba* grown for their winter shoots should be cut back every two years. The large tree-willows should never be planted close to buildings.

Salix alba
This is a vigorous, deciduous tree, usually broadly columnar, with sharply toothed leaves ending in long, tapering points. Young leaves are silvery hairy—becoming green above, blue-green beneath. Small catkins open as the leaves emerge in spring.

Common name: White willow
Native range: Europe, W Asia
Height: 80 ft (25 m)
Spread: 50 ft (15 m)
Hardiness: Zone 2
Variant: The young shoots of 'Britzensis' are bright orange-red in winter.

Salix babylonica
This deciduous tree was once the most commonly grown weeping willow, but it has largely been replaced by *S.* x *sepulcralis* 'Chrysocoma'. It is a spreading tree with pendulous branches and bears dark green, taper-pointed leaves that are blue-green beneath. Small catkins open in spring as the young leaves emerge.

Common name: Babylon weeping willow
Native range: Of cultivated origin in China
Height: 40 ft (12 m)
Spread: 50 ft (15 m)
Hardiness: Zone 6
Variant: 'Tortuosa' (dragon's claw willow) is upright in habit with twisted shoots and leaves.

Salix 'Boydii'
This hybrid between *S. lapponum* and *S. reticulata* was originally found in the Scottish mountains. It makes a slow-growing, dwarf shrub of

Salix alba 'Britzensis'

congested, upright habit, and with rather twisted shoots and small, red buds. The gray-green, rounded, and deeply veined leaves are only about ¾ in (2 cm) long. Small, female catkins are occasionally produced. It does best in a rock garden or trough.

Height: 18 in (45 cm)
Spread: 10 in (25 cm)
Hardiness: Zone 3

Salix caprea 'Kilmarnock'

This is a small, deciduous tree with a dense, spreading head of shoots that weep to the ground. Its broad, dark green leaves are gray-green on their undersurfaces. It is particularly attractive when its silky, gray, male catkins open in early spring before the leaves. Flowers become covered with yellow stamens. It tends to become congested and top-heavy and

Salix daphnoides 'Aglaia'

Salix hastata 'Wehrhahnii'

some of the older shoots should then be cut out. Prune in spring before growth restarts.

Common name: Kilmarnock willow
Height: 5–6 ft (1.5–2 m)
Spread: 8 ft (2.5 m)
Hardiness: Zone 4

Salix daphnoides

This is a fast-growing, small-sized, deciduous tree of broadly conical habit, with bloomy young shoots and slender, dark green, taper-pointed leaves that are blue-green beneath. Small catkins open in spring, as or before the leaves emerge. If required, this species can be cut back every two years in order to induce the production of vigorous and attractive winter shoots.

Common name: Violet willow
Native range: Europe
Height: 33 ft (10 m)
Spread: 33 ft (10m)
Hardiness: Zone 5
Variant: 'Aglaia' produces red shoots in winter and profuse silvery, then yellow, male catkins.

Salix elaeagnos

This is a deciduous shrub producing slender, upright shoots that are densely covered in gray hairs when they are young. Narrow, dark green, rosemary-like leaves, gray-colored at first and blue-white beneath, turn yellow in autumn. Slender catkins open as the young leaves start to emerge in spring.

Common name: Elaeagnos willow
Native range: S and C Europe, SW Asia
Height: 10 ft (3 m)
Spread: 6 ft (2 m)
Hardiness: Zone 4

Salix 'Erythroflexuosa'

This garden-raised hybrid, between the weeping willow S. x sepulcralis 'Chrysocoma' and S. babylonica 'Tortuosa', makes a small, spreading tree with pendulous, twisted shoots, bright orange-yellow in winter. The glossy, green leaves are also twisted, and yellow catkins appear with the leaves in spring.

Height: 16 ft (5 m)
Spread: 16 ft (5 m)
Hardiness: Zone 6

Salix gracilistyla

This is a bushy, deciduous shrub producing gray, hairy shoots and gray-green leaves, which are silky with hairs when young, blue-green beneath. The catkins open in the early to mid-spring period, before the leaves emerge; the males are particularly attractive, with red-tinged, later yellow, anthers.

Native range: Japan, Korea, NE China
Height: 8 ft (2.5 m)
Spread: 13 ft (4 m)
Hardiness: Zone 5
Variant: 'Melanostachys' is a male form producing blackish catkins, showing brick-red later, and yellow-colored anthers.

Salix hastata

This is a small-growing, spreading, deciduous shrub with stout, purple-brown shoots and dark green leaves. The leaves are covered in hairs when they are young, but become smooth as they mature. The catkins open initially gray and silky before or as the young leaves emerge. The females later turn green and the males yellow.

Native range: Europe, W Asia
Height: 3 ft (1 m)
Spread: 3 ft (1 m)
Hardiness: Zone 5
Variant: 'Wehrhahnii' is a male form that flowers profusely.

Salix integra 'Hakuro-nishiki'

Normally grafted on top of a stem, this makes a miniature, deciduous tree with a spreading head of arching shoots. The opposite leaves open nearly white, tinged with pink, later becoming blotched with green. The green-leaved form is native to Japan and makes a graceful shrub with pendulous shoots, but is rarely seen in gardens.

Height: 5 ft (1.5 m)
Spread: 4 ft (1.2 m)
Hardiness: Zone 5

Salix x sepulcralis 'Chrysocoma'

This tree is popular in garden cultivation and is thought to be a hybrid between S. babylonica and S. alba. It makes a very vigorous, wide-spreading tree with slender, pendulous, gold yellow shoots, often reaching to the ground. The slender, taper-pointed, glossy, green leaves are blue-green in color beneath and open early in spring. It is not a suitable specimen for small gardens.

Common name: Golden weeping willow
Height: 50 ft (15 m) or more
Spread: 65 ft (20 m)
Hardiness: Zone 6

Salvia officinalis 'Purpurascens'

Salvia
Labiatae

This is a very large genus comprising some 900 or more species of annual and perennial herbaceous plants, shrubs, and subshrubs, all with opposite leaves. Species are widely distributed—mainly in the warm regions of the world.

The following is the hardiest of the shrubby species, and is grown for its aromatic foliage and its flowers. Sage is suitable for any well-drained garden soil, as long as it is not too rich, and it needs a position in full sun in order to thrive.

Sage can be trimmed back lightly in the spring to retain its compact habit, and again when flowering has finished. If plants have become leggy, cut them back hard in spring to renovate them.

Salvia officinalis
This is a bushy, mound-forming, evergreen shrub producing gray-green, aromatic, and deeply veined leaves. Spikes of two-lipped, whorled, blue-purple flowers open at the ends of the shoots during the summer.

Common name: Garden sage
Native range: Mediterranean region, North Africa
Height: 24 in (60 cm)
Spread: 3 ft (1 m)
Hardiness: Zone 5
Variants: 'Icterina' produces leaves that have yellow margins. 'Purpurascens' produces young foliage that is red-purple in color. 'Tricolor' produces striking-looking foliage, with leaves that are edged with creamy white and pink.

Sambucus
Caprifoliaceae

The elders are a widely distributed genus made up of about 25 species of deciduous shrubs, trees, and herbaceous perennials. All have opposite-growing leaves that are divided up into several leaflets.

Grown for their attractive, sometimes colored foliage as well as for their small flowers and fruits, the elders are suitable for any well-drained garden soil, as long as it is not too dry, and they usually prefer to be given a position in full sun. Once plants are established, they do best if they are cut back hard in the spring to ensure there is a good crop of new foliage for the coming year.

Sambucus nigra

This vigorous and upright, deciduous shrub, sometimes treelike, has bold, dark green leaves divided into five or seven leaflets. Flattened heads of small, fragrant, white flowers open in early summer, followed by black, glossy fruits. It is mainly grown as the selected forms listed below.

Common name: European elder
Native range: Europe, North Africa, SW Asia
Height: 16 ft (5 m)
Spread: 13 ft (4 m)
Hardiness: Zone 5
Variants: 'Aurea' produces yellow leaves. 'Black Beauty' has blackish-purple foliage and pink flowers. 'Guincho Purple' has purple foliage and pink-budded flowers. 'Laciniata' (fern-leaved elder) has leaves with finely cut leaflets. 'Madonna' produces leaves edged with bright yellow. 'Marginata' has leaves edged with creamy white.

Sambucus racemosa

This vigorous, deciduous shrub has arching shoots bearing dark green leaves divided into usually five sharply toothed leaflets. The conical heads of small, pale creamy yellow flowers open in mid-spring, followed by glossy, red fruits in summer.

Common name: European red elder
Native range: Europe, W Asia
Height: 10 ft (3 m)
Spread: 10 ft (3 m)
Hardiness: Zone 4
Variants: 'Plumosa Aurea' produces finely cut, yellow foliage that can scorch if it is positioned in full sun. 'Sutherland Gold' is similar to 'Plumosa Aurea', except with foliage that is of a less intense yellow and not as likely to scorch. 'Tenuifolia' is low and spreading with finely cut leaflets.

Sambucus racemosa 'Sutherland Gold'

Sambucus nigra 'Guincho Purple'

Santolina
Compositae

The lavender cottons make up a small genus comprising some five species of evergreen shrubs, natives of the Mediterranean. They have small, aromatic leaves and tiny flowers on long-stalked heads.

They are suitable for any well-drained garden soil in full sun, and they can be used in the border or for creating a low hedge.

To retain a compact habit, trim them lightly in autumn after flowering, and cut them back hard every two or three years in the spring.

Santolina chamaecyparissus

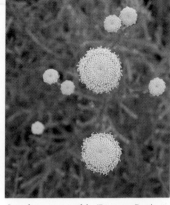

Santolina rosmarinifolia 'Primrose Gem'

Santolina chamaecyparissus

This is a compact and rounded, evergreen shrub, becoming open as it matures. Small, aromatic, white-felted leaves, edged with tiny teeth, are densely arranged on white-hairy shoots. The dense, button-like, bright yellow-colored flowerheads open on long stalks during the mid- to late summer period.

Common name: Lavender cotton
Native range: Mediterranean region
Height: 24 in (60 cm)
Spread: 30 in (75 cm)
Hardiness: Zone 6
Variant: 'Lemon Queen' produces lemon-yellow heads of flowers.

Santolina rosmarinifolia

This evergreen shrub has a compact, rounded habit, and aromatic foliage composed of small, bright green leaves that are deeply cut into toothed lobes. Tiny flowers are borne in dense, button-like, bright yellow flowerheads carried on long, slender, upright stalks in midsummer.

Common name: Holy flax
Native range: SW Europe
Height: 24 in (60 cm)
Spread: 3 ft (1 m)
Hardiness: Zone 7
Variant: 'Primrose Gem' produces pale yellow heads of flowers.

Sarcococca hookeriana var. *humilis*

Sarcococca
Buxaceae

The Christmas boxes comprise a genus of about 14 species of clump-forming or suckering, evergreen shrubs, natives of the Himalayas and East Asia. They are grown for their attractive foliage and their fragrant, winter flowers, as well as for their fruits. Male and female flowers are borne separately on the same plant, both without petals. The male flowers are more conspicuous, with protruding stamens; the female are later followed by the development of fleshy, black or red berries.

They are suitable for any good, moist but well-drained soil, and they prefer a shady position where they make effective ground cover. Little pruning is usually required, but any wayward or weak shoots can be cut to the base in spring.

Sarcococca confusa

This is a dense, clump-forming, evergreen shrub of rounded habit with glossy, dark green, slightly wavy edged leaves. Clusters of small, white, fragrant flowers open in winter as the glossy, black berries from the previous year's flowers ripen.

Native range: Probably China
Height: 5 ft (1.5 m)
Spread: 6 ft (2 m)
Hardiness: Zone 7

Sarcococca hookeriana

This is a vigorous, evergreen shrub producing upright shoots that form a dense thicket. It spreads by underground stems and bears matt, dark green leaves. Clusters of white or pink-flushed, fragrant flowers open in winter, and these are accompanied by black berries.

Native range: Himalayas, Tibet
Height: 5 ft (1.5 m)
Spread: 6 ft (2 m)
Hardiness: Zone 6
Variants: var. *digyna* produces slender-pointed leaves and conspicuously pink-tinged flowers; var. *humilis* is a low-growing form, up to 24 in (60 cm) high.

Sarcococca ruscifolia

This clump-forming, evergreen shrub has arching shoots bearing glossy, dark green, taper-pointed leaves. Clusters of white, fragrant flowers in winter are accompanied by red berries. It is commonly confused in gardens with *S. confusa*.

Sasa veitchii

Native range: China
Height: 4 ft (1.2 m)
Spread: 5 ft (1.5 m)
Hardiness: Zone 7
Variant: var. *chinensis* is the most commonly grown form and has narrow, pointed leaves.

Sasa
Gramineae

The 40 or so species that make up this genus are evergreen bamboos that spread by sending out underground stems. Relatively low-growing and with broad leaves, they are grown for their foliage and are useful for ground cover.

These bamboos are suitable for moist, well-drained soil that has been enriched with organic matter. The following species will grow in sun or shade.

Sasa veitchii

This low, thicket-forming bamboo has slender, upright, green, later purple, canes that spread vigorously by underground stems. The broad, dark green leaves, blue-green beneath, are up to 8 in (20 cm) or more long. In autumn the leaves develop a broad, white margin that lasts through winter, thus creating a variegated effect.

Sassafras albidum

Native range: Japan
Height: 3 ft (1 m)
Spread: 16 ft (5 m) or more
Hardiness: Zone 8

Sassafras
Lauraceae

The three species of deciduous trees in this genus are natives of North America and East Asia. The following is commonly grown for its foliage, which colors well in autumn. It needs a good, moist but well-drained, acidic soil, preferably rich in organic matter, and does best in a sunny position.

Sassafras albidum
This deciduous, usually broadly columnar tree produces suckers from the base. The distinctive, bright green, aromatic leaves are either unlobed or have three prominent lobes, and turn yellow to orange and red in autumn. Clusters of small, yellow flowers, males and females on separate trees, open as the leaves emerge in spring.

Common name: Sassafras
Native range: E North America
Height: 50 ft (15 m) or more
Spread: 33 ft (10 m)
Hardiness: Zone 4

Senecio
Compositae

This very large and widely distributed genus contains more than 1,000 species of annual and perennial

Skimmia japonica 'Rubella'

herbs, shrubs, climbers, and trees. The following is grown for its attractive foliage and requires a well-drained and not-too-rich soil and full sun. For the shrubby New Zealand species sometimes listed here, see *Brachyglottis*.

Senecio viravira
This spreading, evergreen subshrub has young shoots densely covered in white hairs. The silvery leaves are deeply cut into slender lobes. Clusters of small, pale yellow flowerheads open over a long period from summer to autumn.

Native range: Argentina
Height: 24 in (60 cm)
Spread: 3 ft (1 m)
Hardiness: Zone 8

Skimmia
Rutaceae

The four species in this genus are evergreen shrubs and trees, native from the Himalayas to East Asia.

The following are grown for their foliage, flowers (often attractive in bud), and their fruits. They need a moist but well-drained soil rich in organic matter. Forms of S. *japonica* should be grown in shade or semishade, and usually both male and female plants need to be grown to produce fruit. S. x *confusa* 'Kew Green' will tolerate full sun.

Little in the way of pruning is usually necessary, but any wayward shoots can be cut out in the spring. Their compact habit makes them useful in the garden for ground cover in shady places.

Skimmia x confusa 'Kew Green'

Skimmia x *confusa* 'Kew Green'

This vigorous, male shrub is a garden-raised hybrid between S. *anquetilia* and S. *japonica*. It makes a dense, spreading, dome-shaped bush with aromatic foliage. The large, conical clusters of fragrant, creamy white flowers in spring make it perhaps the most attractive of the genus in flower.

Height: 4 ft (1.2 m)
Spread: 6 ft (2 m)
Hardiness: Zone 7

Spread: 3–6 ft (1–2 m)
Hardiness: Zone 7
Variants: 'Fragrans' is a compact, male form that flowers profusely. 'Kew White' is a female form that produces large, white berries. 'Nymans' is a female form that produces red fruits. 'Rubella' is a compact, dome-shaped, male form that has red flowers buds. The buds are conspicuous during winter. 'Veitchii' is a vigorously growing, upright, female form that produces large, bright red berries.

Skimmia japonica

This is an evergreen shrub of very variable habit, ranging from low and spreading to upright, with aromatic, dark green, leathery leaves. In spring, dense clusters of small, fragrant, white flowers open at the ends of the shoots, often from red buds, and these are followed on female plants by bright red, persistent berries that are conspicuous in winter.

Native range: China, Japan
Height: 3–6 ft (1–2 m)

Sophora
Leguminosae

The 50 or so widely distributed species that make up this genus include both deciduous and evergreen trees and shrubs, or herbaceous perennials. They have leaves divided into several to numerous leaflets, and pealike flowers varying in color from white to pink, blue, or yellow.

The following species are grown principally for their flowers. They

Sophora microphylla 'Sun King'

require a well-drained soil and a position in full sun.

Sophora japonica

This spreading, deciduous tree has glossy, dark green leaves, blue-green beneath, with up to 17 leaflets. Fragrant, white, pealike flowers open in large, pendulous clusters in late summer and early autumn, and these are followed by yellow-brown, persistent pods. It does best in regions with hot summers.

Common name: Japanese pagoda tree
Native range: China
Height: 65 ft (20 m)
Spread: 50 ft (15 m)
Hardiness: Zone 4

Sophora microphylla

This is a vigorous, evergreen shrub or small tree that produces leaves that are divided into numerous small, glossy, dark green leaflets. The drooping, golden yellow, tubular flowers open in small clusters from late winter to spring. Except in the mildest of climates, is usually enjoys the protection afforded from being grown against a sunny wall.

Native range: New Zealand, Chile
Height: 20 ft (6 m) or more
Spread: 16 ft (5 m)
Hardiness: Zone 8
Variant: 'Sun King' is a bushy and particularly hardy form, usually reaching up to 10 ft (3 m) in height, and grows and flowers well in the open ground.

Sorbaria
Rosaceae

This is a small genus of four species of deciduous, thicket-forming shrubs that spreads by suckers, with leaves divided up into many leaflets. Grown in gardens for their foliage and their flowers, they are suitable for planting in any well-drained soil.

Since the following is a vigorous species, it may need to be restricted unless there is plenty of room for it to spread into. Cut down some of the older shoots and reduce the length of the remaining ones in late winter. To restrict its spread, remove some of the suckers.

Sorbaria sorbifolia
This vigorous, suckering shrub forms thickets of upright stems bearing dark green leaves divided up into as many as 25 sharply toothed leaflets. Small, white flowers open in dense, conical clusters, up to 10 in (25 cm) long, in the mid- to late summer period.

Native range: N Asia
Height: 6 ft (2 m)
Spread: 16 ft (5 m) or more
Hardiness: Zone 2

Sorbus
Rosaceae

The 100 or so species in this genus are deciduous trees and shrubs widely distributed in temperate regions of the Northern Hemisphere.

The species are very varied in leaf, from toothed to lobed (as in the white beams), while others are divided in several to numerous leaflets (as in the rowans or mountain ashes). The small, clustered flowers are usually white and are followed by white to pink, red, orange, or yellow fruits. The rowans prefer a moist but well-drained, neutral-to-acid soil; white beams are more tolerant and will grow on dry, alkaline soils.

Sorbus alnifolia
This is a conical, deciduous tree with a tendency to spread with age. It has dark green, toothed leaves, which turn to shades of orange, red, and yellow in autumn. Clusters of small, white flowers open in mid-spring, and these are followed by long-persistent, orange-red fruits. In spite of its common name, this species is closely related to the white beams.

Common name: Korean mountain ash
Native range: China, Japan, Korea, Taiwan
Height: 50 ft (15 m)
Spread: 33 ft (10 m)
Hardiness: Zone 4

Sorbus aria
A deciduous tree, conical to broadly columnar in habit, bearing glossy, dark green, sharply toothed leaves densely covered beneath in white hairs. Flattened heads of white flowers in late spring are followed by bright red fruits with white speckles.

Common name: White beam
Native range: Europe
Height: 50 ft (15 m)
Spread: 33 ft (10 m)
Hardiness: Zone 5
Variant: 'Lutescens' is the most popular form and has young foliage that is silvery gray.

Sorbus aucuparia
This is a deciduous tree, rounded and spreading in habit when young, bearing dark green leaves divided up into as many as 15 sharply toothed leaflets, sometimes turning yellow or red in autumn. Broad, flattened heads of small, white flowers in late spring are followed by large clusters of bright red fruits, often heavy enough to weigh down the branches.

Common name: European mountain ash
Native range: Europe, W Asia

Sorbus aria 'Lutescens'

Height: 50 ft (15 m)
Spread: 33 ft (10 m)
Hardiness: Zone 3
Variants: 'Aspleniifolia' has leaflets that are, themselves, divided up into smaller leaflets at the base. 'Fastigiata' is an extremely compact form with upright branches bearing deep red fruits in dense clusters. 'Sheerwater Seedling' is a form with a narrow, upright habit.

Sorbus cashmiriana

This is a small, spreading, deciduous tree. It has dark green leaves divided up into as many as 21 sharply toothed leaflets. The leaves are blue-green beneath and turn a yellow or red color in autumn. Clusters of white or pink flowers open in the late spring, and these are followed by white, pink-tinged fruits carried on red-colored stalks.

Sorbus torminalis

Native range: Himalayas
Height: 26 ft (8 m)
Spread: 26 ft (8 m)
Hardiness: Zone 4

Sorbus commixta

This conical, deciduous tree has bright green leaves divided into about 15 taper-pointed leaflets, blue-green beneath, turning yellow to red or purple-red in autumn. Broad, flattened heads of small, white flowers open in the late spring, and these are followed by bright orange-red fruits.

Native range: Japan, Korea
Height: 33 ft (10 m)
Spread: 26 ft (8 m)
Hardiness: Zone 5
Variant: The foliage of 'Embley' turn bright orange-red in autumn.

Sorbus hupehensis

This broadly columnar, deciduous tree has leaves divided into as many as 17 leaflets, blue-green above and blue-gray beneath. The leaves turn red in autumn. Domed clusters of small, white flowers open in late spring, and these are followed by white fruits, often with a pink flush toward the top.

Native range: China
Height: 33 ft (10 m)
Spread: 26 ft (8 m)
Hardiness: Zone 5

Sorbus intermedia

This is a vigorous, broadly columnar to rounded tree with dark green leaves, gray-green beneath, that are sharply lobed and toothed, more deeply toward the base of the leaf. Dense clusters of small, white flowers open in late spring, and these are followed by broadly egg-shaped, bright red fruits.

Common name: Swedish white beam
Native range: NW Europe
Height: 50 ft (15 m)
Spread: 40 ft (12 m)
Hardiness: Zone 4

Sorbus 'Joseph Rock'

This is a vigorous and deciduous shrub with a broadly columnar habit that produces upright branches. The bright green leaves, divided up into as many as 17 sharply toothed leaflets, turn to colors of orange, red, and purple in autumn. Clusters of white flowers open in late spring to early summer, and these are followed by pale yellow, later orange-yellow fruits. It is probably a form of a Chinese species.

Height: 33 ft (10 m)
Spread: 26 ft (8 m)
Hardiness: Zone 6

Sorbus reducta

This is a small, thicket-forming, deciduous shrub with upright shoots that spreads by sending out underground stems. The glossy, dark green leaves are divided up into as many as 15 leaflets, and foliage turns

Sorbus vilmorinii

a deep red-purple color in the autumn. Small clusters of white flowers open in the late spring, and these are followed by bright pink-colored fruits.

Native range: China
Height: 24 in (60 cm)
Spread: 3 ft (1 m)
Hardiness: Zone 6

Sorbus sargentiana

This broadly columnar to spreading, deciduous tree produces stout shoots bearing large and glossy, red, sticky buds. The bold, deep green leaves have up to 11 leaflets and turn to orange and red in autumn. Broad, flattened heads of small, white flowers open in early summer, and these are followed by large clusters of small, red fruits.

Native range: China
Height: 33 ft (10 m)
Spread: 33 ft (10 m)
Hardiness: Zone 6

Sorbus thibetica

This vigorous, deciduous tree, broadly conical in habit, has bold, dark green leaves densely covered beneath with white hairs. Rather open clusters of small, white flowers open in late spring to early summer, and these are followed by small, rounded, apple-like fruits, orange or yellow when ripe.

Native range: China, Himalayas
Height: 50 ft (15 m)
Spread: 40 ft (12 m)
Hardiness: Zone 6
Variant: 'John Mitchell' has large, rounded leaves.

Sorbus torminalis

A broadly conical, deciduous tree with dark green leaves deeply cut into pointed and toothed lobes, turning yellow, red, or purple in autumn. Clusters of white flowers from the late spring to early summer, and these are followed by small, russet-brown, speckled fruits.

Common name: Wild service tree
Native range: Europe, North Africa, SW Asia
Height: 50 ft (15 m)
Spread: 33 ft (10 m)
Hardiness: Zone 6

Spartium junceum

Sorbus vilmorinii

This is a small, spreading, deciduous tree of graceful habit, with fernlike leaves divided up into as many as 25 small, glossy, green leaflets, gray-green beneath. Clusters of small, white flowers in late spring or early summer are followed by deep red fruits that ripen to pink, then white.

Native range: China
Height: 20 ft (6 m)
Spread: 20 ft (6 m)
Hardiness: Zone 6

Spartium
Leguminosae

The single species in this small genus is a deciduous shrub grown for its showy flowers. Suitable for any not-too-rich, well-drained soil, it should be grown in full sun. Able to withstand considerable exposure in mild areas, it can be grown as a specimen or in the border. In colder regions it does well against a sunny wall. Cutting back in spring helps to retain its compact habit.

Spartium junceum

This vigorous, deciduous shrub has slender, green, upright shoots bearing small, sparse, dark green leaves. The large, fragrant, golden yellow, pealike flowers open in clusters at the ends of the shoots over a long period from summer to autumn.

Common name: Spanish broom
Native range: S Europe, N Africa, SW Asia
Height: 10 ft (3 m)
Spread: 6 ft (2 m)
Hardiness: Zone 8

Spiraea
Rosaceae

This genus has about 80 species of deciduous shrubs widely distributed in the temperate regions of the Northern Hemisphere, and provides numerous ornamental species valuable in gardens.

Grown for their flowers and for their sometimes colored foliage, these plants are excellent for the border or for ground cover, and look best when planted in groups. They are suitable for any moist but well-drained soil, preferring a position in full sun.

Regular pruning and deadheading are beneficial after flowering, and some of the older shoots on mature plants should be cut out. For those flowering from the old shoots early in the year, cut back in summer after flowering. For those flowering on the

Spiraea japonica 'Anthony Waterer'

new shoots late in the year, cut back in early spring before growth restarts.

Spiraea 'Arguta'

This is an old and popular, garden-raised hybrid that makes a vigorous, deciduous shrub with slender, arching shoots producing bright green leaves. Clusters of small, white flowers are profusely borne along the branches in mid- to late spring from the old shoots.

Common name: Garland spiraea
Height: 6 ft (2 m)
Spread: 8 ft (2.5 m)
Hardiness: Zone 4

Spiraea x cinerea 'Grefsheim'

This is an attractive, garden-raised hybrid that makes a spreading, deciduous shrub with a compact habit. It produces arching shoots bearing slender, blue-green leaves with silky undersurfaces. Dense clusters of small, white flowers open along the branches on the old shoots during the mid-spring period.

Height: 5 ft (1.5 m)
Spread: 6 ft (2 m)
Hardiness: Zone 4

Spiraea japonica

This is the most popular species in gardens and is grown in a very wide range of different forms. It is a deciduous shrub with upright shoots and dark green, sharply toothed foliage. The leaves are often bronze-colored when young. Broad, flattened heads of small, pink, occasionally white, flowers open on the new shoots in mid- to late summer.

Native range: China, Japan
Height: 5 ft (1.5 m)
Spread: 5 ft (1.5 m)
Hardiness: Zone 4
Variants: 'Albiflora' produces white flowers. 'Anthony Waterer' has very deep pink flowers and leaves that are

Spiraea thunbergii

Spiraea japonica 'Genpei'

is often grown as 'Shirobana'. 'Gold Mound' is a low-growing, compact form with yellow foliage and pale pink flowers. 'Little Princess' develops into a compact, small mound bearing small heads of deep pink-colored flowers.

Spiraea nipponica 'Snowmound'

This selection of a Japanese species is among the most popular of the early-flowering spiraeas. It is a vigorously growing, yet compact, rounded shrub producing dark green leaves on graceful, arching shoots. Small, profuse clusters of white flowers open along the branches on the old shoots during the spring.

Height: 5 ft (1.5 m)
Spread: 6 ft (2 m)
Hardiness: Zone 4

Spiraea thunbergii

This bushy, deciduous or semi-evergreen shrub has slender, arching shoots and narrow, pale green leaves. The small clusters of white flowers

often marked with white. 'Candlelight' is a compact form with butter yellow young foliage. 'Firelight' has young foliage that is deep orange-red, turning red in autumn, and deep pink flowers. 'Genpei' produces mixed heads of white and pink flowers, and open on the old shoots before or as the new leaves emerge.

Native range: China
Height: 5 ft (1.5 m)
Spread: 6 ft (2 m)
Hardiness: Zone 4

Spiraea x *vanhouttei*

This garden-raised hybrid between *S. cantoniensis* and *S. trilobata* makes a vigorous, usually semi-evergreen shrub that develops into a dense clump of upright, arching shoots bearing dark green leaves, blue-green beneath and lobed toward the tip. Profusely borne, white flowers in dense clusters open along the branches on the old shoots.

Height: 6 ft (2 m)
Spread: 8 ft (2.5 m)
Hardiness: Zone 3
Variants: 'Pink Ice' has leaves that are heavily mottled with white, and it flowers less freely.

Stachyurus
Stachyuraceae

This small genus of about six species of deciduous and semi-evergreen shrubs are natives of the Himalayas and East Asia. The following is the most popular species, and is grown for its early flowers.

The shrub is suitable for growing in a good, moist but well-drained soil that is rich in organic matter. It can be grown in a border or trained against a wall.

Pruning is not usually essential, but some of the old shoots of mature plants can be cut back to the base after flowering.

Stachyurus praecox

This is a vigorous, deciduous shrub with arching, red-brown shoots and bright green leaves ending in a long, tapered point. Slender, stiffly pendulous spikes form in autumn,

Stachyurus praecox

opening to pale yellow flowers on the bare shoots before the leaves emerge in late winter or early spring.

Native range: Japan
Height: 10 ft (3 m)
Spread: 13 ft (4 m)
Hardiness: Zone 6

Staphylea
Staphyleaceae

The bladdernuts comprise a genus of some 11 species of deciduous shrubs, sometimes treelike, with opposite leaves divided into several leaflets.

Grown for their flowers and unusual fruits, the following is suitable for any moist but well-drained soil. It can be grown as a specimen shrub or in a woodland setting. Little pruning is essential, but it can be cut back hard in winter if required.

Staphylea colchica

This deciduous shrub has upright shoots with glossy, green leaves divided into three to five leaflets.

Stewartia pseudocamellia

Clusters of fragrant, white, bell-shaped flowers open at the ends of the shoots in late spring as the young leaves are emerging, followed by pale green, bladder-like fruits divided into two or three lobes.

Native range: Caucasus
Height: 10 ft (3 m)
Spread: 10 ft (3 m)
Hardiness: Zone 6

Stephanandra
Rosaceae

A genus of four species of deciduous shrubs, all natives of East Asia. The following is grown for its foliage, small flowers, and attractive winter shoots.

It does best in good, moist, but well-drained soil, and is suitable for a shrub border. To prune, cut some of the old shoots to the base after flowering and reduce the others to strong side shoots.

Stephanandra incisa
This vigorous, clump-forming, deciduous shrub of graceful habit spreads by sending out suckers. Its arching, zigzag shoots turn to a richly colored brown in winter, and the deeply lobed and toothed, bright green leaves turn orange-yellow to red in the autumn season. Clusters of small, greenish-white flowers open during the late spring and early summer.

Native range: Japan, Korea
Height: 6 ft (2 m)
Spread: 10 ft (3 m)
Hardiness: Zone 4
Variant: 'Crispa' is low-growing and spreading form, reaching up to about 24 in (60 cm) in height, with deeply cut leaves. It is useful as a groundcover plant.

Stewartia
Theaceae

The nine species making up this genus are deciduous and evergreen trees and shrubs found mainly in East Asia, but with two species in the United States of America. Related to the camellias, the following is grown for its foliage, showy flowers, and ornamental bark. It requires a moist but well-drained, lime-free soil rich in organic matter.

Stewartia pseudocamellia
This is a conical to broadly columnar, deciduous tree with red-brown bark that peels to leave attractively contrasting patches of cream and pink showing through. The dark green, taper-pointed leaves turn to brilliant shades of orange, yellow, and red in the autumn. White, camellia-like flowers, growing up to about 2½ in (6 cm) across, and with a conspicuous central boss of yellow stamens, open during the summer months.

Native range: Japan
Height: 50 ft (15 m)
Spread: 33 ft (10 m)
Hardiness: Zone 5

Stewartia pseudocamellia

Styrax japonicus

Styrax
Styracaceae

This is a genus comprising 100 or more widely distributed species of deciduous and evergreen shrubs and trees, found mainly in the warm regions of the Northern Hemisphere.

Grown principally for its flowers, the following species requires a moist but well-drained, lime-free soil. It is ideal as a specimen tree in a woodland setting, where it is sheltered from any strong winds by the other trees.

Apart from the removal of any dead, diseased, or crossing wood, no pruning is usually required.

Styrax japonicus
This is a gracefully spreading, deciduous tree, often producing branching low down bearing glossy, green leaves that turn red or yellow in the autumn. The pendulous, white or pink-tinged, slightly fragrant flowers have conspicuous clusters of yellow stamens in their centers, and they hang along the undersides of the branches in the early to midsummer period.

Common name: Japanese snowbell
Native range: China, Japan, Korea
Height: 33 ft (10 m)
Spread: 33 ft (10 m)
Hardiness: Zone 5
Variant: 'Pink Chimes' produces pink-colored flowers.

Symphoricarpos
Caprifoliaceae

This is a genus made up of some 17 species of deciduous shrubs with opposite, sometimes lobed leaves.

These are densely growing plants, often forming thickets, and they spread by sending out suckers. They are natives mainly of North America, including Mexico, with a single species native to China.

These shrubs are grown for their ornamental fruits and they are suitable for planting in any well-drained soil. They can be used to create low hedges or as groundcover plants.

To restrict their growth, they can be cut back as necessary in early spring before the new season's growth starts.

Symphoricarpos x chenaultii 'Hancock'

This garden-raised hybrid between *S. microphyllus* and *S. orbiculatus* makes a vigorous, wide-spreading, deciduous shrub with dark green, rounded leaves that are bronze-colored when young. It is useful for ground cover. Clusters of small, white, inconspicuous flowers open between early and midsummer, and these are followed by rather sparse, pink fruits.

Height: 5 ft (1.5 m)
Spread: 10 ft (3 m)
Hardiness: Zone 4

Symphoricarpos orbiculatus

This is a bushy, deciduous shrub with a spreading habit and with arching branches bearing dark green to blue-green leaves. Small, white or pink-tinged flowers open in clusters in early to midsummer, and these are followed by small, red-purple, long-persistent fruits. Does best in regions that experience hot summers.

Common names: Coralberry, Indian currant
Native range: United States of America, Mexico
Height: 5 ft (1.5 m)
Spread: 8 ft (2.5 m)
Hardiness: Zone 2
Variant: 'Foliis Variegatis' produces

striking foliage, with leaves that are conspicuously edged with yellow.

Syringa
Oleaceae

The lilacs are a well-known and popular genus of some 20 species of deciduous shrubs and trees, all with opposite leaves, and are native from East Europe to East Asia.

They are grown for their showy clusters of fragrant flowers, and require a good, well-drained soil, preferably in a sunny position. They require little pruning, but they do benefit from dead-heading, particularly when young.

Syringa x laciniata

A bushy, rounded, deciduous shrub of uncertain origin, but is probably a garden-raised hybrid between *S. protolaciniata* and *S. vulgaris*. It is distinct among the commonly grown lilacs in that the leaves are deeply cut into between three and nine narrow lobes. Clusters of fragrant, lilac flowers open in late spring.

Height: 6 ft (2 m)
Spread: 10 ft (3 m)
Hardiness: Zone 7

Syringa meyeri

A compact and bushy, deciduous shrub of rounded habit with small, dark green leaves. Dense clusters of fragrant, violet-purple flowers open in the late spring and early summer period. This species is mainly represented in gardens by the form described below, which is sometimes grown as *S. velutina*.

Native range: N China
Height: 5 ft (1.5 m)
Spread: 6 ft (2 m)
Hardiness: Zone 3
Variant: 'Palibin' is a very compact, slow-growing form, ideally suited for the small garden.

Syringa x laciniata

Syringa vulgaris 'Masséna'

Syringa pubescens

This vigorous, upright shrub, sometimes treelike, has glossy, dark green leaves. Large clusters of fragrant flowers, lilac-purple to nearly white, open at the ends of the shoots in late spring. The typical form is rarely seen, and it is mainly represented in gardens by the forms described below.

Native range: N China
Height: 16 ft (5 m)
Spread: 13 ft (4 m)
Hardiness: Zone 4
Variants: subsp. *microphylla* 'Superba' (*S. microphylla* 'Superba') is smaller, up to 6 ft (2 m), and bears profuse, rose-pink flowers in early summer, and intermittently until autumn. subsp. *patula* 'Miss Kim' (*S. patula* 'Miss Kim') is a compact form, up to about 6 ft (2 m) in height, and has purple-colored buds opening to ice-blue flowers.

Syringa vulgaris

This, the most commonly grown species, makes a vigorous, large shrub, sometimes treelike in stature, with broad, heart-shaped leaves ending in a tapered point. The large, conical clusters of very fragrant flowers open in late spring and early summer. Lilac-purple in the typical form, there are many selections with flowers ranging from white to pink, red, blue, and purple, and in single or double forms.

Common name: Common lilac
Native range: E Europe
Height: 20 ft (6 m)
Spread: 20 ft (6 m)
Hardiness: Zone 3
Variants: 'Andenken an Ludwig
Späth' ('Souvenir de Louis Spaeth')
produces deep wine-red, single
flowers. 'Charles Joly' has deep
purple-red, double flowers.
'Katherine Havemeyer' produces
double, lavender-purple flowers.
'Madame Lemoine' bears white,
double flowers opening from cream
buds. 'Masséna' has clusters of single,
red-purple flowers.

Tamarix
Tamaricaceae

The tamarisks are a genus made up of
some 50 species of deciduous shrubs,
sometimes trees, with feathery,
plumelike foliage that is composed of
tiny leaves.

Grown principally for their graceful
habit and small but profusely borne
flowers, they prefer a well-drained
soil and a position in full sun. They
are an excellent choice for a full
coastal exposure, where they will
tolerate very dry conditions, but
inland they do require more shelter
and a moisture-retentive soil.

It is best to cut plants back hard
annually in order to retain a compact
habit—*T. ramosissima* in spring,
T. tetrandra in summer, when
flowering has finished.

Tamarix ramosissima
This is a vigorous, spreading,
deciduous shrub, sometimes treelike,
with long, slender shoots, densely
covered in tiny, pointed, pale green
leaves. Dense spikes of small, pink
flowers open profusely along the new
shoots in late summer.

Native range: SE Europe to China
Height: 20 ft (6 m)
Spread: 16 ft (5 m)
Hardiness: Zone 2

Variants: 'Pink Cascade' is very
vigorous with rich pink flowers.
'Rubra' has deep pink flowers.

Tamarix tetrandra
This vigorous, spreading shrub or
small tree has a graceful habit,
producing arching, purple-brown
shoots bearing tiny, densely arranged
leaves. The slender clusters of small,
pale pink flowers open in spring from
shoots that have formed in the
previous year.

Native range: SE Europe, SW Asia
Height: 13 ft (4 m)
Spread: 16 ft (5 m)
Hardiness: Zone 5

Telopea
Proteaceae

The four species that make up this
small genus of evergreen shrubs or
trees are all natives of Australia,
including the island state of
Tasmania.

The following species is the most
commonly grown, principally for its
striking flower clusters. It requires a
moist but well-drained, lime-free soil
in order to thrive. It prefers a sunny
position, as long as it is not dry, with
its roots shaded from the hottest of
the sun.

Telopea truncata
This stoutly branched, evergreen
shrub has young shoots densely
covered in dark brown hairs, and
leathery, dark green leaves sometimes
toothed or lobed toward the tip.
Dense heads, up to 3 in (8 cm)
across, of slender, tubular, deep
crimson flowers open at the ends of
the shoots in early summer.

Common name: Tasmanian waratah
Native range: Tasmania
Height: 13 ft (4 m)
Spread: 10 ft (3 m)
Hardiness: Zone 8

Tibouchina urvilleana

Teucrium
Labiatae

This large genus of plants contains aproximately 300 species of often aromatic, herbaceous perennials and shrubs, all with opposite leaves. Species are widely distributed, particularly in the Mediterranean region and Southwest Asia.

The following species is grown for its attractive foliage and its flowers, and it does best in a well-drained soil where it receives full sun.

It can be cut back lightly after flowering to retain a compact habit. It is suitable for a border or for growing on a sunny wall in regions where it is not fully hardy.

Teucrium fruticans
This is a compact and vigorous, evergreen shrub with young shoots that are densely covered with white hairs, and bearing aromatic, bright green foliage. The leaves, which are gray-green when young, are white beneath. The lilac-purple, five-lobed flowers open in spikes at the ends of the shoots during summer.

Common name: Shrubby germander
Native range: Mediterranean region
Height: 3 ft (1 m) or more
Spread: 6 ft (2 m)
Hardiness: Zone 8

Tibouchina
Melastomataceae

This is a large genus comprising some 350 species of evergreen shrubs and herbaceous perennials, natives of Mexico and Central and South America.

The following species is grown for its striking flowers, but it will survive outside only in the mildest of climates. It is also suitable for training against a wall.

When it comes to pruning, young shoots can be shortened in spring to encourage a bushy habit.

Tibouchina urvilleana
This is a vigorous-growing, evergreen shrub that produces stout, four-angled shoots covered in red hairs, and softly hairy, prominently three-veined, dark green leaves. The deep

violet-purple flowers open over a long period from the summer right through to autumn.

Common name: Brazilian glorybush
Native range: Brazil
Height: 10 ft (3 m)
Spread: 6 ft (2 m)
Hardiness: Zone 10

Tilia
Tiliaceae

The lindens comprise a genus of some 25 species of deciduous trees that are widely distributed in North America as well as in Europe and Asia. They make handsome specimen trees and they are particularly valued for their habit, foliage, and flowers. Some limes also produce attractively colored winter shoots.

Linden trees are suitable for any well-drained garden soil that is not too dry. They often respond well to pruning and are commonly pollarded (pruned heavily to reduce the crown and to encourage the production of vigorous shoots) or pleached (kept low by frequent pruning and training the branches to form an interwoven hedge or to grow over a pergola). Those that produce the colored winter shoots are particularly effective when pleached.

Tilia cordata
This broadly columnar tree has glossy, dark green, rounded leaves, blue-green on their undersurfaces, with tufts of brown hair growing from the axils of the leaves. Pendulous clusters of small, pale yellow, fragrant flowers hang from the branches in midsummer.

Common name: Little leaf linden
Native range: Europe, W Asia
Height: 100 ft (30 m)
Spread: 50 ft (15 m)
Hardiness: Zone 4
Variant: 'Greenspire' is compact in habit and is broadly conical.

Tilia x euchlora
A deciduous tree of uncertain origin, possibly a hybrid between *T. cordata* and *T. dasystyla*. It makes a broadly columnar tree with very glossy, dark green leaves edged with fine teeth. Pendulous clusters of small, pale yellow, fragrant flowers hang from the branches in midsummer.

Height: 65 ft (20 m)
Spread: 33 ft (10 m)
Hardiness: Zone 3

Tilia x europaea
This naturally occurring hybrid between *T. cordata* and *T. platyphyllos* is commonly planted in large gardens and or in public spaces. It is a broadly columnar tree with rounded, dark green leaves, paler beneath. It bears pendulous clusters of small, pale yellow, fragrant flowers in midsummer. It is often seen with numerous shoots arising from large burrs at the base of the tree.

Common name: European linden
Native range: Europe
Height: 100 ft (30 m) or more
Spread: 50 ft (15 m)
Hardiness: Zone 3
Variant: 'Wratislaviensis' has attractive foliage that is bright yellow when young.

Tilia platyphyllos
This broadly columnar, deciduous tree has rounded, sharply toothed, and abruptly pointed, dark green leaves, softly downy beneath, turning yellow in autumn. Clusters of small, fragrant, pale yellow flowers open in early to midsummer.

Common name: Big leaf linden
Native range: Europe, SW Asia
Height: 100 ft (30 m)
Spread: 65 ft (20 m)
Hardiness: Zone 4
Variants: 'Aurea' produces yellow shoots in winter. 'Rubra' has bright red winter shoots.

Tilia platyphyllos 'Rubra'

Tilia tomentosa

This is a vigorously growing, broadly columnar tree with rounded, sharply toothed, and sometimes slightly lobed leaves. The leaves, which are dark green above and densely covered in white hairs on their undersurfaces, turn yellow in autumn. Prominent clusters of very fragrant, pale yellow flowers hang down from the shoots in mid- to late summer.

Common name: Silver linden
Native range: SE Europe, SW Asia
Height: 80 ft (25 m)
Spread: 50 ft (15 m)
Hardiness: Zone 4
Variant: 'Petiolaris' (*Tilia* 'Petiolaris'), the weeping silver linden, is a form that produces gracefully pendulous branches.

Toona
Meliaceae

This is a genus of six species of deciduous and evergreen trees, natives of China, Southeast Asia, and northern Australia. Only the following is commonly grown, and it makes a handsome specimen tree. It is suitable for any good, well-drained soil and prefers a position in full sun.

Toona sinensis

This broadly columnar, deciduous tree, sometimes spreading by suckers, has stout shoots and bold leaves, up to 24 in (60 cm) or more long, with as many as 30 dark green leaflets that are onion-scented when crushed. Large, pendulous clusters of

Trochodendron aralioides

small, white, fragrant flowers open at the ends of the shoots in midsummer.

Synonym: *Cedrela sinensis*
Native range: China
Height: 65 ft (20 m)
Spread: 50 ft (15 m)
Hardiness: Zone 5
Variant: 'Flamingo' is slow-growing with brilliant pink young foliage, later creamy white, then green.

Trachycarpus
Palmae

This is a small genus of six species of evergreen palms, with single or clustered stems and fan-shaped leaves, that are natives of the Himalayas and East Asia. The following is the most commonly grown species and is the hardiest palm. It makes an excellent specimen tree, and is suitable for any well-drained soil in a sunny position with shelter from strong winds.

Trachycarpus fortunei
This evergreen, single-stemmed palm has a stout trunk densely covered with the fibrous brown remains of old leaf bases. The very large, fan-shaped leaves, up to 4 ft (1.2 m) across, are deeply cut into numerous slender, dark green segments. Massive, drooping clusters of tiny, pale yellow,

fragrant flowers open in early summer, males and females on separate plants.

Common names: Windmill palm, fan palm
Native range: China
Height: 33 ft (10 m)
Spread: 10 ft (3 m)
Hardiness: Zone 8

Trochodendron
Trochodendraceae

The single species in this genus is an evergreen tree with no obvious close relatives. Handsome in foliage and with unusual flowers, it requires a moist but well-drained, lime-free soil, and does best in a semi-shaded position, sheltered from strong winds perhaps among other trees.

Trochodendron aralioides
A broadly columnar, evergreen tree, often branching low and shrubby, conical when young. Glossy, dark green leaves are borne on long, slender stalks, and end in finely tapered points, and leaves are clustered toward the ends of the shoots. Bright green flowers, consisting of a central disk with numerous stamens radiating out, like the spokes of a wheel, are borne in conical clusters in late spring and early summer.

Ulex europaeus 'Flore Pleno'

Native range: Japan, Korea, Taiwan
Height: 33 ft (10 m)
Spread: 26 ft (8 m)
Hardiness: Zone 8

Ugni
Myrtaceae

This is a genus made up of about 15 species of evergreen shrubs and trees, natives of South America and all with opposite leaves.

Only the following species is commonly grown, and it is valued for its foliage and flowers as well as its edible fruits. It requires a moist but well-drained soil and does best in areas that experience cool, moist summers and mild winters. Where it thrives, however, it can be used for hedging.

Ugni molinae
This is an evergreen shrub that bears small, dark green, untoothed leaves. The leaves have paler undersurfaces and end in a short, abrupt point. Fragrant, nodding, cup-shaped, pale pink flowers open on slender stalks in the late spring, and these are followed by small, red and aromatic, edible berries.

Synonym: *Myrtus ugni*
Common name: Chilean guava
Native range: Chile
Height: 5 ft (1.5 m)
Spread: 3 ft (1 m)
Hardiness: Zone 9

Ulex
Leguminosae

The gorses are a genus made up of about 20 species of spiny shrubs, natives of Western Europe and North Africa. Leaves are present normally only on the young seedlings, and these are replaced by spines as the plants mature.

These shrubs grow best in poor, well-drained soils, in particular sandy soils, and they need a position in full sun in order to do well.

They can be cut back lightly after flowering to retain a compact habit. If plants become leggy, as they do in rich soils, cut them back hard, to within 6 in (15 cm) of the base.

Ulex europaeus
This is a dense, thicket-forming shrub with rigid, green shoots that are formidably armed with sharp-pointed, green spines. Masses of

Ulmus minor 'Dampieri Aurea'

bright golden yellow, fragrant, pealike flowers, growing up to about ¾ in (2 cm) long, open along the ends of the shoots in mid- to late spring, but sometimes earlier, and often intermittently as well at other times of the year.

Common name: Common gorse
Native range: W Europe
Height: 5 ft (1.5 m)
Spread: 8 ft (2.5 m)
Hardiness: Zone 6
Variant: 'Flore Pleno' produces bright yellow, double flowers.

Ulex gallii

This compact, dwarf shrub has a spreading habit with green shoots bearing sharp-tipped spines. The golden yellow, pealike flowers, up to ½ in (1.5 cm) long, open from late summer to autumn.

Common name: Dwarf gorse
Native range: W Europe
Height: 5 ft (1.5 m)
Spread: 6 ft (2 m)
Hardiness: Zone 7
Variant: 'Mizen' is a prostrate form with shoots that creep across the

ground. It comes into flower in the late summer period.

Ulmus
Ulmaceae

This genus is made up of some 45 or so species of elms. They are all deciduous trees and shrubs that are widely distributed in the temperate regions of the Northern Hemisphere. While some species of elm are grown for their attractive foliage, others are favored for their striking bark, but they are all suitable for any well-drained soil. The prevalence of Dutch elm disease has considerably reduced the number and variety of elms that are in cultivation in many parts of the world.

Ulmus x hollandica 'Jacqueline Hillier'

This is a slow-growing and bushy shrub with a rounded habit. It is a compact plant when young, but becomes more open as it matures. The dark green, rough-textured leaves are sharply toothed and neatly arranged in two ranks on both sides of the brown-hairy shoots.

Height: 10 ft (3 m)
Spread: 13 ft (4 m)
Hardiness: Zone 5

Ulmus minor

A deciduous tree of broadly columnar habit, with outer shoots that usually droop, and glossy, green, rather leathery leaves that turn yellow in autumn. Clusters of tiny flowers, made conspicuous by their red stamens, open on the bare shoots in early spring, followed by pale green, winged fruits.

Common name: Smooth-leaved elm
Native range: Europe, North Africa, SW Asia
Height: 80 ft (25 m)
Spread: 50 ft (15 m)

Vaccinium corymbosum

Hardiness: Zone 5
Variant: 'Dampieri Aurea' is a small tree with a conical habit producing golden yellow foliage.

Ulmus parvifolia

This is a rounded-to-upright, deciduous tree with arching shoots and gray, green, and orange-brown, flaking bark. The glossy, dark green, sharply toothed leaves turn shades of yellow, red, or purple in the autumn. Small clusters of tiny, red flowers open among the leaves in autumn, and these are followed by small, pale green, winged fruits. It is resistant to Dutch elm disease.

Common name: Chinese elm
Native range: China, Korea, Japan
Height: 50 ft (15 m)
Spread: 40 ft (12 m)
Hardiness: Zone 5

Vaccinium
Ericaceae

This large genus is made up of about 450 species of deciduous and evergreen shrubs, sometimes trees, widely distributed in the Northern Hemisphere, South Africa and South America. While some species are grown for their edible fruits, the ornamental types are also grown for their foliage—which, in the deciduous species, often colors in autumn—and their urn-shaped to bell-shaped flowers. They require a moist but well-drained, lime-free, and humus-rich soil.

Pruning is not usually essential, but cut *V. corymbosum* back in winter to restrict its growth.

Vaccinium corymbosum

This is a vigorous-growing, deciduous shrub that forms dense clumps of upright shoots bearing dark green leaves turning to shades of orange, yellow, and red in autumn. Small, urn-shaped, white or pink-flushed flowers open in late spring as the young leaves are emerging, and the flowers are followed by edible, blue-black berries.

Common name: Highbush blueberry
Native range: E North America
Height: 6 ft (2 m)
Spread: 6 ft (2 m)
Hardiness: Zone 3

Vaccinium glaucoalbum

This mound-forming, evergreen shrub spreads by sending out underground stems and has dark blue-green, leathery leaves, blue-white beneath. Spikes of small, cylindrical, white flowers and blue-white bracts open in the late spring and early summer periods, and these are followed by blue-black, bloomy berries.

Native range: E Himalayas
Height: 3 ft (1 m)
Spread: 6 ft (2 m)
Hardiness: Zone 8

Vaccinium vitis-idaea

A creeping, evergreen shrub forming dense mats of glossy, dark green, leathery leaves. Clusters of small, bell-shaped, white or pink-tinged flowers open at the ends of the shoots in late spring and early summer, followed by bright red, edible berries.

Common name: Mountain cranberry
Native range: Northern Hemisphere
Height: 12 in (30 cm)
Spread: 6 ft (2 m) or more
Hardiness: Zone 2
Variant: 'Koralle' freely produces large-sized fruits.

Viburnum
Caprifoliaceae

This very important genus has about 150 species of deciduous and evergreen shrubs, sometimes trees, with opposite leaves. They are widely distributed in temperate regions of the Northern Hemisphere, extending to Southeast Asia and South America.

Viburnums are grown for a range of ornamental features, including their often fragrant flowers, fruits, and foliage, which, on the deciduous species, often colors well in autumn. They are suitable for any good, well-drained soil and can be used in the border as specimen shrubs or grown in a woodland setting among other shrubs and trees.

Viburnum betulifolium

This is a vigorous, spreading, deciduous shrub that has arching branches bearing dark green, toothed, and taper-pointed leaves. Broad, flattened heads of small, white flowers open in the early summer, and these are followed by profuse, small, bright red fruits in nodding clusters.

Native range: China
Height: 13 ft (4 m)
Spread: 16 ft (5 m)
Hardiness: Zone 5

Viburnum x bodnantense

This is a garden-raised hybrid between *V. farreri* and *V. grandiflorum*. It makes a stiffly branched shrub of

Viburnum betulifolium

upright habit, becoming more arching with age, and bearing dark green leaves that are bronze-colored when young. The dense clusters of fragrant, tubular, white to pink flowers open on the bare shoots over a long period from the autumn through to early spring. This hybrid is normally grown as one of the selected forms listed below.

Height: 10 ft (3 m)
Spread: 8 ft (2.5 m)
Hardiness: Zone 5
Variants: 'Charles Lamont' produces bright pink-colored flowers. 'Dawn' bears rose-pink flowers that fade with age to a white flushed with pink. 'Deben' produces nearly white flowers that open from pale pink-colored buds.

Viburnum x burkwoodii

This is a garden-raised hybrid between *V. carlesii* and *V. utile* that makes a rounded, semi-evergreen shrub with glossy, dark green leaves, sometimes turning red in autumn. Dense heads of white, very fragrant flowers open in mid- to late spring from pink buds. The flowers are followed by flattened fruits, which ripen from red to black.

Height: 10 ft (3 m)
Spread: 10 ft (3 m)
Hardiness: Zone 5
Variants: 'Anne Russell' is a compact form with very fragrant flowers. 'Mohawk' has profuse, strongly fragrant, white flowers opening from deep pink buds. 'Park farm Hybrid' is spreading with large flowers and orange-red autumn color.

Viburnum x carlcephalum

This garden-raised hybrid between *V. carlesii* and *V. macrocephalum* makes a vigorous and stoutly branched, rounded, deciduous shrub with broad, dark green leaves that turn red in autumn. The very fragrant, tubular, white flowers flushed with pink open from pink buds in large, domed heads during late spring.

Height: 8 ft (2.5 m)
Spread: 10 ft (3 m)
Hardiness: Zone 5

Viburnum carlesii

This very popular species is a deciduous shrub of stiffly branched, rounded habit and with dark green leaves that turn red in autumn. The very fragrant, white to pale pink

Viburnum x carlcephalum

Viburnum davidii

flowers open from deeper colored buds in mid- to late spring, sometimes followed by red, later black, fruits. Normally grown as the selected forms listed below.

Native range: Korea
Height: 6 ft (2 m)
Spread: 6 ft (2 m)
Hardiness: Zone 5
Variants: 'Aurora' produces pale pink-colored flowers opening from red buds. 'Diana' has red flower buds opening pink, and bronze-tinged young foliage.

Viburnum davidii

This evergreen shrub forms a low, spreading mound of compact habit with bold, dark green, conspicuously three-veined leaves. Heads of small, white flowers open in late spring and also at other times of the year, particularly autumn and winter, followed by showy, egg-shaped, metallic blue fruits. Some plants may be either male or female and both need to be planted to obtain fruits. It makes excellent ground cover in sun or shade.

Native range: China
Height: 3 ft (1 m)

Spread: 6 ft (2 m)
Hardiness: Zone 8

Viburnum x juddii

This garden-raised hybrid between *V. carlesii* and the closely related *V. bitchiuense* makes a rounded, deciduous shrub with dark green leaves sometimes turning red in autumn. The domed heads of white, very fragrant flowers, flushed with pink, open from pink buds in mid- to late spring.

Height: 8 ft (2.5 m)
Spread: 8 ft (2.5 m)
Hardiness: Zone 4

Viburnum farreri

This is a stoutly branched, deciduous shrub of upright habit with dark green leaves that are bronze when young and turn red or purple-red in autumn. Clusters of very fragrant, tubular flowers from pink buds, open to white flushed with pink from late autumn and winter to early spring.

Native range: China
Height: 10 ft (3 m)
Spread: 8 ft (2.5 m)
Hardiness: Zone 5

Variant: 'Candidissimum' produces white flowers and foliage that is a pale green color when young.

Viburnum opulus

This is a large, vigorous, deciduous shrub with dark green, maple-like, three- to five-lobed leaves that turn orange-yellow to red in autumn. Broad, flattened, lacecap-like heads of white flowers open in the early summer, and these are followed by glossy, red fruits.

Common name: European cranberry bush
Native range: Europe, North Africa, W and C Asia
Height: 13 ft (4 m)
Spread: 13 ft (4 m)
Hardiness: Zone 3
Variants: 'Aureum' produces foliage that is yellow when young. 'Compactum' is a form with a very compact habit, growing only up to about 5 ft (1.5 m) tall. 'Roseum' has rounded heads of large, sterile, white flowers. 'Xanthocarpum' produces yellow fruits.

Viburnum plicatum

This rounded to spreading, deciduous shrub has branches often arranged in tiers, with dark green, prominently veined leaves turning red-purple in autumn. Large, flattened, lacecap-like heads of white flowers open on long stalks above the foliage in late spring and early summer, and these are sometimes followed by small, red fruits. Normally grown as one of the selected forms listed below.

Native range: China, Japan
Height: 10 ft (3 m)
Spread: 16 ft (5 m)
Hardiness: Zone 5
Variants: 'Grandiflorum' has rounded heads of large, sterile flowers but no fruits. 'Lanarth' has lacecap-like heads with very large, sterile flowers, but is not free-fruiting. 'Mariesii' has

very distinctly layered branches and lacecap-like flowerheads, but few fruits. 'Nanum Semperflorens' is a compact and slow-growing form, with small flowerheads that are produced over a long period during summer and autumn. 'Pink Beauty' is a striking form with the sterile flowers aging to deep pink. 'Rowallane' has lacecap-like flowerheads and profusely borne red fruits.

Viburnum rhytidophyllum

This vigorous, large, evergreen shrub has stout, scurfy shoots and bold, glossy, dark green, leathery leaves, up to 8 in (20 cm) long, conspicuously and deeply veined. Grown mainly for its foliage, it also bears large, domed heads of small, creamy white flowers in late spring and early summer, and these are followed by red fruits that ripen to black.

Native range: China
Height: 16 ft (5 m)
Spread: 16 ft (5 m)
Hardiness: Zone 5

Viburnum sargentii

This is a large, deciduous shrub with dark green, three-lobed leaves, bronze when young and turning yellow or red in autumn. Lacecap-like heads up to 4 in (10 cm) across, of white flowers in late spring are followed by bright red fruits.

Native range: NE Asia
Height: 10 ft (3 m)
Spread: 13 ft (4 m)
Hardiness: Zone 4
Variant: 'Onondaga' is a compact and upright shrub with deep maroon young leaves that turn red-purple in autumn. The fertile flowers are red in bud and these contrast with the sterile, white, outer flowers.

Viburnum sieboldii

This is a large, vigorous, deciduous shrub of spreading habit, sometimes

Vinca minor 'Atropurpurea'

Viburnum carlesii 'Diana'

treelike, and has bold, glossy, dark green, prominently veined leaves. Large clusters of small, tubular, creamy white flowers open in late spring, and these are followed by profuse, persistent, glossy, red fruits maturing to black.

Native range: Japan
Height: 20 ft (6 m) or more
Spread: 20 ft (6 m)
Hardiness: Zone 4

Viburnum tinus

This popular and vigorous, evergreen shrub of compact habit has rather glossy, dark green, usually hairy leaves. The small, white flowers, often tinged pink, open in clusters at the ends of the shoots from pink buds over a long period during the the winter and spring, followed by blue-black fruits. this shrub makes an excellent dense screen or hedge.

Common name: Laurustinus viburnum
Native range: Mediterranean region
Height: 10 ft (3 m)
Spread: 13 ft (4 m)
Hardiness: Zone 8
Variants: 'Eve Price' is very compact with bright pink buds. 'French White' produces pure white flowers. 'Gwenllian' has profusely borne, pink-tinged flowers, and fruits freely. 'Purpureum' has dark green leaves that are purple-flushed when young. 'Variegatum' has pale green leaves conspicuously edged with yellow.

Vinca
Apocynaceae

The periwinkles form a small genus of just six species of subshrubs and herbaceous perennials, all with opposite leaves, and slender, trailing, or arching shoots.

These plants are suitable for any well-drained soil, as long as it is not too dry, and they make excellent ground cover, whether planted in sun or shade. Flowering is usually best, however, in reasonably bright positions. Cutting back hard in spring can increase their vigor.

Vinca major 'Variegata'

Vinca difformis

This is an evergreen subshrub, herbaceous in cold regions, with slender, trailing shoots and bright green leaves up to 3 in (8 cm) long. The pale lilac to nearly white flowers, 1½ in (4 cm) across, with five spreading lobes, open singly along the shoots during the late autumn and early winter.

Native range: SW Europe, NW Africa
Height: 12 in (30 cm)
Spread: 10 ft (3 m) or more
Hardiness: Zone 8
Variant: 'Jenny Pym' has flowers with deep lilac lobes narrowly edged white and with a white center.

Vinca major

This is a vigorous, evergreen shrub with arching, slender shoots bearing dark green leaves, up to 3 in (8 cm) long. Bright blue flowers, up to 1½ in (4 cm) across, with five spreading lobes, are borne singly along upright shoots over a long period from the late spring to early autumn.

Common name: Big periwinkle
Native range: Mediterranean region
Height: 24 in (60 cm)
Spread: 16 ft (5 m) or more
Hardiness: Zone 6
Variants: 'Maculata' has leaves that are blotched in the center with yellow-green. 'Oxyloba' produces deep blue flowers with narrow lobes. 'Variegata' bears leaves that are broadly edged with creamy white.

Vinca minor

This vigorous, trailing, evergreen shrub forms dense mats of glossy, dark green leaves, up to about 2 in (5 cm) long. The five-lobed flowers, about 1 in (2.5 cm) across, in various shades of blue, are produced on the young shoots over a long period from spring to autumn.

Common name: Myrtle periwinkle
Native range: Europe, W Asia

Vitex agnus-castus

Height: 8 in (20 cm)
Spread: 16 ft (5 m) or more
Hardiness: Zone 4
Variants: 'Alba Variegata' produces leaves that are edged with pale yellow and bears white flowers. 'Argenteovariegata' has leaves edged with creamy white and blue-colored flowers. 'Atropurpurea' is a form that produces deep violet-purple flowers. 'Aureovariegata' has yellow-edged leaves and blue flowers. 'Azurea Flore Pleno' produces sky-blue, double flowers. 'Gertrude Jekyll' has profusely borne, white flowers. 'La Grave' bears large, azure-blue flowers. 'Multiplex' has double, plum-purple-colored flowers.

Vitex
Verbenaceae

This large genus consisting of 250 or so species of deciduous and evergreen shrubs and trees is widely distributed in warm, mainly tropical regions of the world. They have opposite-growing leaves, which are often divided into several leaflets.

The following is the most frequently seen species in garden cultivation. It needs a well-drained soil and a position in full sun. In regions where it is not completely hardy, it can be grown against a sun-facing wall. Cut back the shoots that have flowered to strong buds in the spring.

Vitex agnus-castus
A deciduous shrub of open habit with gray, hairy shoots and dark green, aromatic leaves divided into slender leaflets. Large, branched spikes of fragrant, violet flowers open during early autumn. Flowers best in dry weather after a hot summer.

Common name: Chaste tree
Native range: Mediterranean region to C Asia
Height: 10 ft (3 m)
Spread: 10 ft (3 m)
Hardiness: Zone 7

Weigela 'Bristol Ruby'

Weigela
Caprifoliaceae

The ten species of deciduous shrubs of this genus, all with opposite leaves, are grown for their tubular to bell-shaped, pink to red, yellow, or sometimes white flowers. Suitable for the shrub border, they can be grown in any good, well-drained soil. On mature plants, cut some of the oldest shoots back to the base and shorten shoots that have flowered.

Weigela 'Briant Rubidor'

This garden-raised hybrid makes a deciduous, upright shrub. The leaves are either bright yellow or green edged with yellow, and are up to 3 in (8 cm) long. The clusters of deep red, bell-shaped flowers open in late spring and early summer. It does best with a little shade, as the leaves may burn in full sun.

Synonym: Weigela 'Olympiade'
Height: 8 ft (2.5 m)
Spread: 6 ft (2 m)
Hardiness: Zone 5

Weigela 'Bristol Ruby'

This is a vigorous, garden-raised hybrid with an upright habit that has dark green leaves. Clusters of rich red, bell-shaped flowers open in late spring and early summer from very dark red buds.

Height: 8 ft (2.5 m)
Spread: 6 ft (2 m)
Hardiness: Zone 5

Weigela florida

This is a deciduous shrub of a compact, rounded, spreading habit with arching shoots and dark green, taper-pointed leaves up to about 4 in (10 cm) in length. Clusters of funnel-shaped, deep pink flowers, pale pink inside, open in the late spring to early summer period.

Native range: China, Korea
Height: 6 ft (2 m)
Spread: 8 ft (2.5 m)
Hardiness: Zone 5
Variants: 'Foliis Purpureis' is lower-growing and compact in habit, up to 3 ft (1 m) tall, with bronze-purple foliage and purple-pink flowers. 'Variegata' has leaves that are edged with creamy white.

Weigela 'Looymansii Aurea'

This is a garden-raised hybrid of spreading habit producing pale golden yellow-colored young leaves edged with red, later pale green. Clusters of slender, pale pink flowers open in late spring to early summer. Does best given light shade, as it may burn in full sun.

Height: 6 ft (2 m)
Spread: 6 ft (2 m)
Hardiness: Zone 5

Weigela middendorffiana

This is a small, compact shrub producing upright shoots bearing bright green leaves growing up to about 3 in (8 cm) long. Clusters of bell-shaped, pale yellow-colored flowers, often with a conspicuous blotch of deep orange inside, open at

Xanthoceras sorbifolium

the ends of the shoots in the late
spring to early summer.

Native range: Japan, N China, Korea
Height: 5 ft (1.5 m)
Spread: 5 ft (1.5 m)
Hardiness: Zone 5

Weigela 'Victoria'
This is a garden-raised hybrid making
a deciduous shrub of upright habit
with deep bronze-purple leaves
growing up to 3 in (8 cm) long. Deep
purple-pink, funnel-shaped flowers
open in late spring to early summer.

Height: 6 ft (2 m)
Spread: 5 ft (1.5 m)
Hardiness: Zone 5

Xanthoceras
Sapindaceae

The only member of this small
genus is a deciduous shrub. It is not
frequently seen in garden cultivation
and is grown for its striking and
unusual flowers.

It is a suitable plant for any good,
well-drained soil and does best in a
hot, sunny position. It can be grown
in the shrub border or against a warm
wall. Pruning is not normally
required.

Xanthoceras sorbifolium
This is a vigorous, deciduous shrub,
sometimes treelike in stature,
producing stout shoots bearing glossy,
dark green leaves divided up into 17
sharply toothed leaflets. The five-
petalled, white flowers, about 1 in
(3 cm) across, have a yellow-green,
later red, blotch in the center. They
open in clusters at the ends of the
shoots in late spring.

Native range: China
Height: 16 ft (5 m)
Spread: 13 ft (4 m)
Hardiness: Zone 6

400 TREES, SHRUBS, AND BAMBOOS

Yucca
Agavaceae

This is a genus comprising about 40
species of evergreen herbaceous
perennials, shrubs, and trees, natives
of the southern United States of
America, Mexico, and Central
America.

Grown for their bold foliage and
showy flower clusters, they thrive in a
well-drained soil and a warm, sunny
position. Cut the dead flower stalks
back to the base in spring.

Yucca filamentosa
This stemless, evergreen shrub
spreads by sending out suckers and
forms dense clumps of rigid, dark
green, sword-shaped leaves up to
30 in (75 cm) long. Pendulous,
creamy white flowers, 2 in (5 cm)
long, open in summer on spikes
up to 5 ft (1.5 m) tall.

Common name: Adam's needle
Native range: SE United States of
America
Height: 5 ft (1.5 m)
Spread: 5 ft (1.5 m)
Hardiness: Zone 4
Variants: 'Bright Edge' has leaves
edged in yellow. 'Variegata' bears
leaves edged with creamy white.

Yucca flaccida
This is a suckering, stemless,
evergreen shrub resembling
Y. filamentosa but differing in the
slightly shorter, dark green to blue-
green leaves, which bend downward
at the end. Pendulous, creamy white
flowers, up to 2 in (5 cm) long, open
in summer on tall spikes up to 5 ft
(1.5 m) high.

Native range: SE United States of
America
Height: 5 ft (1.5 m)
Spread: 5 ft (1.5 m)
Hardiness: Zone 4
Variants: 'Golden Sword' has leaves
that are banded with yellow in the

center. 'Ivory' produces profuse
flowers that are borne horizontally.

Yucca gloriosa
This evergreen shrub has a short,
stout, usually unbranched trunk
bearing a dense crown of large, rigid,
spine-tipped, dark green leaves, up
to 24 in (60 cm) long, blue-green
when young. Tall spikes of
pendulous, creamy white flowers,
sometimes flushed red or purple,
open in late summer.

Common name: Mound lily yucca
Native range: SE United States of
America
Height: 8 ft (2.5 m)
Spread: 6 ft (2 m)
Hardiness: Zone 6
Variant: 'Variegata' has leaves edged
with yellow.

Yushania
Gramineae

This is a genus of evergreen
bamboos, native of East Asia. The
following is grown for its foliage and
graceful habit, and is suitable for a
good, moist but well-drained soil. It
will stand exposure and can be
planted for shelter, but it will need
protection from strong winds in very
cold areas. It can be invasive and may
need to be restricted at the roots.

Yushania anceps
This is a vigorous, evergreen bamboo
that spreads quickly by sending out
underground stems. The tall,
cylindrical canes are purple at first,
later turning brownish green, and
bear dense clusters of slender, purple
branches and glossy, bright green
leaves, to 4 in (10 cm) long, blue-
green beneath.

Native range: NW Himalayas
Height: 16 ft (5 m)
Spread: 16 ft (5 m) or more
Hardiness: Zone 8

Zauschneria
Onagraceae

This is a small genus made up of four species of deciduous and evergreen, herbaceous perennials and subshrubs, with opposite- or alternate-growing leaves, and are natives of the western United States of America and northern Mexico. The following is grown for its foliage and its contrasting flowers.

It requires a not-too-rich, well-drained soil in full sun, and is suitable for growing in a rock garden or the base of a sunny wall. Cut back to the woody base in spring.

Zauschneria californica
This variable, evergreen, subshrubby perennial forms clumps of upright shoots and spreads by sending out underground stems. It produces slender, green to gray-green leaves and spikes of scarlet, funnel-shaped flowers that open at the ends of the shoots over a long period from summer through to autumn.

Common name: California fuchsia
Native range: California, NW Mexico
Height: 24 in (60 cm)
Spread: 24 in (60 cm)
Hardiness: Zone 8
Variant: 'Dublin' produces profusely borne, bright scarlet flowers and green leaves.

Zelkova
Ulmaceae

This is a genus made up of six species of deciduous trees, grown for their foliage and bark, and natives of southern Europe, the Caucasus, and East Asia. The flowers are tiny and inconspicuous, males and females usually separate but borne on the same tree.

They require a good, deep, moist but well-drained soil and they make excellent specimen trees for the larger garden.

Zelkova serrata
This is a spreading, deciduous tree producing attractive, smooth, gray bark that flakes as the tree ages. Its dark green, slender-pointed, and sharply toothed leaves turn to shades of orange, yellow, and red in the autumn. Tiny green flowers open on the young shoots in the spring, and these are followed by small, spherical-shapedfruits.

Common name: Japanese zelkova
Native range: China, Japan, Korea
Height: 50 ft (15 m)
Spread: 50 ft (15 m)
Hardiness: Zone 5

Zenobia
Ericaceae

The single species of this small genus is grown principally for its attractive foliage and fragrant flowers. It requires a moist but well-drained, acidic soil that is rich in organic matter. It does best if given a sunny or lightly shaded garden position, but it requires more shade in areas where the soil tends to dry out during the hot weather.

Cut the stems that have flowered back to strong shoots when flowering has finished. Cut some of the oldest shoots right back to ground level every year.

Zenobia pulverulenta
This deciduous or semi-evergreen shrub has bloomy, arching shoots and dark green to blue-green leaves that are scalloped at the margins. Nodding, bell-shaped, fragrant, white flowers, up to ⅓ in (1 cm) across, open in clusters toward the ends of the shoots in early to midsummer.

Native range: SE United States of America
Height: 5 ft (1.5 m)
Spread: 5 ft (1.5 m)
Hardiness: Zone 5

Climbers

The versatility of climbing plants enables them to be grown in virtually any garden situation. Those that are self-clinging, with tendril pads, such as *Parthenocissus*, or with aerial roots, such as *Hedera* (ivy), the climbing hydrangeas, and *Campsis*, can be grown on a wall or tree trunk, depending on their requirements for light. Vigorous climbers on a house wall should be kept under control because they can invade loose brickwork and damage guttering.

Other climbers attach themselves by twining their leaf stalks, such as *Clematis*, or stems, such as the honeysuckles (*Lonicera*), or by using tendrils, such as the passion flower (*Passiflora*). If they are grown against a wall, these plants require a suitable support, such as a wire or wooden frame, but they can also be trained into large shrubs or trees, or over a pergola or archway. If they are grown over a support, make sure that it is strong enough, as a vigorous climber can be extremely heavy, especially when wet or laden with snow. Choose climbers that are to be grown into a tree or shrub with care, as some, such as *Actinidia deliciosa* and *Clematis montana*, are very vigorous and demand a large tree to act as a support.

Climbers provide a variety of features to delight the gardener, from the striking flowers of Clematis, which are often followed by ornamental and long-lasting silky seed heads, to the fragrant flowers of several of the honeysuckles (*Lonicera*) and the showy trumpets of *Campsis*. While many climbers flower in spring and summer, they can be chosen to extend this display throughout the year. The dainty *Clematis cirrhosa* var. *balearica* is particularly useful for blooming between late autumn and early spring. Foliage, too, is an important feature, as in the bold-leaved and variegated *Hedera colchica* 'Dentata Variegata', and the striking autumn color of *Parthenocissus*.

Actinidia deliciosa 'Hayward'

Actinidia
Actinidiaceae

This genus of some 40 species of deciduous and evergreen climbers with twining shoots are all natives of East Asia.

Grown for their foliage, flowers, and fruits, they are suitable for any good, well-drained soil, flowering best in a sunny position. They can be trained into a tree or some other appropriate support, or grown against a sunny wall.

Except in some forms of *A. deliciosa*, male and female flowers are borne on separate plants and both need to be grown to produce fruit. Cut back to about 12 in (30 cm) on planting and tie in the resulting shoots as they grow. Reduce the length of vigorous shoots in early spring.

Actinidia arguta
This vigorous, deciduous climber has dark green, finely toothed leaves on red stalks. Clusters of greenish-white, fragrant flowers, ¾ in (2 cm) across, open in early summer, followed by smooth, yellow-green, edible fruits on female plants. Some forms selected for their edible fruits as well as self-fertile forms are sometimes available.

Common name: Bower actinidia
Native range: E Asia
Height: 33 ft (10 m) or more
Hardiness: Zone 3

Actinidia deliciosa
This is a vigorous, deciduous climber with stout, bristly shoots and glossy, dark green leaves. Clusters of fragrant, creamy white flowers, 1½ in (4 cm) across, open in early summer, followed on female plants by the familiar bristly skinned, edible fruits. Several forms selected for their fruits, as well as self-fertile forms, are available. This species has been called *A. chinensis* in gardens.

Common names: Chinese actinidia, kiwi
Native range: China
Height: 33 ft (10 m) or more
Hardiness: Zone 8
Variant: 'Hayward' is popular for its larger-sized fruits.

Actinidia kolomikta

This deciduous climber has slender shoots and dark green, heart-shaped leaves strikingly blotched with white or pink. Clusters of fragrant, white flowers, up to about ¾ in (2 cm) across, open in the late spring to early summer, and these are followed on female plants by smooth, yellow-green fruits about 1 in (2.5 cm) long. The foliage color develops best in conditions of bright light.

Native range: China, Japan
Height: 33 ft (10 m) or more
Hardiness: Zone 4

Akebia
Lardizabalaceae

A genus of four species of deciduous and evergreen climbers with slender, twining stems and leaves divided, fanlike, into several leaflets. Grown for its flowers and unusual fruits, the following species needs a good, moist but well-drained soil. Flowering best in full sun, it is suitable for training into a tree or other support or, with support, for growing against a wall. Restrict its growth if necessary by cutting back after flowering.

Akebia quinata

This vigorous, slender-stemmed, deciduous or semi-evergreen climber has leaves divided into five leaflets. Emerging bronze, they turn to dark green and can be tinged purple during winter. Pendulous clusters of fragrant, purple flowers in early spring are followed by sausage-shaped, bloomy pods up to 4 in (10 cm) long.

Akebia quinata

Native range: E Asia
Height: 33 ft (10 m)
Hardiness: Zone 5

Ampelopsis
Vitaceae

A genus of about 25 species of deciduous climbers, natives of North America and Asia. Closely related to the grape vines (*Vitis*), they attach themselves to supports by slender tendrils growing from the stems. They are grown for their often deeply cut leaves and ornamental fruits and they prefer a good, well-drained soil and fruit best if given a sunny position. To restrict their growth, cut them back as necessary in winter.

Ampelopsis brevipedunculata

This is a deciduous climber that has three- or, sometimes, five-lobed, dark green leaves, to 6 in (15 cm) long. Clusters of tiny, green flowers in summer are followed by striking, bright blue-colored fruits, about ⅓ in (1 cm) across, ripening from yellow and pink.

Native range: E Asia
Height: 20 ft (6 m)
Hardiness: Zone 4
Variant: 'Elegans' has leaves blotched with white and pink and is less vigorous.

Aristolochia
Aristolochiaceae

This genus comprises some 300 species of twining deciduous and evergreen climbers, shrubs, and perennial herbs. They are widely distributed and many are found in tropical regions.

Grown principally for its bold foliage and unusual flowers, the following species does best in a good, well-drained soil. It is suitable for growing over any strong support or into a tree.

Cut any weak shoots to the base and train strong shoots on to a suitable support. Restrict growth, if necessary, by cutting back long shoots in spring or when flowering has finished.

Aristolochia macrophylla
This is a vigorous, deciduous climber that produces twining shoots and dark green, heart-shaped leaves about 10 in (25 cm) or more long. The unusual siphon-shaped flowers, about 1½ in (4 cm) long, are yellow-green with a flared, purple-brown mouth, and are borne singly or in pairs from the shoots in the early summer months.

Common name: Dutchman's pipe
Native range: E United States of America
Height: 33 ft (10 m)
Hardiness: Zone 4

Berberidopsis
Flacourtiaceae

This genus is made up of two species of evergreen climber, natives of Chile and Australia, but only the following is commonly grown. It needs a moist but well-drained, lime-free soil rich in organic matter, and it generally grows best in the shade.

It prefers areas with cool, moist summers and mild winters, and it can be trained against a shady wall or allowed to scramble over small shrubs.

Berberidopsis corallina
This is a slender-stemmed, evergreen or semi-evergreen climber with dark green, spiny margined leaves, up to 4 in (10 cm) long, blue-white beneath. The small, spherical, bright red flowers, up to ½ in (1.5 cm) across, hang from the stems on long, slender shoots, and open over a long period during mid- and late summer.

Common name: Coral Chilevine
Native range: Chile
Height: 16 ft (5 m)
Hardiness: Zone 8

Billardiera
Pittosporaceae

This is a genus of about eight species of evergreen climbers with twining stems, natives of Australia. Only the following species is commonly grown, for its flowers and fruits.

This species requires a moist, well-drained, lime-free soil that is rich in organic matter, and it does best in areas with cool, moist summers and mild winters. It usually needs little pruning.

Billardiera longiflora
This is an evergreen climber with slender, twining shoots bearing narrow, dark green leaves. The slender, tubular, pale yellow-green

Campsis x *tagliabuana* 'Madame Galen'

flowers, up to about 1 in (3 cm) long, open during the summer, and these are followed by rounded, lobed fruits in various colors from deep blue to purple, red, pink, or white.

Common name: Climbing blueberry
Native range: Tasmania
Height: 6 ft (2 m)
Hardiness: Zone 8

Campsis
Bignoniaceae

The two species in this genus are deciduous climbers that cling by sending out aerial roots, and are natives of China and the southeast of the United States of America. They have opposite leaves divided, fernlike, into several leaflets.

Cultivated for their showy flowers, they will grow in any well-drained soil. They can be trained over any suitably strong support, such as a pergola, large tree, or sunny wall. Train against the support initially as they can take time to attach their roots.

Cut back to 6 in (15 cm) after planting and train the strongest-growing shoots to the desired framework. Once established, prune the side shoots to two or three buds in spring.

Campsis radicans
This vigorous, deciduous climber has stout shoots and large, dark green leaves composed of up to 11 sharply toothed leaflets. Clusters of large, trumpet-shaped, bright orange to red flowers, up to 4 in (10 cm) long, open in late summer.

Common name: Trumpet vine
Native range: SE United States of America
Height: 33 ft (10 m) or more
Hardiness: Zone 4
Variant: 'Flava' produces yellow flowers.

Campsis x *tagliabuana*
This is a garden-raised hybrid between C. *grandiflora* and C. *radicans* that makes a very

vigorous, deciduous climber clinging by aerial roots, with leaves divided into up to 11 leaflets. Clusters of large, trumpet-shaped flowers open in the late summer.

Height: 33 ft (10 m) or more
Hardiness: Zone 5
Variant: 'Madame Galen' is the most popular form with large clusters of bright orange-red flowers up to 3 in (8 cm) long.

Celastrus
Celastraceae

This is a genus of about 30 species of widely distributed, deciduous and evergreen shrubs, trees, and climbers. The flowers are small and rather inconspicuous, but the main attraction is the fruits, which split to reveal colored seeds. Male and female flowers are usually borne on separate plants; both sexes need to be present for fruiting.

The following species will grow in any well-drained soil and can be trained over any suitably strong support or trained to grow into a tree.

Celastrus orbiculatus
This vigorous, deciduous climber has twining stems and bright green leaves turning yellow in autumn. Small clusters of tiny, greenish flowers in early summer are followed by yellow, pea-sized fruits. The fruits reveal bright red seeds when they open and have a very striking appearance.

Common name: Oriental bittersweet
Native range: E Asia
Height: 33 ft (10 m) or more
Hardiness: Zone 5

Cissus
Vitaceae

This large genus comprises about 350 species of usually evergreen, herbaceous perennials and shrubs,

succulents, and climbers that are widely distributed, mainly in the tropical and subtropical regions of the world.

The following species is grown for its foliage and fruits. It is suitable for any good, moist but well-drained soil, but it will thrive only in mild climates. It can be grown onto a suitable support, or trained against a wall or into a tree. Cut back long shoots as necessary in spring to restrict size.

Cissus striata
This evergreen climber attaches itself to supports by slender tendrils, and has glossy, dark green leaves divided into usually five toothed leaflets. Clusters of small, green flowers open in summer, and these are followed by red to purple-red or black berries. Does best where winters are mild.

Common name: Ivy of Uruguay
Native range: Chile, S Brazil
Height: 33 ft (10 m)
Hardiness: Zone 8

Clematis
Ranunculaceae

This is a large genus of about 300 species of climbers, subshrubs, and herbaceous perennials, widely distributed, with opposite leaves usually divided into several leaflets. The leaves of climbing species have twining stalks for attaching themselves to supports.

Grown mainly for their flowers—the showy part of which is the sepals—they also often produce conspicuous, silky seed heads that can remain an attractive feature for a long period. Petals are absent, but some flowers have modified petal-like staminodes in their centers.

Grow in well-drained soil rich in organic matter, and keep the base of the plant shaded. Cut back deciduous sorts on planting to a pair of buds at 12 in (30 cm) from the soil.

Clematis 'Alba Luxurians'

Prune early-flowering species to restrict growth if necessary in late the spring when flowering has finished. Prune early, large-flowered hybrids in early spring by cutting shoots back to a strong bud. Removing flowers once they have faded will encourage a second crop of blooms.

Prune late-flowering (from midsummer) species and hybrids in early spring. Late, large-flowered hybrids, Texensis hybrids, and Viticella hybrids can be cut back hard to about within 6–8 in (15–20 cm) from the soil level.

Clematis 'Abundance'

This late-flowering Viticella hybrid bears profuse, wine-red, slightly nodding flowers, up to about 2¾ in (7 cm) across, with centers of golden stamens and deeply veined sepals. Flowering occurs from midsummer to late autumn.

Height: 8 ft (2.5 m)
Hardiness: Zone 6

Clematis 'Alba Luxurians'

A late-flowering Viticella hybrid with gray-green foliage and white flowers, up to 3 in (8 cm) across, with centers of deep purple stamens, the four sepals flushed green toward their tips. Flowering occurs from midsummer to early autumn.

Height: 13 ft (4 m)
Hardiness: Zone 6

Clematis alpina

A slender-stemmed, deciduous climber with leaves divided into nine sharply toothed leaflets. The nodding, bell-shaped, usually blue flowers, with centers of white staminodes, open on slender stalks in mid- to late spring, followed by silky seed heads.

Common name: Alpine clematis
Native range: Europe
Height: 8 ft (2.5 m)
Hardiness: Zone 5
Variants: 'Columbine' produces pale

Clematis 'Barbara Jackman'

Clematis 'Bill Mackenzie'

gray-blue flowers. 'Constance' has semidouble, deep pink flowers. 'Frankie' bears blue flowers, the staminodes of which are attractively blue-tipped. 'Jacqueline du Pré' produces large, mauve-pink flowers with sepals that are narrowly edged with white. 'Pamela Jackman' has large, rich blue-colored flowers with outer staminodes that are tinged blue. 'Pink Flamingo' bears profuse, pink, double flowers. 'Ruby' produces deep pink flowers. 'White Columbine' has pure white flowers. 'Willy' bears mauve-pink flowers that are deep pink at the bases of the sepals.

Clematis armandii

This is a vigorous, evergreen climber with glossy, dark green leaves that are often bronze-colored when young. Leaves are divided into three leathery, prominently veined leaflets. Flowers are fragrant, with four or five sepals, white or pink-tinged, borne in clusters in the early spring. It generally does best if given a sheltered position and grows well against a wall.

Native range: China, N Myanmar (Burma), N Vietnam
Height: 33 ft (10 m)
Hardiness: Zone 7

Variants: 'Apple Blossom' has flowers that are pink in bud. 'Snowdrift' has large, pure white flowers.

Clematis 'Barbara Jackman'

This early, large-flowered hybrid bears mauve-blue flowers, up to 4 in (10 cm) across, with contrasting creamy yellow stamens, each sepal with a central carmine stripe. Flowering occurs in the late spring to early summer period and again in the early autumn.

Height: 10 ft (3 m)
Hardiness: Zone 5

Clematis 'Bees' Jubilee'

This is an early, large-flowered hybrid with deep pink flowers, up to 5 in (12 cm) across, fading to pale pink, with a deeper pink band on each sepal and with a center of pale brown stamens. Flowering occurs in late spring and early summer and again in early autumn.

Height: 8 ft (2.5 m)
Hardiness: Zone 5

Clematis 'Bill Mackenzie'

This vigorous hybrid between *C. tangutica* and *C. tibetana* subsp.

Clematis 'Bees' Jubilee'

vernayi makes a deciduous climber with bright green leaves composed of sharply toothed leaflets. Long-stalked flowers, with four wide-spreading, rather thick, bright yellow sepals, have centers of purple filaments, and its flowers open from midsummer through to autumn.

Height: 16 ft (5 m)
Hardiness: Zone 5

Clematis campaniflora

This is a vigorous, deciduous climber with slender shoots and blue-green leaves with up to 21, usually untoothed, leaflets. The small, wide bell-shaped flowers are pale lilac and open on long, slender stalks in mid- to late summer.

Native range: Portugal, SW Spain
Height: 20 ft (6 m)
Hardiness: Zone 6
Variant: 'Lisboa' has larger, mauve-blue flowers.

Clematis x *cartmanii* 'Joe'

This garden-raised hybrid between C. *marmoraria* and C. *paniculata* makes a trailing evergreen plant that can be tied in to a suitable support. It produces finely divided, glossy, green leaves and masses of white, starlike flowers, up to about 1½ in (4 cm) across, each with six sepals. Flowers are flushed with green in bud and open in early spring.

Height: 5 ft (1.5 m)
Hardiness: Zone 8

Clematis cirrhosa

This is a variable, evergreen climber producing slender shoots and glossy, dark green leaves. Foliage can vary from undivided to lobed or be divided into three leaflets. Bell-shaped, creamy white, fragrant flowers, up to about 2¾ in (7 cm) across, sometimes spotted with purple inside, open from late autumn to early spring, and these are followed by silky seed heads.

Clematis cirrhosa var. balearica

Native range: Mediterranean region
Height: 10 ft (3 m)
Hardiness: Zone 7
Variants: var. *balearica* (fern-leaved clematis) has deeply lobed leaflets that turn a bronze-purple color in the cold weather. 'Freckles' produces flowers that are heavily blotched inside with maroon-purple. 'Wisley Cream' has large, creamy white, unspotted flowers.

Clematis 'Comtesse de Bouchaud'

This late, large-flowered hybrid of vigorous growth bears mauve-pink flowers, growing up to about 4 in (10 cm) across, with deeper pink veins and centers of bright yellow stamens. It flowers profusely from midsummer through to the early autumn.

Height: 13 ft (4 m)
Hardiness: Zone 5

Clematis 'Daniel Deronda'

This is an early, large-flowered hybrid. The strikingly large flowers, which grow up to 8 in (20 cm) across, are violet-blue in color and have paler-colored centers and creamy stamens. The plant blooms in the late spring and early summer, and again in early autumn. The flowers produced early in the year are singles or sometimes semidoubles, and they are at their most impressive when the plant is given a sunny position.

Height: 10 ft (3 m)
Hardiness: Zone 5

Clematis 'Doctor Ruppel'

An early, large-flowered hybrid with bright pink flowers, a deeper pink band in the center of each sepal and pale brown stamens. Flowering occurs in late spring and early summer, and again in early autumn. Flowers fade little even in strong sunlight.

Height: 10 ft (3 m)
Hardiness: Zone 5

Clematis 'Duchess of Albany'

A late-flowering Texensis hybrid bearing upright, tulip-shaped, bright pink flowers shading to lilac-pink at the margins of the fleshy sepals, which are striped deeper pink in the center. Can be grown as a climber or trailing over low shrubs.

Height: 8 ft (2.5 m)
Hardiness: Zone 4

Clematis 'Duchess of Edinburgh'

An early, large-flowered hybrid with fully double, rosette-like, white flowers, 4 in (10 cm) across, with green shading and centers of yellow stamens. Flowers open in late spring and early summer and again in early autumn. Some of the sepal-like

Clematis 'Doctor Ruppel'

leaves below the flowers are often green mottled with white.

Height: 8 ft (2.5 m)
Hardiness: Zone 5

Clematis x *durandii*

A garden-raised hybrid between
C. *integrifolia* and C. 'Jackmanii'. It
makes a stoutly branched, deciduous
climber with glossy, green, undivided
leaves up to 6 in (15 cm) in length.
The large, deep violet-blue flowers,
reaching up to 4 in (10 cm) across,
have centers of yellow stamens and
open during the summer. It is not a
self-clinging climber and so needs to
be tied in or staked.

Height: 8 ft (2.5 m)
Hardiness: Zone 5

Clematis 'Elsa Späth'

This is an early, large-flowered hybrid
producing flowers colored an
attractive shade of deep lavender-
blue. The flowers, which grow up to
about 6 in (16 cm) across, have a
paler-colored flush in the center of
each sepal and red stamens.
Flowering occurs from the late spring
through to early summer and and
there is a repeat flowering from the
late summer to early autumn.

Height: 8 ft (2.5 m)
Hardiness: Zone 5

Clematis 'Ernest Markham'

This late, large-flowered hybrid
climber has a vigorous growth pattern
and bears rich, red-colored flowers
that grow up to about 4 in (10 cm)
across. Each flower has a center of
creamy brown-colored stamens. The
blooms start to open in midsummer
and continue right through to the
autumn. If the plant is left unpruned,
it will come into flower somewhat
earlier—perhaps at the beginning of
the summer.

Clematis 'Duchess of Edinburgh'

Clematis florida 'Sieboldii'

Height: 10 ft (3 m)
Hardiness: Zone 5

Clematis 'Etoile Rose'

This is a late-flowering Texensis
hybrid with nodding, bright rose-
pink, bell-shaped flowers, up to 2 in
(5 cm) across, with sepals recurving
at the tips and edged with silvery
pink. Flowering occurs from late
summer to autumn.

Height: 10 ft (3 m)
Hardiness: Zone 4

Clematis 'Etoile Violette'

This is a late-flowering Viticella
hybrid with profusely borne, nodding,
deep purple flowers, up to about
2¾ in (7 cm) across, with centers of
creamy yellow stamens. Flowering
occurs from midsummer through to
early autumn.

Height: 10 ft (3 m)
Hardiness: Zone 6

Clematis flammula

This is a vigorous, deciduous climber
with bright green leaves divided into
three or five, sometimes lobed,
leaflets. The large clusters of small,
very fragrant, white flowers, 1 in
(2.5 cm) across, open from late
summer into autumn.

Native range: S Europe, North
Africa, SW Asia
Height: 16 ft (5 m)
Hardiness: Zone 6

Clematis florida

This deciduous or semi-evergreen
climber has glossy, deep green leaves
with up to nine leaflets. The large
flowers, 4 in (10 cm) or more across,
have up to six creamy white,
spreading sepals banded with green
on the back, and centers of purple-
black stamens. It is normally grown
as one of the selections listed below.

Clematis 'Henryi'

Native range: China
Height: 10 ft (3 m)
Hardiness: Zone 8
Variants: 'Flore Pleno' has double
flowers, with dense centers of
greenish white, petal-like
staminodes. 'Sieboldii' has white
flowers with contrasting centers of
deep purple staminodes.

Clematis 'Gipsy Queen'

This late, large-flowered hybrid bears
profuse, deep velvety purple, single
flowers, up to about 5 in (12 cm)
across, with centers of red stamens.
It flowers from the midsummer
through to early autumn.

Height: 13 ft (4 m)
Hardiness: Zone 5

Clematis 'Henryi'

An early, large-flowered hybrid whose
creamy white flowers, up to 8 in
(20 cm) across, have pointed sepals
and centers of dark brown stamens.
Flowering occurs in early to
midsummer and again in late
summer and early autumn.

Height: 13 ft (4 m)
Hardiness: Zone 5

Clematis 'HF Young'

This is an early, large-flowered hybrid
bearing pale blue flowers, up to 8 in
(20 cm) across, with overlapping
sepals and centers of cream-colored

Clematis 'Huldine'

Clematis 'Madame Julia Correvon'

stamens. Flowering occurs from the late spring to early summer and and there is a repeat flowering in the early autumn.

Height: 10 ft (3 m)
Hardiness: Zone 5

Clematis 'Huldine'

This is a late-flowering hybrid with a vigorous pattern, bearing small, white-colored flowers, about 2½ in (6 cm) across, banded pale pink on the reverse side of the sepals, and with centers of yellow stamens. Flowering occurs from midsummer to early autumn.

Height: 13 ft (4 m)
Hardiness: Zone 5

Clematis 'Jackmanii'

This is a popular, late, large-flowered hybrid bearing velvety, rich violet-purple colored, slightly nodding flowers, up to about 4 in (10 cm) across, with centers of yellow-green stamens. Flowering occurs freely from the midsummer through to the early autumn.

Height: 13 ft (4 m)
Hardiness: Zone 4

Clematis 'Kermesina'

This is a late-flowering Viticella hybrid bearing freely produced, deep crimson flowers with centers of red-purple stamens. Flowering occurs from midsummer to early autumn.

Height: 13 ft (4 m)
Hardiness: Zone 4

Clematis 'Lasurstern'

This early, large-flowered hybrid bears single, deep lavender-blue flowers, reaching up to about 8 in (20 cm) or more across, with overlapping and wavy-edged sepals and conspicuous centers of creamy colored stamens. Flowering occurs from late spring through to early summer and again in the early autumn.

Height: 10 ft (3 m)
Hardiness: Zone 5

Clematis 'Little Nell'

This is a late-flowering Viticella hybrid with profusely borne, pale pink flowers, up to 2 in (5 cm) across, with sepals edged pale mauve-pink and centers of green stamens. Flowering occurs from midsummer to early autumn.

Clematis macropetala 'Jan Lindmark'

Height: 13 ft (4 m)
Hardiness: Zone 4

Clematis macropetala

This is a slender-stemmed, deciduous climber with leaves that are usually divided up into nine bright green, sharply toothed leaflets. The slightly nodding, blue to violet-blue flowers, up to about 4 in (10 cm) across, open in the spring and early summer, and consist of four spreading sepals with centers that are made up of numerous petal-like staminodes.

Native range: SE Siberia, Mongolia, N China
Height: 10 ft (3 m)
Hardiness: Zone 5
Variants: 'Ballet Skirt' produces large, deep pink-colored flowers. 'Jan Lindmark' bears attractive mauve-pink flowers. 'Lagoon' produces large, deep blue-colored flowers. 'Markham's Pink' bears soft pink flowers. 'White Moth' has small, creamy white flowers.

Clematis 'Madame Julia Correvon'

This is a late-flowering Viticella hybrid bearing freely produced, bright wine red, and widely bell-shaped flowers, reaching up to about 5 in (13 cm) across. The flowers have strikingly contrasting centers composed of cream stamens and four slightly twisted sepals.

Height: 10 ft (3 m)
Hardiness: Zone 4

Clematis 'Marie Boisselot'

This is an early, large-flowered hybrid with a vigorous growth pattern, bearing pure white flowers, up to about 8 in (20 cm) across, composed of overlapping sepals with centers of golden yellow stamens. Flowering occurs from early summer through to early autumn.

Synonym: *Clematis* 'Madame le Coultre'
Height: 10 ft (3 m)
Hardiness: Zone 5

Clematis rehderiana

Clematis montana

This is a very popular and an extremely vigorous, deciduous climber, and bears leaves that are divided up into three leaflets. The profusely borne, usually white or pink-flushed, often scented flowers, growing up to about 2½ in (6 cm) across, open in dense clusters in the late spring. Many of the plants grown under this name may belong to one of the forms listed below. It requires a substantial support.

Native range: Himalayas to China and Taiwan
Height: 50 ft (15 m)
Hardiness: Zone 6
Variants: 'Alexander' produces creamy white-colored flowers that are very fragrant. The young foliage of 'Broughton Star' is bronze-colored and produces semidouble, dusky pink flowers. var. *grandiflora* has large, white flowers, growing up to about 5 in (12 cm) across. 'Mayleen' bears satin-pink, fragrant flowers and young foliage that is an attractive bronze color. var. *rubens* produces pink flowers and purple shoots and also has bronze-colored young foliage. 'Tetrarose' has young foliage that is bronze and bears lilac-pink flowers. 'Vera' has deep pink, fragrant flowers.

Clematis 'Mrs N Thompson'

This early, large-flowered hybrid has a compact growth habit and produces deep violet-purple flowers, reaching up to about 5 in (12 cm) across. The sepals are banded scarlet and the flowers have central clusters of red stamens. Flowering occurs from the late spring to early summer, and again in early autumn.

Height: 8 ft (2.5 m)
Hardiness: Zone 5

Clematis 'Multi Blue'

This is an early, large-flowered hybrid with deep blue-colored, double flowers, growing to about 4 in (10 cm) or more across. Flower centers have dense clusters of pale to silvery blue, petal-like staminodes. Flowering occurs from the late spring through to early summer, and again in late summer and early autumn.

Height: 8 ft (2.5 m)
Hardiness: Zone 5

Clematis 'Niobe'

This is a late, large-flowered hybrid that produces deep red, single flowers reaching up to about 6 in (15 cm) across. The flowers are very dark and blackish red when they first open, and they have central clusters of yellow stamens. Flowering occurs from midsummer through to the early autumn.

Height: 10 ft (3 m)
Hardiness: Zone 5

Clematis 'Perle d'Azur'

This vigorous, late, small-flowered hybrid freely produces slightly nodding, wide, bell-shaped, sky-blue flowers, up to about 3 in (8 cm) across, with sepals recurved at the tips, and with pale yellow stamens at their centers. Flowering occurs from midsummer to early autumn.

Clematis 'The President'

Height: 13 ft (4 m)
Hardiness: Zone 5

Clematis rehderiana

A deciduous climber with leaves divided into as many as nine leaflets. The nodding, bell-shaped, pale yellow, cowslip-scented flowers open in large, upright clusters in late summer and early autumn.

Native range: China
Height: 20 ft (6 m)
Hardiness: Zone 6

Clematis spooneri

This is a vigorous, deciduous climber, with young shoots covered in yellowish hairs and dark green leaves divided into three sharply toothed and softly hairy leaflets. White or pink-flushed flowers, reaching up to about 3½ in (9 cm) across, open between the late spring and early summer. This climber has been grown in gardens as *C. chrysocoma*.

Synonyms: *C. chrysocoma* var. *sericea*, *C. montana* var. *sericea*
Native range: China
Height: 26 ft (8 m)
Hardiness: Zone 6

Clematis tangutica

This is a deciduous climber bearing bright green leaves divided into sharply toothed, slender leaflets. The pendulous, yellow-colored, lantern-shaped flowers have four, slender-pointed sepals. The flowers open on slender stalks in the late summer to autumn, and these are followed by attractive, silky seed pods.

Native range: China
Height: 16 ft (5 m)
Hardiness: Zone 5

Dregea sinensis

Clematis 'The President'

This is an early, large-flowered hybrid that bears rich purple-blue flowers, growing up to about 6 in (15 cm) across. The sepals are silvery beneath and flower centers have clusters of red stamens. Flowering occurs over a long period, from the early summer through to early autumn.

Height: 10 ft (3 m)
Hardiness: Zone 5

Clematis tibetana subsp. *vernayi*

This vigorous, slender-stemmed, deciduous climber has blue-green leaves divided into five to seven or nine untoothed, lobed leaflets. The pendulous, lantern-shaped, yellow flowers, up to about 1½ in (4 cm) long, have thick sepals and centers of purple-colored stamens. The flowers are followed by silky seed pods.

Common name: Orange peel clematis
Native range: Nepal, China
Height: 20 ft (6 m)
Hardiness: Zone 6

Clematis x *triternata* 'Rubromarginata'

This is a vigorous-growing, garden-raised hybrid between *C. flammula* and *C. viticella* that makes a slender-stemmed deciduous climber. The small, profusely borne flowers, growing up to about 2 in (4.5 cm) across, have four to six slender, red-purple sepals, shading to white at the base, with centers of yellow stamens. It flowers during the late summer and autumn period, and does best if given a sunny position in the garden.

Height: 16 ft (5 m)
Hardiness: Zone 6

Clematis viticella

This is a semi-woody, deciduous climber with slender, partially herbaceous shoots and dark green leaves divided into several untoothed leaflets. The nodding, wide, bell-shaped, blue-purple to red-purple colored flowers, growing up to about 2½ in (6 cm) across, open over a long period from the summer through to early autumn.

Common name: Virgin's bower
Native range: S Europe, SW Asia
Height: 13 ft (4 m)
Hardiness: Zone 6
Variant: 'Purpurea Plena Elegans' produces fully double, purple-red flowers.

Dregea
Asclepiadaceae

This is a genus made up of three species of climbers bearing opposite leaves, all natives of the warm regions of the Old World.

The following species is the only one that is generally seen in garden cultivation, and it is grown principally for its attractively fragrant flowers. It is suitable for planting against a warm, sheltered wall and it needs well-drained soil in order to thrive. Tie young shoots in to a suitable support until they attach themselves naturally by twining.

Little pruning is generally needed. However, any dead, damaged, or diseased wood should be removed in spring, or, if it is necessary to restrict growth, cut stems back when flowering has finished.

Dregea sinensis

This vigorous, deciduous climber has heart-shaped, dark green leaves, up to about 4 in (10 cm) long, velvety with hairs beneath. Dense, nodding, long-stalked clusters of small, very fragrant, star-shaped flowers are creamy white spotted with red, and open in early to midsummer.

Synonym: *Wattakaka sinensis*
Native range: China
Height: 16 ft (5 m)
Hardiness: Zone 9

Eccremocarpus
Bignoniaceae

This is a small genus of five species of woody or herbaceous climbers that attach themselves by tendrils, and have opposite leaves divided into several leaflets. The following can be grown in any good, well-drained soil in a sunny position. They can be trained over any suitable support or into a tree. Pinching out the tips of the shoots of young plants encourages a bushy habit.

Eccremocarpus scaber

This vigorous, semiwoody, evergreen climber has glossy, green, fernlike leaves divided into toothed leaflets, and ending in slender, branched tendrils. Clusters of small, tubular flowers, up to 1 in (2.5 cm) long, usually orange but sometimes yellow, red, or pink, open over a long period from the late spring or early summer through to autumn.

Common name: Chilean glory flower
Native range: Chile
Height: 16 ft (5 m) or more
Hardiness: Zone 9

Fallopia
Polygonaceae

This genus, consisting of seven species of herbaceous perennials and woody climbers, is distributed widely in the temperate regions of the Northern Hemisphere. The following species is grown for its vigorous habit and its small flowers. It will grow in any well-drained garden soil and is useful for providing quick cover for walls and fences.

To restrict growth, cut back, hard if necessary, in early spring.

Hedera algeriensis 'Gloire de Marengo'

Fallopia baldschuanica

This is a very vigorously growing, deciduous climber producing long, twining shoots bearing bright green, heart-shaped leaves, bronze-colored when young. Clusters of small, white or pink-tinged flowers open over a long period during the summer and autumn period, and these are followed by small, greenish-white or pink-tinged fruits. Requires a substantial support.

Synonym: *Polygonum baldschuanicum*
Common names: Mile-a-minute, Russian vine
Native range: C Asia to China
Height: 50 ft (15 m)
Hardiness: Zone 4

Hedera
Araliaceae

The ivies are a genus of 12 species of evergreen climbers distributed from western Europe to East Asia. They attach themselves to supports by aerial roots and have two distinct growth phases. In the juvenile phase, the leaves are normally lobed and aerial roots are produced, but not flowers or fruits. Plants spread over the ground or climb vigorously in this stage. The adult stage occurs when plants reach or approach the tops of their supports. The plants then become bushy, do not climb, and start to bear flowers and fruits.

The ivies are useful for growing on a wall or up a tree trunk. They also make good ground cover. They prefer a good, moist but well-drained soil that is rich in organic matter. For

Hedera helix 'Green Ripple'

Hedera hibernica

ground cover in dense shade, vigorous green-leaved forms are most suitable. Variegated forms color best in bright positions, but should be sheltered from strong, cold winds.

Cut them back as necessary in early spring to restrict their growth.

Hedera algeriensis

This vigorous climber has purple-red colored shoots and glossy, dark green, usually three-lobed leaves, sometimes 6–8 in (20 cm) across, on long, red stalks. It makes excellent ground cover in sun or shade, but it is not suitable for colder localities. It is often grown as *H. canariensis*.

Common name: Algerian ivy
Native range: North Africa
Height: 33 ft (10 m) or more
Hardiness: Zone 8
Variant: 'Gloire de Marengo' produces gray-green leaves with margins of creamy white.

Hedera colchica

This is a vigorous climber that produces stout shoots and large, heart-shaped, unlobed or shallowly lobed, leathery, dark green leaves. The leaves sometimes reach as much as 10 in (25 cm) in length. *H. colchica* makes an excellent plant

wherever ground cover is required, but it also climbs very vigorously if given suitable support once it has become established.

Common name: Colchis ivy
Native range: Caucasus, N Iran
Height: 33 ft (10 m) or more
Hardiness: Zone 7
Variants: 'Dentata' produces large leaves with sparsely toothed margins. 'Dentata Variegata' is similar to 'Dentata' except that its leaves are broadly edged with creamy yellow.

Hedera helix

This vigorous, evergreen climber has dark green leaves often with conspicuous paler veins. The leaves are variable in size and shape, but usually have three to five lobes. This species is mainly grown in gardens as selected forms listed below.

Common name: English ivy
Native range: Europe
Height: 33 ft (10 m) or more
Hardiness: Zone 4
Variants: 'Adam' has small, shallowly three-lobed, gray-green leaves edged with white. 'Buttercup' produces golden yellow leaves turning yellow-green in shade. 'Caecilia' has strongly wavy-edged leaves with a cream margin. 'Erecta' does not climb and

produces rigid, upright shoots, up to 3 ft (1 m) in length, bearing small leaves. 'Glacier' has gray-green leaves edged with creamy white. 'Goldchild' has small, bright green leaves that are broadly edged with golden yellow. 'Goldheart' has bright green leaves blotched in the center with golden yellow. 'Green Ripple' has jaggedly lobed leaves with a long, central lobe. 'Ivalace' produces bright green, shallowly lobed leaves with crisped margins and makes a good groundcover plant. 'Little Diamond' is bushy, up to 12 in (30 cm) tall, with unlobed, gray-green leaves edged creamy white. 'Parsley Crested' has rounded leaves with crimped edges. 'Sagittifolia' has arrow-shaped leaves with slender, pointed lobes. 'Spetchley' is slow-growing with very small, dark green leaves.

Hedera hibernica

This is a vigorously growing ivy with broad, usually five-lobed, dark green leaves, up to about 6 in (15 cm) across. It is commonly grown as ground cover, and it is one of the best species for this purpose, thriving even in dense shade. It will also climb vigorously if given support.

Common name: Irish ivy
Native range: W Europe
Height: 33 ft (10 m) or more
Hardiness: Zone 4

Hydrangea
Hydrangeaceae

The climbing species that form a part of this genus make ideal plants for growing against a wall, the side of a house, or on the trunk of a large tree. Although they will cling naturally to their support by their aerial roots, they can also be used very effectively as ground cover.

As young plants, they can be slow to attach themselves to their supporting surface, and during this time they can either be tied in until they become established or be allowed to spread across the ground and attach themselves naturally in their own time. If necessary, cut back after flowering to restrict their growth. (*See also chapter on Trees, Shrubs, and Bamboos.*)

Hydrangea anomala subsp. petiolaris

This vigorous, deciduous climber has peeling, brown bark on older stems, and heart-shaped, glossy, green leaves often turning yellow in autumn. Large, flattened, lacecap-like heads of white flowers, up to 10 in (25 cm) across, edged with large, sterile flowers, open in early summer.

Synonym: *Hydrangea petiolaris*
Common name: Climbing hydrangea
Native range: Japan, South Korea
Height: 50 ft (15 m) or more
Hardiness: Zone 4

Hydrangea seemannii

This is a vigorous, evergreen climber with bold, glossy, dark green leaves up to 8 in (20 cm) long. The stems creep across the ground and attach themselves to such supports as a wall or tree trunk. Domed heads of white flowers open from buds enclosed by conspicuous bracts in summer. Most flowers are small with a few large, sterile flowers on the outside.

Native range: Mexico
Height: 33 ft (10 m) or more
Hardiness: Zone 8

Jasminum
Oleaceae

The climbing species in this genus have twining stems and opposite or alternate leaves that are usually divided into several leaflets. The following species are the ones most frequently seen in gardens and they are grown principally for their very fragrant flowers.

Hydrangea anomala subsp. *petiolaris*

. They are suitable for any good, well-drained soil and they flower best if given a position in full sun. Cut back on planting and then train the resulting shoots over a suitable support, or tie them in against a wall.

To restrict their growth, cut back as necessary after flowering. (*See also chapter on Trees, Shrubs, and Bamboos.*)

Jasminum beesianum

This is a slender-stemmed and twining, deciduous or semi-evergreen climber that bears opposite, dark green, undivided leaves, growing up to about 2 in (5 cm) in length. Clusters of small, fragrant, deep red to pink colored flowers open in late spring to early summer, and these are followed by persistent, glossy, black berries.

Native range: China
Height: 16 ft (5 m)
Hardiness: Zone 7

Jasminum officinale 'Argenteovariegatum'

Jasminum officinale

This is a very vigorous, deciduous climber producing slender, twining shoots bearing opposite, deep green leaves that are composed of up to nine leaflets. Clusters of white, very fragrant flowers, reaching up to ¾ in (2 cm) across, open at the ends of the shoots over a long period from summer to autumn.

Common name: Common white
jasmine
Native range: SW Asia to China
Height: 33 ft (10 m) or more
Hardiness: Zone 8
Variants: f. *affine* has flowers tinged
with pink. 'Argenteovariegatum' has
gray-green leaves edged with creamy
white. 'Aureum' has leaves blotched
with yellow. 'Fiona Sunrise' has soft
yellow foliage. 'Inverleith' has flowers
that are red in bud and open white,
with red on the backs of the lobes.

Jasminum x stephanense

This naturally occurring hybrid,
which is also raised in gardens,
between *J. beesianum* and
J. officinale, makes a vigorous, twining,
deciduous climber. The leaves are
opposite and vary from undivided to
those with up to five leaflets, and are
often edged with creamy yellow and
pink when young. Fragrant, pale pink
flowers open in early to midsummer.

Native range: China
Height: 16 ft (5 m)
Hardiness: Zone 8

Lapageria
Philesiaceae

The single species in this genus is an
evergreen with slender, twining
shoots. It is grown for its striking
flowers and needs a moist but well-
drained, lime-free soil that is rich in
organic matter.

At its best in regions with cool,
moist summers and mild winters, it
generally needs the protection of a
shady wall. Little pruning is usually
required, except to remove any dead
wood in spring.

Lapageria rosea

This is an evergreen climber that
spreads by sending out suckers from
the base. It has slender, twining, wiry
shoots and rigid, glossy, dark green,
taper-pointed leaves, growing up to

Lapageria rosea

4 in (10 cm) long. The showy,
pendulous, bell-shaped, deep pink
flowers, up to 3 in (8 cm) long, open
over a long period during summer
and autumn.

Common name: Red Chile bells
Native range: Chile, Argentina
Height: 13 ft (4 m)
Hardiness: Zone 8
Variant: var. *albiflora* produces white
flowers.

Lonicera
Caprifoliaceae

Although the honeysuckles contain
both shrubs and climbers, it is the
climbers that are the best known and
most popular in gardens.

They are grown for their usually
fragrant flowers, and can be
deciduous or evergreen with twining
shoots; they are suitable for any well-
drained soil. Honeysuckles can be
trained onto any strong support or
grown into a tree.

Lonicera x brownii 'Dropmore Scarlet'

Lonicera x italica

Young plants should be cut back hard on planting and then the resulting shoots tied in to the support. Cut back after flowering if necessary to restrict their growth. (*See also chapter on Trees, Shrubs, and Bamboos.*)

Lonicera x *brownii*

This is an attractive garden-raised hybrid between *L. hirsuta* and *L. sempervirens* that makes a deciduous or semi-evergreen climber with blue-green leaves. The uppermost pairs of leaves are joined into a disk around the stem. Whorls of tubular, slightly two-lipped, unscented, orange-red flowers open in late spring and summer.

Common name: Brown's honeysuckle
Height: 13 ft (4 m)
Hardiness: Zone 5
Variant: 'Dropmore Scarlet' produces scarlet-colored flowers over a long period during the summer and autumn seasons.

Lonicera *caprifolium*

This deciduous climber produces deep blue-green leaves, blue-white on their undersurfaces, with the uppermost pairs joined into a disk around the stem. The fragrant flowers are creamy white, flushed with pink on the outside, and open in

whorls in the summer. The flowers are followed by orange-red berries.

Common name: Sweet honeysuckle
Native range: Europe, W Asia
Height: 20 ft (6 m)
Hardiness: Zone 5

Lonicera x *heckrottii*

This is a garden-raised hybrid that makes a scrambling, deciduous or semi-evergreen shrub with dark green leaves, blue-green on their undersurfaces. The uppermost pairs of leaves are joined to form a disk around the stem. Whorls of fragrant, yellow flowers, flushed with purple-pink on the outside, open in summer and early autumn.

Height: 13 ft (4 m)
Hardiness: Zone 5
Variant: 'Gold Flame' climbs more vigorously and produces flowers that are more brightly colored.

Lonicera x *italica*

This is a garden-raised hybrid between *L. caprifolium* and *L. etrusca* that makes a vigorous, deciduous climber with purple-colored young shoots and dark green leaves, blue-green on their undersurfaces, with the uppermost pairs joined to form a disk around the stem. Whorls of fragrant flowers, purple-pink in bud,

Lonicera japonica 'Aureoreticulata'

open to yellow flushed with red-purple outside during the summer and early autumn. It is sometimes grown as *L. x americana*.

Height: 20 ft (6 m)
Hardiness: Zone 6
Variant: 'Harlequin' produces leaves that are edged with creamy white.

Lonicera japonica

This is a very vigorous, evergreen climber with dark green, sometimes lobed leaves. The fragrant flowers open white, sometimes purple-flushed, in pairs, and turn deep yellow with age over a long period from late spring or early summer to autumn. The flowers are then followed by black berries.

Common name: Japanese honeysuckle
Native range: China, Japan, Korea
Height: 33 ft (10 m)
Hardiness: Zone 4
Variants: 'Aureoreticulata' has leaves that are veined with yellow. 'Halliana' is very vigorous, with white flowers turning to deep yellow. 'Hall's Prolific' is similar to 'Halliana', but flowers

very profusely. var. *repens* has purple-flushed foliage and flowers tinged purple outside.

Lonicera periclymenum

This is a vigorous, deciduous climber with strongly twining shoots and rich green leaves, with blue-green undersurfaces. The flowers are white to yellow, often streaked on the outside with pink, red, or red-purple. They are very fragrant and open in dense whorls at the ends of the shoots in mid- to late summer. The flowers are then followed by glossy, red, fleshy berries.

Common name: Woodbine honeysuckle
Native range: Europe, North Africa, W Asia
Height: 26 ft (8 m)
Hardiness: Zone 4
Variants: 'Belgica' produces flowers that are reddish-purple on the outside, fading to a yellowish color. 'Graham Thomas' has creamy white flowers turning to yellow. 'Serotina' produces flowers that are deep red-purple on the outside. 'Sweet Sue' bears very profuse and fragrant white flowers, turning to yellow.

Lonicera x *tellmanniana*

This garden-raised hybrid between *L. sempervirens* and *L. tragophylla* makes a vigorous, deciduous climber with large, bright green leaves, blue-white beneath. The large, unscented flowers have a long, slender tube and are deep yellow, flushed coppery red, opening from late spring to midsummer.

Height: 16 ft (5 m)
Hardiness: Zone 5

Parthenocissus
Vitaceae

This is a genus comprising about ten species of mostly deciduous

Parthenocissus quinquefolia

climbers, natives of North America, the Himalayas, and East Asia. They attach themselves to their support by tendrils borne from the shoots, which often end in adhesive disks.

These plants are suitable for any well-drained soil and provide some of the best specimens when a large wall, or similar area, needs covering. In addition, they can also be used for ground cover.

To restrict growth, cut them back as necessary in the late autumn.

Parthenocissus henryana

This vigorous, deciduous climber attaches itself by means of tendrils ending in adhesive disks. The leaves are divided, fanlike, into three or five, or sometimes seven, leaflets, which are dark green and conspicuously veined in the center with silver and pink. The leaves turn a bright red color in autumn.

Native range: China
Height: 33 ft (10 m)
Hardiness: Zone 7

Parthenocissus quinquefolia

This vigorous, deciduous climber clings by tendrils ending in adhesive disks. It has bright green leaves divided, fanlike, into five, or sometimes just three, sharply toothed leaflets. Bronze-red foliage turns brilliant red in the early autumn.

Common name: Virginia creeper
Native range: E and C United States of America, Mexico
Height: 50 ft (15 m) or more
Hardiness: Zone 4

Parthenocissus tricuspidata

A vigorous, deciduous climber clinging by tendrils ending in adhesive disks. It has bold, glossy, dark green leaves, usually three-lobed but sometimes with three leaflets on young plants. It grows rapidly, turning brilliant red and purple in autumn.

Common name: Boston ivy
Native range: Japan, China
Height: 50 ft (15 m) or more
Hardiness: Zone 4
Variants: 'Lowii' produces small leaves with deeply cut lobes. 'Veitchii' has leaves turning to a deep red-purple in autumn.

Passiflora
Passifloraceae

The passion flowers make up a large genus of some 400 or more species of mainly deciduous and evergreen climbers and, more rarely, herbaceous perennials, shrubs, and trees. They are widely distributed, mainly in the tropical regions of South America.

The following is the most reliably hardy species and is suitable for planting in any reasonably good, well-drained soil. It performs best, however, when trained on a sun-facing wall.

In the spring, cut back the stems to restrict growth and remove any dead or damaged wood. Shoots that have flowered should be cut back to two or three buds after the blooms are spent.

Passiflora caerulea

This vigorous, evergreen or semi-evergreen climber attaches itself to supports by means of slender, coiling tendrils. It bears deep green leaves, cut nearly to the center into usually five or seven lobes. The striking, slightly fragrant flowers, 4 in (10 cm) across, are white with a conspicuous corona of white filaments, blue at the tips and deep purple at the base. Flowers open over a long period during summer and autumn and are followed by egg-shaped, orange-yellow fruits, to 2 in (5 cm) long.

Common name: Passion flower
Native range: Brazil
Height: 33 ft (10 m)
Hardiness: Zone 7

Passiflora caerulea

Pileostegia
Hydrangeaceae

This is a small genus of four species of evergreen climbers with opposite leaves, natives of East Asia. The following is the most frequently seen species in garden cultivation, and is grown for its bold foliage and attractive flowerheads. It is suitable for any good, well-drained soil and does best grown against a wall or large tree. It will thrive in sun or shade. Prune if necessary in the early spring to restrict its growth.

Pileostegia viburnoides
This is an evergreen climber that attaches itself to supports by aerial roots. It has bold, dark green, leathery leaves up to 6 in (15 cm) long. The broad, flattened clusters, up to 6 in (15 cm) across, of small, creamy white flowers open in late summer and autumn. They resemble those of the climbing hydrangeas, but lack the large, sterile flowers.

Native range: India, China, Taiwan
Height: 20 ft (6 m)
Hardiness: Zone 8

Schisandra
Schisandraceae

This genus comprises about 25 species of deciduous and evergreen climbers with twining shoots, natives mainly of East Asia. One species is native to the southeast of the United States of America.

They are grown principally for their unusual flowers and attractive fruits and prefer a moist but well-drained soil. They can be trained against a wall or some other suitable support. Male and female flowers are usually borne on separate plants and both need to be grown in order for fruit to be produced.

To restrict growth, cut back any very long shoots to a few buds in late winter or early spring. And to encourage vigorous young growth on established plants, cut one of the older shoots back right to the base each year to encourage new growth.

Schisandra rubriflora

This deciduous climber has slender, twining shoots, red when young, and dark green leaves, up to about 5 in (12 cm) long, that turn yellow in autumn. Slender-stalked, deep red flowers, about 1 in (2.5 cm) across, open during mid- to late spring, and these are followed on female plants by clusters of red, pea-sized fruits borne on long, red stalks.

Native range: N India, N Myanmar (Burma), China
Height: 20 ft (6 m)
Hardiness: Zone 8

Schizophragma
Hydrangeaceae

This is a small genus of four species of deciduous climbers with opposite leaves, natives of East Asia. They are grown for their showy flowerheads, which, like the climbing hydrangeas, bear large, sterile flowers. Attaching themselves to supports by means of aerial roots, they are suitable for any reasonably good, moist but well-drained soil that is rich in organic matter. They can be grown against a wall or the trunk of a large tree.

Growth can be restricted by cutting back after flowering.

Schizophragma hydrangeoides

This vigorous, deciduous climber has bold, dark green, sharply toothed leaves, up to 6 in (15 cm) long, blue-green beneath. Broad, flattened heads, up to 10 in (25 cm) across, of small, creamy white flowers, each head edged with large, creamy bracts, open in midsummer.

Native range: Japan
Height: 33 ft (10 m)
Hardiness: Zone 5

Variants: 'Moonlight' has leaves flushed with gray-silver. 'Roseum' has pink-colored bracts.

Senecio
Compositae

While this large genus contains several cultivated climbing species, most are suitable only for a conservatory. The following, however, can be grown outside in mild areas and requires a well-drained soil in a sunny, sheltered position. It is suitable for training against a wall or it can also be allowed to scramble through a bushy shrub.

Cut back lightly on planting and reduce shoots by about one-third after flowering. Cut out any dead wood in spring. (*See also chapter on Trees, Shrubs, and Bamboos.*)

Senecio scandens

This vigorous, scrambling, semi-evergreen shrub has long shoots and bears bright green, sharply toothed, and often lobed leaves. The bright yellow, daisy-like flowerheads open in large clusters over a long period from autumn until the first hard frosts.

Native range: E Asia
Height: 10 ft (3 m) or more
Hardiness: Zone 9

Solanum
Solanaceae

This is a very large genus made up of as many as 1,400 species of annual and perennial herbaceous plants, shrubs, trees, and climbers, very widely distributed, particularly in the tropical regions of South America.

The following climbing species are cultivated for their showy flowers and they will grow in any good, well-drained soil, but they do best in a sunny position. Train the scrambling shoots over a fence or any other suitable support, or grow them against a wall. To restrict growth, cut back long shoots to a few buds in early spring.

Solanum crispum

This is a vigorous, evergreen or semi-evergreen, scrambling shrub bearing dark green, taper-pointed leaves, up to about to 5 in (12 cm) long. The fragrant, blue-purple flowers, reaching about 1 in (3 cm) across, have conspicuous centers of yellow anthers and they open during the summer and early autumn.

Native range: Chile, Peru
Height: 33 ft (10 m)
Hardiness: Zone 8
Variant: 'Glasnevin' flowers over a very long period, sometimes into the winter season.

Solanum jasminoides

This vigorous, evergreen or semi-evergreen climber produces dark green leaves that can be unlobed, lobed, or divided into a few separate leaflets. They are borne on slender stalks, which twine around a support. Fragrant, pale blue, star-shaped flowers with centers of yellow anthers open in large clusters during summer and autumn.

Common name: Jasmine nightshade
Native range: South America
Height: 20 ft (6 m)
Hardiness: Zone 8
Variant: 'Album' produces white flowers.

Stauntonia
Lardizabalaceae

This is a genus made up of about 16 species of evergreen climbers. All have twining shoots and leaves that are divided, fanlike, into several individual leaflets.

The following is the most commonly seen species in garden cultivation. Grown for its foliage,

flowers, and fruits, it requires a good, well-drained soil and a sunny position. It can be trained against a wall or other suitable support, or it will climb into the branches of a tree. Little pruning is needed. Tie in the long shoots as they grow and cut back lightly in early spring.

Stauntonia hexaphylla

This is a vigorous, twining, evergreen climber with bold leaves divided in as many as seven dark green leaflets. Drooping clusters of white, fragrant flowers, ¾ in (2 cm) across, flushed with violet, open in late summer, and these are followed by egg-shaped, purple fruits up to 2 in (5 cm) long.

Native range: Japan, South Korea
Height: 33 ft (10 m)
Hardiness: Zone 8

Tecoma
Bignoniaceae

A genus of about 12 species of shrubs, trees, and scrambling climbers with opposite leaves divided into several leaflets. They are natives from the southern United States to South America, and South Africa. The following is grown for its showy flowers and is suitable for any well-drained soil in full sun. Cut back long shoots in early spring.

Tecoma capensis

This is a vigorous, scrambling, evergreen climber with bright green leaves divided into five to nine sharply toothed leaflets. The trumpet-shaped flowers, up to about 2¾ in (7 cm) long, are bright orange to red, sometimes yellow, and open in clusters at the ends of the shoots in summer.

Common name: Cape honeysuckle
Native range: S and E Africa
Height: 16 ft (5 m) or more
Hardiness: Zone 10

Trachelospermum jasminoides 'Variegatum'

Trachelospermum
Apocynaceae

This is a genus of some 20 species of twining evergreen climbers with opposite leaves, natives mainly of South Asia, but with one species in the southeast of the United States of America.

Suitable for any good, well-drained garden soil, they are ideal for growing on supports against a wall or over a trellis or pergola.

Trachelospermum asiaticum

This is a vigorous, evergreen climber with glossy, dark green, often white-veined leaves, growing up to about 2 in (5 cm) in length. Very fragrant, five-lobed, creamy white, later yellow flowers, about ¾ in (2 cm) across, open in clusters in mid- to late summer.

Native range: Japan, Korea
Height: 16 ft (5 m)
Hardiness: Zone 7

Trachelospermum jasminoides

This vigorous, scrambling, evergreen climber has glossy, dark green leaves up to 3 in (8 cm) long. The very fragrant flowers, about 1 in (2.5 cm) across, open pure white in small clusters during the mid- to late-summer season and then turn more cream with age.

Common name: Chinese star jasmine
Native range: China, Japan
Height: 20 ft (6 m)
Hardiness: Zone 8
Variants: 'Variegatum' has leaves that are edged with creamy white. 'Wilsonii' has slender leaves conspicuously veined with white.

Vitis
Vitaceae

This is a genus consisting of about 65 species of deciduous climbers with peeling bark, widely distributed in the temperate regions of the Northern Hemisphere, particularly North America. Firmly atttaching themselves to supports with their tendrils, they can be grown in any well-drained garden soil that is rich in organic matter.

Many hybrids are grown for their fruits, but the following is the most commonly seen of the ornamental species, and is prized for its autumn color. It is suitable for growing into a large tree or for training on a wall, pergola, or other similarly substantial support.

Vitis coignetiae

This vigorous, deciduous climber has stout shoots densely covered with gray hairs when young. The large, shallowly lobed leaves, up to 12 in (30 cm) long, are dark green and deeply veined above and thickly covered with brown hairs beneath. They turn brilliant shades of red in autumn.

Native range: Japan
Height: 65 ft (20 m)
Hardiness: Zone 5

Wisteria floribunda 'Multijuga'

Wisteria floribunda 'Alba'

Wisteria
Leguminosae

This genus of some five species contains some of the best known of all the climbers. Natives of East Asia and the southern United States of America, they have deciduous leaves divided into numerous leaflets and showy, pendulous clusters of pealike flowers. Good, well-drained soil is ideal for them, and they flower best in full sun. They can be trained into a tree, against a wall, or over a pergola or similar support. They will also grow as free-standing plants. Plants do not usually flower when they are young and full blooming is enhanced by correct pruning.

Until established, reduce the length of the long shoots in winter and again in summer, training and tying in the resulting shoots to cover the desired space. Once established, cut back the side shoots in summer to about 6 in (15 cm) of a branch, and in winter prune these back again to two or three buds.

Wisteria floribunda

This vigorous, deciduous climber has dark green leaves composed of up to 19 leaflets. Pendulous clusters, up to about 12 in (30 cm) long, of fragrant, purple-blue, pealike flowers, spotted yellow inside, open in early summer.

Common name: Japanese wisteria
Native range: Japan
Height: 33 ft (10 m) or more
Hardiness: Zone 5
Variants: 'Alba' produces white flowers. 'Domino' has pale lilac-blue flowers. 'Multijuga' bears very long flower clusters up to 24 in (60 cm) or more in length. 'Rosea' produces bronze young leaves and long clusters of pink-colored flowers.

Wisteria sinensis

A vigorous and popular, deciduous climber with dark green leaves divided into as many as 13 leaflets. Foliage is usually bronze when young, and it sometimes turns to yellow in the autumn. Violet-blue, fragrant, pealike flowers open in compact, pendulous clusters in late spring, and these are followed by attractive, hanging pods with a velvety texture.

Common name: Chinese wisteria
Native range: China
Height: 33 ft (10 m) or more
Hardiness: Zone 5
Variant: 'Alba' is a woody stemmed, large-leaved climber with fragrant, pealike, white flowers.

Conifers

Conifers have always had a special place in the garden. Although lacking the striking flowers of many other trees and shrubs, they provide bold contrasts of foliage color and texture as well as habit. Many conifers grow into large trees and are seen at their best only in larger gardens. Planted as specimen trees, many of them —such as the pines, spruces, and silver firs—make prominent focal points of distinctive habit and foliage in the garden landscape.

Large conifers are an excellent choice if you need a windbreak at the edge of your property. The conical habit of such trees as Lawson cypress (*Chamaecyparis lawsoniana*) and western red cedar (*Thuja plicata*) provide a tall, dense screen with enough space between the tops to let sufficient wind filter through. Combining different forms with colored foliage makes the screen as ornamental as it is practical.

In smaller gardens, conifers can also be used for screening and hedging, but they may then need regular trimming to prevent them dominating the scene. Many conifers, however, are suitable for the smallest of positions. Not only are there many species that are naturally low-growing, but there is also a large number of dwarf and slow-growing selections of various habits and in colors ranging from silvery blue to bright yellow. These plants often mimic the original large tree, only in miniature form. *Abies lasiocarpa* var. *arizonica* 'Compacta', for example, is at most a small tree, conical in habit, and with striking, silvery foliage, while *Picea glauca* var. *albertiana* 'Conica' makes a dense cone of bright green. In addition to plants such as these, the numerous selections of the cypresses (*Chamaecyparis*) and the prostrate or spreading selections of junipers grown for ground cover, mean that conifers can make a valuable contribution to even the smallest of gardens.

Abies concolor 'Compacta'

Abies lasiocarpa var. arizonica 'Compacta'

Abies
Pinaceae

The silver firs are a genus of some 50 species of evergreen trees with whorled branches, widely distributed in the Northern Hemisphere—mainly in temperate regions. Their needle-like, usually bluntly pointed leaves vary from dark green to blue-green and often have blue-white bands of stomata on their undersides. Male and female flowers are borne separately on the same tree, usually only on the upper branches; the female flowers are followed by upright cones.

Silver firs mostly prefer a moist but well-drained, lime-free soil, and are best as specimen trees. *A. cephalonica* and *A. pinsapo*, as well as the dwarf forms, will tolerate drier, more alkaline soils.

Abies balsamea
This is a conical tree with gray bark marked with resin-bearing blisters. The bright green needles are often notched at the tip and have two silvery white bands beneath. Flowers open in early summer: male clusters are pendulous and yellow; females upright and purple before turning green and forming brown cones up to 4 in (10 cm) long.

Common name: Balsam fir
Native range: North America
Height: 50 ft (15 m) or more
Spread: 33 ft (10 m) or more
Hardiness: Zone 3
Variant: 'Nana' is a dwarf, rounded bush, up to about 24 in (60 cm) high, with leaves that are densely arranged around the shoots.

Abies cephalonica
A conical tree with glossy, dark green, sharp-pointed needles marked with two white bands of stomata beneath. Flowers open in late spring: male clusters are pendulous, red at first and opening to yellow; females are upright and green, ripening to a brown cylindrical cone up to 6 in (15 cm) long.

Abies koreana

Common name: Greek fir
Native range: Greece
Height: 100 ft (30 m)
Spread: 33 ft (10 m)
Hardiness: Zone 5
Variant: 'Meyer's Dwarf' ('Nana') is
a dwarf, bushy form up to 6 ft (2 m).

Abies concolor

This is a vigorous, narrowly conical
tree with smooth, gray bark that is
often marked with resin blisters. The
slender, blue-gray, blunt-tipped
needles are mostly upswept from the
shoots and are a similar color on both
sides. Flowers open in late spring:
the male clusters are yellow,
pendulous beneath the shoots; the
females upright and green, maturing
to a green or purple, later brown,
cone up to 4 in (10 cm) long.

Common name: Colorado fir
Native range: W United States of
America, NW Mexico
Height: 80 ft (25 m) or more
Spread: 50 ft (15 m)
Hardiness: Zone 4

Variant: 'Compacta' is rounded,
growing up to 8 ft (2.5 m) in height.

Abies grandis

A vigorous, conical tree with slender,
bright green needles spreading in two
ranks either side of the shoots,
marked with two white bands
beneath. It flowers in late spring:
male clusters beneath the shoots, red
at first, opening yellow; females
upright, green, maturing to brown
cones 4 in (10 cm) long.

Common name: Grand fir
Native range: W North America
Height: 100 ft (30 m) or more
Spread: 50 ft (15 m)
Hardiness: Zone 6

Abies koreana

This is a conical tree of compact
habit with densely arranged, glossy,
dark green leaves that are a brilliant
blue-white color beneath. The tree
flowers in late spring or early
summer: the male clusters are

Abies cephalonica 'Meyer's Dwarf'

pendulous beneath the shoots and yellow; the female flowers are upright and reddish purple, maturing to purple and then brown cones up to 3 in (7.5 cm) long.

Common name: Korean fir
Native range: South Korea
Height: 33 ft (10 m)
Spread: 16 ft (5 m)
Hardiness: Zone 5
Variants: 'Flava' produces yellow-green flowers that mature into yellow-brown cones at the end of the season. 'Silberlocke' produces leaves that curve upward and show their attractively and conspicuously colored, silvery undersides.

Abies lasiocarpa

This is a tree with a conical habit with smooth, gray bark marked with resin blisters. The gray-green, often notched leaves have two white bands beneath. Its flowers open in late spring or early summer: male clusters are pendulous, red at first and opening yellow; female flowers are upright and purple, maturing to purple brown cones about 4 in (10 cm) long.

Common name: Alpine fir
Native range: W North America
Height: 80 ft (25 m)
Spread: 33 ft (10 m)
Hardiness: Zone 5
Variants: var. *arizonica* (corkbark fir) has blue-gray foliage and corky bark, and in most areas it is the best form. 'Compacta' is a form of this, making a large, dense shrub or small tree, up to 16 ft (5 m) high, with blue-gray-colored foliage.

Abies nordmanniana

This is a conical tree with lush foliage. The densely arranged needles, notched at the tip, are glossy and bright green above with two greenish-white bands beneath. Flowers open in late spring: the males are pendulous and reddish, opening yellow; the females are upright and green, maturing to purple-brown cones up to 6 in (15 cm) long.

Common name: Nordmann fir
Native range: Caucasus, Turkey
Height: 100 ft (30 m)
Spread: 50 ft (15 m)
Hardiness: Zone 4

Variant: 'Golden Spreader' is slow-growing and bushy, up to 5 ft (1.5 m), with bright yellow foliage.

Abies pinsapo

This broadly conical tree has rigid, bluntly pointed needles arranged all around its stout shoots. The shoots are gray-green to blue-gray in color, with white bands displayed on both sides. The flowers open in late spring: males are pendulous and reddish, opening yellow; the female flowers are upright and green, maturing to brown cones up to 6 in (15 cm) long.

Common name: Spanish fir
Native range: S Spain
Height: 80 ft (25 m)
Spread: 50 ft (15 m)
Hardiness: Zone 6
Variant: 'Glauca' has blue-gray foliage.

Abies procera

A narrowly conical tree with blue-green needles, blunt or notched at the tip, with white bands on both sides—more conspicuous below. Flowers open in late spring: males pendulous, red opening to yellow; females upright, red or green, maturing to purple-brown cones 10 in (25 cm) long.

Common name: Noble fir
Native range: NW United States of America
Height: 100 ft (30 m) or more
Spread: 33 ft (10 m)
Hardiness: Zone 5
Variants: Members of the Glauca Group have blue-gray foliage.

Araucaria
Araucariaceae

The 19 species making up this genus of evergreen trees are found in South America, Australia, New Guinea, and Norfolk Island. The following is the only species that is hardy in cool, temperate regions. It is suitable for any good, moist, but well-drained soil, if given a sunny position where it is sheltered from strong winds. It is the hardiest relative of the Wollemi pine (*Wollemia nobilis*).

Araucaria araucana

This is a conical tree when young, with gray, wrinkled bark, but develops a more spreading, rounded head with age. The glossy, dark green, spine-tipped and triangular, overlapping leaves, up to 2 in (5 cm) long, densely cover the shoots and persist for many years. Male and female flower clusters grow on separate trees: males cylindrical, green then brown; females rounded, green maturing to brown cones 6 in (15 cm) long.

Common name: Monkey puzzle tree
Native range: S Chile, S Argentina
Height: 65 ft (20 m) or more
Spread: 33 ft (10 m)
Hardiness: Zone 7

Calocedrus
Cupressaceae

The three species of evergreen trees making up this small genus are natives of the western regions of the United States of America, northern Mexico, and Southeast Asia. The following is the only species that is commonly found in garden cultivation, where it is grown for its characteristic habit. It is suitable for any well-drained soil.

Calocedrus decurrens

A narrowly columnar, evergreen tree with red-brown, scaly bark and dark green, aromatic foliage borne in flattened sprays. Tiny, pointed, scalelike leaves densely cover the slender shoots. Male and female flowers are separate on the same tree in spring. Both are small, the females ripening to oblong, yellow-brown cones to 1 in (2.5 cm) long.

Araucaria araucana

Common name: California incense
cedar
Native range: W North America
Height: 80 ft (25 m)
Spread: 16 ft (5 m)
Hardiness: Zone 5
Variant: 'Aureovariegata' has foliage
that is blotched with yellow.

Cedrus
Pinaceae

The cedars form a genus of four
species of large evergreen trees that
are natives of North Africa,
Southwest Asia, and the Himalayas.
They produce two types of foliage:
single needles are borne on long
shoots; short, slow-growing shoots

bear needles in dense whorls. The
male flower clusters are often
conspicuous above the shoots in
autumn, and the small female flowers
are followed by barrel-shaped cones.

These trees are suitable for any
well-drained soil in a sunny position.
However, in their typical forms they
are suitable only for large gardens.

Cedrus atlantica
This is a conical tree with ascending
branches when young, sometimes
spreading as the tree matures. The
slender needles, about 1 in (2.5 cm)
long, are dark green to gray-green or
blue-green. Purple-brown, later brown
cones, 3 in (8 cm) long, are borne
upright on the branches in autumn.

Common name: Atlas cedar
Native range: Algeria, Morocco
Height: 80 ft (25 m)
Spread: 50 ft (15 m)
Hardiness: Zone 6
Variants: 'Aurea' has golden yellow foliage when young. 'Fastigiata' is a form with a conical habit and with upright branches and blue-gray foliage. Glauca Group (blue atlas cedar) has blue-gray foliage. 'Glauca Pendula' has this blue-gray foliage as well as weeping branches.

Cedrus deodara

A conical tree with spreading branches and drooping young tips. Bright green to gray-green, slender needles, 2 in (5 cm) long, are borne in dense whorls. Male flower clusters, upright above the shoots, are purple at first, opening yellow in autumn; female flowers are followed by barrel-like, purple-brown cones 5 in (12 cm) long.

Common name: Deodar cedar
Native range: Afghanistan to W China
Height: 100 ft (30 m)
Spread: 65 ft (20 m)
Hardiness: Zone 7
Variants: 'Aurea' has golden yellow, later yellow-green foliage. 'Feelin' Blue' is shrubby, with gray-blue foliage. 'Golden Horizon' is a form with a low, spreading habit and golden yellow foliage.

Cedrus libani

A conical tree, columnar to spreading with age, with level, tiered branches. The short, dark green to gray-green needles, up to 1 in (3 cm) long, are arranged in dense whorls. Flowers open in autumn: males blue-green, opening yellow, upright above the shoots; females maturing to barrel-shaped green cones, up to 5 in (12 cm) long, ripening to brown.

Common name: Cedar of Lebanon
Native range: Lebanon, Syria,

Cephalotaxus harringtonii 'Fastigiata'

SW Turkey
Height: 100 ft (30 m)
Spread: 80 ft (25 m)
Hardiness: Zone 5
Variant: 'Sargentii' forms a low-growing mound up to about 24 in (60 cm) in height.

Cephalotaxus
Cephalotaxaceae

A genus of ten species of evergreen shrubs and trees, natives of the Himalayas to East and Southeast Asia, with needle-like leaves. Male and female flowers are borne on separate plants.

Grown for its habit and foliage, the following is an excellent and tough specimen plant suitable for any good, well-drained soil—in sun or shade.

Cephalotaxus harringtonii

A slow-growing, evergreen shrub or spreading tree with red-brown, peeling bark. Slender, blunt-tipped, leathery, dark green needles spread in two ranks, either side of the shoots. The small, creamy white flowers open in spring, males beneath the

Chamaecyparis lawsoniana 'Ellwoodii'

Chamaecyparis lawsoniana 'Aurea Densa'

shoots, females at the tip, followed by fleshy coated seeds, up to 1 in (2.5 cm) long, green at first, later turning purple-brown.

Common name: Cow tail pine
Native range: Korea, Japan, Taiwan
Height: 20 ft (6 m)
Spread: 20 ft (6 m)
Hardiness: Zone 6
Variant: 'Fastigiata' is compact and narrow, with upright branches, the leaves arranged around the shoots. Can revert, producing spreading branches with normal foliage, which should be removed.

Chamaecyparis
Cupressaceae

The cypresses are a genus of six species of evergreen trees, natives of North America and East Asia. The tiny, scalelike leaves are arranged in flattened sprays of aromatic foliage, often marked with white beneath. The spring-opening flowers are small, males and females separate on the same tree. The female flowers are followed by small cones. Juvenile forms may have small, needle-like leaves and no cones.

Forms of *C. lawsoniana* are often used for hedging. These should be clipped regularly as necessary between spring and autumn, cutting only into the young shoots.

Chamaecyparis lawsoniana

A narrow, conical tree with flattened, drooping sprays of usually dark green to blue-green aromatic foliage, marked with white beneath. The small flowers open at the tips of the shoots in early spring: males red; females blue-green, maturing to small cones to ⅓ in (1 cm) across.

Common name: Lawson cypress
Native range: W United States of America
Height: 100 ft (30 m) or more
Spread: 26 ft (8 m)
Hardiness: Zone 5
Variants: 'Alumigold'—compact and columnar, to 33 ft (10 m), with bright yellow young foliage. 'Alumii'— columnar, to 50 ft (15 m), with sprays of blue-gray foliage. 'Aurea Densa'— conical, to 6 ft (2 m), with golden yellow foliage. 'Bleu Nantais'— conical and shrubby, to 10 ft (3 m), with silvery blue foliage. 'Broomhill Gold'—bushy and upright, to 26 ft (8 m),with yellow foliage. 'Chilworth Silver'—broadly columnar, to 8 ft (2.5 m), with silvery blue juvenile foliage. 'Columnaris'—compact and

narrowly conical, to 33 ft (10 m), with blue-green foliage. 'Ellwoodii'—conical, to 26 ft (8 m), with blue-green juvenile foliage. 'Ellwood's Gold'—similar to 'Ellwoodii', but with yellow-flushed young foliage. 'Erecta Viridis'—upright, to 50 ft (15 m), with bright green foliage. 'Fletcheri'—conical, to 40 ft (12 m), with semi-juvenile gray-green foliage. 'Gimbornii'—rounded bush, to 6 ft (2 m), with blue-green foliage. 'Golden Wonder'— conical, to 16 ft (5 m), with golden yellow foliage. 'Green Globe'—compact, to 18 in (45 cm), with bright green foliage. 'Lane'—conical with golden yellow foliage. 'Minima Glauca'—slow-growing, rounded bush, 5 ft (1.5 m), with blue-green foliage. 'Pembury Blue'—conical, to 50 ft (15 m), with silvery blue foliage. 'Pygmaea Argentea'— dense and conical, to 6 ft (2 m), with white-tipped foliage. 'Silver Threads'—dwarf, conical form with foliage splashed in silver-white and yellow. 'Snow White'—dwarf and compact with juvenile, white-tipped foliage. 'Summer Snow'—small and bushy shrub, young foliage white in summer, later turning green. 'Wisselii'—narrowly columnar, to 65 ft (20 m), with congested sprays of blue-green foliage.

Chamaecyparis nootkatensis

A conical, evergreen tree with orange-brown, peeling bark and pendulous, flattened sprays of dark green foliage. Small flowers open in early spring: males yellow; females blue-green, maturing to a cone about ⅓ in (1 cm) across.

Native range: NW North America
Height: 80 ft (25 m) or more
Spread: 26 ft (8 m)
Hardiness: Zone 4
Variants: 'Lutea' produces bright yellow foliage that later turns yellow-green in color. 'Pendula' has very pendulous foliage.

Chamaecyparis pisifera 'Boulevard'

Chamaecyparis obtusa

This is a broadly conical, evergreen tree with attractive, red-brown bark peeling in strips. The dark green and aromatic foliage has white markings beneath and is borne in flattened sprays. Small flowers open in late winter or early spring: males are yellow tinged with red; females are green at first, then turning brown and maturing to small, brown cones about ⅓ in (1 cm) across. It is mainly grown in gardens as selected forms, many of which are dwarf.

Common name: Hinoki false cypress
Native range: Japan
Height: 65 ft (20 m)
Spread: 26 ft (8 m)
Hardiness: Zone 5
Variants: 'Crippsii'—golden yellow foliage. 'Fernspray Gold'—conical, to 10 ft (3 m), with golden bronze, fern-like foliage. 'Kosteri'—makes a dwarf, conical bush, to 4 ft (1.2 m), with dense sprays of bright green foliage. 'Nana Aurea'—a compact and conical plant, to 6 ft (2 m), with yellow foliage. 'Nana Gracilis'—a popular slow-growing, dwarf form, to 10 ft (3 m) tall, with dark green foliage. 'Tetragona Aurea'—a small, conical tree, up to 33 ft (10 m) tall, with yellow foliage in four-sided, but not flattened, sprays.

Chamaecyparis obtusa 'Crippsii'

Chamaecyparis pisifera

This is a broadly conical, evergreen tree with an open habit and gray to brown bark peeling in thin strips. The glossy green, aromatic foliage is conspicuously marked with white beneath and is borne in flattened sprays. Small flowers open in the early spring: male flowers are brown; female flowers green, maturing to brown cones about ¼ in (6 mm) across, that are blue-green when young. It is mainly grown as selected forms noted below.

Common name: Sawara false cypress
Native range: Japan
Height: 65 ft (20 m)
Spread: 26 ft (8 m)
Hardiness: Zone 4
Variants: 'Boulevard' is columnar, up to about 33 ft (10 m), with blue-green juvenile foliage, and prefers moist soil. 'Filifera Aurea' is bushy, to about 16 ft (5 m), with golden yellow, thready foliage. 'Nana' is a flat-topped dome of dark green foliage up to 24 in (60 cm) high.

Chamaecyparis thyoides

This is a narrowly columnar, evergreen tree with gray to red-brown bark peeling in strips. The blue-green to green foliage is borne in small, flattened sprays, marked with white beneath, and it is often speckled with resin above. Its small flowers open in late winter or early spring: males are red; females green, maturing to small, bloomy cones up to ¼ in (6 mm) across.

Common name: White cedar cypress
Native range: E United States of America
Height: 50 ft (15 m)
Spread: 16 ft (5 m)
Hardiness: Zone 4
Variants: 'Andelyensis' is a narrow, conical form growing to 16 ft (5 m). 'Ericoides' is a conical bush, to 6 ft (2 m), with blue-green juvenile foliage turning bronze in winter. 'Rubicon' is compact and upright, to 30 in (75 cm), with gray-green juvenile foliage turning red in winter.

Cryptomeria
Cupressaceae

The single species that makes up this small genus is a tree that is grown principally for its attractive habit, foliage, and bark, and is suitable for any good, well-drained soil. It does grow to become a large tree, and so is not suitable for smaller gardens. However, many smaller selections can be grown in the rock garden or as specimen trees, depending on their eventual size.

Cryptomeria japonica

This is a large, evergreen tree with a conical habit and soft orange-brown bark peeling in vertical strips. The taper-pointed, bright green needles are borne pointing forward all around the slender shoots. The tree's small flowers open in the late winter or early spring: males are yellow-brown in color and grow in clusters; females

Cryptomeria japonica 'Vilmoriniana'

are green initially and grow singly at the ends of the shoots, maturing to brown cones up to about ¾ in (2 cm) across.

Common name: Japanese cedar
Native range: China, Japan
Height: 100 ft (30 m)
Spread: 50 ft (15 m)
Hardiness: Zone 5
Variants: 'Bandai-sugi' is a densely branched, slow-growing form, up to about 6 ft (2 m) high, with foliage turning bronze-red in winter. 'Compressa' is a very compact and rounded bush, up to 24 in (60 cm) in height, with densely arranged, upright foliage that turns bronze in winter. 'Elegans' is a medium-sized tree, reaching a height of up to 33 ft (10 m) or more, with soft juvenile foliage that is bronze-colored in winter. 'Sekkan-sugi' is a conical form, up to about 33 ft (10 m) in height, and bearing soft creamy colored foliage. 'Spiralis' is a shrub or small tree, up to approximately 20 ft (6 m) high, with leaves that are conspicuously twisted around the shoots. 'Vilmoriniana' is a slow-growing form that produces very densely arranged foliage. It eventually develops into a compact, bun-shaped plant, about 24 in (60 cm) in height, and its foliage turns bronze in winter.

Cryptomeria japonica 'Spiralis'

Cunninghamia
Cupressaceae

This is a small genus made up of just two species of evergreen trees that are natives of China, Taiwan, and Vietnam. The following species is the most frequently seen, mainly in substantial gardens or parks, and it attains its largest size in regions that experience moist summers.

This species requires a moist but well-drained soil and is usually grown as a specimen tree in a woodland setting, where it benefits from the

Cunninghamia lanceolata

are vigorous, evergreen trees with tiny, scalelike leaves borne in pendulous, flattened sprays.

The following is the most commonly seen example, planted for its habit and fast growth. It is useful as a specimen tree or as a large screen, but is much too vigorous and large for a hedge in small gardens. It needs clipping several times during the summer to keep it under control.

x *Cupressocyparis leylandii*

This is a garden-raised hybrid between *Chamaecyparis nootkatensis* and *Cupressus macrocarpa* and makes a large and very fast-growing, evergreen tree with a columnar habit. The green to blue-green, aromatic foliage is composed of tiny, pointed, scalelike leaves. It produces small flowers that open in the early spring. The male flowers are yellow, while the females are very small and inconspicuous, and are sometimes followed by rounded cones up to ¾ in (2 cm) across.

Common name: Leyland cypress
Height: 100 ft (30 m)
Spread: 20 ft (6 m)
Hardiness: Zone 6
Variants: 'Castlewellan' produces young foliage that is bright yellow but turns more yellow-green with age. 'Gold Rider' is similar to 'Castlewellan', but has brighter yellow foliage. 'Haggerston Gray' is the most commonly grown form, with gray-green foliage, and is usually sold as x *C. leylandii*.

shelter from the wind afforded by the surrounding trees. It does best where it receives full sun.

Cunninghamia lanceolata

This conical, evergreen tree, with ridged, red-brown bark, becomes increasingly columnar with age. Taper-pointed leaves, up to 2½ in (6 cm) long, spread out either side of the shoots. The leaves are glossy and dark green above and have two greenish-white bands beneath. Flowers open in late spring: the males yellow-brown and in clusters; the females yellow-green and single at the ends of the shoots. Female flowers mature to green, later brown cones up to 1½ in (4 cm) across.

Common name: China fir
Native range: China, Vietnam
Height: 65 ft (20 m)
Spread: 23 ft (7 m)
Hardiness: Zone 7

x *Cupressocyparis*
Cupressaceae

This is a genus comprising garden-raised hybrids between species of Chamaecyparis and Cupressus. They

Cupressus
Cupressaceae

The cypresses make up a widely distributed genus of 17 species of evergreen trees, natives of North and Central America, the Mediterranean region, North Africa, the Himalayas, and China. Closely related to *Chamaecyparis*, though not as easy to grow, cypresses have tiny, scalelike leaves that are only occasionally arranged in flattened sprays.

Grown for their habit, foliage, and sometimes their bark, they require a well-drained soil and—since not all are fully hardy—a position in full sun, sheltered from strong winds. Pruning is not necessary and young trees should be securely staked for their first few years until they have put out a securing root system.

Take care in choosing the correct site for a cypress. Young trees tend to establish more successfully than larger, more mature specimens, but they do not tolerate being transplanted once in the ground.

Cupressus arizonica var. glabra

A conical, evergreen tree with red-brown and red-purple bark peeling in rounded patches. The blue-gray, aromatic foliage is borne in sprays all around the shoots, and the tiny, scale-like leaves feature a spot of white resin on their backs. Small, bright yellow male flowers are conspicuous in late winter. The green female flowers are followed by rounded cones, up to 1 in (2.5 cm) across, which can persist for several years.

Synonym: *Cupressus glabra*
Native range: Arizona
Height: 50 ft (15 m)
Spread: 16 ft (5 m)
Hardiness: Zone 7
Variant: 'Blue Ice' has silver blue foliage.

Cupressus cashmeriana

This is a conical, evergreen tree that adopts a more spreading habit as it matures, and features red-brown bark that peels in vertical strips. This is one of the most attractive of the cypresses and is particularly valued for its foliage, which hangs from the shoots in long, flattened, blue-gray sprays. The very small flowers open in the late autumn to winter. The female flowers are followed by blue-

x *Cupressocyparis leylandii* 'Castlewellan'

green, later brown, cones, the scales of which finish in hooked points.

Common name: Kashmir cypress
Native range: Bhutan
Height: 33 ft (10 m) or more
Spread: 20 ft (6 m) or more
Hardiness: Zone 9

Cupressus macrocarpa

This is a vigorously growing, evergreen tree, dense and conical in shape when young, but becoming spreading and more open with age. The bright green, aromatic foliage—which consists of tiny, scalelike leaves—is borne in dense sprays all around the shoots. The tree's small flowers open in the late spring: male flowers are yellow; females green, followed by rounded, red-brown cones up to about 1½ in (4 cm) across. Although this species is popular and is commonly found in garden cultivation, it occurs in only a very small region in the wild.

Common name: Monterey cypress
Native range: California

Cupressus macrocarpa 'Goldcrest'

Cupressus cashmeriana

Height: 100 ft (30 m)
Spread: 33 ft (10 m)
Hardiness: Zone 7
Variants: 'Gold Spread' is a low-growing and wide-spreading form, reaching a height of only about 3 ft (1 m), and has golden yellow young foliage. 'Goldcrest' produces bright yellow foliage.

Cupressus sempervirens

This is an evergreen tree of variable columnar to spreading, or even sometimes pendulous, habit. It has dark green foliage arranged all around the shoots and has little or no scent. The small flowers open in spring: male flowers are yellow-brown; females green, followed by green, later brown cones up to about 1½ in (4 cm) across, and they are slightly longer than they are broad.

This species is prone to damage during severe winters and so requires a sheltered site.

Common name: Italian cypress
Native range: E Mediterranean region, N Africa, SW Asia
Height: 65 ft (20 m)
Spread: 6 ft (2 m) or more
Hardiness: Zone 7
Variants: Stricta Group is the most commonly seen form in garden cultivation, with trees of a narrowly columnar to narrowly conical habit. Some branches may tend to arch outward after bearing cones. 'Swane's Gold' is narrowly conical, reaching a height of about 26 ft (8 m), and has yellow foliage.

Ginkgo
Ginkgoaceae

As is indicated by its appearance, the single species that comprises this genus is not a true conifer, but it is the only living relative of a group of plants once widely distributed in the Northern Hemisphere. This is the

Ginkgo biloba (detail)

Ginkgo biloba

surviving member of a genus that is thought to be in the region of 200 million years old.

Unique among trees for its leaf shape, it is grown for its interesting foliage, which colors in autumn, and is usually planted as a specimen tree. It is suitable for any well-drained soil in full sun, and it is at its best in regions with hot summers. Its tolerance of pollution makes it excellent for cities.

Male and female flowers are borne on separate trees and both are required for fruits to be produced. The fruits are unpleasantly scented and can be messy when they fall. For this reason, selected male forms are often grown where fruits would prove to be a problem.

Ginkgo biloba

This is a deciduous, upright and conical tree when young, broadly columnar to rounded with age. The wide, fan-shaped leaves, up to 3 in (8 cm) long, are variously notched, sometimes deeply at the tip, and turn bright yellow in autumn. Small flowers may be borne, but only after about 20 years or more growth. This is when pollinated females trees produce their edible nuts enclosed within a fleshy, yellow-green, and malodorous covering.

Common name: Maidenhair tree
Native range: China
Height: 65 ft (20 m)
Spread: 50 ft (15 m)
Hardiness: Zone 4

Juniperus
Cupressaceae

The junipers are a diverse genus of evergreen shrubs and trees with 54 species widely distributed in the Northern Hemisphere, extending to tropical Africa. They bear two types of foliage. All species as seedlings have juvenile foliage composed of needle-like leaves, and some retain this leaf form into maturity. Others have adult foliage that is composed of tiny, scalelike leaves. Some species can bear both types of foliage. Male and female flowers are normally borne on separate plants, the females followed by berry-like cones.

Junipers will grow in any well-drained soil and prefer a sunny position. They can be used for a variety of purposes—from specimen trees and shrubs through to rock garden plants or as ground cover. As

Juniperus chinensis 'Kaizuka'

described here, the upper surface of the leaf is that facing the end of the shoot.

Juniperus chinensis

This is a conical, evergreen tree with red-brown bark peeling in vertical strips. Foliage is aromatic, and both juvenile and adult forms are usually borne on the same tree. The juvenile foliage consists of sharp-pointed, needle-like leaves banded with blue-white above. Small flowers open in early spring followed, on female plants, by bloomy, berry-like cones to ⅓ in (8 mm) long.

Common name: Chinese juniper
Native range: E Asia
Height: 50 ft (15 m)
Spread: 20 ft (6 m)
Hardiness: Zone 4
Variants: 'Aurea' is a small, narrowly conical tree of compact habit with yellow foliage. 'Blaauw' is shrubby and upright, with gray-blue, mainly adult foliage. 'Blue Alps' is shrubby, to

13 ft (4 m), with steel-blue juvenile foliage. 'Expansa Variegata' is low and spreading, to 3 ft (1 m) tall and 10 ft (3 m) across, with gray-green juvenile foliage blotched creamy white. 'Kaizuka' (Hollywood juniper) is shrubby or a small tree of irregular shape, with bright green adult foliage and profuse, bloomy cones. 'Pyramidalis' is a conical tree with blue-green, mainly juvenile foliage.

Juniperus communis

This widely distributed species is very variable in habit—from prostrate to upright, shrubby or tree-like. The aromatic foliage is always juvenile, with sharp-pointed, needle-like leaves marked with a broad white band on the upper surface. Female plants bear small, green, later bloomy, then glossy black, berry-like cones to ¼ in (6 mm) long.

Common name: Common juniper
Native range: Northern Hemisphere
Height: to 20 ft (6 m)
Spread: to 20 ft (6 m)
Hardiness: Zone 2
Variants: 'Compressa' is dwarf and narrowly conical, to 24 in (60 cm). 'Depressa Aurea' is wide-spreading, to 3 ft (1 m) tall and 10 ft (3 m) across, with golden yellow young foliage. 'Gold Cone' is conical, to 4 ft (1.2 m), with golden foliage. 'Green Carpet' is a creeping form with bright green foliage. 'Hibernica' is narrowly upright, to 16 ft (5 m) tall. 'Repanda' is low and wide-spreading, to 12 in (30 cm) tall, and is good for ground cover. 'Sentinel' is very narrowly upright, to 6 ft (2 m) tall.

Juniperus horizontalis

This is a creeping, evergreen shrub with long, trailing shoots, or sometimes with short, upright, or arching shoots. The gray-green to blue-green colored foliage can be adult or juvenile, or a mixture of both. Female plants bear bloomy cones to ⅓ in (8 mm) long. It makes an

Juniperus virginiana 'Grey Owl'

Juniperus sabina 'Tamariscifolia'

excellent species for ground cover in a rock garden.

Common name: Creeping juniper
Native range: Canada, N United States of America
Height: 12 in (30 cm)
Spread: 16 ft (5 m) or more
Hardiness: Zone 4
Variants: 'Blue Chip' has bright blue foliage, bronze-tinged in winter. 'Hughes' has silvery blue foliage. 'Wiltonii' is very low-growing with bright blue-green foliage, purple-tinged in winter.

Juniperus x *pfitzeriana*

This garden-raised hybrid between *J. chinensis* and *J. sabina* makes a wide-spreading, evergreen shrub, sometimes treelike in habit, with arching shoots. It is mainly grown as selected forms, of which there are many. They are invaluable landscape plants as specimens, for mass plantings and for ground cover. They were originally known in gardens as forms of *J. chinensis* or *J.* x *media*.

Common name: Pfitzer juniper
Height: 10 ft (3 m)
Spread: 16 ft (5 m)

Hardiness: Zone 4
Variants: 'Carbery Gold' is low and wide-spreading with creamy yellow foliage. 'Gold Coast' is compact, to 3 ft (1 m) tall, with golden yellow foliage. 'Mint Julep' has bright green foliage. 'Old Gold' is compact with bronze-yellow foliage. 'Pfitzeriana Aurea' is wide-spreading, to 10 ft (3 m) tall, with golden yellow young foliage. 'Sulphur Spray' is spreading, to 6 ft (2 m) tall, with pale sulphur-yellow foliage. 'Wilhelm Pfitzer' is the form once grown as *J.* x *media* 'Pfitzeriana' and has bright green juvenile and adult foliage.

Juniperus procumbens

This is a low, wide-spreading, evergreen shrub with stout, creeping shoots turned up at the ends. The foliage is mainly juvenile with slender, spine-tipped, blue-green leaves with two blue-white bands on the upper surface. Fruit is rarely produced in cultivation, but it makes an excellent groundcover plant.

Native range: S Japan
Height: 18 in (45 cm)
Spread: 10 ft (3 m) or more
Hardiness: Zone 4

Juniperus procumbens 'Nana'

Variant: 'Nana' is a compact form producing dense, layered foliage.

Juniperus sabina

This is a spreading, evergreen shrub featuring attractive, red-brown, peeling bark and graceful, arching branches. The aromatic foliage is mainly adult in form, although occasionally there are some sharp-pointed juvenile leaves. In this species, both male and female flowers are sometimes borne on the same plant.

Common name: Savin juniper
Native range: Europe to China
Height: 10 ft (3 m)
Spread: 16 ft (5 m)
Hardiness: Zone 3
Variant: 'Tamariscifolia' develops into a low, spreading mound, reaching about 3 ft (1 m) in height, and has the blue-green, mainly juvenile form of foliage.

Juniperus scopulorum

This is a narrowly conical, evergreen tree featuring red-brown bark peeling in thin strips. The slightly aromatic foliage is adult in form and varies in color from gray-green to blue-green. Female plants bear bloomy, blue-black, berry-like cones up to about ¼ in (6 mm) long.

Common name: Rocky mountain juniper
Native range: W North America (Rocky Mountains region)
Height: 50 ft (15 m)
Spread: 13 ft (4 m)
Hardiness: Zone 4
Variants: 'Blue Arrow' is very narrow with silvery blue foliage. 'Skyrocket' is narrow and upright in habit, with blue-gray foliage.

Juniperus squamata

This is an evergreen shrub or tree of very variable habit, and can be found as a creeping, spreading, or upright plant. The foliage is all juvenile and is composed of densely arranged, sharp-pointed, needle-like leaves, green banded with silvery white above. Female plants bear blue-black, berry-like cones. It is mainly grown as dwarf selections and is most often seen in the rock garden or is used for ground cover.

Common name: Single seed juniper
Native range: Himalayas, China, Taiwan
Height: to 16 ft (5 m)
Spread: to 16 ft (5 m)
Hardiness: Zone 4
Variants: 'Blue Carpet' is low and spreading in habit, to 12 in (30 cm) tall, with blue-gray foliage. 'Blue Star' makes a dense mound, up to about 18 in (45 cm) high, with silvery blue foliage. 'Holger' is spreading in habit, up to 3 ft (1 m) tall, with blue-gray foliage that is creamy yellow when young. 'Meyeri' is dense and upright, reaching a height of 16 ft (5 m) or more, and has arching shoots and blue-gray foliage.

Juniperus virginiana

This is an evergreen tree of narrowly columnar habit, with red-brown bark peeling in vertical strips. The aromatic, gray-green to deep green foliage consists of both adult, scalelike leaves and juvenile leaves, which are sharp-pointed and needle-like. Female plants bear bloomy, blue-black, berry-like cones.

Common name: Eastern red cedar
Native range: E North America
Height: 50 ft (15 m)
Spread: 16 ft (5 m)
Hardiness: Zone 4
Variants: 'Blue Cloud' is spreading in habit, reaching a height of about 5 ft (1.5 m), with gray-blue foliage. 'Grey Owl' is a vigorous, spreading shrub, up to about 8 ft (2.5 m) tall, with arching shoots and silvery gray-colored foliage.

Larix
Pinaceae

The larches are a genus of deciduous trees with 11 species distributed in the Northern Hemisphere. Like cedars, the larches bear foliage of two types. Long shoots produce single, needle-like leaves arranged spirally, while short shoots produce dense whorls of leaves. Male and female flowers are borne separately on the same tree, the females ripening to woody, upright cones.

They are suitable for any good, moist but well-drained soil, and they do best if given a position where they receive full sun.

Larix decidua
This is a conical, deciduous tree with spreading branches and drooping branchlets. It bears slender, bright green, needle-like leaves, which open early in the year on yellowish shoots and turn yellow in autumn. The flowers open in early spring as the young foliage emerges. Male flowers are yellow and pendulous, females red, upright above the shoots, maturing to brown, egg-shaped cones up to about 1½ in (4 cm) long.

Common name: European larch
Native range: Europe
Height: 80 ft (25 m) or more
Spread: 33 ft (10 m)
Hardiness: Zone 3

Larix kaempferi
A vigorous, broadly conical-growing, deciduous tree with spreading branches. The blue-green, needle-like leaves open early in the year on red-purple shoots and foliage turns yellow to orange in autumn. The flowers open in early spring. Male flowers are yellow and pendulous; females cream to pink or red, upright above the shoots, maturing to brown, rosette-like cones up to about 1 in (3 cm) long.

Common name: Japanese larch
Native range: Japan
Height: 80 ft (25 m) or more
Spread: 33 ft (10 m)
Hardiness: Zone 4
Variant: 'Pendula' is a form with conspicuously pendulous branchlets.

Metasequoia
Cupressaceae

The single species in this genus is remarkable because it was discovered only very recently—in the 1940s. Before this time it was known only from the fossil record. It is very fast-growing and prefers a moist but well-drained soil and a sunny position. Male catkins are usually borne only in regions that experience reliably hot summers.

Metasequoia glyptostroboides
This is a vigorous, deciduous tree featuring attractive, red-brown bark and a trunk that is deeply fluted at the base when mature. The slender, deep green leaves emerge early in the year and spread out either side of opposite, deciduous shoots. In autumn, the leaves turn yellow to

Metasequoia glyptostroboides

pinkish or red-brown before they fall. Pendulous male catkins open on the shoots in the early spring, and the small female flowers are followed by rounded, green—later brown— cones, up to about 1 in (2.5 cm) across, even if male flowers are not present.

Common name: Dawn redwood
Native range: China
Height: 100 ft (30 m)
Spread: 33 ft (10 m)
Hardiness: Zone 5
Variant: 'Gold Rush' produces golden yellow young foliage.

Microbiota
Cupressaceae

The single species in this genus is an evergreen shrub closely related to the junipers. It requires a moist but well-drained soil and a position in full sun. Valued in gardens for its great hardiness and foliage, it can be grown in a rock garden or be mass-planted to provide ground cover.

Microbiota decussata
This is a low-growing and wide-spreading evergreen shrub with bright green, aromatic foliage arranged in arching sprays of tiny, scale-like, occasionally needle-like, leaves. Foliage turns bronze in winter. The small cones, to ⅛ in (3 mm) long, resemble those of a juniper, but have woody scales and break open when ripe.

Native range: E Siberia
Height: 12 in (30 cm)
Spread: 10 ft (3 m) or more
Hardiness: Zone 3

Picea
Pinaceae

This is a genus of 34 species of evergreen trees, widely distributed in the Northern Hemisphere. Needle-like, usually sharply pointed leaves are borne singly on the shoots, and are sometimes marked with white bands beneath. Male and female flowers are borne separately on the same tree: the males usually yellow or red-flushed; the upright females developing into woody cones, pendulous when mature.

They require a good, moist but well-drained soil and do best if provided with a sunny position. They will often not grow well on very dry or shallow, chalky soils.

Picea abies
This is a conical, evergreen tree with red-brown to gray bark and spreading branches bearing pendulous branchlets. The dark green, four-sided and bluntly pointed needles are densely borne on orange-brown shoots. The flowers open in the late spring, the red females maturing to brown cones up to about 6 in (15 cm) long.

Picea abies 'Little Gem'

Picea breweriana

Common name: Norway spruce
Native range: Europe
Height: 100 ft (30 m)
Spread: 26 ft (8 m)
Hardiness: Zone 4
Variants: Numerous, often dwarf forms have been selected. 'Acrocona' is a small, shrubby tree, to 10 ft (3 m), producing cones at the tips of the shoots, even when young. 'Little Gem' is a slow-growing dwarf of a bun-shaped habit. 'Nidiformis' is a low-growing dwarf, to 5 ft (1.5 m), spreading widely.

Picea breweriana

This elegant species is among the most popular of the larger spruces. An evergreen conical tree with spreading branches bearing long, pendulous branchlets, giving a weeping appearance. The flattened, needle-like, dark green leaves are banded with whitish green beneath. The flowers open in late spring, the red females maturing to dark brown cones to 5 in (12 cm) long. This species can be slow to establish and develop its weeping habit.

Common name: Brewer spruce
Native range: W United States of America
Height: 50 ft (15 m)

Spread: 20 ft (6 m)
Hardiness: Zone 5

Picea glauca

A narrowly conical tree with scaly, gray-brown bark. The slender, needle-like, blue-green leaves are four-sided and densely arranged on white shoots. The flowers open in spring, the purple-red females followed by pale brown cones 2½ in (6 cm) long. Only the dwarf forms are commonly grown.

Common name: White spruce
Native range: Canada, N United States of America
Height: 65 ft (20 m) or more
Spread: 20 ft (6 m)
Hardiness: Zone 2
Variants: var. *albertiana* (Alberta white spruce) is a form from the Rocky Mountains, which has given rise to the following selections: 'Alberta Blue' is compact and conical, to 6 ft (2 m), with striking blue foliage; 'Conica' is compact and conical, to 6 ft (2 m), with green foliage. 'Alberta Globe' is a dwarf, bun-shaped plant of dense, rounded habit. 'JW Daisy's White' is conical with creamy young foliage turning green. 'Laurin' is a slow-growing dwarf of narrowly conical habit with upright branches.

Picea omorika

Picea mariana

This is a narrowly growing conical, evergreen tree producing gray-brown colored, flaking bark. The slender, blue-green, four-sided leaves end in a sharp point and are densely borne on yellow-brown shoots. The flowers open in the spring months, the red-colored female flowers maturing to small, red-brown cones up to about 1½ in (4 cm) in length. It is mainly found in garden cultivation as the form listed below.

Common name: Black spruce
Native range: Canada, N United States of America
Height: 65 ft (20 m)
Spread: 20 ft (6 m)
Hardiness: Zone 3
Variant: 'Nana' is a dwarf and compact form that makes a dense mound up to 24 in (60 cm) tall.

Picea mariana 'Nana'

Picea omorika

This narrowly conical, evergreen tree has orange-brown to purple-brown, scaly bark. The slender, glossy, dark green leaves are banded with white on the reverse. Flowers are red, opening in late spring, the females maturing to purple-brown cones up to 2½ in (6 cm) long. The pendulous branches that make this species so attractive take several years to develop on seedlings.

Common name: Serbian spruce
Native range: Serbia
Height: 65 ft (20 m)
Spread: 16 ft (5 m)
Hardiness: Zone 4
Variant: 'Pendula' resembles mature plants of the typical form, but it develops the desirable, weeping habit from an earlier age.

Picea orientalis

This is a narrowly conical tree that becomes columnar with age. The distinctive, four-sided and bluntly pointed, glossy and dark green leaves are very short and densely arranged on the shoots. The flowers open in spring: males bright red, opening yellow; females red, maturing to slender, purple, later brown cones up to 4 in (10 cm) long.

Common name: Oriental spruce
Native range: Caucasus, N Turkey
Height: 100 ft (30 m)
Spread: 26 ft (8 m)
Hardiness: Zone 4
Variants: 'Aurea' has strikingly attractive, bright yellow young foliage, which later turns green. 'Skylands' is a slow-growing, small tree, with golden yellow foliage throughout the year.

Picea pungens

This is a conical, evergreen tree with purple-brown, scaly bark and stout shoots. The four-sided, needle-like leaves are rigid and sharply pointed, varying in color from gray-green to silvery blue. The flowers open in the late spring or early summer: males red, opening yellow; females green, maturing to pale brown cones up to 4 in (10 cm) long.

Common name: Colorado spruce
Native range: W United States of America
Height: 65 ft (20 m)
Spread: 20 ft (6 m)
Hardiness: Zone 3
Variants: 'Erich Frahm' makes a small, dense, conical tree, to 33 ft (10 m), with blue foliage. 'Fat Albert' is densely conical, 16 ft (5 m), with rich blue foliage. 'Globosa' is a dense, rounded bush, to 5 ft (1.5 m), with blue-gray foliage. 'Hoopsii' is conical with densely arranged and striking, blue-white foliage. 'Iseli Fastigiate' has strongly upright branches and steel-blue foliage. 'Koster' is conical with silvery blue foliage.

Picea pungens 'Koster'

Pinus
Pinaceae

The pines are a genus of about 120 species of evergreen trees, sometimes shrubs, widely distributed in the Northern Hemisphere. The needle-like leaves are mainly borne in bundles of two, three, or five, and vary in color from green to blue or blue-green. Male and female flowers are borne separately on the same plant: males yellow; females ripening to cones that may persist for some time. They are generally suitable for any well-drained soil, preferring a sunny position. Those with needles in bundles of five do not grow well on shallow, chalky soils.

Pinus aristata

This is a conical, evergreen tree, often branching low, and shrubby in habit. The short, bright green and pointed needles, up to about 1½ in

Pinus aristata

(4 cm) long, are borne in dense bundles of five on stout shoots covered in red hairs, and are marked with conspicuous spots of white resin. Flowers open in the early summer season, the female flowers developing into to brown cones, up to about 4 in (10 cm) long, with prickly scales.

Common name: Bristle-cone pine
Native range: W United States of America
Height: 20 ft (6 m) or more
Spread: 13 ft (4 m) or more
Hardiness: Zone 4

Pinus armandii

This is a broadly conical, evergreen tree with smooth, gray bark. The slender, drooping needles, up to 6 in (15 cm) long, are green on the outer surfaces, blue-green on the inner, and are borne in clusters of five. Flowers open in early summer— the females maturing to pendulous cones up to about 8 in (20 cm) in length.

Native range: China, N Myanmar (Burma)
Height: 65 ft (20 m)
Spread: 33 ft (10 m)
Hardiness: Zone 5

Pinus cembra

Pinus bungeana

This is a conical, evergreen tree, often branching low down with several stems, and featuring bark that flakes in conspicuous patches of gray-green and creamy white. Rigid and sharply pointed, dark green leaves, growing up to about 3 in (8 cm) long, are borne in clusters of three. Flowers open in the early summer. The females are red and mature to form small, egg-shaped, brown cones, reaching up to about 2½ in (6 cm) in length, with spine-tipped scales.

Common name: Lace-bark pine
Native range: China
Height: 50 ft (15 m)
Spread: 33 ft (10 m)
Hardiness: Zone 5

Pinus cembra

This evergreen tree is conical when young and later becomes narrowly columnar, with densely hairy young shoots. The glossy, green needles are blue-green on their inner surfaces and are borne in dense bundles of five. Flowers open in late spring to early summer: males red when young; the females red, maturing to form red-brown cones, up to 3 in (8 cm) long, purple-blue when young. The cones contain edible seeds and do not open.

Common name: Swiss stone pine
Native range: C Europe
Height: 65 ft (20 m)
Spread: 20 ft (6 m)
Hardiness: Zone 4
Variant: 'Aurea' ('Aureovariegata') produces yellow-flushed foliage.

Pinus densiflora

This is an evergreen tree that is conical when it is young and becomes increasingly spreading and flat-topped as it matures. Its upper bark has a distinct reddish-brown color. The slender, dark green needles, up to about 5 in (12 cm) in length, are borne in pairs. The flowers open in the late spring—the females red, maturing to form pale brown cones up to about 2 in (5 cm) in length.

Common name: Japanese red pine
Native range: Japan, Korea, Russian Far East
Height: 50 ft (15 m)
Spread: 40 ft (12 m)
Hardiness: Zone 4

Pinus densiflora 'Umbraculifera'

Pinus heldreichii 'Compact Gem'

Variants: 'Alice Verkade' makes a dense, bun-shaped, dwarf form up to about 24 in (60 cm) high. 'Pendula' grows into a low, wide-spreading mound up to about 3 ft (1 m) in height. 'Umbraculifera' is a slow-growing, shrubby form, eventually making a height of about 13 ft (4 m) and with a flattened, spreading head of foliage.

Pinus heldreichii

This is a compact, evergreen tree with a conical habit, featuring gray bark that cracks into small, square plates. The rigid, dark green needles are densely borne in pairs. The flowers open in the early summer, the purple-red females maturing to form egg-shaped cones, up to about 4 in (10 cm) long, deep blue the first year, yellow-brown when ripe after the second year.

Synonyms: *P. leucodermis*, *P. leucodermis* var. *heldreichii*
Common name: Bosnian pine
Native range: SE Europe
Height: 50 ft (15 m)

Spread: 16 ft (5 m)
Hardiness: Zone 5
Variant: 'Compact Gem' is a slow-growing, dwarf form eventually making about 10 ft (3 m) in height.

Pinus mugo

This is an evergreen shrub, more rarely treelike in habit, of rounded growth and with upright or spreading branches. The dark green, rigid, and bluntly pointed leaves are often slightly twisted and are borne in pairs. The flowers open in the early summer, the female flowers followed by brown cones, up to about 2½ in (6 cm) in length, that are prickly when young.

Common name: Swiss mountain pine
Native range: Europe
Height: 16 ft (5 m)
Spread: 20 ft (6 m)
Hardiness: Zone 3
Variants: *P. mugo* is very variable when grown from seed and many forms have been selected. 'Gnom' makes a dense, rounded bush up to 6 ft (2 m) tall. 'Humpy' is very slow

Pinus mugo

growing and produces short needles.
'Mops' is a dense, rounded, slow-growing shrub. 'Ophir' is dwarf and
rounded in form, making up to 24 in
(60 cm) in height, with foliage that
turns golden yellow in winter. 'Winter
Gold' is a spreading shrub, up to
about 3 ft (1 m) tall, with golden
yellow winter foliage.

Pinus nigra

This evergreen tree has nearly black
bark and is conical in form when
young, becoming more columnar as it
ages with stout, spreading branches.
The rigid, sharp-pointed needles, up
to 6 in (15 cm) long, are dark
blackish-green and densely borne in
pairs. The flowers open in late spring
to early summer, the red female
flowers maturing to form brown
cones up to about 3 in (8 cm) long.

Common name: Black pine
Native range: Europe
Height: 80 ft (25 m)
Spread: 33 ft (10 m)
Hardiness: Zone 4
Variants: 'Hornibrookiana' is a dense,

Pinus nigra 'Hornibrookiana'

shrubby form, up to 6 ft (2 m), with
short needles; subsp. laricio (var.
maritima), the Corsican pine, has
more slender branches and gray-green foliage.

Pinus parviflora

This is an evergreen tree, conical in
form when young and becoming

Pinus parviflora

broadly columnar to spreading as it ages, with gray, scaly bark. The slender, slightly twisted needles, growing up to about 2½ in (5 cm) long, are green on their outer surfaces, with blue-white insides, and are borne in clusters of five. The flowers open in the early summer season: males are red, opening yellow; females are red, maturing to red-brown cones, up to about 3 in (7 cm) long, and are green colored when young.

Common name: White Japanese pine
Native range: Japan
Height: 50 ft (15 m)
Spread: 26 ft (8 m)
Hardiness: Zone 4
Variant: 'Adcock's Dwarf' is slow-growing, up to 8 ft (2.5 m), with dense, blue-green needles.

Pinus patula

This very beautiful species makes a rounded, evergreen tree that is conical when young, and with thick, red-brown bark. The slender, bright green needles, about 8 in (20 cm) or more long, hang in pendulous clusters of three. The flowers open in summer, the females followed by brown cones, up to 4 in (10 cm) long, persisting for many years.

Common name: Jelecote pine
Native range: Mexico
Height: 50 ft (15 m)
Spread: 33 ft (10 m)
Hardiness: Zone 8

Pinus pumila

This is an upright to spreading, evergreen shrub with stout shoots.

Pinus strobus 'Radiata'

The bluntly pointed, dark green leaves are blue-white on their inner surfaces and are borne in dense clusters of five. The flowers open in spring: males red-purple in color; females red when young, maturing to yellow- or red-brown cones up to 2½ in (6 cm) long.

Common name: Dwarf Siberian pine
Native range: NE Asia
Height: 16 ft (5 m)
Spread: 13 ft (4 m)
Hardiness: Zone 3
Variants: 'Glauca' produces gray-blue foliage. 'Globe' makes a dense, rounded bush, up to about 6 ft (2 m) across, with gray-blue foliage.

Pinus radiata

This is a vigorous, evergreen tree with a broadly conical to columnar habit, and with thick, dark gray bark. The slender, bright green needles, up to 6 in (15 cm) long, are densely borne in clusters of three. The flowers open in early summer, the purple-red females maturing to green, later orange-brown, cones up to 6 in (15 cm) long. The cones persist on the shoots for many years.

Common name: Monterey pine
Native range: California

Height: 100 ft (30 m)
Spread: 33 ft (10 m)
Hardiness: Zone 8

Pinus strobus

This vigorous, conical evergreen tree has smooth, gray bark that becomes fissured with age. The slender, gray-green needles are whitish on their inner surfaces and are borne in clusters of five. The flowers open in early summer, the pink females maturing to slender, curved, pendulous cones, up to about 6 in (15 cm) long, that are often marked with resin.

Common names: Eastern white pine, Weymouth pine
Native range: E North America
Height: 100 ft (30 m)
Spread: 26 ft (8 m)
Hardiness: Zone 3
Variant: 'Radiata' ('Nana') is a dwarf, shrubby form growing up to about 5 ft (1.5 m) in height.

Pinus sylvestris

This is an evergreen tree, conical in form when young and becoming more spreading-to-domed shape with age. The bark on the upper trunk is conspicuously orange, while lower

Pinus sylvestris 'Aurea'

down it is purple-gray in color and flaking. The stout, twisted, blue-green leaves are borne in pairs. The flowers open in late spring to early summer, the red females maturing to green, later brown, cones up to about 3 in (7 cm) long.

Common name: Scotch pine
Native range: Europe, Asia
Height: 100 ft (30 m)
Spread: 33 ft (10 m)
Hardiness: Zone 3
Variants: 'Aurea' has bright yellow foliage in winter. 'Beuvronensis' is a slow-growing, dwarf form, to 3 ft (1 m) tall, with short, blue-gray needles. 'Fastigiata' is narrow with upright branches, to 33 ft (10 m). 'Gold Coin' is dwarf, to 6 ft (2 m), with yellow winter foliage. 'Watereri' is shrubby, to 26 ft (8 m) tall and across, with blue-green foliage.

Platycladus
Cupressaceae

The single species in this genus is closely related to *Thuja* and is better known in gardens under its synonym. Grown for its foliage and attractive cones, it is suitable for any good, well-drained soil. It prefers a position in full sun—if it is planted in cold areas, it should be sheltered from strong winds. Useful as a specimen plant or for hedging, it can be trimmed in spring and late summer.

Platycladus orientalis
This is a densely branched, evergreen shrub of upright habit, more rarely a tree, with tiny scale-like leaves arranged in vertically held, flattened sprays. The conspicuous cones, up to about ¾ in (2 cm) long, are covered

with a blue-white bloom when young and have prominent hooks on the backs of their scales.

Synonym: *Thuja orientalis*
Native range: China, Korea, Russian Far East
Height: 33 ft (10 m)
Spread: 16 ft (5 m)
Hardiness: Zone 6
Variants: 'Aurea Nana' is a dwarf form, to 5 ft (1.5 m), with bright yellow foliage. 'Elegantissima' is narrow and upright, to 16 ft (5 m), with bright yellow young foliage that is yellow-green in summer and bronze in winter. 'Rosedalis' is dwarf, to 3 ft (1 m), with foliage that is creamy yellow when young, bronze-purple in winter.

Podocarpus
Podocarpaceae

This genus of just over 100 species of evergreen trees and shrubs is mainly confined to the warm regions of the Southern Hemisphere, extending to Central America, Mexico, and East Asia. Species are variable in foliage and have male and female flowers on separate plants. The fruit is borne on a flesh-colored receptacle that is attractive to birds, and is produced only when both male and female plants are present.
   Plants are suitable for any good, moist but well-drained soil.

Podocarpus nivalis
This is an evergreen shrub that makes a dense mound with leathery, yellow-green leaves, to ¾ in (2 cm) long, ending in short points. Male plants bear clusters of small, yellow flowers. Female plants may bear small cones with a fleshy, red base.

Common name: Alpine totara
Native range: New Zealand
Height: 5 ft (1.5 m)
Spread: 6 ft (2 m)
Hardiness: Zone 7

Podocarpus salignus
This graceful, evergreen tree has a conical habit and red-brown colored bark that peels in long strips. The slender, glossy, green leaves are distinctly curved, up to about 4 in (10 cm) long, and are borne on slender, green shoots. Male plants produce clusters of small, yellow-colored flowers in spring; females, small cones on a fleshy, green to violet base. It is at its best in areas that experience cool, moist summers and mild winters.

Native range: Chile
Height: 50 ft (15 m)
Spread: 20 ft (6 m)
Hardiness: Zone 8

Pseudolarix
Pinaceae

The single species in this small genus is a deciduous tree superficially similar to the larches.
   Grown for its autumn color, it requires a good, moist but well-drained, lime-free soil in full sun, and it should be sheltered from the effects of strong winds.

Pseudolarix amabilis
This is a slow-growing, conical, deciduous tree with foliage similar to that of the larches. The slender, bright green leaves are borne singly on long shoots and in dense whorls on short side shoots. Leaves turn golden yellow in autumn. Male and female flowers are yellow and are borne separately at the ends of the short shoots in late spring. The egg-shaped cones, to 2 in (5 cm) long, ripen from blue-green to yellow-green, then brown, breaking up on the tree before they fall.

Common name: Golden larch
Native range: E China
Height: 50 ft (15 m)
Spread: 33 ft (10 m)
Hardiness: Zone 5

Pseudotsuga menziesii 'Fletcheri'

Pseudotsuga
Pinaceae

The four species in this small genus are evergreen trees native of western North America, south to Mexico, and East Asia. The following is the only species commonly found in gardens. Frequently grown commercially for forestry, it makes a very large tree, but has produced a few forms for smaller gardens. Grow in moist, well-drained, lime-free soil. Reaches its greatest size in areas with high rainfall.

Pseudotsuga menziesii
This is a very fast-growing, evergreen tree with a conical habit, and producing thick, red-brown bark. The slender, dark green leaves are borne all around the shoots and have two whitish bands beneath. The flowers open in spring, males and females separately but on the same tree: the male flowers are yellow; the females green flushed with pink. The pendulous, red-brown cones that develop are up to about 4 in (10 cm) long, and have characteristic three-pronged bracts emerging from between the scales.

Common name: Pacific Coast Douglas fir
Native range: W North America, Mexico
Height: 130 ft (40 m) or more.
Spread: 33 ft (10 m)
Hardiness: Zone 4
Variant: 'Fletcheri' is bushy and spreading, up to 6 ft (2 m) high, with blue-green foliage.

Sciadopitys
Sciadopityaceae

The single species in this genus is the only member of its family, and it is a very distinct and unusual evergreen tree. Grown for its foliage, it is suitable for any good, moist but well-drained, lime-free soil. It makes an excellent specimen tree for a sunny position, but is also tolerant of shade.

Sciadopitys verticillata
A densely growing, conical evergreen tree with red-brown bark. It is slow-growing when young and often multi-stemmed. The slender, deep green, needle-like leaves, up to 5 in (12 cm) long, are grooved on both sides and

Sequoia sempervirens

Sequoia sempervirens 'Prostrata'

arranged in whorls at the ends of the shoots. Male and female flowers are separate on the same tree and open in spring: males yellow-brown; females green maturing to red-brown cones up to 3 in (8 cm) long.

Common name: Japanese umbrella pine
Native range: Japan
Height: 50 ft (15 m)
Spread: 26 ft (8 m)
Hardiness: Zone 5

Sequoia
Cupressaceae

The single species in this small genus is a large, evergreen tree grown for its vigorous growth, habit, attractive bark, and foliage. In the wild, trees live to a great age and there is a specimen in California that is the tallest tree anywhere in the world. In cultivation it is tolerant of a range of conditions, although it does require a good, moist but well-drained soil and a site in full sun. The most rapid growth and largest size are attained in areas with cool, moist summers. Owing to its rapid growth rate and final size, this tree is suitable only for large gardens or public spaces.

Sequoia sempervirens

This is a fast-growing, conical, evergreen tree with soft, thick, red-brown bark and spreading branches. The yewlike foliage consists of small, dark green leaves marked with two white bands beneath. The leaves decrease in length toward the end of the shoots. The flowers open in late winter to early spring, males and females separate but on the same tree. The male flowers are yellow-brown; the females green, followed by red-brown cones up to about 1 in (3 cm) in length.

Common name: Redwood
Native range: W United States of America
Height: 100 ft (30 m) or more
Spread: 33 ft (10 m)
Hardiness: Zone 7
Variants: 'Adpressa' is slow-growing, up to 33 ft (10 m) or more in height, with white-tipped young foliage. 'Prostrata' is low and spreading, up to 3 ft (1 m) high, with broad, blue-green leaves.

Sequoiadendron giganteum

Common names: Giant redwood, Wellingtonia
Native range: California
Height: 100 ft (30 m) or more
Spread: 33 ft (10 m)
Hardiness: Zone 6
Variants: 'Glaucum' is narrowly conical with blue-green foliage. 'Pendulum' is slender with main branches hanging vertically.

Sequoiadendron
Cupressaceae

The single species in this genus is frequently confused with *Sequoia sempervirens*, although the two trees are quite distinct. Despite the fact that it is not generally as tall as *Sequoia*, it reaches a greater girth, and a specimen of this species is the world's most massive tree. It will grow in any good, well-drained soil, but is suitable only for large gardens.

Sequoiadendron giganteum
This fast-growing, conical, evergreen tree has thick, soft, red-brown bark. The downswept branches are clothed with small, sharp-pointed leaves arranged all around the shoots, making the foliage rough to the touch. Separate male and female flowers open in early spring on the same tree. Males are yellow; females green, maturing to barrel-shaped, brown cones up to 3 in (8 cm) long.

Taxodium
Cupressaceae

The two species in this genus—one deciduous, one evergreen—are natives of the southeast of the United States of America through Mexico to Guatemala. The following species has attractive foliage, which colors up in autumn, and it is the only one that is commonly grown.

It prefers a moist, or even wet, lime-free soil and does best in full sun. The cypress "knees" (woody protuberances growing vertically from the roots) are best produced on moist soils, most prolifically in regions with hot summers.

Taxodium distichum
A conical, deciduous tree with gray-brown bark, and with a trunk often buttressed and fluted when mature. Two types of leaves are borne: small, scalelike leaves on persistent shoots, and slender leaves, up to ¾ in (2 cm), spreading out either side of deciduous shoots. In autumn, the leaves turn reddish brown and fall with the shoots. The flowers form in autumn, but open in spring. Male flowers are yellow-green, in hanging catkins. The females are green, followed by rounded, brown cones up to 1 in (3 cm) across. Cypress knees, up to 3 ft (1 m) tall, may form where conditions are favorable.

Common name: Common bald cypress
Native range: SE United States of America

Height: 100 ft (30 m) or more
Spread: 26 ft (8 m)
Hardiness: Zone 4
Variant: var. *imbricatum* (*T. ascendens*)
is a smaller, narrower tree, reaching a
height of up to about 65 ft (20 m),
and has leaves, up to ⅓ in (1 cm) in
length, closely pressed against the
upright, deciduous shoots.

Taxus
Taxaceae

The yews form a genus of about ten
species of evergreen shrubs and trees
that are widely distributed mainly in
the temperate regions of the
Northern Hemisphere, extending to
Central America and Malaysia.

   The following is the most
commonly grown species. It is
suitable for any well-drained soil,
even shallow, chalky soils, and will
grow either in sun or shade. The
variegated forms color best if given a
bright position. It is a useful plant for
hedging and topiary and can be
trimmed in both the summer and
early autumn.

   Old plants can be rejuvenated by
cutting them back hard in spring.

Taxus baccata
A broadly conical, evergreen with
smooth, purple-brown, flaking bark
and dark, blackish green leaves.
Small male and female flowers are
borne on different trees in spring, but
only the pale yellow male flowers are
conspicuous. The fruit produced is a
single seed partly enclosed in a fleshy,
red covering. All parts of the fruit,
except the seed coat, are poisonous.

Common name: English yew
Native range: Europe, N Africa,
W Asia
Height: 33 ft (10 m) or more
Spread: 33 ft (10 m)
Hardiness: Zone 6
Variants: 'Fastigiata' (Irish yew) is a
female form, narrowly upright when
young, with leaves spreading around

Taxus baccata 'Standishii'

the shoots. 'Fastigiata Aureomarginata'
is an upright, male form with yellow-
edged leaves. 'Repens Aurea' is a low
and spreading, female form bearing
yellow-edged leaves, and it makes
attractive ground cover. 'Semperaurea'
is male with golden yellow foliage.
'Standishii' is female, narrowly
upright, with yellow-edged leaves.

Thuja
Cupressaceae

The five species that make up this
genus are all evergreen trees, natives
of North America and East Asia.
There is one species from China, but
this is now extinct in the wild. The
trees usually have aromatic foliage
composed of tiny, scalelike leaves
borne in flattened sprays. The small,
male and female flowers are borne
separately on the same plant.

   Thujas do best if given good, moist
but well-drained soil and a position
where they are sheltered from the

effects of strong winds. They are useful as specimen plants, while dwarf forms are suitable for rock gardens. They can also be used for hedging.

Thuja occidentalis

This is a conically shaped, evergreen tree with a dense habit, and with orange-brown bark that peels in vertical strips. Tiny, scalelike leaves, of a similar color on both sides, are borne in flattened, aromatic sprays. The flowers open in the spring. The male flowers are red; females yellow-brown, followed by upright cones, up to about ⅓ in (1 cm) long, ripening from a yellow-green color to brown.

Common name: American arborvitae
Native range: E North America
Height: 65 ft (20 m)
Spread: 16 ft (5 m)
Hardiness: Zone 3
Variants: 'Danica' is a compact, rounded, dwarf form with foliage growing in vertical sprays. The leaves turn bronze in winter. 'Hetz Midget' is an extremely compact and slow-growing, rounded bush. 'Holmstrup' is a large, narrowly conical shrub, up to about 13 ft (4 m) in height. 'Rheingold' is a rounded bush, up to 3 ft (1 m), with bronze-yellow foliage that is pinkish when young. 'Smaragd' is a slow-growing, narrowly conical form, to 10 ft (3 m) tall, with bright green foliage. 'Tiny Tim' is a slow-growing dwarf up to 12 in (30 cm) tall. 'Yellow Ribbon' is narrowly conical, to about 10 ft (3 m) tall, with golden yellow foliage.

Thuja plicata

This is a vigorously growing, densely conical, evergreen tree with attractive, purple-brown bark that peels in vertical strips. Tiny, scalelike leaves are borne in flattened sprays of aromatic foliage marked with white beneath. The flowers open in the spring. The males are reddish black, while the females are yellow-green, followed by small, upright cones, up to about ⅓ in (1 cm) long, ripening from yellow-green to brown.

Common name: Giant arborvitae
Native range: W North America
Height: 100 ft (30 m)
Spread: 26 ft (8 m)
Hardiness: Zone 5
Variants: 'Atrovirens' has glossy, dark green leaves. 'Aurea' has soft yellow-colored foliage. 'Rogersii' is a slow-growing form, reaching a height of about 3 ft (1 m), with bronze-yellow foliage. 'Stoneham Gold' is a conical form, up to about 10 ft (3 m) high, with golden yellow young foliage. 'Zebrina' is vigorous and has foliage banded with yellow and dark green.

Thujopsis
Cupressaceae

The single species that makes up this small genus is an evergreen tree that is grown for its handsome foliage. The tree is suitable for any good, moist but well-drained soil, and it does best if provided with a position that is in full sun, yet where it is still sheltered from strong winds.

Thujopsis dolabrata

This is a conical, evergreen tree with purple-brown bark peeling in vertical strips. The slightly aromatic foliage is borne in broad, flattened sprays composed of small, scalelike, bright green leaves. The leaves are conspicuously marked with large patches of white on their undersurfaces. The small flowers open in the spring. The males are blackish green in color, while the females are blue-gray, maturing to a brown, bloomy cone, up to ½ in (1.2 cm) long, blue-green when young.

Native range: Japan
Height: 65 ft (20 m)
Spread: 26 ft (8 m)
Hardiness: Zone 5
Variants: 'Aurea' produces young foliage that is flushed with yellow.

Thuja occidentalis 'Danica'

'Nana' is a dwarf shrub reaching a maximum height of about 3 ft (1 m). 'Variegata' has foliage that is sparsely blotched with white.

Tsuga
Pinaceae

The hemlocks make up a small genus of nine species of graceful, evergreen trees that are natives of North America and East Asia. The following species are those most widely seen in garden cultivation, usually as selected dwarf forms. Male and female flowers are borne separately but on the same tree.

The hemlocks do best if they are provided with a moist but well-drained soil rich in organic matter. They can be grown in sun or shade.

Tsuga canadensis
A broadly conical, evergreen tree with red-brown bark and bearing slender, flattened leaves that narrow slightly toward their tips. The leaves spread out either side of the shoots and are marked with two white bands on their undersurfaces. Flowers open in late spring. The males are yellow and the females green, maturing to small, pale brown, pendulous cones up to about ¾ in (2 cm) long.

Common name: Canada hemlock
Native range: E North America
Height: 80 ft (25 m)
Spread: 33 ft (10 m)
Hardiness: Zone 4
Variants: 'Jeddeloh' is a small bush, up to about 3 ft (1 m) tall, with arching shoots. 'Minuta' is a very compact and slow-growing, dwarf form up to about 24 in (60 cm) tall.

Tsuga heterophylla
A conical, evergreen tree with purple-brown bark and dark green leaves with parallel sides and two white bands beneath. The reddish male and female flowers open in spring, the females maturing to pale brown, pendulous cones up to about ¾ in (2 cm) long.

Common name: Western hemlock
Native range: W North America
Height: 100 ft (30 m)
Spread: 33 ft (10 m)
Hardiness: Zone 6

INDEX